RG78

1-8-97

DISCARDED

Mental Health
DISORDERS
SOURCEBOOK

Health Reference Series

Volume Nine

Mental Health
DISORDERS
SOURCEBOOK

*Basic Information about
Schizophrenia, Depression, Bipolar
Disorder, Panic Disorder, Obsessive-
Compulsive Disorder, Phobias and
Other Anxiety Disorders, Paranoia and
Other Personality Disorders, Eating
Disorders, and Sleep Disorders,
along with Information about
Treatment and Therapies*

Edited by
Karen Bellenir

Omnigraphics, Inc.

Penobscot Building / Detroit, MI 48226

BIBLIOGRAPHIC NOTE

This volume contains the following numbered publications produced the National Institute of Mental Health: 00-0009, 00-0013, 00-0018, 00-0025, 00-4015, 00-4081, 85-1265; the following numbered publications of the National Institutes of Health: 87-1541, 89-1138, 89-1495, 90-1457, 90-1675, 91-1792, 92-1509, 92-1680, 92-1950, 93-3417, 93-3499, 93-3509, 93-3697, 94-3477, 94-3585, 94-3775; excerpts from 94-3737; and the Consensus Development Conference Statement Volume 5 Number 11. This volume also contains a copyrighted document produced by the Psychiatric Institute, "The Trauma of Sexual Abuse," and several copyrighted documents produced the Anxiety Disorders Association of America: "Panic and Agoraphobia," "Phobias," "Post-Traumatic Stress Disorder," "Social Phobias," "Anxiety Disorders in the Elderly," "Anxiety Disorders: Helping a Family Member," and "Generalized Anxiety Disorder." All copyrighted documents are all reprinted with the permission of the copyright holders.

Edited by Karen Bellenir

Peter D. Dresser, Managing Editor, *Health Reference Series*

Omnigraphics, Inc.

Matthew P. Barbour, *Production Coordinator*
Laurie Lanzen Harris, *Vice President, Editorial*
Peter E. Ruffner, *Vice President, Administration*
James A. Sellgren, *Vice President, Operations and Finance*
Jane J. Steele, *Vice President, Research*

Frederick G. Ruffner, Jr., *Publisher*

Library of Congress Cataloging-in-Publication Data

Mental health disorders sourcebook : basic information about schizophrenia, depression, bipolar disorder, panic disorder, obsessive-compulsive disorder, phobias and other anxiety disorders, paranoia and other personality disorders, eating disorder, and sleep disorders, along with information about treatment and therapies / edited by Karen Bellenir.

     p.   cm. — (Health references series ; v. 9)
     Includes bibliographical references and index.
     ISBN 0-7808-0040-0 (lib. bdg. : alk. paper)
     1. Mental illness. 2. Psychiatry. ~~I. Bellenir, Karen.~~
~~II. Series.~~
~~RC454.4.M458~~   1995   95-36873
    616.89 ~~dc20~~   CIP

∞

Printed in the United States

Contents

Part III—Mood Disorders, continued

Part IV—Anxiety Disorders

Part V—Other Mental Health Disorders

Part VI—Mental Health Treatments and Therapies

Preface

About this Book

According to statistics compiled by the U.S. Department of Health and Human Services, mental illness will strike 20 percent of Americans at some point during their lives. Most of them will not seek help because the disorders continue to be stigmatized by society. In addition, sufferers and their families often view the symptoms of mental health disorders as signs of personal weakness.

Mental health disorders are not personal weaknesses, however. Although scientists still do not understand all factors contributing to mental illness, chemical imbalances and other biological dysfunctions have been identified and are treatable. According to one projection, up to 80 percent of the people afflicted with depression, manic depression, or schizophrenia could be helped with currently available medication and therapy.

This volume contains basic information for the layperson about mental health disorders. Patients, family members, friends, and the interested general public will find medical explanations along with advice on seeking treatment and coping with the problems that often accompany a diagnosis of mental illness.

How to Use this Book

This book is divided into parts and chapters. Parts focus on broad areas of interest. Chapters are devoted to single topics within a part.

Part I: Introduction presents an overview of mental health disorders in America. It includes encouragement for mental health patients along with historical and statistical information about mental health disorders.

Part II: Schizophrenic Disorders offers basic information about schizophrenia, antipsychotic medications, and current research efforts aimed at identifying the cause or causes of schizophrenia and developing more effective therapies.

Part III: Mood Disorders provides information about depressions, bipolar disorder (also known as manic depressive disorder), and seasonal affective disorder, along with information about helping a depressed person get help, pharmacologic treatments, and psychotherapy.

Part IV: Anxiety Disorders includes information about panic disorders, obsessive-compulsive disorders, phobias, and post-traumatic stress disorders.

Part V: Other Mental Health Disorders gives information about personality disorders, eating disorders, sleep disorders, and wife abuse.

Part VI: Mental Health Treatments and Therapies summarizes available mental health services, medications, and treatments.

Acknowledgements

The editors gratefully acknowledge the assistance of the many people who helped produce this volume. Special thanks go to Dr. David Missar for providing guidance as we attempted to sort out the vast topic of mental health disorders; to Margaret Mary Missar for obtaining the documents reproduced in this volume; and to Bruce the Scanman for making its production a reality.

Note from the Editor

This book is part of Omnigraphics' *Health Reference Series*. The series provides basic information about a broad range of medical concerns. It is not intended to serve as a tool for diagnosing illness, in prescribing treatments, or as a substitute for the physician/patient relationship. All persons concerned about medical symptoms or the possibility of disease are encouraged to seek professional care from an appropriate health care provider.

Part One

Introduction

Chapter 1

You Are Not Alone

Preface

If you have a mental illness, you are not alone. One in five adult Americans will have a mental illness during their lifetime that is severe enough to require treatment. Many more have problems that prevent them from enjoying their lives.

Fortunately, effective treatments are now available for many mental illnesses. Unfortunately, most people do not seek help. Many wrongly believe their symptoms are their own fault or are caused by personal weakness. They think if they try hard enough they can overcome their problems by themselves, and they suffer unnecessarily.

In actuality, mental illnesses often involve biological dysfunctions that require professional treatment. An individual with a mental illness needs treatment and help in coping with everyday problems. In contrast, individuals who do not have a mental illness can usually deal with ordinary problems by themselves. At times of particular stress, however, even mentally healthy persons will find professional assistance useful.

The following discussion of mental health and mental illnesses is designed to provide information that can help people lead happier, healthier lives.

DHHS Pub. No. (ADM) 92-1178.

What Is Mental Health?

While mental health can mean many things to many people, self-esteem and the capacity to care about others are universally important components of mental health. Mentally healthy people understand that they are not perfect nor can they be all things to all people. They experience a full range of emotions including sadness, anger, and frustration as well as joy, love, and satisfaction. While they typically can handle life's challenges and changes, they can reach out for help if they are having difficulty dealing with major traumas and transitions—loss of loved ones, marriage difficulties, school or work problems, the prospect of retirement.

Helping Yourself—and Others—to Mental Health

There are a number of steps you can take to help maintain good mental health. When you reduce your own stress level, you put others at ease too. When you are cooperative and outgoing, you bring out the cooperative spirit in others. Here are some suggestions:

Take a realistic approach. If there's a job to do, get it done without ruffling the feathers of other people. Accept a challenge. Take command of the situation. Set goals. Keep them in perspective and see them as part of a larger purpose. Compromise with others who may not see eye-to-eye with you on every point. Remember, they also have rights. Enlist cooperation rather than arouse antagonism. Suggest a family or staff meeting to encourage cooperation and compromise.

Learn to recognize and express your feelings. Try not to label feelings—yours or others—as "good" or "bad." It is human to experience a wide range of feelings. It is generally healthy to express feelings as soon as possible in a suitable way since, when pent up, they can result in inappropriate responses. For example, if you feel put down or ignored and suppress your feelings, you may later vent your anger on someone else or you may turn it inward and feel depressed. Know why you feel angry and express your feelings as calmly as possible. Or talk matters over with a sensible, trustworthy person—a wise friend, a clergyman, a physician, a relative, or a professional counselor. This approach may help you to think more clearly, handle your feelings appropriately, and better understand the feelings of others as well.

Don't brood. Often a simple change of pace or a refocusing of energies is a constructive way of "getting away from it all." Instead of brooding, do something—no matter how small—positive and useful about a problem. Try not to worry about the things you cannot change.

Proceed one step at a time. To escape the feeling that you're trapped, evaluate your problem, consider each step necessary to solve it, and work toward a solution. This "one-step-at-a-time" approach will allow you to take pride in your ability to handle the situation. By diverting your tensions and anger to worthwhile and reachable goals, you will be amazed by how much control you can exert in managing your life.

What to Watch for

Even when you try your best, you will still experience periods of frustration and unhappiness. Usually, with time, you will overcome your distress. But you should learn to recognize when your problems—or those of your loved ones—are too much to handle alone. You can help yourself, your family, and your friends by knowing when to ask for professional help. Some of the warning signs include:

Undue prolonged anxiety. This is an anxiety out of proportion to any identifiable reason or cause. Of course, everyone experiences problems that make them tense and anxious. But a deep, continuing anxiety—a state of almost constant tension and fear that may fasten itself to one cause after another—is a signal that help is needed. Unrelieved anxiety not only causes mental anguish but also can lead to physical problems.

Prolonged or severe depression. Clinical depression—which is quite different from normal depressed feelings or "the blues"— strongly affects thinking, feelings, and behavior. Persistent feelings of inadequacy, sadness, helplessness, hopelessness, undue pessimism, and loss of confidence are some of the symptoms of depression. Changes in behavior patterns are a key sign that depression may be getting out of hand and help should be sought.

Depressed individuals often withdraw from friends they normally enjoy, from loved ones, and from the usual occupation and hobbies that give pleasure. Their eating and sleeping habits change. Some suffer from loss of appetite and insomnia, especially an inability to stay asleep; others seek solace in overeating and excess sleeping.

Other symptoms of depression include low energy, chronic fatigue, decreased effectiveness at school, work, or home, and loss of sexual interest. Depressed individuals are those most likely to think of suicide as a solution, although people with other mental and emotional disturbances may also be suicidal. During periods of crisis, people should be with others, avoiding isolation.

Abrupt changes in mood and behavior. These changes do not include deliberate steps a person adopts for self-improvement. They refer to changes in mood and behavior that reflect serious alterations in an individual's normal habits or way of thinking. For example, the good student whose grades abruptly drop or the frugal man or woman who suddenly begins gambling away large sums of money is very likely to be experiencing emotional problems. Also, frequent or regular mood changes from highs to lows, whether gradual or abrupt, can signal a mood disorder (see description under **Mood disorders**).

Physical symptoms that may be related to tension. Some bodily ailments and complaints—headaches (including migraines), nausea, or unexplained pains—may have no identifiable physical cause. These symptoms are very real. But only a physician is qualified to determine whether they are caused by medical illness. Because medical tests may reveal an organic cause, any persistent physical ailment should be checked by a doctor.

If any of the warning signs described above are severe or long lasting, whether caused by a medical illness or not, professional help may be needed.

"Kinds" of Mental Illness

Definitions of mental illnesses in this section were derived from the *Diagnostic and Statistical Manual of Mental Disorders, Third Edition—Revised.* American Psychiatric Association, 1987.

Schizophrenic disorders. In any given year, approximately 1.8 million people in this country, or 1 percent of the population, are affected by a form of schizophrenia. (Rates are based on estimates of the

U.S. 1989 population—184,000,000 persons aged 18 and over. Source is unpublished data from the Epidemiology and Psychopathology Branch, Division of Clinical Research, National Institute of Mental Health.) This complex and extremely puzzling type of mental illness is particularly disabling, generally interfering with the ability to work, relate to others, and take care of oneself.

Generally, symptoms of schizophrenia become apparent during adolescence or early adulthood, but can begin later in life. Symptoms may include delusions (false beliefs, sometimes paranoid in nature, whereby the individual wrongly feels persecuted or endangered), hallucinations (hearing voices that are not present), disconnected or incoherent speech, withdrawal from the outside world, grossly inappropriate feelings, or abnormal psychomotor activity (rocking, pacing, or immobility). While some who experience an apparent schizophrenic episode will recover fully, schizophrenia is a chronic or recurrent illness for most people.

In order to obtain the most appropriate treatment, accurate diagnosis by a qualified psychiatrist is essential since other psychotic conditions—those induced by such drugs as LSD or PCP, or by mania, depression, or organic brain disturbances—may mimic symptoms of schizophrenia.

Mood disorders. Depression, mania, and bipolar disorder (bipolar disorder is also called manic-depressive illness and is characterized by cycles of depression and mania) are referred to as *mood disorders*. Mood disorders affect an estimated 11.6 million adults in the United States, or 6.3 percent of the population, each year.

Depressive disorders change the way people think, feel, and behave. Unlike the normal "down" mood that we all experience at one time or another, *major depression* lingers on and becomes more pronounced than warranted by the events of daily living. Depression interferes with the ability to think, to concentrate, and to enjoy the normal pleasures of life. Depressed people may brood about death and dying, and may exhibit suicidal behavior. Some people experience depressive episodes—onsets of symptoms that can be severe and disabling. Others can continue to function, but feel depressed and "under the weather" all the time, a condition called *dysthymia*.

Manic episodes, by contrast, are marked initially by elation, hyperactivity, irritability, decreased need for sleep, inflated self-esteem, and increased loud speech, with abrupt changes of topic. As the episode progresses, the person with mania can, like those with schizophrenia, become overtly psychotic, experiencing delusions, hallucinations, and bizarre behavior.

Individuals suffering from *bipolar disorder* alternate between episodes of excitement/mania and major depression. Symptoms can be severe and disabling, or relatively mild, a condition called *cyclothymia*.

Anxiety disorders. Anxiety is a normal, necessary part of life that everyone experiences at times. As a symptom, it is not uncommon in the early stages of schizophrenia when the individual is experiencing strange new sensations; and it often accompanies mood disorders. In another group of disorders, however, anxiety is the core symptom. Anxiety disorders affect approximately 10.1 percent of the general population, or more than 18 million people, during any year. These disorders can take several forms.

Generalized anxiety disorders are marked by jumpiness, irritability, tension, sweating, racing or pounding heart, and a variety of other symptoms associated with anxiety. The person is apprehensive, on edge, and has problems getting to sleep. To be considered a disorder, the symptoms should be persistent, generally continuing for more than a few weeks.

People with *panic disorder* are subject to attacks of panic from out of nowhere, with no obvious cause. They become extremely frightened and often think they are going to die. They suffer heart palpitations, dizziness, chest pains, a sense of unreality, and other symptoms. The disorder can be limited to a period of a few weeks or months, but more commonly it recurs over time. Although the attack itself generally lasts only a few minutes, anticipating the feeling of helplessness or loss of control that accompanies the panic can make the person reluctant to be alone or to leave home.

The individual whose frequent attacks have increasingly constricted normal activities is usually diagnosed as having *agoraphobia*. This is the most disabling of all the phobias, which are also considered anxiety disorders. The person with agoraphobia usually avoids situations where escape would be difficult or impossible—crowds, tunnels, stores, bridges, elevators, or public transportation. Some people with agoraphobia become so fearful that they never leave their homes for years at a time.

Other types of phobia include *simple phobias*, the persistent and irrational fear of a specific object, activity, or situation, and *social phobias*, the irrational fear of humiliating or embarrassing oneself in public.

Yet another anxiety disorder is *posttraumatic stress disorder*, which is an often recurrent reaction to a psychologically traumatic event that is outside the range of usual human experience. Wartime combat, bombing, rape, floods, or torture are examples of this type of experience. Symptoms include reexperiencing the event, nonresponsiveness to others, little interest in outside activities, sleeplessness, memory problems, and loss of concentration.

Obsessive-compulsive disorder (OCD) is an anxiety disorder involving repetitive thoughts and behaviors that are difficult if not impossible to control. The intrusive and obsessive thoughts may revolve around a fear of harming others or of being harmed. In response to obsessive thoughts, OCD victims often feel obligated to perform certain rituals—behaving in a specific way a specific number of times—to ward off harm, even though they know that the behavior is illogical. Two of the most common OCD rituals are handwashing and checking. For example, persons who fear either being contaminated or contaminating others will wash their hands numerous times for long periods of time every day. Or persons who fear harming others, such as running over them with a car, will stop their car repeatedly to check on whether there is a victim lying dead on the road.

Some people with OCD are obsessed with self-doubt and compulsively check to see if they have locked doors or turned off equipment or carried out other tasks for which they feel responsible.

Personality disorders. The individual with a personality disorder demonstrates personality traits that are inflexible and cause him or her either to adjust poorly in social relationships or to suffer internal distress. Characteristic of these disorders are rigid and deeply rooted dysfunctional patterns in relating, perceiving, and thinking. Personality disorders typically become apparent in adolescence or earlier and are often less obvious in middle and old age. This age-related pattern is especially true of the individual with an *antisocial personality*, usually a person in the late teens or the twenties who is in continuous social or legal trouble and appears to profit little from parental or social punishment.

The characteristics of *borderline personality* are manifested in sudden changes in mood, unstable interpersonal relationships, and proneness to unpredictable actions which could be self-damaging. Individuals with this disorder may also have a mood disorder.

An individual with *paranoid personality* characteristically behaves toward others with unwarranted suspicion, envy, jealousy, and stubbornness. He is ready to believe that others have taken advantage of him, even when evidence to the contrary is presented.

Mental Illnesses Can Be Treated

Thanks to research, many effective therapies are available for the treatment of mental illnesses. Medications and different types of psychosocial therapies have been used alone or in combination. The treatment chosen for an individual depends on the diagnosis and severity of the illness. For severe disorders, such as schizophrenia, depression, and bipolar disorder, as well as some anxiety disorders, a doctor usually prescribes medication and some form of psychosocial therapy. These include individual psychotherapy, group and family therapy, behavior therapy, marital counseling, recreational therapy, occupational therapy, hypnotherapy, behavior modification, art therapy, and psychodrama. With some other disorders, psychosocial therapy may be all that is needed for a successful recovery.

At times, electroconvulsive therapy, often referred to as ECT or "shock" therapy, can be lifesaving for severely depressed and suicidal individuals, some of whom may not respond to other therapies.

These People Can Help

Psychiatrists, psychologists, psychiatric social workers, psychiatric nurses, mental health counselors and aides, or teachers who are specially trained in the area of mental illnesses and their treatment are among those who can be of assistance. It is beneficial to discuss problems with a family doctor or clergyman who can offer referral information. Self-help organizations can also be beneficial.

How to Find Help

There are many services available to persons experiencing mental and emotional problems:

- Mental health associations, consumer organizations, and mutual help groups can provide assistance and information about mental health resources available in your community.

- Professional associations usually have State or local chapters that can help in finding an appropriate professional in the community. These include the State psychiatric and psychological associations or medical societies.

- Family service agencies may also provide information, referrals, and counseling for individuals and families.

- State and local departments of social services, city or county health departments, or county medical associations and others, including Veterans Administration hospitals, school counseling programs, and private clinics, can also provide help.

- State mental hospitals usually maintain special units for intensive short-term treatment and specialized programs for disorders of longer duration. Some private hospitals also have short-term psychiatric, intensive-care units.

- Community mental health centers provide a myriad of mental health services including inpatient, outpatient, partial hospitalization, and aftercare services. Also included are services for children and the elderly.

To obtain the name and telephone number of mental health services in your community, scan the front cover of your telephone book where police and fire departments list their telephone numbers. Often mental health programs are listed on this page. You can check the Yellow Pages under "mental health," "health," "social services," "suicide prevention," "hospitals," or "physicians." For appropriate numbers, you can also call directory assistance or the operator and request the telephone number of your local mental health center.

11

Once you make contact with your local mental health clinic, you will meet trained personnel who can answer your questions, provide assistance, or direct you to a further source of help.

If an emergency exists—someone is threatening suicide or acting in a violent or extremely bizarre manner—call the police or an ambulance. You can also contact a mental health hotline or suicide prevention center.

Three Important Tips

How much you are helped depends on several factors: (1) Obtaining the right diagnosis is important; some mental illnesses have one or more symptoms in common, so careful evaluation is required; (2) Your therapist should have the training and most up-to-date information needed to treat your mental illness; (3) There should be a "fit" between your personality and that of the therapist. It pays to seek help from another if you feel dissatisfied or unaided by a particular therapist.

Most of us experience stress in the course of living. If you have a mental or emotional problem from time to time, try not to be unduly discouraged. But if the problem persists, or is severe, you should seek help. Remember, you are not alone.

For Further Information on Mental Health and Mental Illness, Write to:

Information Resources and Inquiries Branch
Office of Scientific Information
National Institute of Mental Health
5600 Fishers Lane, Room 15C-05
Rockville, MD 20857

National Mental Health Association, Inc.
1021 Prince Street
Alexandria, VA 22314-2971

National Alliance for the Mentally Ill
2101 Wilson Blvd., Suite 302
Arlington, VA 22201

National Depressive and Manic Depressive Association
730 N. Franklin, Suite 501
Chicago, IL 60601

Anxiety Disorders Association of America
6000 Executive Blvd. Suite 200
Rockville, MD 20852-4004

Chapter 2

Mental Illness in America

Introduction

In its report on the Fiscal Year 1992 budget for the Department of Health and Human Services, the Senate Committee on Appropriations stated:

> *The Committee appreciates the ongoing work of the National Advisory Mental Health Council and the National Mental Health Leadership Forum. The Committee requests that reports of these groups be transmitted to the Committee, as authorized under section 406(g) of the Public Health Service Act.* (Senate Report No. 102-104, p. 153)

The following report has been prepared by the National Advisory Mental Health Council in response to this request.

Background

America faces an extraordinary health crisis: lack of adequate care for millions of its citizens who suffer from mental illness. Almost four million Americans, including one-third of the Nation's homeless,

---

Excerpts from *Mental Illness in America: A Series of Public Hearings,* A Report to Congress prepared by the National Advisory Mental Health Council, December 1991.

are now suffering from severe mental illness. For them, treatment delayed is treatment denied.

Mental illness is a no-fault disease. It can and does strike down Americans from all walks of life. Tragically, one in five Americans will suffer from mental illness at some point in their lives, and only 20 percent of them will receive any type of professional care. The prevalence of mental disorders is a real and pervasive problem. In the United States, approximately 22 percent of the population will experience a diagnosable mental disorder during their lives. The economic costs of mental illness are increasing rapidly and constitute an enormous burden to society. Only 37 percent of all health insurance policies provide inpatient coverage for mental illness comparable to coverage for other illnesses, and only 6 percent have a comparable outpatient coverage. Such poor insurance coverage hardly seems appropriate for problems as debilitating and costly as mental illness.

The victims of severe, persistent, and disabling disorders—like anxiety disorders, schizophrenia and manic depressive disease—are too frequently left to suffer alone, without hope. They suffer needlessly, without the knowledge of medical research into possible treatments and medications that could bring relief and a return to productivity.

How can this be? Clearly, something is terribly wrong. The unfortunate truth is that most Americans do not yet understand that mental illness is a disease, and like heart disease or diabetes, it can be effectively treated. For example, 80 to 90 percent of those suffering from depression respond quickly to treatment. Available treatments can help up to 80 percent of those suffering from manic depressive disorder, and 80 percent of the victims of schizophrenia can be relieved of acute symptoms with proper medication.

Mental disorders are still shrouded in myth and ignorance. These combine to produce widespread public stigma. This pervasive and pernicious stigma robs its victims of their ability to seek treatment and condemns them to long-term and unnecessary agony.

In December 1989, members of the National Advisory Mental Health Council and the National Mental Health Leadership Forum planned an unprecedented series of three National public hearings—**Mental Illness in America**—to bring these problems into full public view in order to confront, and at long last, to overcome them. The hearings were held in Marshall, MN, Los Angeles, CA, and Chicago, IL during 1990 and 1991.

Established in 1946, The National Advisory Mental Health Council is an advisory body of 12 experts in the fields of mental health and public policy relevant to The National Institute of Mental Health (NIMH). Council members, appointed by the Secretary of the Department of Health and Human Services, advise the NIMH on policies and programs concerning the nation's mental health. The National Mental Health Leadership Forum, established in 1988, is a coalition of 38 professional and voluntary mental health interest groups.

The shared objective of the Council and the Forum in sponsoring these extraordinary hearings was to reach out to America and to hear firsthand, the problems and barriers, as well as the opportunities and possible solutions to enhancing our knowledge and improving care for persons suffering from mental illness. The programmatic content of the three hearings differed, but they shared a common format. Panel presentations allowed patients, service providers, health administrators, researchers, public officials, and legislators from across the country to testify to members of the Council and the Forum. Their testimony formed the basis for policy recommendations outlined in this report. Before, during, and after each hearing, impressive media campaigns focused the attention of an estimated 100 million people on critical issues concerning mental illness.

Testimony presented at these unique hearings defined the problems we face and underscored the urgency of our unfinished agenda:

- One in five Americans, at some point in their lives, will have a diagnosable mental disorder.

- An estimated 7.5 million American children under the age of 18 suffer from a mental disorder.

- Many of the approximately 29,000 Americans per year who commit suicide suffer from a treatable mental illness, such as depression or manic depressive illness.

- Suicide is the second leading cause of death for our youth between the ages of 15 and 19 years. Among adolescents, suicide has increased over 30 percent since 1950.

- Schizophrenia strikes more than 2.5 million Americans over the course of their lifetimes. Approximately 30 percent of all hospitalized psychiatric patients in the United States suffer from this most disabling group of mental disorders.

- Major depression and manic-depressive disorders affect approximately one out of every 10 Americans.

- One-third of the 600,000 homeless persons in the country are also victims of severe mental illness.

The long shadow of mental illness stretches back through time. President Abraham Lincoln suffered from depressive illness. He stated, "I am now the most miserable man living. If what I feel were equally distributed to the whole human family, there would not be one cheerful face on earth." But Abraham Lincoln saved the Union while he endured a mental disorder. He was not called "mentally ill"; he was called "Mr. President."

This Nation's inattention to mental illness has been tolerated far too long. It troubles our national conscience that the problem of mental illness is too unpleasant to mention, too easy to put off, and seemingly devoid of solution.

No one doubts the destructive consequences of an untreated mental disorder. Nonetheless, the most recurrent, reverberating themes of these hearings documented the ways in which mentally ill individuals and their loved ones are victims of widespread and enduring stigma and ignorance. Numerous scientific studies have shown that stigma is the most debilitating handicap faced by mentally ill Americans. Ignorance is the breeding ground for stigma, and stigma exists among people regardless of their place of residence, socioeconomic level, intelligence, or education.

Recent data document the corrosive effects of stigma. In one study, 71 percent of respondents said mental illness is due to some emotional weakness; 65 percent said bad parenting is at fault; 35 percent pointed to sinful behavior; 45 percent believed mentally ill people can bring on or turn off their illnesses at will; and 43 percent said such illness is incurable. Only 10 percent believe severe mental disorders have a biological basis involving the brain. Scientific studies have documented that mental illnesses are real diseases and not the result of personal failure, lack of willpower, or moral weakness.

As President Bush stated in his 1991 proclamation for Mental Illness Awareness Week:

> *Mental illness is becoming more widely understood. Thanks to dramatic advances in basic biomedical research and in the behavioral sciences, we have been able to achieve significant improvements in the diagnosis, treatment, and prevention of emotional and mental disorders. Scientific progress has also helped to alleviate the stigma associated with mental illness, as more and more Americans learn about its origins and effects.*

Hearing on Mental Illness in Rural America
Marshall, Minnesota, April 12, 1990

Program Description

The Council and Forum met in Marshall, Minnesota to hear witnesses from across the nation speak about the problems of mental illness in rural America. Mental disorders are not unique to rural communities, but a long term declining rural economy is placing many more people at risk. Farms are vital to the rural economic base, but during the last decade their financial vigor has dwindled. Community tax bases have eroded, young people have fled to jobs in urban areas, and rural educational and human service programs have declined.

The Senate Committee on Appropriations expressed its concern about mental disorders and access to care in a 1989 report (Senate Report 101-127). The Committee report refers to rural America's increasing unemployment and poverty—its loss of people and resources. The report notes that at the same time, rural rates of substance abuse, mental disorders, and suicide have climbed alarmingly. It also states that American Indians and Alaskan Native Americans in rural areas face the consequences of even greater poverty and other risk factors associated with mental illnesses, yet these groups have fewer mental health services available and very poor access to care compared to other rural residents.

During the hearing, consumers, families, mental health professionals, researchers, service providers, and public representatives discussed the psychobiological and social causes of mental illnesses in rural areas and possible solutions. Senator David Durenberger; Congressman Vin Weber; Alcohol, Drug Abuse, and Mental Health Administrator Frederick Goodwin, M.D.; and the then NIMH Director, Lewis L. Judd, M.D. opened the discussion. Members of the Council and Forum served as hearing officers for four panels addressing overall rural mental health issues and the specific issues of depression, teenage suicide, and stigma. The panels were followed by an open town meeting attended by 350 people interested in rural mental health.

Findings

Rural Mental Health Issues. Many Americans in rural areas have suffered mental and emotional anguish. Witnesses testified that such anguish, exacerbated by economic crisis and hardship, has taken its toll. There are increased dysfunctional family patterns, alcohol and substance abuse, and related problems. In the face of an increased risk of mental disorders, rural residents are often unable to get needed help. Few psychiatrists, psychologists, and other mental health professionals are available in rural America; specialists in specific mental disorders are practically nonexistent. Also missing are supervised housing and group homes; thus hospitals are often forced to keep patients well enough to be discharged. Too often, emergency care for those in crisis is the local jail.

Even where services are available, delay and distance are additional barriers—but not the only ones. Too many in need are unable to pay for care. Many rural residents are without third-party health coverage; many who are covered are underinsured. Many farmers and small rural businesses cannot afford adequate mental health coverage.

Rural Native Americans face special hardships. Available mental health services for Native American children, youth, and adults are minimal; access to care is poor.

Depression. Witnesses cited evidence indicating the depth of depressive illness in rural America. A 1988 Iowa State University study reported that 22 percent of (a representative sample of 400) rural Iowans suffered symptoms of depression. A 1986 Minnesota study of 2200 rural young people found that 18 percent were moderately or severely depressed.

The National Rural Mental Health Association cited a study showing that during the worst of the farm crisis, 80 percent of adults in rural families with serious economic setbacks suffered from a range of emotional problems. Seventy-three percent had sleep problems, 62 percent had feelings of worthlessness, and 56 percent were withdrawn. A North Dakota mental health Helpline received 9000 calls in 1988. Forty percent of the calls were related to the farm crises; most of the callers discussed depression and suicide.

Consumer witnesses speaking about personal consequences of the farm crisis vividly substantiated these statistics. They discussed the onset of serious depression due to changes in family and home caused by economic hardship. In rural areas, the stress factor seems greater than in urban areas. Loss of farm or employment in rural areas means a family or some of its members must face additional stress because of the need to find work and move to another locale. Both those moving and those left behind feel increased despair and hopelessness.

Witnesses also told how unemployment and underemployment place special burdens on rural women, especially those in farming families. Farm women often have many and diverse responsibilities that include homemaking, child-rearing, and elder-care responsibilities, as well as work on and off the farm. As a result, witnesses said they are at special risk for stress and depression.

Teenage Suicide. Teenage suicide in rural America is an all too frequent human tragedy. A 1986 University of Minnesota study found that six percent of 2200 rural Minnesotans between 15 and 19 reported an attempted suicide during the prior six months. Suicide rates among rural young Native Americans are nearly twice the national average. Suicide is not confined to those of school age in rural areas. Witnesses cited data in which suicide rates in a population of rural farmers were significantly higher than the national average.

Although mental disorders are the most common cause of suicide, witnesses cited stress from a deteriorating rural economy as a contributing factor. Youngsters who took their lives said in suicide notes that their death might help ease the family's financial burden. Other possible influencing factors in suicides, according to witnesses, are alcohol abuse (especially among young rural Native American suicide victims), violence, substance abuse, apathy, neglect, and sexual abuse.

Witnesses stressed that given the magnitude of suicide and other problems in rural areas, there are far too few resources available to treat mental and addictive disorders, to prevent suicides, and/or to treat suicidal youth. Rural communities often lack emergency facilities; treatment is often delayed.

Stigma. According to many witnesses, stigma stops people with mental illness from seeking appropriate help. Those who do seek help place themselves at risk of humiliation. Why is there the strong stigma against mental illness in rural culture? It may result from the particularly strong rural pride in self reliance and independence. Mental and emotional problems threaten that image and are seen as signs of irrationality and weakness. Added to the aversion against mental disorders in rural areas is a lack of privacy for those who overcome the isolation imposed by the illness.

Witnesses further noted that rural residents, faced with strong stigma against mental illness, are very reluctant to admit to personal problems. As a result, both those afflicted with mental disorders and their families often find the stigma harder to overcome than the illness. In some cases, stigma may take more subtle but serious forms; it may originate from those supposed to help. Parents may hesitate to seek help for themselves or their children out of fear that service providers will infer a dysfunctional or abusive family situation. Where communities rely on law enforcement officials for restraint in the absence of emergency care, stigma can be exacerbated. Persons incarcerated or even accompanied by police can feel like and be perceived as criminals.

Stigma affects not only the individual considering whether to seek help. It also influences reimbursement policies. Too many health insurers, according to witnesses, fail to understand there are a number of both successful and cost-effective treatments for mental illnesses. Instead, they retain the belief that mental health services are a "bottomless pit" that will overwhelm health care financing; the result can be failure to provide adequate coverage.

Town Meeting. Town meeting participants testified on a range of issues confirming and providing new depth to perspectives offered in the panel sessions. For example, a psychologist cited his research findings that indeed economic turmoil is a factor in interpersonal stress, anxiety, and depression. Other witnesses cited that environmental factors important for recovery, such as affordable housing and transportation, are often absent in rural economies.

The lack of available or accessible mental health professionals was again frequently mentioned. In Minnesota, a predominantly rural state, only 40-50 out of 400 psychiatrists practice in rural areas. There are insufficient incentives to recruit and retain mental health professionals in rural areas. Salaries, for example, lag behind those in urban areas. Lesser Medicare and Medicaid reimbursement levels to mental health programs in rural areas exacerbate the imbalance.

Some rural communities are able to provide care by utilizing available health professionals—for example, primary care physicians and psychiatric social workers. Community resource people—clergy, agricultural extension agents and even bankers—serve informally to refer people to professional caregivers. In some cases, people without professional health training, including consumers, are hired to identify and offer counsel to those possibly needing help, but hesitating to seek it.

The special value of utilizing community resource people is not only extension of or substitution for scarce resources. Community resource people are often better able to overcome the impediment that stigma exerts on access to mental health services. Located in the community and immersed in its culture, community resource people are able to extend outreach more effectively than professionals—particularly those from outside the rural community.

Hearing on Child and Adolescent Mental Disorders
Los Angeles, California, October 9, 1990

Program Description

The focus of the second hearing was on the status of research and services concerning mental disorders in children and adolescents, and on steps that must be taken to free our youth of the costly, tragic burdens of mental illness. Care for children and adolescents suffering mental illnesses has been identified by Congress, the Council, and the NIMH as a focal concern. The United States Congress received from Council a *National Plan for Research on Child and Adolescent Mental Disorders* in order to further knowledge in this crucial area.

The opening plenary session of the hearing, entitled "Faces of Mental Illness," consisted of personal stories intended to reveal the human face of child and adolescent mental disorders. It was co-chaired by actress Patty Duke and Lewis L. Judd, M.D., then Director of the NIMH and Chairman of the Forum. Children suffering from mental illness and from all walks of American life and members of their families described the effects of these disorders from personal, family, and financial perspectives. They related success stories of winning the battle to overcome mental illness, as well as tragedies of death at the end of a difficult search for effective treatment.

The plenary session was followed by four panels meeting concurrently: Risk Factors for Mental Disorders in Children and Adolescents; a two-part panel covering depression and suicide in children and adolescents and stigma and its impact on children and adolescents; Service Systems for Children and Adolescents with Mental Disorders; and an at-large public hearing covering a wide range of service and financing issues.

Because of the breadth and scope of participation, the hearing was successful in bringing together a full spectrum of viewpoints and knowledge resources on child and adolescent mental disorders. The perspectives included those of basic and clinical scientists, of service providers and consumers, and of those with expertise in the organization, financing, and delivery of care.

Findings

In addition to reinforcing the need for a broad, well-organized research effort in the area of child and adolescent mental disorders, the hearing focused attention on and brought new light to other critical issues in the mental health needs of American youth: the presentation and candid discussion of both successes and failures of child mental health service systems; review of financial issues and problems of access to care; a highlight of the need for more successful public-private sector coordination and of the need for better graduate education programs for professionals preparing to conduct research and/or provide care to children and adolescents; broad-based presentation of issues specific to the hospital-based care of children and adolescents.

One remark by a consumer witness served to synthesize the human and scientific issues succinctly: "Active treatment . . . rendered by psychiatrists who kept up with current scientific findings enabled my daughter to get the proper medical treatment (medication) for her condition and to progress. The brain research supported by NIMH resulted in immediate and obvious benefit to her and made the difference in her life."

The most poignant "finding" came from the panel "Faces of Mental Illness": no one is immune to mental illness. All who attended this session were made acutely aware that mental illness can bring torment and destruction to the lives of rich and poor alike, regardless of race, age, sex, or residence.

Risk Factors. In the General Risk Factors panel, researchers and other professionals addressed issues concerning the distribution of risk of developing mental illness. If risk is unevenly distributed, what are the differentiating factors? In addition to risk factors, are there "protective factors" which reduce the risk of mental illness?

All children are not at equal risk of developing mental disorders. Rather, studies suggest that certain factors can contribute toward a disorder. The probability of developing a mental illness increases progressively with the number of risk factors present.

Risk factors include genetic predisposition, which increases a child's vulnerability to autism, Tourette's syndrome, and affective, anxiety, attentional, and learning disorders. Poor prenatal care, which leads to increased risk of premature birth and a host of related problems, can also contribute to the risk of developing mental disorders, as can chronic physical illness—such as leukemia, diabetes mellitus, asthma, cystic fibrosis, epilepsy, and AIDS. Cognitive impairments, such as those resulting from mental retardation, as well as deficits in sensory perception, including deafness and blindness, can also be contributing factors.

There is an increased risk for developing mental disorders in children surrounded by persistent psychological adversity, such as violence, poverty, disorganized and inadequate schooling, and homelessness. Child abuse or neglect, disturbed family relationships, and parental mental illness may also contribute to increased risk. Conversely, some children—even when raised in extremely adverse conditions—do not become mentally ill, possibly because of "protective factors." What these "protective factors" are remains unclear. Elucidation of their nature, however, would be invaluable in furthering efforts to prevent mental disorders in our youngsters.

Comorbidity. New research suggests that adolescents and young adults with mental disorders often have co-occurring substance abuse disorders as well. The panel on Alcohol, Drug, and Other Risk Factors for Mental Disorders in Children and Adolescents discussed issues of comorbidity.

Some research findings suggest that substance use plays a role in the etiology of affective disorders, anxiety disorders, conduct disorders, and antisocial personality. The peak age (15-19) for developing an alcohol or drug disorder is also the peak age of onset for developing bipolar and depressive disorders. Heavy use of substances like alcohol or cocaine may produce severe depression or paranoid behavior.

Conversely, mental disorders may play a role in the vulnerability of adolescents for developing substance-use disorders. For example, prior depression or anxiety may lead to "self-medication" in an effort to relieve a disturbed mood.

Since genetic predisposition may determine which individuals are most susceptible to addictive and mental disorders, an understanding of the genetic bases of mental illnesses and substance abuse disorders may provide markers to determine who is at risk.

Depression and Suicide. Suicide is the eighth leading cause of death in the U.S. and the second leading cause among those 15-19. Approximately 4900 people between 15 and 24 take their lives each year. Estimates vary widely on the number of attempted suicides for each completion. In 1988 (the most recent year for which National Center for Health statistics are available), the suicide rate among those 15 to 19 was 11.3 in 100,000.

The panel concerning Depression and Suicide in Children and Adolescents addressed questions about the causes of the high rate of suicide in the 15 to 24 age range, and about symptoms or other factors suggesting a high risk for suicidal behavior.

Causal factors for youth suicide include mental illnesses. One recent study demonstrated that approximately 90 percent of adolescent suicides were committed by individuals with a diagnosable mental disorder, including depression, antisocial behavior, drug and alcohol abuse, and learning disorders.

Depression, even though largely treatable, is one of the leading causes of suicide in children and adolescents. Depression causes the sufferer to experience a persistent sadness, a loss of pleasure from ordinarily enjoyable activities, fatigue, and often overwhelming feelings of pessimism or hopelessness that may lead to suicide.

The various stresses of adolescent life, including change of schools and homes, unstable parenting figures, and unreasonable expectations are also suspected risk factors for adolescent depression and suicide.

Stigma and Its Impact on Children and Adolescents. The main cause of stigma is ignorance. The extent of mental disorders in our children far outreaches the general level of understanding which the nation has of them. Ignorance about the biological and sociocultural bases of mental disorders and the availability and effectiveness of treatment regimens is common.

The stigma associated with mental disorders can be especially damaging to our young people. Parents with a mistaken belief of fault often "cover up" the mental disorders of their children. The result could be the tragic avoidance of diagnosis and treatment possibly effective in alleviating the child's suffering.

Media portrayal of the mentally ill as unstable or dangerous has been cited as a possible contributing factor to the stigmatization of mental illness and treatment. Additionally, the incorrect belief that mental disorders are permanent and irreversible persists in a large portion of the population, along with the fear that seeking treatment for a mental disorder is tantamount to admitting one is "insane."

Service Systems for Children and Adolescents Suffering from Mental Disorders. The complexity of serving the mental health needs of children and adolescents was highlighted by the following quotation from a witness describing the California mental health service systems: "California has approximately 160 children-and-youth-serving programs, overseen by 37 different state entities, located in seven different State departments. These State programs are implemented through 20 different types of programs at the county level, with consumer access determined by over 25 different and often conflicting eligibility criteria."

The major question raised at the California and Pennsylvania Service Systems for Children and Adolescent Mental Disorders panel was: what are the key issues that must be addressed in order to decrease the complexity and increase the efficiency and effectiveness of service programs? The panels also addressed the related issue of how Federal, state and local governments can more effectively work together to improve services. In other words, is there a sound basis in systems research to guide service system development?

Additionally, many of the problems that face children in volatile situations—in which they are confronted with violence, homelessness, addiction, or endogenous mental disorders—could be alleviated or entirely averted through more appropriate, accessible, and effective therapeutic intervention. A system of care is required in which youths who present a number of co-occurring mental and addictive disorders can receive coordinated treatment for all the factors underlying their condition.

The demand for meeting the unique mental health needs of children and adolescents is complicated in that services provided to children are the responsibility of a great many uncoordinated organizations and agencies. Cost shifting among agencies with shared responsibility creates further substantial confusion and makes it difficult to track treatment costs and other economic impacts.

Complex and often conflicting eligibility requirements are also a significant access barrier. This factor often contributes to frustrating and counterproductive service fragmentation. Different types of mental health-related services for youth operate in isolation from each other. The result is a vertical-type service system in which each type specializes only in a particular aspect of the child or adolescent.

In many cases the parents of children and adolescents in need of mental health care are forced to make choices among limited and uncoordinated resources. Until just recently, several states required parents to relinquish custody of their children in order to get treatment for them.

A less extreme but still unacceptable situation is the prevailing out-of-state placement of disturbed children who need residential service. Emotionally disturbed children are all too frequently bounced from one service system to another because of poor or non-existent service coordination, or because of their families' inability either to afford proper treatment or to meet state or Federal criteria for assistance.

Other Issues. Additional panels focused on a variety of issues including access to care, financial issues, advocacy, and public/private sector coordination.

It is important to determine the forces that inhibit or facilitate access to appropriate care. Definition of these forces can make appropriate care available to all children and adolescents suffering from mental illnesses.

Financing of care for mentally ill children and adolescents must be reexamined. Do reimbursement streams define service programs? How does cost shifting affect the cost of care in public and private settings?

Questions surfaced about the organization and delivery of care to children and adolescents. What are the prerequisites of effective public/private coordination that will produce an integrated system of care?

In the broad view, the hearing resulted in enrichment of the substantive knowledge of the issues for each participant and for the field at large, and in enhancement of public awareness of the need to focus national attention on the mental health needs of our young people. With the help of Patty Duke and others, the stigma associated with mental illness was challenged and, for many observers, reduced.

Hearing on Severe Mental Illness and Homelessness
Chicago, Illinois, September 5, 1991

Program Description

Severe mental illness and homelessness was the subject of the third hearing in this series. It convened on September 5, 1991 in Chicago, Illinois. Unique to this hearing was the active participation of the Federal Interdepartmental Task Force on Homelessness and Severe Mental Illness. The purpose of this Task Force is to assist the Executive Branch of Government in developing a national strategy to assist states, localities, and the private sector better to meet the housing, treatment, and support needs of severely mentally ill persons.

The hearing's theme was chosen because of the tragic and growing public health problem confronting this nation in its quest to develop improved methods of treating and caring for the severely mentally ill. Although there have been major research advances in clinical and basic neurosciences and in behavioral sciences in recent years, millions of severely mentally ill people have not yet been the beneficiaries of those advances.

- At any time, there are approximately 600,000 homeless people in America. It is estimated that 200,000 homeless persons suffer from severe mental disorders.

- Only two percent of the citizens of the United States with health care coverage have policies that adequately and fairly cover mental illness.

- Among health maintenance and preferred provider organizations in this country, over 60 percent now specifically exclude treatment for those with severe mental disorders.

The hearing explored the medical, behavioral, sociological and financial issues associated with severe mental illness. In addition to raising public awareness, the hearing generated findings and recommendations suggesting significant changes in mental health programs and policy on the Federal, state, and local levels, as well as for the private sector.

The opening session presented a distinguished group of dignitaries who provided background information and discussed their own unique perspectives on severe mental illness and homelessness. Academy Award-winning actor Rod Steiger (who has suffered from severe depression) and nationally syndicated columnist Ann Landers were honorary guest speakers. Leading national experts in the field of mental health as well as local and state political and religious figures, including Chicago Mayor Richard Daley and His Eminence Joseph Cardinal Bernardin, also addressed the audience of over 1,000 people.

Following this opening session, witnesses in a special panel entitled "Faces of Severe Mental Illness and Homelessness" presented testimony describing their own personal battles with these devastating disorders. The speakers told how these illnesses affect families, friends, and careers; they spoke of the successes and failures of treatment. The audience repeatedly heard that these illnesses affect people regardless of social class, ethnic background, gender, or age.

At the end of the main plenary session, the hearing divided into five concurrent panels: Knowledge Development and Dissemination and New Treatments; Severe Mental Illness and Homelessness; Treatment Delivery Systems; Criminal Justice Issues and Insurance Issues; and Successful Programs and Advocacy.

Members of the Council, Forum and Federal Interdepartmental Task Force on Homelessness and Severe Mental Illness served as officers of the hearing. A wide array of consumers, mental health professionals, researchers, service providers and public officials provided testimony. Findings and recommendations from these panels covered a wide range of research, service, resource, and public education issues.

Findings

Knowledge Development and Dissemination and New Treatments. This panel discussed the mounting research evidence demonstrating that untreated mental disorders may lead to increased utilization of primary care medical services and also contribute to the burden on the criminal justice system. Currently only 20 percent of adults suffering from a diagnosable mental illness are receiving professional treatment for their disorder. In the past ten years, research has made possible the development of reliable diagnostic systems, sophisticated epidemiological information, and new pharmacologic and psychosocial therapies—all of which have made rigorous treatment outcome research possible. The capacity to "tailor" treatments to specific conditions is increasing. Research is on the threshold of breakthroughs in the understanding of the biological and behavioral bases of mental illness. These advances will lead to even better technologies and therapies for the diagnosis and treatment of devastating and costly severe mental disorders.

Testimony revealed a need for targeted epidemiological studies of severe, persistent, and disabling mental disorders to determine prevalence and to identify variations in rates that might provide important information regarding risk factors for mental illness. Panelists also suggested that advances in imaging technology have greatly enhanced our knowledge about the human brain. To exploit this technology fully, we must move beyond the discovery of anatomical abnormalities and begin to examine their causes. Speakers raised concern about the need to improve diagnostic accuracy, including comprehensive assessment of functional impairments, and the need to address problems of impaired quality of life and the potential for successful rehabilitation. Other areas demanding further study include methods to reduce or eliminate symptoms, to improve social or vocational functioning, to increase personal sense of well being, and to change relationships to

31

family and community. Also needed is research on new and innovative techniques being integrated into psychotherapy and on the effectiveness of these approaches.

There was concern about the potentially toxic side effects of many drugs used to treat mental illness. Side effects are a major reason for the lack of patient compliance in taking medication. Research is needed to develop new medications and to profile new dose strategies that reduce side effects. New and more efficacious treatments need to be developed for individuals resistant to conventional pharmacologic treatments.

Witnesses at a services-research roundtable testified that the current mental health system is fragmented and difficult to access. Formulation of a comprehensive, integrated service delivery system, perhaps including case managers, is needed. A major cross-cutting issue is the relationship of the mental health system to the general medical care system. Further research could clarify the most effective role for the primary, care provider, nonmedical providers, the local community hospital, nursing homes, social service departments, schools, and penal institutions. Increased linkages are needed between mental health services researchers and other components of the mental health services community including state departments of mental health, community mental health facilities, and state hospitals. Also necessary is increased communication among mental health, public health, and substance abuse service agencies.

Concomitant with increasing attention to the organization of mental health services should be recognition that many mentally ill individuals are incarcerated in jails, prisons, and juvenile facilities. There is a need to study the extent of the problem and to devise strategies to improve the response of these facilities to these issues and the provision of care.

All panelists agreed that stigmatization of mental illness and mentally ill persons has contributed to longstanding problems in the organization, financing, and delivery of mental health care. Effective ways to overcome barriers resulting from stigma and to identify the best strategies to reintegrate those with mental disorders into the community must be developed. In addition, lack of adequate insurance coverage and reimbursement and the nationwide variability of coverage constitute major barriers to successful treatment of persons with severe mental illness. Finance mechanisms must be improved in both the public and private sectors.

Severe Mental Illness and Homelessness. In this portion of the hearing, expert witnesses provided an overview of issues related to housing, income support, and access to health and mental health care for homeless individuals with severe mental illness. Three separate panels addressed the most pressing problems of homeless mentally ill persons. They were:

- **Knowledge Gaps.** This panel concentrated on defining the problem and the areas which needed further research. Also discussed were research findings on the characteristics and needs of homeless mentally ill persons;

- **Housing and Services.** This panel emphasized innovative service approaches, with a particular view to the coordination of treatment, housing, and services for homeless mentally ill individuals;

- **Perspectives.** In this panel, experts who have worked with homeless persons discussed homelessness and severe mental illness from varying perspectives. The witnesses included a Circuit Court Judge, a representative from the Department of Health and Human Services Office of the Inspector General, and a representative from the National Mental Health Consumer Self-Help Clearinghouse.

All of the panels shared the common goal of defining and implementing a comprehensive strategy to end homelessness among homeless mentally ill persons. Now that the high percentage of mental disorders among homeless persons is recognized, it is clear that mental health service systems must be coordinated with the housing, health, and social services already utilized in fighting homelessness.

The homeless population is comprised of discrete subgroups. Each group has distinct and varying needs to be addressed in a comprehensive manner linking housing with necessary supportive services. This approach is especially important for those who are also severely mentally ill.

Studies during the past ten years reveal several major findings: homeless individuals with a severe mental illness often have other problems, such as co-occurring substance abuse, physical health problems, or involvement with the criminal justice system; these individuals also suffer from economic distress that makes securing and retaining affordable housing extremely difficult; these persons lack basic human services and face multiple institutional barriers to meeting basic human needs, including fragmented mental health services, lack of transportation, and stigmatization by service providers.

Although some residential treatment facilities exist, some homeless people refuse to live in them. Problems with rules and controls in some of these facilities result in many residents leaving and becoming homeless once again. Self-help, client-run programs supporting and advocating independent living exist as an alternative to "system" solutions. Mental health systems and programs involving consumers in their decision-making bodies benefit from and improve due to that involvement. Many of the expert witnesses felt that independent living remains the only viable option for the homeless. Support services that enable people, particularly the mentally ill, to secure and maintain their homes must also be available.

Many mentally ill and homeless individuals, women, adolescents, and children, are victims of family violence. There is a relationship between physical and sexual violence and homelessness and mental illness. Also, among the homeless population, families with children comprise the fastest growing subpopulation. Estimates indicate that a third of the nation's homeless are families with children, 23 percent are children, and at least 3 percent are unaccompanied youth. Homeless children have a greater prevalence of risk factors for impaired emotional development and poor mental health, such as acute and chronic physical health problems, developmental and academic delays, and reported physical abuse. There is a paucity of studies examining the mental health needs of homeless children, and many research questions remain to be answered.

One of the most pressing service delivery questions that must be answered is finding the most cost-effective approaches to delivering these services. Research and policy-making groups eagerly await new knowledge concerning alternatives or combinations of alternatives that may be most effective. What organizational structures for service delivery should be recommended? And with budget restrictions, what should be the priorities for services provision? These issues should be an immediate and high priority area of intensive study.

Treatment Delivery Systems for Persons with Severe Mental Illness. A great many organizations and agencies currently have the responsibility for meeting the mental health needs of this nation. For example, it is not unusual for any one state to have as many as 10 departments, divisions, offices, and commissions involved in serving the same population. This cumbersome multiplicity of shared responsibility often contributes to service fragmentation.

It is distressingly commonplace that people seeking mental health treatment are sent from one service to another because there is poor or nonexistent service coordination, because they cannot afford proper treatment, or because they do not meet state or Federal criteria for assistance. All this occurs in an atmosphere of current fiscal crisis that is taking a heavy toll on all these agencies. They are cutting back on the number of programs offered and staff employed.

At the state level, witnesses cited the need for strong support from the Governor's office for mental health services and for state legislatures to develop strong comprehensive health and mental health systems. Concern was expressed regarding the infrastructure for mental health service delivery. Planning and communication between state agencies and local providers remains a major problem.

Witnesses suggested that the key to serving the growing demands of persons with mental disorders is the development of a multidisciplinary group of professionals. Pools of well-trained providers should include staff who are sensitive to cultural differences, language barriers, and ethnic family customs and traditions. Families have a great deal of personal knowledge and experience in caring for their mentally ill relatives. They can collaborate with and motivate providers to implement beneficial interventions; families can have an impact on the service delivery system.

Testimony also underscored the growing problem of substance abuse co-occurring with mental illness.

Criminal Justice Issues. Just as "warehousing" victims of mental illness in state hospitals in the first half of the 20th century made no sense, locking them up in jails, sedating them in nursing homes, or ignoring them on our city streets makes no sense as we approach the 21st century.

Many mentally ill Americans enter the penal system, sometimes repeatedly. For example, the Los Angeles County Jail houses approximately 3,600 severely mentally ill individuals on any given day—700 more than the largest public mental hospital in the United States.

Although drug and alcohol abuse and mental retardation are not strictly considered "mental health" problems, the behavioral and emotional manifestations are often very similar, and at times indistinguishable. Many inmates have a combination of these conditions and present substantial custodial, treatment, and correctional problems to a criminal justice system poorly trained and ill equipped to manage the combination.

Pervasive stigma, absence of effective advocates, absence of effective administrative structures and services, and lack of interagency coordination and collaboration are all interrelated factors negatively affecting service delivery and development for mentally impaired persons involved in the criminal justice system.

Service development and delivery for severely mentally impaired persons involved with the criminal justice system require administrative and clinical leadership in both the human service and criminal justice systems. Concern was voiced that services be organized to function as a continuum that fosters the effective coordination and collaboration of **all** service components of the criminal justice system and the human service system.

Panelists raised the need to work with the inmate while he/she is in jail to enhance independent living skills and functioning. Providers should be sensitive to cultural differences and be knowledgeable about the offender's resistance to anything connected with his or her incarceration, including a pre-arranged appointment after release. There is also a need to expand liaisons with the community mental health systems in order to provide for more continuity of care of mentally ill offenders upon their discharge from prison.

Law enforcement officers will benefit from knowledge that gives them the opportunity to make sound professional judgments when they are dealing with a person possibly suffering from mental illness. Correctional officers may lack knowledge about the verbal and physical clues displayed by a mentally ill person. Training would enable the officers to interpret these clues correctly, rather than to jump to a conclusion that might place both officer and consumer at risk. Lack of information about the effects of medications and lack of training concerning verbal intervention techniques is also a problem.

Public and Private Third Party Reimbursement. Mental illnesses are among the most widespread, destructive, and costly public health problems in the United States. Many mentally ill Americans cannot access appropriate care and thus remain undertreated or worse yet, untreated.

A major reason access to care is limited is that insurance coverage and reimbursement mechanisms for the treatment of mental illnesses, particularly the most severe episodes, are grossly inadequate for most Americans, irrespective of their socioeconomic status. The disparity between insurance coverage for mental illness and physical illness is documented. An all too frequent discovery of a mentally ill patient is the way the health insurance industry can turn its back on a patient who becomes a casualty of the "fine print." Current well-known examples include coverage caps applied to both inpatient and outpatient mental health treatment, but not applied to general health treatment; and the difference between outpatient-treatment co-payments for physical problems as opposed to significantly higher copayments required under virtually all public and private insurance programs for outpatient mental health services. Limitations and exclusions for individuals suffering from mental illnesses are found throughout the myriad of health insurance plans offered by the public and private sectors. These limitations are especially true for the under- or uninsured, two-thirds of whom are employed by small businesses.

The Nation lacks a model mental health benefit plan which could be adopted by private insurers as a means of providing cost effective protection for mental health services.

Successful Programs. Coordination is critical for linking hospital and community services, housing with support services, and clinical treatment and rehabilitation. The legacy of problems created by deinstitutionalization can be clearly shown by the current state of inner cities and shelters overflowing with severely mentally ill persons in various stages of illness.

In addition to service coordination, another important role of community mental health services is to provide opportunities for rehabilitation. Rehabilitation is a continuing process that helps individuals improve their functioning so they can be more successful and satisfied in the living, learning, and working environments of their choice.

37

There are numerous successful programs in operation throughout the United States. Several were highlighted at the hearing as "model programs." These highly successful programs serve many ethnic populations in both urban and rural settings. Specialized services have been developed for children, adults, and the aged. Other target populations are comprised of homeless persons, people in jails, or alcohol and other drug abusers.

Characteristic of these successful programs is a culturally sensitive and highly trained staff capable of providing a wide range of services. Services provided frequently include good assessment of intake, case management services, vocational training, residential services, as well as medication therapy and emergency screening and assessment services. All treatment units are composed of highly trained staff from a variety of mental health disciplines. Some programs are also fully committed to careful monitoring of the effectiveness of their interventions and have regularly conducted evaluations showing that these programs dramatically reduce rehospitalization rates. Close coordination and integration with other community services is essential to success.

Advocacy Panel. Despite the existence of effective models of mental health service delivery in this country over the past 25 years, many states and communities have yet to develop long range plans for organizing, financing, and implementing truly integrated systems of care that are capable of addressing the complex needs of the severely and chronically mentally ill.

Money alone is not necessarily the determining factor when configuring a cost-effective system. The proof is that a number of states actually spend far less per capita, yet achieve far more with their mental health dollars.

Few would disagree that many problems will ultimately require strategic agreements between elected officials, administrators, and professionals. The situation is not helped when the stigma still attached to mental illness makes such resolution a low priority item on the public agenda.

What are the difficulties in developing humane and effective mental health systems and how can we direct our efforts towards moving public policy in this area? The advocacy panel raised this question, along with others.

Attempts to shift costs from one level of government to another (Federal, state, local) keep many public sector systems in constant flux and impede effective program design. Cost reduction, rather than clinical effectiveness, often serves as the primary evaluation criterion for program proposals. In this regard, mental health advocates and professionals note with dismay how admission diversion efforts from state hospitals, more often than not, create another set of continuity and recidivism problems in the absence of established viable alternative community-based services.

Certain problems presented by severely mentally ill client populations, such as violent behavior or refusal of services, are repeatedly glossed over or ignored in the design of programs. In practice, many provider agencies may focus disproportionate attention on more treatment-compliant clients. This practice leaves the most difficult clients with little or no access to services. Special populations of mentally ill persons are severely underserved—including children and adolescents, the elderly, minorities, the dually diagnosed substance abuser. and the working poor.

Efforts to limit both financial costs and political liability often result in distortion of assessment and eligibility determination to fit predetermined results. Observers of the public sector mental health scene are all too familiar with the great debates that seem to surround such issues as the prevalence of the mentally ill in homeless populations, jails, and nursing homes—with estimates ranging anywhere from 10 to 90 percent.

Planning is inadequate. Communication and cooperation between state agencies and local providers are erratic and often nonexistent. The planning process should include professionals, family members, advocates, and clients. Outreach is vital. An approach offering the best means of effectively delivering services to those most in need is for community teams to offer services to clients rather than requiring clients to contact individual and disparate agencies.

Chapter 3

Suicide Facts

Completed Suicides. U.S., 1991

Suicide is the 8th leading cause of death in the United States.
The 1991 age-adjusted rate was 11.4/100,000, or 0.0114%, down
from 11.5/100,000 in 1990.

- Contrast this with the leading cause of death, diseases of the
  heart, at 148.2/100,000
- Over 99.9% of Americans did not die by suicide

Suicide by firearms is the most common method for both men
and women, accounting for 60% of all suicides.
More men than women die by suicide.

- The gender ratio is over 4:1
- 73% of all suicides are committed by white men
- Nearly 80% of all firearm suicides are committed by white
  men

The highest suicide rates are for persons over 65; however, it is
not a leading cause of death in this age group.

- The 1991 suicide rate for white men over 85 was 75.1/100,000

NIMH Pub. No. OM-00-4081.

Suicide is the third leading cause of death among young people *15 to 24* years of age, following unintentional injuries and homicide. In this age group:

- Suicide rates are lower than for any other group except children less than 14 years of age
- The rate was 13.1/100,000 in 1991, down from 13.2/100,000 in 1990
- The total number of deaths in 1991 was 4,751, compared with 30,810 for all ages
- The gender ratio was nearly 6:1 (men:women)

Among young people *15 to 19* years of age the suicide rate was 11.0/100,000 in 1991, down from 11.1/100,000 in 1990.

- The total number of deaths was 1,899, compared with 30,810 for all ages
- Rates among both young women and young men in this age group have increased since 1979, rates for young men have increased at a greater rate than rates for young women
- The gender ratio was nearly 5:1

Among young people *20 to 24* years of age the suicide rate was 14.9/100,000 in 1991, down from 15.1 /100,000 in 1990.

- The total number of deaths was 2,852, compared with 30,810 for all ages
- The rate among young women in this age group has steadily decreased since 1979; the rate among young men has remained relatively flat
- The 1991 gender ratio was 6.5:1

Risk Factors

Scientific research has shown that almost all people who kill themselves have a diagnosable mental or substance abuse disorder; the majority have more than one disorder.

Suicide and suicidal behavior are not normal responses to the stresses experienced by most people.

Suicide is a complex behavior. The risk factors for suicide frequently occur in combination. Many people experience one or more risk factors and are not suicidal.

More Risk Factors

Familial factors in highly dysfunctional families can be associated with suicide.

- Family history of mental or substance abuse disorder
- Family history of suicide
- Family violence, including emotional, physical, or sexual abuse

Adverse life events in combination with other strong risk factors such as mental or substance abuse disorders and impulsivity, may lead to suicide. Other risk factors include:

- Prior suicide attempt
- Firearm in the home
- Incarceration
- Exposure to the suicidal behavior of others, including family members, peers, and/or via the media in news or fiction stories

Attempted Suicides

No national data on attempted suicide are available; reliable scientific research, however, has found that:

- There are an estimated 8-25 attempted suicides to one completion; the ratio is higher in women and youth and lower in men and the elderly
- More women than men report a history of attempted suicide, with a gender ratio of about 2:1
- The strongest risk factors for attempted suicide in adults are depression, alcohol abuse, cocaine use, and separation or divorce

- The strongest risk factors for attempted suicide in youth are depression, alcohol or other drug use disorder, and aggressive or disruptive behaviors

The majority of suicide attempts are expressions of extreme distress that need to be addressed.

Prevention

Because suicide is a highly complex behavior, preventive interventions must also be complex and intensive if they are to have lasting effects over time.

Based on reliable findings from scientific research, recognition and appropriate treatment of mental and substance abuse disorders is the most promising way to prevent suicide and suicidal behavior in all age groups.

Because most elderly suicides have visited their primary care physician in the month prior to their suicides, recognition and treatment of depression in the medical setting is a promising way to prevent elderly suicide.

Limiting young people's access to firearms and other forms of responsible firearms ownership, especially in conjunction with the prevention of mental and addictive disorders, also may be beneficial avenues for prevention of firearm suicides.

Most school-based, information-only, prevention programs focused solely on suicide have *not* been evaluated to see if they work.

- New research suggests that such programs may actually increase distress in the young people who are most vulnerable

School and community prevention programs designed to address suicide and suicidal behavior as part of a broader focus on mental health, coping skills in response to stress, substance abuse, aggressive behaviors, etc., are most likely to be successful in the long run.

All suicide prevention programs need to be scientifically evaluated to demonstrate whether or not they work.

Chapter 4

Nursing Home Residents: Mental Health Status

In Brief

- In 1987, about 59 percent of nursing home residents had some type of mental disorder, 47 percent had behavior problems, and 68 percent had psychiatric symptoms.

- Almost 43 percent of residents had dementia, either alone or in combination with other mental disorders. The probability of having dementia increased with age, but the prevalence of other mental disorders declined with age.

- Female residents were more likely to have dementia and to exhibit psychiatric symptoms, while male residents were more likely to exhibit behavior problems.

Background

The aging of the U.S. population, together with the high and increasing costs of providing long-term institutional care, make it important to understand the characteristics of persons who reside in nursing homes. Data from phase 1 of the 1987 National Medical Expenditure Survey (NMES) provide estimates of mental disorders, be-

AHCPR Pub. No. 92-0113.

havioral problems, and psychiatric symptoms of persons who resided in nursing and personal care homes in the United States on January 1, 1987.

Selected Findings

Mental Disorders

Of the 1.5 million people age 18 or over living in nursing or personal care homes in 1987, almost 41 percent had no mental disorders; 29 percent had dementia only (including chronic or organic brain syndrome); 14 percent had dementia in combination with one or more other mental disorders; and 16 percent had one or more mental disorders without dementia (Figure 4.1).

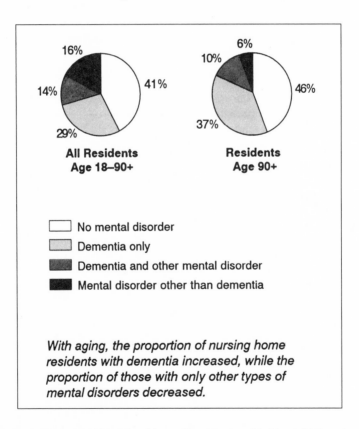

Figure 4.1. Percent of Nursing Home Residents with Mental Disorders, January 1, 1987

The pattern of mental disorders varied considerably by age. Few residents under age 65 had dementia, although 36 percent had a mental disorder other than dementia. With increasing age, smaller proportions of residents had mental disorders that were not dementia. For residents age 90 and older, the most prevalent classification was either no mental disorder (46 percent) or dementia only (37 percent) (Figure 4.1).

Patterns of mental disorders differed little between men and women; where there were statistically significant sex differences, a higher proportion of women than men had a diagnosis of mental disorder.

Behavioral Problems

Slightly less than half of all nursing home residents exhibited problem behaviors. The most prevalent behavior problem was getting upset and/or yelling (31 percent), followed by wandering (11 percent) and physically hurting others (11 percent). Nearly 52 percent of male residents had behavioral problems, compared with 46 percent of female residents (Figure 4.2). In particular, men were nearly twice as likely as women to hurt others (16 percent versus 9 percent, respectively).

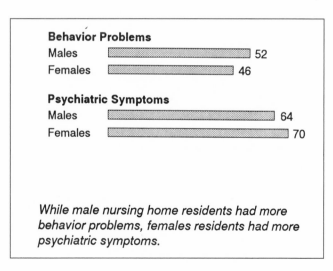

Behavior Problems
Males 52
Females 46

Psychiatric Symptoms
Males 64
Females 70

While male nursing home residents had more behavior problems, females residents had more psychiatric symptoms.

Figure 4.2. *Percent of Male and Female Nursing Home Residents with Behavioral Problems and Psychiatric Symptoms, January 1, 1987*

Psychiatric Symptoms

More than two-thirds (68 percent) of all nursing home residents had one or more psychiatric symptoms, including dullness, withdrawal, impatience, delusions, and hallucinations. Almost two-thirds (64 percent) exhibited at least one symptom of depression, and nearly 30 percent experienced psychotic symptoms. Women were more likely than men to experience multiple symptoms at nearly all ages.

Resident Composition by Facility Characteristics

Independent for-profit facilities had a higher proportion of residents with mental disorders (63 percent) than did nonprofit chains (52 percent). The proportion of residents with dementia residing in facilities with fewer than 50 beds (35 percent) was lower than in facilities with 150 or more beds (45 percent). These differences were not apparent, however, when all mental disorders were considered. A far smaller proportion of residents of noncertified facilities had dementia (27 percent) than those in facilities with any type of program certification (43-49 percent).

Implications

The data indicate that a significant proportion of nursing home residents had some type of mental disorder, and the data reveal information about differences by age and sex. One reason younger persons enter nursing homes may be the presence of chronic mental disorders. By contrast, residents age 65 or over tended to suffer from dementia. Female residents were more likely to have dementia and psychiatric symptoms, while male residents were more likely to have behavior problems. These differences may reflect sex-related patterns of disability or differences in the way men and women express emotional stress.

Given the increasing number of persons over age 85 in the United States, the availability of family support for mentally frail elders may decrease, placing a greater burden on institutional care. Information about nursing home residents is important for planning to meet the increasing need for such care.

This issue of *Intramural Research Highlights* is based on the following publication:

Lair, T. and D. Lefkowitz. (1990, September). *Mental health and functional status of residents of nursing and personal care homes.* (DHHS Publication No. (PHS) 90-3470). National Medical Expenditure Survey Research Findings 7, Agency for Health Care Policy and Research. Rockville, MD: Public Health Service.

For further information on the subject of this issue, please call the Division of Medical Expenditure Studies, (301) 227-8400.

Chapter 5

Combating the Stigma of Mental Illness

Among people who have been treated for mental illness, what is the biggest problem they face when trying to resume life in the community?

Most will say it is simply their inability to be accepted by other people. They have difficulty finding friends, housing, and work. They feel the sting of discrimination in almost everything they attempt. Many times they feel old friends are uncomfortable in their presence. They feel cut off from society.

They are the victims of the stigma that still surrounds mental illness. Numerous scientific studies have shown that stigma, often overt, is directed toward former mental patients by society. It becomes their most debilitating handicap.

Since 1980, the National Institute of Mental Health has been a leader in a nationwide attempt to remove the stigma associated with mental illness through an effort to encourage employers to hire people who have come through such illness and who are now able and eager to work. It has been proven that the dignity of work provides stability and meaning to these people as much as to those who have never experienced mental illness.

By forming a partnership with the private sector, the Institute has inaugurated an information program for employers that is paying dividends. Employers have learned that former mental patients, in-

DHHS Pub. No. (ADM) 90-1470.

cluding the chronically mentally ill, comprise a valuable labor pool for American business.

But, employer knowledge and acceptance are not enough. The problems of stigma are everywhere. They affect all of us. We have found, also, that as the general public learns more about the devastating problems caused by stigma, even greater understanding and help will follow.

One in five families in the United States knows the devastating impact of mental illness. But its effects are far-reaching as family, friends, and co-workers suffer by the changes inflicted on them by another's mental illness.

Thirty percent of the population will suffer from cancer during their lifetimes, while 15 percent will be touched by mental illness. However, victims who have suffered both mental illness and cancer report that the mental illness caused them the greater pain.

In truth—the obstacles faced by recovering mental patients following treatment for their illness are often as difficult to overcome as was the illness.

Here, the question must be asked, "What is mental illness?" To begin with, mental illness is not a homogeneous entity which a general discussion of mental illness seems to imply. However, included under the rubric of mental illness are symptoms and problems that affect many persons but which may not be evident in others. These symptoms may not seriously—or even markedly—impair personal or social functioning. On the other hand, there are persons who may suffer from more serious, obvious, and incapacitating degrees of illness. These latter persons may well require hospitalization and intensive care and treatment.

Since the passage of the National Mental Health Act by Congress in 1946, care and treatment of mentally ill people has improved dramatically, assisted immeasurably by improvement in the use of psychoactive drugs (such as tranquilizers) and the development and use of other new therapies.

Improving Treatment

Today, research has unraveled many of the mysteries about the origins of mental illness. It has revealed that many mental illnesses are actually caused by biochemical imbalances, as is the case with many physical illnesses.

The mentally ill should not be blamed for their condition any more than diabetics should be blamed for having diabetes. Uncovering many of the biochemical imbalances has led to treatments restoring the needed chemical balances, just as insulin controls the balances for diabetes. As long as a diabetic person takes the proper dosage of insulin, that person can live a normal life. It is much the same with mental illness. As long as the victim follows prescribed treatments, that person, too, can lead as normal a life as possible.

As care has been upgraded, so, too, have the settings in which treatment is given. For many decades, the usual responses to the mentally ill were to hide them away at home or to relegate them to asylums. As the number of admissions increased, care in the asylum became mostly custodial.

Problems of Deinstitutionalization

The populations of public mental hospitals grew until, about 30 years ago, more than 550,000 were housed in State and county facilities. Since then, deinstitutionalization—the process of releasing mental patients to communities—has lowered the number to fewer than 150,000.

At first, deinstitutionalization was hailed as a momentous advance by those who advocated treatment and services in community-based facilities—community mental health centers, halfway houses, psychosocial rehabilitation programs, and the like.

However, practice outpaced practicality; where the mentally ill were once caged as animals, chained to walls, mistreated, and even beaten, new understanding of mental illness has given many of them freedom. But the price of that freedom has often been aimless wandering through the streets, without homes or jobs. And, in too many instances, Americans who have had the misfortune to suffer mental illness—even those who approach a societal definition of normal—daily face an unsympathetic, unfair, and hostile society.

Historical physical abuse or neglect has been replaced by a less visible but no less damaging psychic cruelty.

Generally, in these enlightened days, we do not physically remove from our midst those we do not wish to have around; and we no longer send them to a far-away asylum. Instead, we isolate them socially, a much more artful though equally debilitating form of ostracism. A paradox now exists. In a time of vastly increased medical sophistication, which virtually guarantees greater numbers of restored mental patients, discrimination against them continues. Although we as a society have come far in the way we respond to those with mental illness, there is still a great distance to go.

For example, research studies have found that most Americans think the two worst things that can happen to a person are leprosy and insanity. In American society, ex-convicts stand higher on the ladder of acceptance than former mental patients. Asked to rank 21 categories of disability, from the least offensive to the most, respondents placed mental illness at the bottom of the list.

Attitude Changes

Public attitudes toward the mentally ill have changed in the past few decades, but the changes appear to be minimal. A 1979 study updating an earlier attitudes survey found "no noteworthy changes in attitudes toward the mentally ill 23 years later."

People continue to discriminate against the mentally ill, although it may be less socially acceptable to admit it openly. Discrimination crosses all boundaries of society and exists among people of all ages, socioeconomic levels, intelligence, education, and places. Nearly everyone, it seems, regards victims of mental disorders as "fundamentally tainted and degraded."

Even more astounding, mental patients sometimes face rejection from professionals who are paid to treat and help them. A key finding of a 1980 forum on stigma was that many health-care professionals harbor unconscious, unstated negative feelings about their mental patients. A 1980 survey found some psychiatric nurses showed prejudice toward their patients. Other studies have shown that it is not unusual for some staff members in psychiatric facilities to abuse their patients physically.

What is behind the stigma directed at mental patients? Some researchers think the term stigma is itself the problem. Too strong a word to be useful in describing the full range of reactions toward the mentally ill, they believe, it discourages objective thinking about the problem it encompasses. That is, they believe simply talking about stigma may cause it.

Other investigators suggest that behavior, not a label, is what evokes negative response. For example, relatively well-adjusted and well-educated people who develop a psychiatric disorder but recover are unlikely, in this view, to suffer extensively from the problems of the stigma. It is the more or less permanently disabled persons who tend to be the objects of fear and avoidance.

Fears of Dangerousness

One of the reasons for this view, perhaps, is that people fear the mentally ill because they are thought to be unpredictable. But the truth is that the behavior of former mental patients is, on nearly every occasion, no different from the rest of society.

Thus, it should be said clearly: The vast majority of mentally ill persons are not dangerous. Here as elsewhere it is unfair to stigmatize the many for the acts of the few. The unfairness is apparent when danger from former mental patients is compared with the danger from drunk drivers. Some of the most predictably and demonstrably dangerous persons in our society are drunk drivers who account for about half of all fatal automobile accidents (about the same number as all criminal homicides each year), but Americans demonstrate a truly astonishing tolerance for this group of dangerous persons.

Then compare this to the record of former mental patients. Fewer than 2 percent of them pose any kind of danger to society. The reality is that persons who have been through emotional disturbances are typically anxious, passive, and fearful.

But the myth of dangerousness is perpetuated through a lack of knowledge by most members of the public. The belief that mentally ill persons are to be feared has been described in the research literature as a "core belief of the American public." Further, a recent California survey found only 17 percent of respondents agreed with the statement that mental patients are not dangerous.

The facts belie these beliefs. There has been an increase in the arrest rates of former mental patients over the past 29 years, but this increase pertains to former patients who had arrest records *prior* to being hospitalized.

Though there have also been a few studies showing *higher* rates of violent crimes by mentally ill persons, those who do not have prior arrest records have post-discharge arrest rates *equal to or lower* than those of the general population.

Why then the continuing public perception of them as dangerous individuals to be feared and shunned?

Role of the Media

Many observers fix a large share of the blame on the communications media. Newspapers in particular stress a history of mental disorder when they find it in the backgrounds of people who commit crimes of violence. Television news programs also sustain this view with their sensationalization of crimes where former mental patients are involved.

In television dramas, mentally ill persons are often portrayed as violent or victims of violence. Such stereotyping illustrates one of the many uses of mental illness by television producers or directors—to excite fear in the audience. One critic has pointed out that, on television, mental illness is synonymous with danger. Although that idea cannot be supported by known facts, it lends authenticity to the myth.

In this respect, the media—in the interests of fairness and in recognition of their power to influence public opinion—have a responsibility to provide a broader perspective on the mentally ill. A leading scientific investigator in this area has commented, "That the mass media can condition a subtle set of attitudes which influences the behavior of society toward those who have been hospitalized for mental disorder is unequivocal."

The media usually reflect the beliefs of the public. Thus, it follows that when a majority of Americans are convinced that there are benefits in helping to change beliefs about mental illness, these beliefs will be positively altered. And the media must be convinced that at least some of the credit for helping change beliefs would accrue to them.

Possibility of Change

A summary of several studies indicates important areas where change is likely: in increased positive images of mental patients, in decreased fear ratings of them, in decreased fear of becoming insane, and (by patients themselves) in increased self-confidence. This likelihood is borne out by university-based studies which show that negative and stigmatizing images of mental patients can be altered.

For example, a Minnesota mental health education program informs the public in a straightforward way of the struggles of real people with emotional problems. Early indications are that awareness of such people's experiences and perceptions results in increased resistance to negative mass media images of current and former mental patients.

There are other encouraging signs of greater public understanding and acceptance of mental illness. Women, for example, have been found to be far more accepting of mental patients than are men. Recent Canadian and U.S. studies have shown positive acceptance of community mental health residential facilities, even in situations where residents have been labeled "mentally disordered offenders."

A survey by the National Restaurant Association, the first ever to investigate employment of the mentally restored in a single industry, produced solid evidence of the value of former mental patients to employers. The most outstanding result of the survey concerned work performance. More than 75 percent of employers who had hired mentally restored people rated them "as good as or better" than their co-workers in motivation, quality of work, attendance, job punctuality, and job tenure.

Fellow employees were described as cooperative and helpful toward their mentally restored coworkers, supporting the findings of another study of a shift toward understanding and acceptance when mental patients are given a chance to fill normal roles in work and other activities.

Thus, as impressive as the gains in treatment of mental illness have been over the past few decades, they are not enough. It is also necessary to alter society's perceptions of mental illnesses and the mentally ill. People must understand that mental illnesses are real, that they are common, and that no one is beyond help. It is important to spread the message that, thanks to research, effective treatments are now available to help most mentally ill people lead satisfying and productive lives at home, at work, and in the community. These treatments are continually being improved through ongoing research. There is now more hope than ever for people who are mentally ill, and there should be more acceptance of these individuals by society at large. Only when they can take their place among us as valued employees, tenants, and friends will their struggle against mental illness be won.

This text was produced by the National Institute of Mental Health (NIMH), the U.S. Government agency that supports and conducts research to improve the diagnosis, treatment, and prevention of mental illness. NIMH-supported studies alleviate suffering and bring hope to people who have a mental disorder, to those who are at risk of developing one, and to their families, friends, and coworkers. Thus, mental health research benefits millions of Americans and reduces the burden that mental disorders impose on society as a whole. NIMH is part of the Alcohol, Drug Abuse, and Mental Health Administration, a component of the U.S. Department of Health and Human Services.

Chapter 6

Plain Talk about Handling Stress

You *need* stress in your life! Does that surprise you? Perhaps so, but it is quite true. Without stress, life would be dull and unexciting. Stress adds flavor, challenge, and opportunity to life. Too much stress, however, can seriously affect your physical and mental well-being. A major challenge in this stress-filled world of today is to make the stress in your life work *for* you instead of against you.

Stress is with us all the time. It comes from mental or emotional activity and physical activity. It is unique and personal to each of us. So personal, in fact, that what may be relaxing to one person may be stressful to another. For example, if you are an executive who likes to keep busy all the time, "taking it easy" at the beach on a beautiful day may feel extremely frustrating, nonproductive, and upsetting. You may be emotionally distressed from "doing nothing." Too much emotional stress can cause physical illness such as high blood pressure, ulcers, or even heart disease; physical stress from work or exercise is not likely to cause such ailments. The truth is that physical exercise can help you to relax and to handle your mental or emotional stress.

Hans Selye, M.D., a recognized expert in the field, has defined stress as a "non-specific response of the body to a demand." The important issue is learning how our bodies respond to these demands. When stress becomes prolonged or particularly frustrating, it can become harmful—causing *distress* or "bad stress." Recognizing the early signs of distress and then doing something about them can make an impor-

DHHS Pub. No. (ADM) 91-502.

59

tant difference in the quality of your life, and may actually influence your survival.

Reacting to Stress

To use stress in a positive way and prevent it from becoming distress, you should become aware of your own reactions to stressful events. The body responds to stress by going through three stages: (1) alarm, (2) resistance, and (3) exhaustion.

Let's take the example of a typical commuter in rush-hour traffic. If a car suddenly pulls out in front of him, his initial alarm reaction may include fear of an accident, anger at the driver who committed the action, and general frustration. His body may respond in the alarm stage by releasing hormones into the bloodstream which cause his face to flush, perspiration to form, his stomach to have a sinking feeling, and his arms and legs to tighten. The next stage is resistance, in which the body repairs damage caused by the stress. If the stress of driving continues with repeated close calls or traffic jams, however, his body will not have time to make repairs. He may become so conditioned to expect potential problems when he drives that he tightens up at the beginning of each commuting day. Eventually, he may even develop a physical problem that is related to stress, such as migraine headaches, high blood pressure, backaches, or insomnia. While it is impossible to live completely free of stress and distress, it is possible to prevent some distress as well as to minimize its impact when it can't be avoided.

Helping Yourself

When stress does occur, it is important to recognize and deal with it. Here are some suggestions for ways to handle stress. As you begin to understand more about how stress affects you as an individual, you will come up with your own ideas of helping to ease the tensions.

Try physical activity. When you are nervous, angry, or upset, release the pressure through exercise or physical activity. Running, walking, playing tennis, or working in your garden are just some of the activities you might try. Physical exercise will relieve that "up tight" feeling, relax you, and turn the frowns into smiles. Remember, your body and your mind work together.

Share your stress. It helps to talk to someone about your concerns and worries. Perhaps a friend, family member, teacher, or counselor can help you see your problem in a different light. If you feel your problem is serious, you might seek professional help from a psychologist, psychiatrist, social worker, or mental health counselor. Knowing when to ask for help may avoid more serious problems later.

Know your limits. If a problem is beyond your control and cannot be changed at the moment, don't fight the situation. Learn to accept what is—for now—until such time when you can change it.

Take care of yourself. You are special. Get enough rest and eat well. If you are irritable and tense from lack of sleep or if you are not eating correctly, you will have less ability to deal with stressful situations. If stress repeatedly keeps you from sleeping, you should ask your doctor for help.

Make time for fun. Schedule time for both work and recreation. Play can be just as important to your well-being as work; you need a break from your daily routine to just relax and have fun.

Be a participant. One way to keep from getting bored, sad, and lonely is to go where it's all happening. Sitting alone can make you feel frustrated. Instead of feeling sorry for yourself, get involved and become a participant. Offer your services in neighborhood or volunteer organizations. Help yourself by helping other people. Get involved in the world and the people around you, and you'll find they will be attracted to you. You will be on your way to making new friends and enjoying new activities.

Check off your tasks. Trying to take care of everything at once can seem overwhelming, and, as a result, you may not accomplish anything. Instead, make a list of what tasks you have to do, then do one at a time, checking them off as they're completed. Give priority to the most important ones and do those first.

Must you always be right? Do other people upset you—particularly when they don't do things your way? Try cooperation instead of confrontation; it's better than fighting and always being "right." A little give and take on both sides will reduce the strain and make you both feel more comfortable.

It's OK to cry. A good cry can be a healthy way to bring relief to your anxiety, and it might even prevent a headache or other physical consequence. Take some deep breaths; they also release tension.

Create a quiet scene. You can't always run away, but you can "dream the impossible dream." A quiet country scene painted mentally, or on canvas, can take you out of the turmoil of a stressful situation. Change the scene by reading a good book or playing beautiful music to create a sense of peace and tranquility.

Avoid self-medication. Although you can use prescription or over-the-counter medications to relieve stress temporarily, they do not remove the conditions that caused the stress in the first place. Medications, in fact, may be habit-forming and also may reduce your efficiency, thus creating more stress than they take away. They should be taken only on the advice of your doctor.

The Art of Relaxation

The best strategy for avoiding stress is to learn how to relax. Unfortunately, many people try to relax at the same pace that they lead the rest of their lives. For a while, tune out your worries about time, productivity, and "doing right." You will find satisfaction in just *being*, without striving. Find activities that give you pleasure and that are good for your mental and physical well-being. Forget about always winning. Focus on relaxation, enjoyment, and health. If the stress in your life seems insurmountable, you may find it beneficial to see a mental health counselor. *Be good to yourself.*

—by Lous E. Kopolow, M.D.

Part Two

Schizophrenic Disorders

Chapter 7

Schizophrenia: Questions and Answers

Foreword

We expect that nearly 3 million Americans will develop schizophrenia during the course of their lives, and about 100,000 schizophrenic patients are in public mental hospitals on any given day. The treatments available for schizophrenia, while very important in relieving at least some of the suffering for many of the people affected, are not yet preventing the common pattern of repeated relapse with chronic disabilities in social and occupational functioning. Schizophrenia remains poorly understood and largely feared by the public.

This booklet addresses five main questions about schizophrenia: What is it? What causes it? How is it treated? How can other people help? What is the outlook? Accurate information may help to remove misconceptions and thereby reduce the fear, shame, and hopelessness that are too often associated with the disorder.

Shervert H. Frazier M.D.
Director
National Institute of Mental Health

DHHS Pub. No. (ADM) 90-1457. Single copies of this booklet are available at no charge from the Public Inquiries Branch, National Institute of Mental Health, Room 15C-05, 5600 Fishers Lane, Rockville, MD 20857.

What Is It?

Schizophrenia is a term used to describe a complex, extremely puzzling condition—the most chronic and disabling of the major mental illnesses. Schizophrenia may be one disorder, or it may be many disorders, with different causes. Because of the disorder's complexity, few generalizations hold true for all people who are diagnosed as schizophrenic.

With the sudden onset of severe psychotic symptoms, the individual is said to be experiencing acute schizophrenia. "Psychotic" means out of touch with reality, or unable to separate real from unreal experiences. Some people have only one such psychotic episode; others have many episodes during a lifetime but lead relatively normal lives during the interim periods. The individual with chronic (continuous or recurring) schizophrenia often does not fully recover normal functioning and typically requires long-term treatment, generally including medication, to control the symptoms. Some chronic schizophrenic patients may never be able to function without assistance of one sort or another.

Approximately 1 percent of the population develop schizophrenia during their lives. This disorder affects men and women with equal frequency, and the information in this text is equally applicable to both. The first psychotic symptoms of schizophrenia are often seen in the teens or twenties in men and in the twenties or early thirties in women. Less obvious symptoms, such as social isolation or withdrawal or unusual speech, thinking, or behavior may precede and/or follow the psychotic symptoms.

Sometimes people have psychotic symptoms due to undetected medical disorders. For this reason, a medical history should be taken and a physical examination and laboratory tests should be done during hospitalization to rule out other causes of the symptoms before concluding that a person has schizophrenia.

The World of People with Schizophrenia

Unusual Realities: Just as "normal" individuals view the world from their own perspectives, schizophrenic people, too, have their own perceptions of reality. Their view of the world, however, is often strikingly different from the usual reality seen and shared by those around them.

Living in a world that can appear distorted, changeable, and lacking the reliable landmarks we all use to anchor ourselves to reality, a person with schizophrenia may feel anxious and confused. This person may seem distant, detached, or preoccupied, and may even sit as rigidly as a stone, not moving for hours and not uttering a sound. Or he or she may move about constantly, always occupied, wide awake, vigilant, and alert. A schizophrenic person may exhibit very different kinds of behavior at different times.

Hallucinations: The world of a schizophrenic individual may be filled with hallucinations; a person actually may sense things that in reality do not exist, such as hearing voices telling the person to do certain things, seeing people or objects that are not really there, or feeling invisible fingers touching his or her body. These hallucinations may be quite frightening. Hearing voices that other people don't hear is the most common type of hallucination in schizophrenia. Such voices may describe the patient's activities, carry on a conversation, warn of impending dangers, or tell the person what to do.

Delusions: Delusions are false personal beliefs that are not subject to reason or contradictory evidence and are not part of the person's culture. They are common symptoms of schizophrenia and can involve themes of persecution or grandeur, for example. Sometimes delusions in schizophrenia are quite bizarre—for instance, believing that a neighbor is controlling the schizophrenic individual's behavior with magnetic waves, or that people on television are directing special messages specifically at him or her, or are broadcasting the individual's thoughts aloud to other people. Delusions of persecution, which are common in paranoid schizophrenia, are false and irrational beliefs that a person is being cheated, harassed, poisoned, or conspired against. The patient may believe that he or she, or a member of the family or other group, is the focus of this imagined persecution.

Disordered Thinking: Often the schizophrenic person's thinking is affected by the disorder. The person may endure many hours of not being able to "think straight." Thoughts may come and go so rapidly that it is not possible to "catch them." The person may not be able to concentrate on one thought for very long and may be easily distracted, unable to focus attention.

The person with schizophrenia may not be able to sort out what is relevant and what is not relevant to a situation. The person may be unable to connect thoughts into logical sequences, as thoughts may become disorganized and fragmented. Jumping from topic to topic in a way that is totally confusing to others may result.

This lack of logical continuity of thought, termed "thought disorder," can make conversation very difficult and contribute to social isolation. If people cannot make sense of what an individual is saying, they are likely to become uncomfortable and tend to leave that person alone.

Emotional Expression: People with schizophrenia sometimes exhibit what is called "inappropriate affect." This means showing emotion that is inconsistent with the person's speech or thoughts. For example, a schizophrenic person may say that he or she is being persecuted by demons and then laugh. This should not be confused with the behavior of normal individuals when, for instance, they giggle nervously after a minor accident.

Often people with schizophrenia show "blunted" or "flat" affect. This refers to a severe reduction in emotional expressiveness. A schizophrenic person may not show the signs of normal emotion, perhaps using a monotonous tone of voice and diminished facial expression.

Some people with symptoms of schizophrenia also exhibit prolonged extremes of elation or depression, and it is important to determine whether such a patient is schizophrenic, or actually has a bipolar (manic-depressive) disorder or major depressive disorder. Persons who cannot be clearly categorized are sometimes diagnosed as having a schizoaffective disorder.

Normal Versus Abnormal: At times, normal individuals may feel, think, or act in ways that resemble schizophrenia. Often normal people are unable to think straight. They can be made extremely anxious, for example, speaking in front of groups so that they could feel confused, be unable to pull their thoughts together, and forget what they had intended to say.

Just as normal people may occasionally do strange things, many schizophrenic people often think, feel, and act in a normal fashion. Unless in the midst of an extremely disorganized state, a schizophrenic person will have some sense of common reality, for instance, knowing that most people eat three times each day and sleep at night. Being out of touch with reality (which is one way to describe the psychotic symptoms of schizophrenia) does not mean that an individual is living *totally* in another world. Rather, there are certain aspects of this individual's world that are not shared by others and that seem to have no real basis. Hearing a voice of warning that no one else can hear is not an experience shared by most people and is clearly a distortion of reality, but it is only a distortion of one part of reality. A schizophrenic person may, therefore, appear quite normal much of the time.

Schizophrenia Is Not "Split Personality"

There is a common notion that schizophrenia is the same as "split personality"—a Dr. Jekyll–Mr. Hyde switch in character. This is *not* an accurate description of schizophrenia. In fact, split or multiple personality is an entirely different disorder that is really quite rare.

Is Schizophrenia a New Disease?

Although the term "schizophrenia" was not used until the early 20th century, the disorder has existed for a great many years and has been found in all types of societies.

In Western society, "madness" or "insanity" was not generally regarded as a health problem until the early 19th century. At that time, a movement to offer more humane treatment to the mentally ill made it possible for them to receive more scientific, medical treatment. The mentally ill were unchained, released from prisons, and given more appropriate care. Several categories of mental disease were subsequently identified. By the early 20th century, schizophrenia had been distinguished from manic-depressive illness, and subcategories had been described. In 1911, Dr. Eugen Bleuler, a Swiss psychiatrist, first used the term, "the group of schizophrenias." Despite disagreement among scientists as to precisely what conditions should or should not be included in this group, the term has been commonly used since then.

Can Children Be Schizophrenic?

Children over the age of 5 can develop schizophrenia, but it is very rare before adolescence. Moreover, research is needed to clarify the relationship of schizophrenia occurring in childhood to that occurring in adolescence and adulthood. Although some people who later develop schizophrenia may have seemed different from other children at an early age, the psychotic symptoms of schizophrenia (for example, hallucinations, delusions, and incoherence) are rarely seen in children.

Are People with Schizophrenia Likely to Be Violent?

Although news and entertainment media tend to link mental illness and criminal violence, studies tell us that if we set aside those persons with a record of criminal violence before hospitalization, mentally ill persons as a whole are probably no more prone to criminal violence than the general public. Studies are underway to refine our understanding of the different forms of mental illness to learn whether some groups are more prone to violence than others.

Certainly most schizophrenic individuals are not violent; more typically, they prefer to withdraw and be left alone. Some acutely disturbed patients may become physically violent, but such outbursts have become relatively infrequent following the introduction of more effective treatment programs, including the use of antipsychotic medications. There is general agreement that most violent crimes are not committed by schizophrenic persons, and that most schizophrenic persons do not commit violent crimes.

What about Suicide?

Suicide is a potential danger in those who have schizophrenia. If an individual tries to commit suicide or expresses plans to do so, he or she should receive immediate professional help. People with schizophrenia appear to have a higher rate of suicide than the general population. Unfortunately, the prediction of suicide in schizophrenic patients may be especially difficult.

What Causes Schizophrenia?

There is no known single cause of schizophrenia. As discussed later, it appears that genetic factors produce a vulnerability to schizophrenia, with environmental factors contributing to different degrees in different individuals. Just as each individual's personality is the result of an interplay of cultural, psychological, biological, and genetic

70

factors, a disorganization of the personality, as in schizophrenia, may result from an interplay of many factors. Scientists do not agree on a particular formula that is necessary to produce the disorder. No specific gene has yet been found; no biochemical defect has been proven responsible; and no specific stressful event seems sufficient, by itself, to produce schizophrenia.

Is Schizophrenia Inherited?

It has long been known that schizophrenia runs in families. The close relatives of schizophrenic patients are more likely to develop schizophrenia than those who are not related to someone with schizophrenia. The children of a schizophrenic parent, for example, each have about a 10 percent chance of developing schizophrenia. By comparison, the risk of schizophrenia in the general population is about 1 percent.

Over the past 25 years, two types of increasingly sophisticated studies have demonstrated the importance of a genetic factor in the development of schizophrenia. One group of studies examined the occurrence of schizophrenia in identical and fraternal twins; the other group compared adoptive and biological families.

Recent studies of twins have confirmed the basic findings of earlier, scientifically less rigorous studies. Identical twins (who are genetically alike) generally have a higher rate of "concordance" for schizophrenia than fraternal twins (who are no more genetically alike than ordinary siblings). "Concordance" occurs when both members of a twin pair develop schizophrenia. Although studies of twins provide convincing evidence of an inherited factor in schizophrenia, the fact that concordance for schizophrenia among identical twins is only 40 to 60 percent suggests that some type of environmental factor or factors also must be involved.

A second major group of studies looked at adopted children to examine the effects of heredity and environment. In Denmark, an exhaustive investigation of the mental health of adopted-away children of schizophrenic parents was conducted. These children were compared with adopted children whose biological parents had no history of mental illness. A comparison was also made of the rates of mental disorder among the biological relatives of two groups of adoptees—one known to be schizophrenic and the other without a history of mental illness. Findings of adoption studies have indicated that being biologically related to a schizophrenic person increased the risk for schizophrenia, even when the related individuals have had little or no personal contact.

These studies indicate that schizophrenia has some hereditary basis, but the exact extent of this genetic influence needs further exploration. Most scientists agree that what may be inherited is a vulnerability or predisposition to the disorder—an inherited potential that, given a certain set of factors, can lead to schizophrenia. This predisposition may be due to an enzyme defect or some other biochemical abnormality, a subtle neurological deficit, or some other factor or combination of factors. We do not yet understand how the genetic predisposition is transmitted and cannot predict accurately whether a given person will or will not develop the disorder. In some people, a genetic factor may be crucial for the development of the disorder; in others, it may be relatively unimportant.

Are the Parents at Fault?

Most schizophrenia researchers now agree that parents do not cause schizophrenia. In past decades, there was a tendency for some mental health workers to blame parents for their children's disorder. Today, this attitude is generally seen as both inaccurate and counterproductive. Mental health workers now commonly try to enlist family members' aid in the therapeutic program and also show a heightened sensitivity to the very real feelings of burden and isolation many families experience in their attempts to care for a schizophrenic family member.

Is Schizophrenia Caused by a Chemical Defect?

Although no neurochemical cause has yet been firmly established for schizophrenia, basic knowledge about brain chemistry and its link to schizophrenia is expanding rapidly. Neurotransmitters—substances that allow communication between nerve cells—have long been thought to be involved in the development of schizophrenia. It is likely that the disorder is associated with some imbalance of the complex, interrelated chemical systems of the brain. Although we have no definite answers, this area of schizophrenia research is very active and exciting.

Is Schizophrenia Caused by a Physical Abnormality in the Brain?

Interest in this research question has been stimulated by the development of CAT scans (Computerized Axial Tomography)—a kind of x-ray technique for visualizing the structures of living brains. Some studies using this technique suggest that schizophrenic patients are more likely to have abnormal brain structures (for example, enlargement of the cavities in the interior of the brain) than are normal persons of the same age. It should be emphasized that some of the abnormalities reported are quite subtle. These abnormalities have been found neither to be characteristic of *all* schizophrenic patients nor to occur *only* in individuals with schizophrenia.

A more recent development is the PET (Positron Emission Tomography) scan. In contrast to the CAT scan, which produces images of brain structures, the PET scan is a way of measuring the metabolic activity of specific areas of the brain, including areas deep within the brain. Only very preliminary research has been done with the PET scan in schizophrenia, but this new technique, used in conjunction with other types of scans, promises to provide important information about the structure and function of the living brain.

Other special imaging studies that may increase our understanding of schizophrenia include MRI, rCBF, and computerized EEG measures. MRI stands for magnetic resonance imaging, a technique involving precise measurements of brain structures based on the effects of a magnetic field on different substances in the brain. This technique has sometimes been referred to as nuclear magnetic resonance (NMR) imaging. In rCBF, or regional cerebral blood flow, a radioactive gas is inhaled, and the rate of disappearance of this substance from different areas of the brain gives information about the relative activity of brain regions during various mental activities. The computerized EEG (electroencephalogram) is a kind of brain wave test that maps electrical responses of the brain as it reacts to different stimuli. All of these imaging techniques are being used for research. They are not new forms of treatment.

How Is It Treated?

Since schizophrenia may not be a single condition and its causes are not yet known, current treatment methods are based on both clini-

cal research and experience. These approaches are chosen on the basis of their ability to reduce schizophrenic symptoms and lessen the
chances that symptoms will return. A number of treatments and treatment combinations have been found to be helpful and more are being
developed.

What about Antipsychotic Drugs?

Antipsychotic medications (also called neuroleptics) have been
available since the mid-1950's. They have greatly improved the outlook for individual patients. These medications reduce the psychotic
symptoms of schizophrenia and usually allow the patient to function
more effectively and appropriately. Antipsychotic drugs are the best
treatment now available, but they do not "cure" schizophrenia or ensure that there will be no further psychotic episodes. The choice and
dosage of medication can be made only by a qualified physician who
is well trained in the medical treatment of mental disorders. The dosage of medication is individualized for each patient, since patients
may vary a great deal in the amount of drug needed to reduce symptoms without producing troublesome side effects.

Antipsychotic drugs are very effective in treating certain schizophrenic symptoms (for example, hallucinations and delusions). A large
majority of schizophrenic patients show substantial improvement.
Some patients, however, are not helped very much by such medications and a few do not seem to need them. It is difficult to predict
which patients will fall into these two groups and to distinguish them
from the large majority of patients who *do* benefit from treatment
with antipsychotic drugs.

Sometimes patients and families become worried about the
antipsychotic medications used to treat schizophrenia. In addition to
concern about side effects (discussed elsewhere in this text), there may
be worries that such drugs may lead to addiction. Antipsychotic medications, however, do not produce a "high" (euphoria) or a strong physical dependence, as some other drugs do.

Another misconception about antipsychotic drugs is that they act
as a kind of mind control. Antipsychotic drugs do not control a person's
thoughts; instead, they often help the patient to tell the difference between psychotic symptoms and the real world. These medications may
diminish hallucinations, agitation, confusion, distortions, and delu-

sions, allowing the schizophrenic individual to make decisions more rationally. Schizophrenia itself may seem to take control of the patient's mind and personality, and antipsychotic drugs can help to free the patient from his or her symptoms and allow the patient to think more clearly and make better informed decisions. While some patients taking these medications may experience sedation or diminished expressiveness, antipsychotic medications used in appropriate dosage for the treatment of schizophrenia are not chemical restraints. Frequently, with careful monitoring, the dosage of the medication can be reduced to provide relief from undesirable effects. There is now a trend in psychiatry that favors finding and using the lowest dosage that allows the schizophrenic person to function without a return of psychosis.

How Long Should Schizophrenic Patients Take Antipsychotic Drugs?

Antipsychotic drugs also reduce the risk of future psychotic episodes in recovered patients. With continued drug treatment, about 40 percent of recovered patients will suffer relapses within 2 years of discharge from a hospital. Still, this figure compares favorably with the 80 percent relapse rate when medication is discontinued. In most cases, it would not be accurate to say that continued drug treatment *prevents* relapses; rather, it reduces their frequency. The treatment of severe psychotic symptoms generally requires higher dosages than those used for maintenance treatment. If symptoms reappear with a lower dosage, a temporary increase in dosage may prevent a full-blown relapse.

Some patients may deny that they need medication and may discontinue antipsychotic drugs on their own or based on someone else's advice. This typically increases the risk of relapse (although symptoms may not reappear right away). It can be very difficult to convince certain schizophrenic people that they continue to need medication, particularly since some may feel better at first. For patients who are unreliable in taking antipsychotic drugs, a long-acting injectable form may be appropriate. *Schizophrenic patients should not discontinue antipsychotic drugs without medical advice and monitoring.*

What about Side Effects?

Antipsychotic drugs, like virtually all medications, have unwanted effects along with their beneficial effects. During the early phases of drug treatment, patients may be troubled by side effects such as drowsiness, restlessness, muscle spasms, tremor, dry mouth, or blurring of vision. Most of these can be corrected by lowering the dosage or can be controlled by other medications. Different patients have different treatment responses and side effects to various antipsychotic drugs. A patient may do better with one drug than another.

The long-term side effects of antipsychotic drugs may pose a considerably more serious problem. Tardive dyskinesia (TD) is a disorder characterized by involuntary movements most often affecting the mouth, lips, and tongue, and sometimes the trunk or other parts of the body. It generally occurs in about 15 to 20 percent of patients who have been receiving antipsychotic drugs for many years, but TD can occur in patients who have been treated with these drugs for shorter periods of time. In most cases, the symptoms of TD are mild, and the patient may be unaware of the movements.

The risk-benefit issue in any kind of treatment for schizophrenia is an extremely important consideration. In this context, the risk of TD—as frightening as it is—must be carefully weighed against the risk of repeated breakdowns that can terribly disrupt patients' efforts to reestablish themselves at school, at work, at home, and in the community. For patients who develop TD, the use of medications must be reevaluated. Recent research suggests, however, that TD, once considered irreversible, often improves even when patients continue to receive antipsychotic medications.

What about Psychosocial Treatments?

Antipsychotic drugs have proven to be crucial in relieving psychotic schizophrenic symptoms such as hallucinations, delusions, and incoherence, but do not consistently relieve *all* the symptoms of the disorder. Even when schizophrenic patients are relatively free of psychotic symptoms, many still have extraordinary difficulty establishing and maintaining relationships with others. Moreover, because schizophrenic patients frequently become ill during the critical trade-learning or career-forming years of life (ages 18 to 35), they are less likely to complete the training required for skilled work. As a result, many schizophrenic patients not only suffer thinking and emotional difficulties, but they lack social and work skills as well.

It is with these psychological, social, and occupational problems that psychosocial treatments help most. In general, psychosocial approaches have limited value for acutely psychotic patients (those who are out of touch with reality or have prominent hallucinations or delusions), but may be useful for those with less severe symptoms or those whose psychotic symptoms are under control. Numerous forms of psychosocial therapy are available for patients with schizophrenia, and most focus on improving the patient's functioning as a social being—whether in the hospital or community, at home or on the job. Some of these approaches are described here. Unfortunately, the availability of different forms of treatment varies greatly from place to place.

Rehabilitation: Broadly defined, rehabilitation includes a wide array of nonmedical interventions for those with schizophrenia. Rehabilitation programs emphasize social and vocational training to help patients and former patients overcome difficulties in these areas. Programs may include vocational counseling, job training, problem-solving and money management skills, use of public transportation, and social skills training. These approaches are important for the success of the community-centered treatment of schizophrenia, because they provide discharged patients with the skills necessary to lead productive lives outside the sheltered confines of a mental hospital.

Individual Psychotherapy: Individual psychotherapy involves regularly scheduled talks between the patient and a mental health professional such as a psychiatrist, psychologist, psychiatric social worker, or nurse. These talks may focus on current or past problems, experiences, thoughts, feelings, or relationships. By sharing their experiences with a trained, empathic person and by talking about their world with someone outside it, schizophrenic individuals may gradually come to understand more about themselves and their problems. They can also learn to sort out the real from the unreal and distorted.

Recent studies tend to indicate that supportive, reality-oriented therapy is generally of more benefit to schizophrenic outpatients than more probing psychoanalytic or insight-oriented psychotherapy. In one large-scale study, patients given psychotherapy oriented toward reality adaptation and practical interpersonal skills generally did as well or better than patients given more frequent and intensive insight-oriented therapy.

Family Therapy: As usually practiced, family therapy involves the patient, the parents or spouse, and a therapist. Brothers and sisters, children, and other relatives may also be included. The purposes vary. Meeting in a family group can enable various family members and the therapist to understand each others' viewpoints. It also can help with treatment planning (such as discharge from the hospital) and enlisting the aid of family members in the therapeutic program. Family therapy can also provide a way for the therapist to offer the family needed support and understanding in a time of crisis.

Very often, patients are discharged from the hospital to their families' care, so it is important that family members have a clear understanding of schizophrenia and are aware of the difficulties and problems associated with the illness. It is also helpful for family members to understand the ways of minimizing the chance of future breakdowns and to be aware of the different kinds of outpatient and family services that are available in the period after hospitalization.

Group Therapy: Group therapy sessions usually involve a small number of patients (for example, 6-12) and one or two trained therapists. Here the focus is on learning from the experiences of others, testing out one person's perceptions against those of others, and correcting distortions and maladaptive interpersonal behavior by means of feedback from other members of the group. This form of therapy may be most helpful after symptoms have subsided somewhat and patients have emerged from the acute psychotic phase of the illness, since psychotic patients are often too disturbed or disorganized to participate. Later, when patients are beginning to recover, participation in group therapy will often be helpful in preparing them to cope with community life.

Self Help Groups: Another kind of group that is becoming increasingly common is the self-help group. Although not led by a professional therapist, the groups are therapeutic because members— usually ex-patients or the family members of people with schizophrenia—provide continuing mutual support as well as comfort in knowing that they are not alone in the problems they face. These groups also serve other important functions. Families working together can more effectively serve as advocates for needed research and hospital and community treatment programs. Ex-patients as a group may be better able to dispel stigma and draw public attention to such abuses as discrimination against the formerly mentally ill.

Family and peer support and advocacy groups are now very active and provide useful information and assistance for patients and families of patients with schizophrenia and other mental disorders.

The National Alliance for the Mentally Ill is composed exclusively of family groups, with 550 of them as of the end of 1985 and adding about 150 to 200 new groups each year. The National Mental Health Association, the nation's oldest and largest nongovernmental citizen's voluntary organization, is concerned with all aspects of mental disorders and mental health. The National Mental Health Consumers' Association, a network of self-help organizations across the country, now has about 150 affiliates and operates a Self-Help Clearinghouse. These groups can be contacted at the following addresses:

The National Alliance for the Mentally Ill
1901 North Fort Myer Drive, Suite 500
Arlington, Virginia 22209
(703) 524-7600

National Mental Health Association
1021 Prince Street
Alexandria, Virginia 22314-2971
(703) 684-7722

The National Mental Health Consumers' Association
311 South Juniper Street, Room 902
Philadelphia, Pennsylvania 19107
(215) 735-2465

Residential Care

Prolonged hospitalization is now very much less common than it was 20 or 30 years ago, when approximately 300,000 schizophrenic patients were residents of State and county mental institutions. Despite this trend, a minority of patients still seem to require long-term inpatient care. For most patients, prolonged hospital stays are not recommended because they increase dependence on institutional care and result in a loss of social contacts with family, acquaintances, and the community. Short-term residential care in well-staffed facilities can give patients needed relief from stressful situations, provide a protective atmosphere for the troubled patient, allow restarting or adjustment of medication, and reduce pressure on the family.

Many schizophrenic persons can benefit from partial hospitalization (day care or night care), from outpatient treatment (going to a clinic or office regularly for individual, group, or occupational therapy), or from living in a halfway house (designed to aid patients in bridging the gap between 24-hour hospitalization and independent living in the community).

What about Other Forms of Treatment?

Electroconvulsive Therapy (ECT) and Insulin Coma: These two forms of treatment are rarely used today in the treatment of schizophrenia. In particular situations, however electroconvulsive therapy may be useful. It can be of help, for example, if a severe depression occurs in the course of a schizophrenic episode. Insulin coma treatment is virtually never used now because of the availability of other effective treatment methods that have fewer potentially serious complications.

Psychosurgery: Lobotomy, a brain operation formerly used in some patients with severe chronic schizophrenia, now is performed only under extremely rare circumstances. This is because of the serious, irreversible personality changes that the surgery may produce and the fact that far better results are generally attained from less drastic and hazardous procedures.

Large Doses of Vitamins: Good physical hygiene, including a nourishing diet and proper exercise, is important to good health. Well-controlled studies have shown that the addition of large doses of vitamins to standard therapy regimens does not significantly improve the treatment of schizophrenia. Also, although vitamins have been thought to be relatively harmless, reports of side effects raise the possibility that these substances may have detrimental consequences when used in very high doses. Reliance on high-dose vitamins as a treatment for schizophrenia is not scientifically justified and does have risks.

Hemodialysis: Preliminary reports that some schizophrenic patients appeared to improve following hemodialysis, a blood-cleansing treatment used in certain kidney disorders, attracted a great deal of attention. However, several more recent controlled scientific studies have reported that the procedure has no beneficial effect on the symptoms of schizophrenia. The weight of scientific evidence now indicates that hemodialysis is not useful in the treatment of schizophrenia.

How Can Other People Help?

A patient's support system may come from several sources, including the family, a professional residential or day program provider, shelter operators, friends or roommates, professional case managers, churches and synagogues, and others. Because the majority of patients live with their families, the following discussion frequently uses the term "family." However, this should not be taken to imply that families ought to be the primary support system.

There are numerous situations in which patients with schizophrenia can be helped by people in their support systems. First of all, for patients who do not recognize that they are ill, family or friends may need to take an active role in having them seen and evaluated by a professional. Often, a schizophrenic person will resist treatment, believing that delusions or hallucinations are real and that psychiatric help is not needed. Since laws regarding involuntary commitment have become very strict, families and community organizations may be frustrated in their attempts to see that a severely mentally ill individual gets needed help. These laws vary from State to State, but generally people who are dangerous to themselves or others due to a mental disorder can be taken by the police for emergency psychiatric evaluation and, if necessary, hospitalization. In some cases, a member of a local community mental health center can evaluate an individual's illness at home if he or she will not voluntarily go in for treatment.

Sometimes only the family or others close to the patient will be aware of strange behavior or ideas that the patient has expressed. Since schizophrenic patients may not volunteer such information during an examination, family members or friends should ask to speak with the person evaluating the patient so that all relevant information can be taken into account.

Seeing that a schizophrenic patient continues to get treatment after hospitalization is also important. Patients may discontinue medications or stop going for followup treatment—often leading to a return of psychotic symptoms. Encouraging and assisting the patient to continue treatment can be very important to recovery. Without treatment, some schizophrenic patients become so psychotic and disorganized that they cannot care for their basic needs, such as food, clothing, and shelter. All too often people with severe mental illnesses such as schizophrenia wind up on the streets or in jails, where they rarely receive the kinds of treatment they need.

Those close to people with schizophrenia are often unsure of how to respond when patients make statements that seem strange or are clearly false. The schizophrenic patient's bizarre beliefs or hallucinations seem quite real—they are not just "imaginary fantasies." Instead of going along with a patient's delusions, family members or friends can tell the patient that they do not see things the same way or do not agree with his or her conclusions, while acknowledging that things may seem that way to the patient.

It may also be useful for those who know the patient well to keep a record of what types of symptoms have appeared, what medications (including dosage) have been taken, and what effects various treatments have had. By knowing what symptoms have been present before, family members may know better what to look for in the future. Families may even be able to identify some "early warning signs" of potential relapses (such as increased withdrawal or changes in sleep patterns) better and earlier than the patients themselves. Return of the psychosis may thus be detected early and treatment may prevent a full-blown relapse. Also, by knowing which medications have helped and which have caused troublesome side effects in the past, the family can help those treating the patient to find the best treatment more quickly.

In addition to involvement in seeking help, family, friends, and peer groups can provide support and encourage the person with schizophrenia to regain his or her abilities. It is important that goals be attainable, since a patient who feels pressured and/or repeatedly criticized by others will probably experience this as a stress that may lead to a worsening of symptoms. Like anyone else, people with schizophrenia need to know when they are doing things right. A positive approach may be helpful and perhaps more effective in the long run than criticism, and this advice applies to all those who interact with the patient.

A common question raised by family and friends concerns "street drugs." Since some people who take street drugs may show symptoms similar to those typical of schizophrenia, people with schizophrenia may be accused of being "high on drugs." To help understand the cause of the patient's behavior, blood or urine samples can be tested for street drugs at many hospitals or physician's offices. While most researchers do not believe that schizophrenic patients develop their symptoms because of drug use, people who have schizophrenia often have particularly bad reactions to certain street drugs. Stimulants (such as amphetamines or cocaine) may cause major problems for schizophrenic patients, as may drugs like PCP or marijuana. In fact, some patients experience a worsening of their schizophrenic symptoms when they are taking such drugs. Schizophrenic patients may also abuse alcohol or other drugs for delusional reasons or in an attempt to lessen their symptoms. This can cause additional problems requiring multiple treatment approaches. Such patients may be helped by a combination of therapies such as medication, rehabilitation, psychotherapy, or Alcoholics Anonymous or other substance abuse programs.

What Is the Outlook?

The outlook for people with schizophrenia has improved over the last 25 years. Although no totally effective therapy has yet been devised, it is important to remember that many schizophrenic patients improve enough to lead independent, satisfying lives. As we learn more about the causes and treatment of schizophrenia, we should be able to help more schizophrenic patients achieve successful outcomes.

Studies that have followed schizophrenic patients for long periods, from the first breakdown to old age, reveal that a wide range of outcomes is possible. A review of almost 2,000 patients' life histories suggests that 25 percent achieve full recovery, 50 percent recover at least partially, and 25 percent require long-term care. When large groups of patients are studied, certain factors tend to be associated with a better outcome—for example, a pre-illness history of normal social, school, and work adjustment. Our current state of knowledge, however, does not allow for a sufficiently accurate prediction of long-term outcome.

The development of a variety of treatment methods and facilities is of crucial importance because schizophrenic patients vary greatly in their needs for treatment. In particular, better alternatives are needed to fill the gap between the relatively nonintensive treatment offered in outpatient clinics and the highly regulated treatment (including 24-hour supervision) provided in hospitals. With a wide variety of facilities available, mental health professionals will be better able to tailor treatment to the different needs of individual patients. Some patients require constant care and attention, while others need a place to learn how to function more independently without constant supervision.

Given the complexity of schizophrenia, the major questions about this disorder—its cause or causes, prevention, and treatment—are unlikely to be resolved in the near future. The public should beware of those offering "the cure" for (or "the cause" of) schizophrenia. Such claims can provoke unrealistic expectations that, when unfulfilled, lead to further disappointment. Although progress has been made toward a better understanding of schizophrenia, there is an urgent need for a more rigorous and broad-based program of basic and clinical research. Research on schizophrenia has benefited greatly from recent basic scientific discoveries, and we hope that a better understanding of neurobiological and psychosocial factors in schizophrenia will be achieved in the next decade.

To Subscribe to the Schizophrenia Bulletin

The *Schizophrenia Bulletin* is a quarterly journal prepared by the Schizophrenia Research Branch of the National Institute of Mental Health. Intended as a forum for the multidisciplinary exchange of information about schizophrenia, the *Bulletin* is the only periodical exclusively devoted to the exploration of this severe and puzzling disorder.

Frequently, an issue of the *Bulletin* focuses on one critical topic. Themes of past issues, for example, have been the role of heredity in schizophrenia, psychosocial approaches to treatment, biological factors in the disorder, subtypes of schizophrenia, childhood psychoses, community support systems, stress and social networks, prognosis and long-term outcome, advances in diagnostic procedures, and research on individuals at high risk for the development of schizophrenia.

The *Bulletin* publishes articles on all facets of schizophrenia research and treatment. Special emphasis is placed on the publication of detailed state-of-the-art reviews of critical areas in the study of schizophrenia. Although the *Bulletin* wishes to encourage a variety of subscribers, most articles published in the journal are primarily directed to the scientific community.

[The *Schizophrenia Bulletin* is available by subscription from the Superintendent of Documents, Government Printing Office, Washington, DC 20402. Back issues, when available, are sold at the single copy price. Contact the Superintendent of Documents for current pricing information.

Chapter 8

Medications for the Treatment of Schizophrenia

Introduction

Schizophrenia, a severe mental disorder characterized by psychotic symptoms (thought disorder, hallucinations, delusions, paranoia) and impairment in job and social functioning, affects more than two million Americans. Current treatment programs for schizophrenia include combinations of medication, psychotherapy, education, and social-vocational rehabilitation.

This text was prepared in response to inquiries reflecting a growing public need for information on the medications used to treat schizophrenia and related illnesses. In this text, meant to serve as a companion to *Schizophrenia: Questions and Answers* [see Chapter 7], we have addressed concerns and questions from the public that are frequently directed to us.

General Information about Antipsychotic Medications

The primary medications used to treat schizophrenic disorders are the antipsychotic medications, also called neuroleptics. Although these medications are not a cure for schizophrenia, they are effective in alleviating or reducing symptoms. Chlorpromazine (Thorazine), the

DHHS Pub. No. 92-1950. Single copies of this booklet are available at no charge from the Public Inquiries Branch, National Institute of Mental Health, Room 15C-05, 5600 Fishers Lane, Rockville, MD 20857.

first medication of this kind, became available for use in the United States during the early 1950s. Since its discovery, several other classes of antipsychotic medications have been developed.

All of the widely used traditional antipsychotic medications are equally effective in treating schizophrenia; however, some individuals may prefer one medication to another because they experience different side effects. Some patients may respond better or experience fewer side effects with those traditional antipsychotic medications that are available in a long-acting, injectable form. Long-acting, injectable medication may also be helpful to patients who do not take their medication reliably.

On the other hand, clozapine (Clozaril), an atypical antipsychotic medication, was first marketed in February 1990 and has been found to be superior to traditional antipsychotic medications for some patients with treatment-resistant schizophrenia. Clozapine appears to cause less muscle stiffness and restlessness (extrapyramidal side effects) than traditional antipsychotic medications and is less likely to produce tardive dyskinesia (TD). However, close monitoring via weekly blood testing is necessary for patients who are treated with clozapine, as described [in this text].

The traditional antipsychotic medications are believed to help relieve psychotic symptoms by blocking the binding sites (receptors) for certain chemicals (neurotransmitters) found in the brain. The neurotransmitter dopamine has been the focus of much interest in learning how many of the antipsychotic medications work. Receptors for dopamine and other chemical transmitters in the brain are targets of the antipsychotic medications, different classes of which may affect one receptor type more than another. Specific side effects may result because a particular binding site is affected by a certain medication.

One way to classify antipsychotic agents is by the dosage of medication, or the potency (strength) in milligrams, that is typically recommended. Antipsychotic agents are often classified on this basis as high, middle, or low potency. Figure 8.1 lists some common antipsychotic medications and their usual daily dosage. Individual doses of medication taken by patients may vary because of differences among individuals in both the severity of their illness and the rate at which they metabolize (break down) medication. This latter factor is influenced by age, race, sex, body build, diet, use of cigarettes or alcohol, and other medications being taken.

The lowest possible dosage of medication effective in relieving symptoms is usually prescribed. Sometimes symptoms of schizophrenia will flare up, requiring a temporary (weeks to months) increase in medication dosage. After an initial or acute episode of illness has been treated with medication, the doctor usually will taper the dosage very slowly to the lowest possible level necessary to keep the symptoms from returning. In a few circumstances, especially when symptoms are mild, some individuals may not require medication. Others may be able to use very low doses except when symptoms are severe. Because of all these factors, it is important that patients consult with their doctor before making changes in medication dose.

Generic name	Trade name	PDR dose range (mg/day)[1]
Chlorpromazine	Thorazine	100–1000
Chlorprothixene	Taractan	75–600
Clozapine	Clozaril	300–900
Fluphenazine	Prolixin, Permitil	1–20
Haloperidol	Haldol	1–15
Loxapine	Loxatane	60–100
Molindone	Moban	15–225
Mesoridazine	Serentil	100–400
Perphenazine	Trilafon	8–64
Thiothixene	Navane	20–60
Thioridazine	Mellaril	200–800
Trifluoperazine	Stelazine	10–40

Note. — PDR = Physician's Desk Reference.

Figure 8.1. Antipsychotic medications available in the United States. [1]As discussed in this text, the daily dosage of medication varies among individuals. The lowest dosage possible to relieve symptoms should be prescribed.

Can a Patient Become Addicted to Antipsychotic Medications?

Addiction to antipsychotic medications does not occur. However, some individuals who have taken such medications for more than a few weeks experience mild, unpleasant symptoms such as nausea, vomiting, abdominal cramps, diarrhea, or sweating when the medication is abruptly stopped. If it becomes necessary to stop medication, the dosage should be slowly tapered to avoid an increase in psychotic symptoms or the effects mentioned above.

How Long Will a Patient Have to Take Antipsychotic Medication?

Duration of therapy with antipsychotic medication is highly individual. Most patients with chronic schizophrenia require some type of medication, usually antipsychotic, for most of their lives. However, some individuals, especially those who have insight into the nature of their illness and understand that increased symptoms may be a warning sign for relapse, are able to take a reduced dose or discontinue medication periodically.

What Are the Major Side Effects of Antipsychotic Medications?

As noted previously, the side effects of antipsychotic medications are a result of their action on chemical receptors. The different classes of antipsychotic medications may affect one receptor more than another, causing different side effects. For example, the lower potency antipsychotic medications are more likely to produce sedation, dry mouth, episodic low blood pressure, and dizziness, whereas the higher potency agents are more likely to produce drooling and muscle stiffness.

Other side effects of antipsychotic medications include constipation, skin rash, sun sensitivity, cholestatic jaundice (slowing of bile flow in the liver), and lowered white blood cell count (agranulocytosis). For all of the currently available antipsychotic medications except clozapine, the risk for lowered white blood cell count is extremely low. With clozapine, however, the risk is high enough (1% to 2% during the first year) to require weekly blood cell monitoring to ensure early detection of this disorder.

Antipsychotic medications are also capable of lowering the seizure threshold. This is an especially critical side effect of clozapine, as patients taking higher doses are at greater risk for seizure than patients taking lower doses. Additional important side effects (e.g., movement disorders, including muscle stiffness and TD; neuroleptic malignant syndrome; and side effects involving the reproductive system) are discussed separately.

Although most patients develop some mild side effects to antipsychotic medications, the risk for developing severe side effects is relatively low overall, and most such side effects can be controlled or tolerated with another medication.

What Types of Movement Disorders Are Produced by Antipsychotic Medications?

Antipsychotic medications may produce several types of abnormal movements and muscle stiffness. Dystonia is the powerful, involuntary contraction or spasm of a muscle or group of muscles. It may occur in any muscle group and may be dramatic in appearance. Dystonia typically occurs within the first week of treatment with, or during an increase in dose of, the antipsychotic medication. Akathisia is a feeling of internal restlessness, which may result in continuous leg movements and leaves some patients feeling compelled to pace. Both dystonia and akathisia are reversible when antipsychotic medication is lowered or stopped, and both can be treated with anticholinergic medications such as benztropine mesylate (Cogentin) and trihexyphenidyl (Artane). Akathisia is also sometimes treated with propranolol (Inderal), amantadine (Symmetrel), or lorazepam (Ativan).

Antipsychotic medications can also produce slowed or stiff movements resulting in a condition resembling Parkinson's disease called pseudoparkinsonism. This condition can occur during the first few weeks of treatment and is characterized by stiffness or rigidity of arms and legs, shuffling when walking, a tremor occurring at rest, and slowed movements of facial muscles causing a lack of facial expression. Pseudoparkinsonism caused by antipsychotic medication may improve with time, is reversible when medication is lowered or stopped, and may be treated with anticholinergic medication.

TD is another movement disorder that can result from the use of antipsychotic medications. This syndrome is discussed in the next section.

91

What Is TD?

TD is a syndrome of abnormal involuntary muscle movements that occurs in some patients who take antipsychotic medications. Research studies show the risk of developing TD to be about 5 percent per year, with 25 to 40 percent of patients developing TD after several years of taking these medications. Certain factors such as being older, being female, and having a diagnosis of affective or organic mental disorder may increase the risk of developing TD. In addition, a high total cumulative dose (the total of all the doses and length of time that medications were taken by a patient) may increase the risk of developing TD.

The muscles of the face, especially those of the mouth and tongue, are most frequently involved in TD, although muscles of the neck, trunk, and extremities may also be affected. TD may appear in various forms and degrees of severity, from mild to severe and disabling. The abnormal muscle movements may appear as muscle spasms, twitching, chorea, or athetosis. The movements characteristic of chorea are sudden and brisk, appearing as a flicking or jerking in the trunk, pelvis, arms, and legs, or as a grimace, frown, tic, or smirk in the muscles of the face. Athetosis is a slow twisting or writhing movement of the muscles. Chorea and athetosis may occur alone or together in TD and other neuropsychiatric conditions.

Because other neuropsychiatric disorders may be mistaken for TD, a doctor must take a history of the patient to include information about past and present use of antipsychotic medications, neurological and psychiatric symptoms, medical illnesses, and psychiatric and medical illnesses in the family. The doctor should also do a complete physical examination with emphasis on the nervous system. It may be necessary to perform blood tests and a magnetic resonance imaging examination of the brain to rule out other causes of the abnormal movements.

Patients who take antipsychotic medications should be examined periodically for TD. Whenever possible, an evaluation for the presence of abnormal movements should be performed before such medication is started. Examinations should then be performed after 3 months, 6 months, and at least every 6 months thereafter. Patients who develop TD should be examined every 3 months.

In some patients, symptoms of TD may be reversed or reduced when antipsychotic medication is reduced to the lowest dosage possible that will still control psychotic symptoms. Similarly, TD symptoms may lessen or disappear (i.e., be "masked") when antipsychotic medication dosages are increased. Some patients experience brief symptoms of TD, known as withdrawal dyskinesia, when antipsychotic medication is stopped or lowered.

However, anticholinergic medications, such as trihexyphenidyl (Artane) and benztropine mesylate (Cogentin), which are useful for treating muscle stiffness, may worsen the symptoms of TD. Anxiety and emotional distress may aggravate the symptoms of TD; therefore, antianxiety medications may be helpful to reduce TD symptoms in anxious patients. Recent research studies on medications effective in treating TD suggest that some medications may reduce symptoms in some patients, so any patients identified as having TD should consult their doctor regarding possible treatments.

What Is Neuroleptic Malignant Syndrome (NMS)?

NMS is a relatively rare but potentially serious side effect of antipsychotic (neuroleptic) medications. It is characterized by muscle rigidity, fever, and dysfunction of the autonomic nervous system (a part of the nervous system that helps regulate blood pressure and body temperature) leading to changes in blood pressure and heart rate, and to increased sweating. Breakdown of muscle tissue can occur in severe cases of NMS, causing high levels of an enzyme creatinine phosphokinase, also called CPK, to accumulate in the bloodstream. Patients who develop severe NMS usually need to be immediately admitted to a medical facility for treatment with intravenous fluids to prevent dehydration, and they may be given muscle-relaxing medications to treat muscle rigidity. Antipsychotic medications should be used very cautiously in patients with a history of NMS.

Questions Frequently Asked about the Effect of Antipsychotic Medications on the Reproductive System

Will Taking Antipsychotic Medications Affect Sexual Performance?

Some men and women who take antipsychotic medications experience a lowering of their sexual drive. Antipsychotic agents may slightly lower blood levels of testosterone, the hormone responsible for maintaining the libido (sex drive) in both men and women. The lower potency antipsychotic medications, such as thioridazine (Mellaril) and chlorpromazine (Thorazine), occasionally cause delayed or retrograde ejaculation in men. During retrograde ejaculation, orgasm is reached without the simultaneous emission of semen; semen is instead propelled backwards into the bladder and eliminated with the next urination (which may appear cloudy as a result).

Will Antipsychotic Medications Affect the Menstrual Cycle or the Ability To Have Children?

Antipsychotic medications lead to an increased level of the hormone prolactin. High prolactin levels may cause irregularity or lengthening of the menstrual cycle, breast swelling, and lactation (breast milk production) in women. Breast enlargement may also occur in men taking antipsychotic medications; this is called gynecomastia. These changes are reversible when the dose of antipsychotic medication is reduced or stopped, causing prolactin levels to be lowered or return to normal.

Women with schizophrenia, regardless of their medication status, may have a lower level of fertility compared with nonschizophrenic women. Conceiving a child may be even more difficult for a woman taking antipsychotic medications because of lowered fertility or menstrual irregularities associated with such medications. Therefore, it is important for women taking these medications to discuss family planning with their doctor and other clinicians.

Do Antipsychotic Medications Cause Birth Defects?

There are no birth malformations known to be caused by antipsychotic medications. As previously discussed in this text, antipsychotic medications are thought to reduce symptoms of schizophrenia by helping to correct chemical imbalances in the brain; it is unknown if the changes in neurochemical levels or their receptors that occur in the brain of a developing fetus exposed to antipsychotic medications will affect the developing nervous system connections of the fetus. Further research is needed in this important area.

As all circumstances are not the same and each patient may have different medical and emotional needs, any woman who takes antipsychotic medications (or other medications) and considers becoming pregnant should seek advice from her physician to discuss the risks and benefits for her.

What Additional Medications Are Available for Patients Who Do Not Achieve Full Relief of Their Symptoms with Antipsychotic Medications?

Some patients receive only partial relief of their symptoms from antipsychotic medications. Research studies suggest that three other medications—lithium, carbamazepine (Tegretol), and some of the benzodiazepine antianxiety medications—may be useful in the treatment of schizophrenic patients when taken in conjunction with traditional antipsychotic medications. Lithium may help to reduce psychotic symptoms further; may increase the length of time between episodes of illness: may reduce excitement; and may lead to improved social functioning, cooperation with treatment, and personal hygiene. Patients do not need to have mood swings to benefit from lithium treatment. Research studies of carbamazepine, an antiseizure medication also used to treat bipolar affective disorder (manic-depressive illness), have found this medication useful in reducing hostile and aggressive behavior in some schizophrenic patients. Benzodiazepines such as lorazepam (Ativan) and alprazolam (Xanax), which are primarily used to treat anxiety, have been found to help reduce agitation during acute episodes of schizophrenic illness and may, if given early in the course of an acute episode of schizophrenia, prevent relapse. Results from research studies of the use of benzodiazepines in patients with chronic schizophrenia show mixed results as to the benefit of these medications for long-term use. Benzodiazepines may help to reduce symptoms of psychosis in very anxious patients, but further research needs to be done into the types and dosages of these medications and the symptoms that may best respond to treatment with benzodiazepines.

Antidepressant medications are often helpful in treating depression when it occurs in schizophrenic patients. More recently, clozapine has been used to treat patients with chronic schizophrenia who do not respond well to traditional treatment regimens. Clozapine is more thoroughly discussed in the next section.

Many other medications have been studied for their effectiveness in treating schizophrenia, with inconsistent results. Medications not generally considered useful for treatment of schizophrenia include propranolol (Inderal), levodopa, vitamins in high dosages, and valproate (Depakote, Depakene).

Electroconvulsive therapy (ECT) was one of the earliest treatments of schizophrenia. Although ECT is not useful for most schizophrenic patients, it may be useful in treating acute symptoms in certain patients who are in severe states of withdrawal (catatonia) or who present with significant affective symptoms such as uncontrolled mania.

Clozapine and Other Atypical Antipsychotic Medications

As a group, the atypical antipsychotic medications differ from the traditional antipsychotic medications in two ways. First, atypical antipsychotic medications are believed to produce less muscle stiffness and may be less likely to cause TD than the traditional antipsychotic agents. Accordingly, because they are less likely to produce neurological side effects, they do not compound or worsen negative symptoms such as flat affect, lack of motivation, and poverty of thought and speech. Second, they do not cause an increase in the hormone prolactin. Thus, specific endocrine side effects, such as enlarged breast tissue and menstrual irregularities, occur to a much lesser extent. (See section on "Questions Frequently Asked About the Effect of Antipsychotic Medications on the Reproductive System.")

Clozapine (Clozaril), the only atypical antipsychotic agent currently marketed in the United States, has been found to be beneficial to some patients who have not responded to treatment with traditional antipsychotic medications or could not tolerate traditional antipsychotic medication because of severe side effects. In a large research study conducted at several medical centers across the United States, it was found that 30 percent of chronic schizophrenic patients who had not responded to treatment with traditional antipsychotic agents improved at least somewhat on clozapine. While there have been a few reports of seriously ill schizophrenic patients making a dramatic recovery from treatment with clozapine, this is a relatively rare event. As previously noted, clozapine can also cause agranulocytosis (low white blood cell count), a serious side effect that can lead to death if not diagnosed and treated immediately. The risk of developing some degree of agranulocytosis on clozapine is between 1 and 2 percent during the first year. If detected and promptly treated, however, this condition is completely reversible. Therefore, patients who take clozapine must have blood tests done every week. Because the high cost of this medication and the weekly blood test requirements have limited its availability, government agencies, consumer groups, and the manufacturer of clozapine have been seeking ways to make this medication more available to patients who may benefit from it.

Will Any New Antipsychotic Medications Be Available Soon?

Research is ongoing to develop newer, safer antipsychotic medications. Two promising medications, remoxipride (available in Europe under the trade name Roxiam) and risperidone, appear to be as effective as the traditional antipsychotic medications and they may cause less muscle stiffness and other movement disorders. These medications are still being tested in the United States and are not expected to be available here for some time.

Questions Frequently Asked about Drugs of Abuse and Their Effects on Schizophrenia

Do Street Drugs Cause Schizophrenia?

Abusing drugs does not cause schizophrenia, but certain street drugs can produce symptoms similar to acute schizophrenia, such as hallucinations (both visual and auditory), paranoia, delusions, disorganized thinking, and excited behavior. Psychostimulant medications (amphetamines and cocaine) and hallucinogenic drugs such as lysergic acid diethylamide (LSD), phencyclidine (PCP), mescaline, and marijuana (especially marijuana high in tetrahydrocannabinol or laced with other drugs) are more likely to produce psychosis than other street drugs. Individuals with a biological vulnerability toward schizophrenia or other psychotic illness may be at greater risk for developing drug-induced psychosis.

What Effects Do Drugs of Abuse or Alcohol Have on Patients With Schizophrenia?

Drugs of abuse or alcohol may worsen schizophrenic symptoms or lead to a relapse. Therefore, schizophrenic patients who abuse drugs or alcohol may require a higher dose of antipsychotic medication to control their schizophrenic symptoms.

Comments

Although the antipsychotic medications are not a cure for schizophrenia, they help to relieve the symptoms of illness and prevent the recurrence of those symptoms for many patients. Since the introduction of these medications in the 1950s, many individuals have been able to lead improved lives outside mental institutions. Some of the newer medications under development are as effective as the traditional agents and are likely to produce fewer extrapyramidal side effects. This may result in better medication compliance in patients who experience troubling side effects. Researchers are working to find new medications that are more effective than the traditional antipsychotic agents, especially for the treatment of negative symptoms of schizophrenia, and to find ways to produce the best possible treatment outcome using the currently available medications.

Chapter 9

Research in Schizophrenia

General Overview

Schizophrenia remains the most puzzling, chronic, and disabling of the severe mental disorders. Clinical trials over the past 30 years have demonstrated the efficacy of antipsychotic medications in reducing the positive symptoms of schizophrenia and adding psychosocial treatment further enhances patient outcome. Nevertheless, most people who develop schizophrenia will have some continuing or recurring symptoms, and an estimated 10 percent of people with schizophrenia resort to suicide. Research on schizophrenia during the past 50 years has ruled out many suspected causes of schizophrenia and discovered a variety of important "clues" to its underlying pathology. Many recent advances in medical technology are now being applied to the study of schizophrenic disorders. The following articles will describe active research areas, recent findings, and new approaches that we believe will lead us to understand better the causes of schizophrenia and improve its treatment.

The last *Special Report* was published in the *Schizophrenia Bulletin* in 1987 and included seven topic articles and a theoretical overview perspective. The current *Special Report* contains 11 major articles. Rather than a single chapter on biological studies, we now

"Nontechnical Summaries of Articles," excerpted from NIH Pub. No. 93-3499, *Special Report: Schzophrenia 1993*. For the complete articles, refer to the *Special Report* or to the *Schizophrenia Bulletin*, Vol. 19, No. 2, 1993.

have separate articles on infection and autoimmune processes, neurochemistry and neuroendocrinology, and neuropathology. Instead of a single chapter on treatment, we now have articles on psychopharmacologic treatment, tardive dyskinesia, and psychosocial treatment. This expansion of scope reflects an increase in the breadth and intensity of research on schizophrenia and recent advances in a variety of areas.

One major factor influencing the developments reported in this issue has been the *National Plan for Schizophrenia Research* (published in 1987 and 1988 as reports of the National Advisory Mental Health Council). There were four general purposes for this plan, whose chief architect was Dr. Samuel Keith. The first was to appraise the current state of the science regarding schizophrenia. Seven panels met to make specific recommendations for future research efforts, based on what we knew in 1987 and what we still needed to know in order to make additional progress.

The *National Plan for Schizophrenia Research* presented a 5-year blueprint for research on schizophrenia, and since we have reached the end of that projection, we believe this *Special Report: Schizophrenia 1993* can assist with our reappraisal of the state of the science. During this year, we plan to reconvene some of the key individuals involved in development of the *National Plan* to determine which goals have been accomplished and decide which new areas require additional research focus, recommend "mid-course" modification and expansion, and develop a research agenda for the coming years.

The second purpose of the *National Plan for Schizophrenia Research* was the stimulation of research initiatives. A number of new mechanisms for funding schizophrenia research have been developed during the past 5 years, including several focused on neuroscience and behavioral sciences. Program announcements, requests for applications, cooperative agreements, and other mechanisms have been used to stimulate the field, and major efforts have been undertaken by all three National Institute of Mental Health (NIMH) Research Divisions. In 1987, NIMH spent approximately $34 million dollars on schizophrenia research; by 1992, that figure had risen to over $100 million. While the growth of research budgets overall has been slowed in recent years due to national economic concerns, we believe that a great deal can and will be accomplished.

The third goal of the *National Plan* was to provide technical resources to promote scientific research on schizophrenia. A variety of new programs are underway to follow up on especially promising leads. One example is the NIMH Molecular Genetics Initiative, which should serve as a national resource and complement the many investigator-initiated projects aimed at finding the genes responsible for producing vulnerability to schizophrenia and related disorders. Workshops on neuroimaging, atypical antipsychotic medications, future developments in molecular genetic research on schizophrenia and related disorders, and women's and minority issues in schizophrenia research are other examples of NIMH efforts to stimulate research and provide technical resources to promote such research.

The *National Plan* was also crafted to increase the number and quality of research scientists studying schizophrenia. Since the development of the *Plan*, the Institute has funded many FIRST (First Independent Research Support and Transition) Awards, Research Scientist Development Awards, and Research Training Positions with a focus on schizophrenia. The NIMH Intramural Research Program continues to be a premier research site providing unparalleled research opportunities for basic and clinical scientists interested in schizophrenia.

The clinical problems produced by schizophrenia are clear: whether we measure these effects in the disruption of individuals' lives, in the number of homeless mentally ill on the streets of our cities and towns, or the financial costs of treatment and lost income to this nation. The NIMH goals for schizophrenia research are likewise quite clear: finding its causes, improving treatments and services through research, and eventually developing preventive strategies to reduce its incidence. The discovery of new classes of antipsychotic medications and our improved understanding of how these medications work in the brain may revolutionize treatment in the next few years. New neuroimaging techniques and radioreceptor studies may finally allow us to see the brain abnormalities that relate directly to specific symptoms of schizophrenia. Finding the relevant genes should allow us to discover the basic biological vulnerability to schizophrenia, and the potential implications of this are truly profound. The revolutions in basic, clinical, and services research provide extraordinary opportunities. We hope to take full advantage of these scientific advances and see that they improve our understanding of schizophrenia's causes and lead to better treatments.

—*David Shore*

101

Diagnosis and Classification

Efforts to understand the nature of schizophrenia are ultimately linked to a disease model. That is, schizophrenia is assumed to be a specific illness or group of illnesses defined ultimately on the basis of its pathophysiological mechanisms and its causes. At present, our definitions of schizophrenia rely primarily on its clinical presentation. In this respect, schizophrenia is similar to many other diseases within medicine, which are defined at a clinical and syndromic level. For example, like schizophrenia, diabetes mellitus has characteristic presenting features, such as difficulty in regulating blood sugar, but has considerable variation in severity and age of onset. Just as we do not fully understand why schizophrenia presents with so much clinical diversity, we also have not yet determined how and why diabetes may have juvenile- and adult-onset forms with different courses and treatment needs.

The diagnostic complexity of schizophrenia can be better understood if one reviews the various streams of thinking that have flowed into the concept. The original definition by Emil Kraepelin (who called the disorder *dementia praecox*) primarily stressed the importance of an early age of onset and a pervasive and persistent impairment in many aspects of cognitive and behavioral function. His formulation was complemented by the ideas of Eugen Bleuler, who was more interested in the cross-sectional symptoms that patients showed on a given occasion and was also interested in identifying which of these symptoms could be considered the most important or fundamental, in the sense that they characterize the essence of the disorder. For Bleuler, the most important symptom was fragmentation in the formulation and expression of thought; he renamed the disorder *schizophrenia* to emphasize splitting of associations as its most fundamental feature. A third stream flowing into the concept of schizophrenia derives from the German psychopathologist Kurt Schneider, who believed that particular kinds of delusions and hallucinations represented the defining features of the disorder. While Kraepelin and Bleuler influenced concepts of schizophrenia throughout most of the 20th century, Schneider's ideas became especially popular in the 1960s and 1970s, when investigators began trying to develop systematic approaches to evaluating schizophrenia for research, leading to the development of structured interviews and other rigorous formulations. Schneiderian first-rank symptoms were given considerable primacy in these assessment instruments, since psychotic symptoms such as delusions and hallucinations were especially easy to identify and to define reliably. These features, therefore, had an important impact on the development of standardized diagnostic criteria in the 1980s.

The definition of schizophrenia that is currently used for clinical work and for most research studies is embodied in the *Diagnostic and Statistical Manual of Mental Disorders (DSM)* of the American Psychiatric Association. This manual has been revised several times during the past decade. The first version to contain explicit diagnostic criteria, *DSM-III*, made a clear break with the broader definitions of schizophrenia that were widely used in the United States during the 1960s and 1970s. These criteria were developed in the context of several important clinical and research developments. For example, research studies comparing diagnostic practices in the United States and other parts of the world indicated that the American definition of schizophrenia was far broader than that used elsewhere, suggesting a need to narrow the definition. In addition, clinical realities such as the developing awareness of the risks of tardive dyskinesia, the possible efficacy of lithium, and the availability of effective antidepressants led to a recognition that placing affective disorders high on the differential diagnostic hierarchy was beneficial to patient care. The definition of schizophrenia was narrowed in *DSM-III* by introducing a requirement that some symptoms of the disorder must be present for at least 6 months, emphasizing psychotic symptoms, and deemphasizing Bleulerian fundamental symptoms.

In spite of these salutary effects, the *DSM-III* definition has also had some negative effects, which are being at least partially ameliorated in the most recent revision, *DSM-IV*. Perhaps the most serious problem with *DSM-III* was that the concept of schizophrenia became somewhat distorted by emphasizing psychotic features at the expense of other defining features. In particular, negative (or deficit) symptoms (which are quite similar to those Bleuler considered fundamental) were given little prominence. Not only do these symptoms have important historical significance and support from a large clinical literature, but they are also the symptoms that prevent patients with schizophrenia from holding jobs, forming normal interpersonal relationships, or leading happy and productive lives. In the economic and social sphere, emphasis on negative symptoms is also needed, so that compensation and treatment agencies will recognize that such symptoms should be given prominence in planning clinical care. In the scientific domain, failure to emphasize negative symptoms has led to failure to design new medications that may be specifically effective for these symptoms or to attempt to understand the symptoms in terms of their underlying brain mechanisms.

A related problem with the *DSM* system is the failure, particularly among young clinicians and laypersons, to recognize that the criteria for schizophrenia provide only a brief description, are arbitrary, and are useful for defining schizophrenia only for certain purposes. The criteria do not represent a comprehensive statement about either the defining features of the disorder or its essential nature. Diagnostic criteria such as those provided in *DSM-III* or *DSM-IV* have a tantalizing simplicity that gives people the sense that we know what schizophrenia is when in fact we do not. It is important to remember that schizophrenia remains a clinical syndrome comprising an unknown number of disease entities or pathological domains.

Research in schizophrenia over the next several decades will rely heavily on efforts to improve our definitions of schizophrenia and ultimately to develop definitions based on pathophysiological mechanisms and etiology. To this end, three general explanatory constructs or models for dealing with the observed heterogeneity of the disorder are being explored: (1) a single etiopathological process leading to diverse manifestations, similar to disorders such as syphilis; (2) multiple disease entities leading to schizophrenia by different etiopathological processes, similar to the syndrome of mental retardation; and (3) specific symptom clusters within schizophrenia, each of which reflects different disease processes and which combine in different ways and different patients. Each of these models attempts to address core questions about the diagnosis and classification of schizophrenia: how we can explain the diversity of the symptoms of the illness—within an individual cross-sectionally, within an individual over time, or within the groups of individuals that we refer to as having "schizophrenia."

Model 1 assumes that schizophrenia is in fact a single disease with a single cause. In this respect, it would resemble syphilis. Syphilis has been known in medicine as "the great imitator," because patients with syphilis can express the disease in many different ways: delusions, memory impairment, personality change, depression, and a host of other symptoms. Yet these diverse symptoms arise because the brain is infected with a single agent, the spirochete. Differences in site and severity of infection with the spirochete probably lead to the diversity of symptoms. Identifying the spirochete as the cause of syphilis ultimately led to the discovery of the disease's essential nature and to a successful treatment, which has now nearly eradicated the disease. Most simple diagnostic systems, such as *DSM*, operate according to model 1. If schizophrenia does indeed have a single cause, this model is quite robust. If not, however, the consequences are poor reproducibility of studies and slowing of the overall research endeavor, since individuals whose illness has different causes are lumped together and referred to as having "schizophrenia."

Model 2, which has been called the multiple disease entities approach, argues that schizophrenia should be conceptualized as similar to mental retardation. Patients who present with the diverse symptoms of this disorder could have developed them for a variety of reasons, ranging from purely genetic to purely environmental, with many combinations possible as well. As with mental retardation, all individuals are somewhat alike, but their common features have a variety of different causes. For example, one form of mental retardation, phenylketonuria, is purely genetic; discovering that it is caused by a fundamental error in metabolism due to a genetic defect has led to improved treatments. At the opposite extreme is another form of mental retardation, fetal alcohol syndrome, caused by environmental injury. In this instance, understanding the cause leads to preventive measures, such as encouraging pregnant women to avoid alcohol. Many forms of mental retardation are, however, as yet poorly understood at the etiopathological level. As with syphilis, different pathological processes can affect the brain differently, causing the variability in clinical presentation that is so frequently observed.

Model 3, which explores domains of psychopathology, assumes that different discrete disease processes lead to different specific symptom domains. For example, one process might lead to prominent negative symptoms, while a different process might underlie hallucinations. The domains are conceptualized as categories that are not mutually exclusive. Any patient can be afflicted with one or more of the various possible disease processes. This model has a variety of advantages, since it points out that several core processes could be associated with specific aspects of schizophrenia rather than only one process.

As the preceding overview suggests, the conceptualization of schizophrenia has become more sophisticated during the past decade. Simple, concise, and practical definitions have been developed that have demonstrated clinical utility, like those in *DSM*. On the other hand, at the level of scientific research, more complex strategies are being developed, which offer the potential of linking understanding of the clinical presentation of schizophrenia to underlying disease processes occurring at the neural level. When combined with the various research technologies described elsewhere (e.g., molecular genetics, neuroimaging), this increase in knowledge and sophistication offers the promise that improved understanding of mechanisms may ultimately lead to improved treatment or even, ultimately, prevention.

—Nancy C. Andreasen and
William T. Carpenter, Jr.

Relations of Symptoms to Cognitive Deficits

The symptoms of schizophrenia include a variety of disturbances in thought, feeling, and action. The clinical symptoms of a patient with schizophrenia, such as hallucinations, delusions, thought disorder, and withdrawal from social interactions, can vary over time, and patients differ markedly from each other in the severity of these symptoms. Behavioral scientists have identified several abnormalities in attention, perception, and other aspects of cognition that seem to characterize schizophrenia. An important question for understanding the psychological and neurobiological bases of symptoms is whether the cognitive dysfunctions and clinical features of the disorder are related to each other, and if so, whether the symptoms and information-processing deficits result from the same neuropsychological processes.

Several subtypes of schizophrenia are recognized. One long-appreciated distinction is that between the paranoid form of the illness, in which delusions are prominent, and nonparanoid forms. More recently, the distinction between positive symptoms and negative symptoms of schizophrenia has received a great deal of attention from both clinical and biological researchers. These two classes of symptoms—which reflect distortions of normal psychological functions and loss of such functions, respectively—may have different neurobiological bases and responses to treatment.

Research evidence suggests that these clinical distinctions are related to the cognitive and neuropsychological deficits seen in schizophrenia. Research in cognitive psychology and neuropsychology has discovered that mental tasks can often be accomplished in several different ways. That is, there is a certain redundancy of processes in perception, attention, and thinking, and a certain flexibility in the brain's information-processing approaches. There appear to be different information-processing styles in patients with delusions and those without delusions. People with paranoid schizophrenia are more attentive to context and connotative aspects of stimuli. Their cognitive processing approach tends to be governed by expectations, general schemata, or templates, while nonparanoid patients are more attuned to the perceptual features of the environment and tend not to categorize information adequately.

Both subtypes of schizophrenia show deficits in a range of information-processing tasks, including attention, memory, and the integration of visual information with motor performance. The extent of positive and negative symptoms shown by a patient is related to the particular kind of information processing that is most difficult for that patient. Difficulty in processing auditory verbal information, especially on tests of distraction, is related to positive symptoms, while motor deficits and impairments in memory and visual information processing are more highly related to negative symptoms.

Recently, the field has moved from discovering associations between clinical and cognitive aspects of schizophrenia to developing and testing theories about how symptoms may be caused by neurocognitive and associated neurobiological dysfunctions. Brain imaging studies by several research teams have shown reduced physiological activation in the frontal cortex of the brain during mental tasks in schizophrenia. These results, together with neuropsychological studies of brain-injured patients and patients with schizophrenia, as well as neuroscience research with nonhuman animals, suggest that a widely distributed system of brain regions is impaired in schizophrenia. This complex circuit, in addition to the frontal lobes, consists of the striatal and septohippocampal areas.

Each of these brain regions appears to be involved in the specific behaviors and psychological processes that are impaired in schizophrenia, such as memory, attention, and controlled motor movement. Moreover, as several research teams have proposed, working as a system, these regions are responsible for the self-regulation and self-monitoring of behavior, which is markedly impaired in schizophrenia. The disruptions in the integration of behavior and experience, first noted as central features of schizophrenia by Kraepelin and Bleuler earlier in this century, appear to reflect abnormalities in the interaction of the frontal, septohippocampal, and striatal brain regions.

Advances in understanding the neuropsychology of schizophrenia depend on discoveries about both the neurobiology and the cognitive psychology of schizophrenia. Through careful description of the psychological aberrations observed in schizophrenia, hypotheses about underlying abnormalities in brain structure and physiology can be developed and tested. Both hallucinations and delusions have been the subject of extensive psychological research in the past decade. This research on schizophrenia has made extensive use of the expanding knowledge of normal cognitive processes.

Humans generally can distinguish between sensory events and events that occur only in imagination and can differentiate between the memory of an experience and the memory of an earlier thought. Sometimes, however, people confuse perception and imagination. Failures in this aspect of self-monitoring are particularly pronounced in patients who have prominent hallucinations and delusions. These misattributions, especially of fragmentary sensory and perceptual experiences, in conjunction with abnormal inference processes and overconfidence in judgments, have been suggested as critical in the genesis of the positive symptoms of hallucinations and delusions. As noted above, abnormalities in the interaction of frontal and septohippocampal brain regions have been proposed to produce positive symptoms and so may underlie these cognitive abnormalities as well.

These developments in theory linking brain systems to both specific symptoms and particular cognitive deficits in schizophrenia are an important advance. Empirical studies of the working brain in schizophrenia through neuroimaging and cognitive research, emerging from common theoretical grounding in cognitive science and neuroscience, will clarify the validity of these theoretical developments. Schizophrenia is a developmental disorder in which clinical state and clinical picture fluctuate over time, so it is important to study the links between cognitive abnormalities and symptoms as the symptoms wax, wane, and change over time.

—Milton E. Strauss

Information Processing and Attention Dysfunctions

Abnormalities in information processing have played a central role in understanding schizophrenia since the time of Kraepelin and Bleuler. Schizophrenia-spectrum patients have profound problems in focusing attention on salient cues and in overcoming the disruptive effects of distracting stimuli. Such patients, theories suggest, are thus rendered vulnerable to stimulus inundation, cognitive fragmentation, and thought disorder induced by this inability to adequately process cognitive cues from the stimulus-laden, complex world that surrounds us. Adding to the strength of such theories, investigators have made considerable progress in clarifying the functional significance and neurobiological basis of information processing and attention dysfunctions.

This review focuses on our understanding of information processing and attention dysfunctions in schizophrenia. The relevant material is presented in four parts. First is an overview of theories of information processing and attention with special reference to their relevance for understanding schizophrenia. Second is a review of specific conceptual issues in information-processing research on the group of schizophrenias. Specifically, it seems clear that information-processing deficits are characteristic of schizophrenia per se and are not the result of nonspecific state variables, such as general distractibility, nor are these deficits due to the effects of antipsychotic medication. Information-processing dysfunctions clearly have profound implications for how the schizophrenia patient functions in normal tasks and activities of daily living. Third is a review of 10 common techniques used to tap the information processing and attention dysfunctions of schizophrenia patients. Recent advances and novel applications of these techniques in "boundary" populations such as high-risk children and schizotypal patients are discussed. Psychopharmacologic probes, animal models, and basic strategies are also reviewed. Fourth, an integration and suggestions for future directions in information processing and attention research in schizophrenia is presented.

William Blake noted that, "If the doors of perception were cleansed, everything would appear ... as it is, infinite" (William Blake as quoted by Aldous Huxley 1954). There is a rich tradition of looking at the critically important information processing and attention dysfunctions that disrupt the "doors of perception" in schizophrenia-spectrum patients. Careful descriptive clinicians, such as Kraepelin, noticed "a certain unsteadiness of attention" in dementia praecox patients. Syntonic with these observations, Bleuler recognized that acute attention is lacking in schizophrenia patients. Since McGhie and Chapman focused on "disorders of attention and perception in early schizophrenia" from a descriptive and phenomenological viewpoint, investigators have consistently tried to identify and understand the neurobiological substrate of these information-processing deficits that seem characteristic of schizophrenia patients.

Attempts to demythologize and quantify information processing and attention deficits in schizophrenia patients note that patients have critical deficiencies in information-processing abilities that are elicited and especially enhanced when high processing loads, multiple tasks, distraction, or other "stressors" demand the rapid and efficient processing of information. Along with the long-term, trait-linked reduced capacity or inefficient processing of task-relevant cognitive operations in schizophrenia patients, other attention deficits may be state-linked. These state-linked collapses of information processing may be more characteristic of psychosis in general (e.g., schizophrenia, mania, drug-induced) than the trait-linked deficits seen in schizophrenia patients and persons at the "boundaries of schizophrenia" (e.g., schizotypal patients, high-risk children, unaffected family members), for whom these deficits seem unremitting.

An integrated information-processing framework provides us with a critical viewpoint that enhances our understanding of the complex and far-reaching neurobiological and psychosocial facets of the group of schizophrenias. In an upward analysis, information-processing dysfunctions correlate with cognitive, neuropsychological, and symptomatic impairments in several important ways. The symptom- and state-related correlates of information-processing deficits in schizophrenia patients are a fascinating area of research. Ever since the early reaction-time studies, it has been useful to see that information-processing impairment does not simply correlate with gross (i.e., nonspecific) symptomatology. In some paradigms, information-processing deficits are accentuated in schizophrenia patients with negative symptoms compared to those with positive symptoms. This finding tends to invalidate explanations of information-processing deficits as accruing from the distracting effects of positive symptoms, such as hallucinations and delusions. It also

110

appears that there are relatively nonspecific information-processing deficits that covary with a psychotic state per se but selectively persist in some poor-prognosis schizophrenia patients. It is interesting to note that many studies point to the utility of information-processing measures in predicting outcome, an important validating and practical issue for future research. This fact leads to an important area in the upward analysis: the occurrence of trait-related deficits in information-processing functions in schizophrenia and boundary patients.

In an upward analysis, studies of trait-related variables have assumed and will continue to assume a critical role. If subjects at the boundaries of schizophrenia (e.g., schizotypal patients, high-risk children, unaffected family members) have information-processing deficits similar to those of schizophrenia patients, then the observed deficits are unlikely to be due to the gross disruption caused by generalized symptoms or treatment variables (e.g., antipsychotic medications, institutionalization). The results of numerous studies dramatically illustrate the centrality of these trait-related studies. Boundary subjects have information-processing dysfunctions in a clear schizophrenia-like direction. These deficits are demonstrable across a wide spectrum of information-processing measures, including virtually all of the 10 measures discussed in this review. In sum, almost every information-processing technique that taps into a schizophrenic deficit also taps into a deficit in some boundary population. The ubiquity of trait-linked deficits in these nonpatient boundary subjects is perhaps the most compelling and dramatic interlocking series of findings in this area of schizophrenia research. There appears to be something very basic and central about information-processing deficits in the group of schizophrenias, especially when these tasks are time-linked and tap into high processing loads. In future work, these information-processing measures should be correlated with each other and with other psychological and biological measures. Researchers must probe for sensitive phenotypic markers to characterize the mode of inheritance of these schizophrenia-linked information-processing deficits; such markers can be used in family molecular genetic studies.

In a "top-down" analytic direction from information processing, we can examine the neurobiological substrate of stimulus processing in the group of schizophrenias. The established anatomic substrate of information-processing functions interacts dramatically with the known neurobiological substrate of the group of schizophrenias, with the frontal lobes, temporal lobes, hippocampus, striatum, pallidum, and thalamus implicated (parts of the cortico-striato-pallido-thalamic circuit).

The most prominent theme in this research area is the shift in thinking from concepts of single locus/single neurotransmitters to more elaborate schemes involving integrated networks or cascades of neurotransmitters located in widely distributed but related or connected areas of the central nervous system. One means of tapping into the neural substrate of information-processing functions is by systemic drug challenges in humans and by systemic and local drug challenges in animal model studies. Studies of schizophrenia patients and normal subjects have also begun to correlate brain images of structure (e.g., using magnetic resonance imaging) and function (e.g., using positron emission tomography [PET]) with information processing and neuropsychological measures. Combining PET with cognitive tasks is an exciting new area that needs to be fully explored.

Animal model studies of techniques that can be tested in humans (e.g., prepulse inhibition of the acoustic startle reflex, P50 gating, latent inhibition, event-related potentials) have been very important in augmenting our understanding of information processing in normal and biologically altered states. These exciting and imaginative studies will undoubtedly be a central and critical area of inquiry in future years.

Information-processing measures will continue to provide a critically important window for observing and probing the clinical characteristics and neural substrate of the group of schizophrenias. Because these disorders appear to be heterogeneous, much care and patience must temper our enthusiasm about the emerging complex but rational picture of schizophrenia that is being painted by investigators working at an intricate level of detail in their laboratories. As more studies use converging measures (e.g., prepulse inhibition and P50 gating) and combine old with new technologies (e.g., continuous performance task and PET), the picture of the group of schizophrenias will undoubtedly grow clearer and more stimulating to our intellects and imaginations.

—*David L. Braff*

Genetics

The study of the genetics of schizophrenia dates back to the first decades of this century. Many of the issues we now struggle with were first articulated then. The first question in considering a possible role for genetic factors in the cause of schizophrenia has to be the degree to which the disorder aggregates (or "runs") in families. Historically, this research can be divided into two periods. At first, studies were usually performed nonblind (with the investigator knowing that the relatives assessed were related to an individual with schizophrenia), without control groups (i.e., relatives of individuals without schizophrenia), and without use of operationalized diagnostic criteria that we now know make psychiatric diagnosis considerably more reliable. While many of these studies were performed by thoughtful and careful researchers, their results—that schizophrenia consistently and substantially aggregates in families—were open to these methodological criticisms. In the early 1980s, the validity of these studies was questioned, and the observed familial aggregation was attributed to consistent methodological biases. In particular, it was suggested that the diagnosis of schizophrenia was overly broad.

In 1993, we can now evaluate these claims, because since 1980 a substantial number of what might be termed second-generation family studies of schizophrenia have been completed. These studies share three key methodological features in their use of (1) "normal" control groups, (2) structured psychiatric assessment and operationalized diagnostic criteria, and (3) blind assessment and diagnosis. Seven studies meeting all these criteria were performed in four countries: the United States, Greece, Germany, and Ireland. Risk of schizophrenia (the probability of developing schizophrenia for persons living through the age at risk—until around 50) in relatives of control subjects was quite similar across studies and averaged 0.5 percent. Risk of schizophrenia in first-degree relatives of schizophrenia subjects (full siblings, parents, and offspring) was much more variable, ranging from 1.4 to 6.5 percent, and averaging 4.8 percent. Statistical analysis suggests that the variation in these estimates could easily have occurred by chance.

Three major conclusions can be drawn from our review of recent family studies of schizophrenia. First, the earlier family studies were substantially correct in concluding that schizophrenia strongly aggregates in families. Their findings do not appear to have been systematically biased by methodological flaws. Second, the seven recent studies suggest that the degree of familial aggregation of schizophrenia is substantial. Risk of schizophrenia in first-degree relatives of an individual with schizophrenia is 9.7 times as great as the risk for relatives of a matched control. Third, we have no convincing evidence that familial aggregation of schizophrenia differs significantly across populations.

The past 10 years have not been active ones for twin or adoption research in schizophrenia. Results of only one new twin study of schizophrenia, performed in Norway, have been published. As in all previous studies, when one twin has schizophrenia, the probability that the other twin also has schizophrenia is much higher if the twins are monozygotic (one-egg, or identical, twins) than if they are dizygotic (two-egg, or fraternal, twins). In this study, these two figures were 48 and 4 percent, respectively. Updated findings from two major adoption studies of schizophrenia, being conducted in Denmark and Finland, continue to support the role of genetic factors in the etiology of schizophrenia. Thus, family studies demonstrate that schizophrenia strongly aggregates in families, and twin and adoption studies continue to suggest that genetic factors account for most of this aggregation.

Accurate definition of who is affected by a disease is crucial in any genetic investigation. A major focus in genetic studies of schizophrenia has been to use family, twin, and adoption data to try to determine precisely which psychiatric disorders might represent alternative expressions of an underlying liability (or vulnerability) to schizophrenia. Since the time of Kraepelin and Bleuler, many clinicians and researchers have noted that some close relatives of patients with schizophrenia, though never psychotic, had odd or eccentric personalities that were clinically reminiscent of schizophrenia. This finding led to the hypothesis that familial liability to schizophrenia can be expressed, at least in part, as a predisposition to schizophrenia-like, or schizotypal, traits. Seven rigorous family or adoption studies have now addressed this question using the criteria of the third edition of the *Diagnostic and Statistical Manual of Mental Disorders* of the American Psychiatric Association (*DSM-III*) or its revision (*DSM-III-R*). Although rates of schizotypal personality disorders fluctuate substantially across studies, all find such cases more commonly in relatives of schizophrenia patients than in relatives of matched control subjects. These results provide strong support for the above hypothesis.

It has also been unclear whether familial liability to schizophrenia predisposes to a broader range of psychotic disorders that, in *DSM-III-R*, would be termed schizo-affective disorder, schizophreniform disorder, delusional disorder, or atypical psychosis. In five modern, rigorous family studies, these psychoses were substantially more common in relatives of schizophrenia patients than in relatives of matched controls, while two other studies did not find this pattern.

Is it possible that familial liability to schizophrenia increases risk for *all* psychiatric disorders? We found nine recent controlled studies that addressed this issue using modern operationalized criteria, blind diagnosis, and control groups. Most studies found no evidence of a familial coaggregation of schizophrenia and mood disorders (major depression and bipolar illness). No studies found any consistent familial relationship between schizophrenia and anxiety disorders or alcoholism.

Thus, we conclude that familial liability to schizophrenia is neither very narrow nor very broad, and includes not only narrowly defined schizophrenia, but also schizotypal personality traits and probably some nonschizophrenic, nonaffective psychotic disorders.

We believe it is now firmly demonstrated that genetic factors play the major role in the familial aggregation of schizophrenia and related disorders. However, it is extremely important to keep in mind that "complexity" and "heterogeneity" are very likely to underlie this genetic etiology. Carriers of disease genes do not always manifest the disorder (a phenomenon known as incomplete penetrance, or delayed age of onset). Affected individuals need not carry any mutant genes (environmental forms, or phenocopies). Diagnostic uncertainties are unavoidable. Furthermore, different families may carry different genes that confer susceptibility (genetic heterogeneity). These factors have crucial implications for the interpretation of genetic studies of schizophrenia.

To date, the mode of transmission of genetic liability to schizophrenia remains uncertain, except that it is unlikely to be due solely to the action of a single major gene that is common to all cases and families. The issues of complexity and heterogeneity greatly limit the power of any statistical method used to address this question.

Similarly, successful application of linkage analysis to identify specific genes that influence susceptibility is likely to be far more difficult for schizophrenia than for simple, Mendelian genetic disorders.

Given these problems, it is not too surprising that the field has yet to produce replicated linkage findings for schizophrenia. The studies to date have had relatively little power to detect such a linkage, especially in the presence of the complexities outlined above. Nevertheless, if one or several genes of major effect exist for schizophrenia, large sample studies using new statistical and laboratory methods have a good chance of detecting them. While success is definitely not guaranteed, if resources allow sufficient time for this approach to mature, truly unprecedented insights into the etiology of schizophrenia may be attainable.

Linkage analysis of schizophrenia should be neither prematurely spurned nor excessively embraced as the only form of viable genetic research in schizophrenia. We recommend a balanced research approach to the genetics of schizophrenia, including both the traditional methods of family, twin, and adoption studies and a major effort in large-sample linkage studies.

—Kenneth S. Kendler
and Scott R. Diehl

Psychopharmacologic Treatment

The treatment of schizophrenia continues to be a major challenge to clinicians, not only because of the severity and complexity of the disease, but because of the need to integrate and address biological, psychosocial, and environmental effects and influences. In addition, with increasing restraints on health care expenditures, the emphasis on cost-effectiveness and community treatment will increasingly influence clinical decisions.

Despite numerous advances in a variety of areas relevant to our understanding of schizophrenia (e.g., brain imaging, genetics, neurochemistry), the medications used to treat schizophrenia have not changed markedly over the past 30 years. With the introduction of clozapine, however, there is increasing interest and effort in developing new drugs and renewed hope that truly better medications can be discovered.

At the same time, considerable progress continues to be made in our ability to use available treatments in the most effective manner with the fewest possible adverse effects. As we await new breakthroughs, we should not forget that even incremental advances in the safe and effective use of currently available treatments can greatly improve the lives of many patients and their families.

Drug dosage continues to be an important issue in acute treatment. Dosages that are too high can lead to an unnecessarily high level of side effects that may be personally distressing and lead to noncompliance in medication taking or interfere with psychosocial and vocational adjustment. In addition, the dosage patients receive when they leave the hospital may influence the long-term dosage level. Recent research suggests that there is no advantage for the average patient in using dosages above 10-20 mg/day of oral haloperidol (Haldol) or fluphenazine (Prolixin) during acute treatment, and for many patients even at these doses prophylactic antiparkinsonian medication should be used to reduce the risk of side effects such as muscle spasms, restlessness, or slowing of movements. Even among patients who do not respond well to an initial course of a specific medication, there is little evidence that increasing the dosage beyond this range produces any added benefit. For patients who fail to respond, obtaining a blood level may sometimes be useful in identifying patients with unusually low (or unusually high) levels, but blood level is not usually an explanation of lack of response. Switching to a different class of neuroleptic is occasionally helpful. Clozapine appears to offer the most promise for patients who have failed to respond to two or three different medications. If clozapine proves either ineffective or impractical, a trial of adjunctive lithium would be the next alternative, followed by a trial of adjunctive benzodiazepines in moderate dosages.

A variety of new antipsychotic medications are currently in various stages of investigation. The goal is to develop compounds with some advantages over existing drugs in terms of effectiveness or side effects. The drug that is closest to becoming available in the United States is risperidone, followed by remoxipride. Both drugs have been shown to be efficacious in large-scale clinical trials and to be less likely than other drugs to produce neurological side effects. Whether they will share clozapine's advantages in treating refractory patients remains to be seen. There is room for renewed optimism, however, that the drug treatment of schizophrenia could be further improved in the not-too-distant future.

There is increasing recognition that many persons suffering from schizophrenia also experience other conditions such as anxiety disorders, depression, obsessive compulsive disorder, or substance abuse. These disorders can produce additional suffering and complicate treatment efforts. It is hoped that further research will guide clinicians in dealing most effectively with such concomitant problems.

Maintenance pharmacotherapy remains a critical modality in the long-term management of schizophrenia and is an essential ingredient in achieving optimum levels of adjustment and functioning in the community. In recent years clinical studies in this area have focused on improving the benefit-to-risk ratio of long-term drug treatment, exploring alternative maintenance strategies, and studying how environmental and psychosocial factors interact with drug treatment. The two major alternative strategies have been continuous low-dose treatment and targeted or intermittent treatment, which is an attempt to take advantage of the fact that many patients will not relapse for several (or even many) months following complete drug discontinuation. Following drug withdrawal, patients are carefully observed with the goal of reinstituting medication at the earliest (or prodromal) signs of relapse. On balance, our review of the literature would suggest that the continuous low-dose treatment may offer more advantages than targeted or intermittent treatment; however, the results of a recently completed study directly comparing the two approaches will allow more definitive conclusions. Although these different dosage-reduction strategies have as one of their most important goals to reduce the risk of tardive dyskinesia (TD), their impact in this regard has not been dramatic to date. It may be, however, that dosage-reduction strategies focused on those patients at highest risk of developing TD would have a more obvious impact. For patients who have developed TD, dosage reduction to the extent possible is desirable.

Continued treatment research conducted in conjunction with many of the perspectives and disciplines represented in this special report will undoubtedly lead to further breakthroughs.

—John M. Kane and
Stephen R. Marder.

Tardive Dyskinesia

The advent of antipsychotic, or neuroleptic, drugs in the early 1950s heralded a new era in drug treatment for schizophrenia patients. These drugs have allowed patients who would otherwise be institutionalized to lead more normal, productive lives. Even today, neuroleptics constitute the most effective drug treatment available for schizophrenia patients. Unfortunately, long-term use of neuroleptics, while ideal for controlling symptoms, also produces tardive dyskinesia (TD), a potentially serious side effect in some patients.

TD is characterized by abnormal movements of the mouth and face, sometimes of the hands and feet, and occasionally of the trunk. The prevalence of TD reported in different studies varies. However, the overall estimate is that TD is present in about 24 percent of all patients treated long term with neuroleptics. Among patient-related variables, aging appears to be a major risk factor for the syndrome. In a current study, we found that the likelihood of developing TD within a year of starting neuroleptic treatment is approximately six times greater among patients aged 45 to 90 than among younger subjects. TD is more prevalent in women than in men. Women also tend to develop more severe symptoms, and the risk continues to rise after age 70, while in men it seems to peak in the 50-70 age group. Other risk factors for TD include mood disorders (especially depression), organic mental syndromes, diabetes mellitus, and a history of neuroleptic-induced parkinsonism.

Studies of drug treatment variables as risk factors for TD have shown no obvious differences among commonly used neuroleptics, except for a lower incidence associated with clozapine. Studies of an association between TD and neuroleptic dosage have also failed to demonstrate a connection. Drug holidays have been shown to have no effect in decreasing the risk of developing TD and may actually increase the risk of persistence of TD as well as of psychotic relapse in some patients. We find that TD may develop in nonpsychiatric patients (e.g., those with complications of diabetes mellitus) treated with metoclopramide, a dopamine D_2 receptor blocker. Although metoclopramide-induced TD is not rare, there is much less awareness of the risks associated with this drug than for the neuroleptics used in psychiatric patients.

Distinguishing TD from other movement disorders, such as drug-induced parkinsonism, is important. Other problems in the assessment of TD include voluntary suppression of the abnormal movements by the patient, the effect of ancillary motor activity and psychological stress on the severity of symptoms, and the tendency of neuroleptics to mask symptoms. However, the development of standardized rating scales and of objective instrumental assessments such as accelerometry, force procedures, and ultrasound has greatly enhanced our ability to evaluate TD, at least for research purposes.

Time appears to be a critical factor in the course of TD, with most studies reporting that the symptoms appear to improve gradually or stabilize over a period of years rather than within the first year of followup. This finding supports the view of TD as a syndrome that follows a continuum from resolved to persistent, rather than being either a reversible or irreversible condition.

While TD is usually mild, it can produce physical and psychosocial complications. Severe oral dyskinesia may result in dental and denture problems that can progress to ulceration and infection of the mouth, as well as muffled or unintelligible speech. Gait disturbances due to limb dyskinesia may leave patients more vulnerable to falls and injuries. Psychosocially, ambulatory patients with obvious TD may experience shame, guilt, anxiety, and anger that can result in depression.

While there has been some progress in assessing the value of different treatments for TD, as yet there are no consistently reliable therapies. Neuroleptic withdrawal, while the most desirable treatment method, is impractical for some patients with chronic schizophrenia. Using neuroleptics to treat TD has been temporarily effective, but since symptoms quickly return when treatment is withdrawn, these drugs appear to merely mask the symptoms, and their use is not recommended for treating TD except in severe cases. "Atypical" neuroleptics such as clozapine may be useful to treat some patients with severe TD, especially the dystonic form.

Many experimental treatments have been used in TD patients, including noradrenergic antagonists and gamma-amino-butyric acid (GABA)ergic agents, with varying degrees of success. On the theory that chronic use of neuroleptics may lead to excessive production of free radicals that damage catecholaminergic and other neurons, vitamin E, a highly potent scavenger of free radicals, has been used to treat TD. Vitamin E appears to be more effective than placebo in some patients with a short duration of TD, but it, too, is not consistently beneficial.

There is no proven way to prevent TD in patients who need long-term treatment with neuroleptics. The best strategy involves restricting these drugs to well-defined indications, using them in the lowest effective doses, and assessing patients at frequent intervals for early signs of TD. While the use of clozapine may reduce the risk of TD, weekly monitoring of blood counts is required because of an increased danger of agranulocytosis.

In the future, the study of TD should focus on several issues, including the underlying mechanisms that lead to the development of TD and the relative contribution of each known risk factor. Investigators will likely continue to improve in their ability to assess TD, but the most critical needs are for new strategies to treat and, preferably, to prevent the syndrome.

—Dilip V. Jeste and
Michael P. Caligiuri

Psychosocial Treatment

A wealth of evidence has accumulated over the past several decades documenting that schizophrenia is a biological illness, rather than the product of faulty child-rearing practices, family conflict, or other family or psychological processes. Despite the biological nature of schizophrenia, however, it is also known that environmental factors can have an important influence on the course of the illness. For example, stressful life events, such as the death of a loved one, and emotionally charged living environments have both been found to increase the chances that a schizophrenia patient will have a symptom relapse requiring hospitalization. In addition to the role of biological and environmental factors in schizophrenia, there is also evidence that patients can be taught new skills to improve the quality of their social relationships and to better manage the stresses of everyday living. Research on the psychological treatment of schizophrenia indicates that the most effective approaches focus on improving patients' personal and interpersonal competencies through learning techniques, while decreasing stress in the home environment by working with family members. The development of "insight" into problems and family dynamics is *not* a goal for either individual or family treatment.

Several issues that have affected the progress of research on psychological treatment for schizophrenia are addressed, including the need for long-term treatment, individual differences in treatment needs, the role of the patient in the treatment process, and the limitations imposed by cognitive deficits associated with schizophrenia. Research indicates that psychological intervention is an important adjunctive treatment for schizophrenia that needs to be provided in the context of a comprehensive, coordinated treatment program. Other components of effective treatment include, but are not limited to, individual and family psychoeducation; medication and ongoing psychiatric evaluation; day hospital, vocational rehabilitation, and educational opportunities; access to crisis counseling; availability of psychiatric inpatient care; supervised residential living arrangements; and case management to obtain entitlements and coordinate the various facets of treatment. When psychological treatment is provided to schizophrenia patients along with an array of other services needed to manage the illness in the community, there is reason to be optimistic that this additional treatment may improve patient functioning and decrease rehospitalizations.

The most widely studied psychological treatment method for schizophrenia patients is social skills training. This treatment approach, which can be provided to patients either individually or in groups, involves systematically teaching patients specific behaviors that are critical for success in social interactions. These skills are taught through a combination of therapist modeling (demonstration), patient role-playing (using the skill in a simulated interaction), positive and corrective feedback to the patient, and homework assignments to practice the skill outside the training session. Controlled research on social skills training for schizophrenia indicates that patients are capable of learning new social skills. This research also suggests that skills training may produce some benefits in other areas of functioning, such as symptoms or social adjustment. However, it is not clear how much improvement occurs, and it is likely that skills training programs need to be provided over extended periods for patients to benefit.

Most patients with schizophrenia have significant cognitive deficits (also referred to as "information-processing deficits") that impair their interpersonal adjustment. Common problems in thinking include poor memory, concentration difficulties, distorted or inaccurate perceptions (e.g., facial expression recognition), and difficulty grasping concepts. There has been a recent surge in interest in developing psychological interventions designed to help patients overcome or compensate for these cognitive impairments. This is an exciting new area of study, but at present there is little controlled research demonstrating that such "cognitive rehabilitation strategies" actually improve patients' cognitive processing or facilitate patient functioning in other areas, such as social adjustment, vulnerability, or symptoms.

A final area in which progress has been made in psychological treatment is family therapy. Family members who care for a relative with schizophrenia, or who are in close contact with an ill relative, experience substantial distress and burden in trying to cope with the illness. Furthermore, negatively charged interactions between patients and relatives may increase the vulnerability of patients to symptom relapses, resulting in a vicious circle of increased patient symptoms leading to increased relative negativity. Over the past decade several different models of family intervention have been developed and tested for schizophrenia. The different approaches to working with families share the common elements of (1) establishing a collaborative, respectful relationship with the family; (2) providing information about schizophrenia and its treatment; and (3) teaching family members less stressful and more constructive strategies for communicating and solving problems. Carefully controlled studies have shown that patients in families who receive this type of family therapy over at least several months have better outcomes than patients in families who do not receive therapy, and some evidence suggests that family members report less distress as well. Further research is needed to clarify how family treatment helps patients and relatives, and who benefits most from which family therapy approach.

Research on the psychological treatment of schizophrenia has made important strides in recent years, and the results of recent studies provide a realistic basis for hope. It is likely that as more breakthroughs occur in the biological treatment of schizophrenia, such as the use of clozapine to improve the functioning of treatment-refractory patients, psychological treatments will assume an even more important role in facilitating the adjustment of patients as they move from institutional settings into the community.

—Alan S. Bellack
and Kim T. Mueser

Neuroimaging

Neuroimaging studies have been used more in schizophrenia than in any other psychiatric disorder. Investigators of brain function in schizophrenia have had to meet the challenge of using developing technology in a complex and heterogeneous disorder. Advances have been made in two related domains of neuroimaging research: structure and function. Structure is examined in neuroanatomic studies, which provide parameters of brain volume. Function is examined in neurophysiologic studies, which measure brain energy metabolism (glucose, oxygen) and blood flow, and neurochemical studies, which measure neuroreceptor density and affinity. Neuroimaging techniques have been able to both inform and advance hypotheses currently influencing schizophrenia research.

With progress in research, including the introduction of new methods, it has become apparent that initial hypotheses regarding schizophrenia were rather simple. It is unlikely that a disorder as complex as schizophrenia would be associated with a single structural or functional lesion in a single neuroanatomical location. Indeed, no such lesion has been identified. However, several findings have emerged consistently, and researchers have made initial attempts to link regional brain abnormalities to symptom patterns and cognitive deficits.

Neuroanatomical Studies: Magnetic Resonance Imaging (MRI)

Initial studies with MRI have attempted to replicate and extend the research with computerized tomography (CT) that showed increased ventricular cerebrospinal fluid (CSF) relative to brain tissue. This finding was considered evidence for structural abnormalities caused by either developmental abnormalities or loss of brain tissue. MRI studies have by and large confirmed that there is an increase in CSF in the ventricles and sulci of the brains of schizophrenia patients.

Attention has now turned to the study of specific brain regions implicated in the neurobiology of schizophrenia. Relatively few studies of the frontal lobe region have been performed in schizophrenia; the results are still inconclusive, and better definitions of substructures are needed. The temporal lobe has been studied more extensively. Reports of abnormalities in schizophrenia implicate lateral temporal regions and medial temporolimbic structures. Decreased brain volume in some of these regions is related to severity of hallucinations, especially auditory ones, and to severity of thought disorder. These anatomical abnormalities are consistent with postmortem neuropathologic findings in schizophrenia. MRI studies in the basal ganglia have yielded somewhat inconsistent findings, and further studies are needed.

Regional volumetric studies are underway, and there is a need to integrate neuroanatomical data with data from other major domains, including phenomenology, neuropsychology, and functional neuroimaging.

Functional Studies: Metabolism and Cerebral Blood Flow (CBF)

Studies of metabolism and blood flow have attempted to address fundamental questions in the study of brain function in schizophrenia. The main imaging techniques applied were the xenon-133 method, positron emission tomography (PET), and single photon emission computerized tomography (SPECT). Investigators have sought to assess whether resting blood flow and glucose metabolism differ between patients with schizophrenia and normal controls. Another important question is whether clinical variables such as symptoms, chronicity of illness, and pharmacologic intervention are related to these physiologic parameters. Incorporating behavioral tasks into physiologic studies can help answer such questions by linking behavioral performance data with physiological measures and examining the pattern of activated relative to resting parameters in schizophrenia.

Three major brain dimensions have been examined complementing current emphases in the study of brain-behavior relations in schizophrenia: anterior-posterior, lateral (with a focus on the temporal lobe), and subcortical-cortical.

The frontal lobes were implicated in early physiologic studies of CBF reports that patients with schizophrenia did not show the normal pattern of increased anterior relative to posterior CBF. This "hypofrontal" disturbance in the anterior-posterior gradient has been supported in some, but not all, studies of resting CBF by the xenon-133 method and of glucose metabolism by PET. The relationship between this pattern of metabolic activity and clinical variables has been examined. Associated with decreased frontal metabolic activity is duration of illness, with longer duration reported with lower anterior-posterior gradient and negative symptoms.

Defective function of the specific regions of the frontal cortex in schizophrenia was evident in reduced CBF seen in subjects executing cognitive tasks believed to depend on the integrity of that region. In contrast to resting glucose PET studies that sometimes show relative hypofrontality, prefrontal flow at rest appears normal and is revealed as abnormal only during specific tasks. Functional changes in temporal lobe regions have also been examined. That schizophrenia patients have dysfunction in temporolimbic structures is supported by recent neuroanatomical and neuropsychological studies. Lateralized abnormalities in these regions, with greater left than right hemispheric dysfunction, are implicated by characteristic clinical features, such as thought disorder, auditory hallucinations, and language disturbances. PET studies of temporal lobe metabolism include findings of both increased and decreased glucose utilization. Metabolism and flow pattern in these regions have also been related to positive symptoms, such as hallucinations, in both PET and SPECT studies.

Functional changes in the basal ganglia have been examined as neuroimaging has been used to measure subcortical-cortical relationships. Several PET studies implicate basal ganglia dysfunction in schizophrenia. While the contribution of PET metabolic and flow studies so far has been to add to the growing evidence for involvement of basal ganglia in schizophrenia, the exact nature of the dysfunction remains elusive. In particular, relationships between basal ganglia and frontal lobe in schizophrenia need exploration. There is emerging evidence of interrelationships between the various key regions, revealed by structural-functional imaging. The study of neuroreceptors provides a direct means of assessing the nature of subcortical abnormalities in schizophrenia.

Functional Studies: Neuroreceptors

There is evidence suggesting that symptoms common in schizophrenia are closely associated with dysfunction of dopamine (DA). This dysfunction may represent an excess of DA. PET studies first focused on a subtype of DA receptors (D_2) because of its clinical relevance and potential to discriminate between illness and treatment effects. Two quantitative PET methodologies evolved to measure D_2 receptors, and the initial reports disagreed.

The disagreement could be due to dissimilarities in the patient populations and methodologies applied and potentially to the fact that the studies were not actually measuring the same neurochemical properties. PET and SPECT neuroreceptor research complements postmortem studies of neuroreceptors in schizophrenia. Furthermore, these methods can elucidate clinically relevant neuroleptic mechanisms by examining drug actions on receptors.

Neuroimaging studies, when placed in the context of the overall effort to establish neural substrates for schizophrenia, have contributed to, and will continue to advance, the understanding of brain dysfunction related to behavior. The field has reached some maturity in establishing paradigms, and there is now a need for adequate sample size in patient and normal populations, with attention to variability in brain function in relation to individual differences, gender, and age. Two types of probes can enhance our understanding of brain function in schizophrenia. The first is the application of tracers for measuring neuroreceptor systems, which is the way to proceed for neuropharmacologic studies. The second is neurobehavioral probes, which are most useful for metabolic studies. Neurobehavioral probes are challenge tasks presented to subjects while the metabolic study is being performed. One of the major challenges in this research is to integrate neuroimaging data across anatomic and functional measures with clinical and neurobehavioral variables.

Toward Integration of Neuroimaging With Neurobiology

Structural and functional studies in schizophrenia suggest that multiple brain regions are affected. Convergent research implicates specific regions. Several lines of evidence imply that the frontal cortical region, in particular the dorsolateral prefrontal cortex, is dysfunctional in schizophrenia. Abnormalities affecting this region seem linked to impaired motivation, socialization, and complex problem solving. Neuropsychological deficits in schizophrenia also suggest frontal lobe involvement. Anatomy of the prefrontal cortex in nonhuman primates indicates multiple links to other cortical areas involved in association, as well as to basal ganglia.

Another region implicated in schizophrenia is the temporal lobe. Early students of schizophrenia suggested the temporal cortex as a pathological locus for auditory hallucinations and thought disorder, based on neural representations of auditory and language function.

Indeed, temporal lobe regions are implicated in functional and anatomic neuroimaging studies. Evidence for temporolimbic circuit involvement in schizophrenia is strong. Primacy of temporolimbic
dysfunction is suggested by the occurrence of positive symptoms following damage to these areas and in some cases of temporal lobe epilepsy. Functions localized to this region may be relevant in disorders
of language, memory, drive, and emotions in schizophrenia. The well-
replicated memory deficits of schizophrenia may be a consequence of
limbic-diencephalic pathology. These brain areas share major connections to prefrontal areas and may serve as a port through which neo-
cortical information reaches the hippocampus and thereafter other
structures within the limbic system.

Of the key regions reviewed earlier, the basal ganglia have many
behaviorally relevant functions, due in part to their connection to multiple brain regions. Clear evidence, however, for primary involvement
of basal ganglia in the pathogenesis of schizophrenia is still lacking.

The initiating event in schizophrenia remains obscure, but new
neuropathologic methods may shed some light. The neuropathologic
findings are most compatible with acquisition in late fetal development or in the perinatal period. Longitudinal MRI studies performed
1 to 2 years after the onset of schizophrenic symptoms do not show
striking increases in ventricular size as the illness evolves. Thus, static
damage early in development could still be reflected as a clinical syndrome characteristically appearing in adolescence and with a waxing
and waning course.

As key functional, structural, and clinical measures within the
same patient population are studied, a more comprehensive system-
wide picture of the disease is likely to emerge. The field is now poised
to conduct such integrative research, which is likely to advance the
understanding of the neural basis of schizophrenia.

Summary and Future Directions

Structural and functional findings emerging from neuroimaging
studies in schizophrenia have begun to provide a bridge linking basic
and clinical behavioral sciences. As we gain experience, findings such
as hypofrontality or DA receptor increases in PET studies are revealed
to be more complex than initially thought. The relationship between
structural and functional changes in the brains of patients with
schizophrenia also requires elucidation. From the viewpoint of speci-

ficity, changes initially hypothesized to be specific to schizophrenia are also reported to occur in affective disorders. These include both functional changes (DA receptor abnormalities and reduced relative frontal glucose metabolism) and structural changes (increased CSF and reduced temporal lobe volume).

We are now equipped to examine hypotheses that address fundamental questions on brain-behavior relations in schizophrenia: (1) What happens to initiate the pathophysiological process ultimately manifested as schizophrenia? (2) When does it happen, in terms of neurodevelopmental versus neurodegenerative processes and their timing? (3) Where does the process first occur regionally? (4) Which areas are then affected secondarily? (5) How do these changes develop and unfold? (6) How do these abnormalities relate to the clinical syndrome of schizophrenia? (7) Are the processes consistent across subtypes? The commitment and excitement experienced by students of schizophrenia should be accompanied by responsibility and care as these lines of investigation are pursued.

—Raquel E. Gur and
Godfrey D. Pearlson

Infection and Autoimmunity

This special report describes many exciting advances recently emerging from schizophrenia research. Most of the individual reports focus on new findings regarding the symptoms of schizophrenia, varied aspects of brain dysfunction in the illness, and effective methods of treatment. Yet, while much important progress has been made in schizophrenia research, we still do not know exactly what originally causes the disorder. Although many abnormalities in brain function have now been convincingly demonstrated, their source remains unknown. Genetic factors have received considerable attention as a potential cause of schizophrenia. Considerable indirect evidence suggests that one or more abnormal genes contribute to at least some cases of schizophrenia. It is important to understand that factors other than genes ultimately also may be identified as causes of schizophrenia. For example, several studies have questioned whether physical trauma during birth might contribute to the development of schizophrenia.

One possibility being studied is that schizophrenia is caused by an infection of the brain (most probably by a virus) or by the immune system of the body reacting against its own brain tissue (a process called autoimmunity). Autoimmunity and infection may be related to each other insofar as autoimmune reactions are thought, in some cases, to be stimulated by an infection. Several investigators have been studying how infection or autoimmunity could affect the brain to result in schizophrenia.

Indirect Evidence

The conventional wisdom has been that the fraction of the population affected with schizophrenia (the prevalence of the disorder) is about the same throughout the world. If infection were a causative factor in schizophrenia, one might expect to see geographic variation in the prevalence. In fact, some investigators have reported such variation, identifying geographic areas with unusually low or high numbers of schizophrenia patients.

Another piece of evidence often cited in support of infection as a cause of schizophrenia is the observation that an excess number of individuals born in the late winter and early spring months subsequently develop schizophrenia. This has been called a "season-of-birth effect." While there is some controversy among researchers about this finding, it is apparent that such an excess of schizophrenia births in late winter and early spring might be the result of increased fetal exposure to maternal viral infections in the late fall and early winter months.

In a related type of finding, investigators have now produced data indicating that fetal exposure to viral epidemics (such as the influenza epidemics that swept the world in the mid-1950s) may be associated with a higher rate of developing schizophrenia. These studies have indicated that a fetus exposed to infection during the second 3-month period (trimester) of pregnancy appears to be more likely to develop schizophrenia in later life. The second trimester is an important time in the growth of the fetus, a period in which the cortex of the brain is being formed. It is possible that influenzal illness in the mother during this phase of pregnancy disrupts brain development of the fetus in a manner that predisposes to the later development of schizophrenia.

Thus, indirect evidence does exist that implicates viral infection as a cause of schizophrenia. Such evidence has spurred investigators to look more directly at schizophrenia patients for laboratory proof of infection or an autoimmune reaction.

Testing for Infection or Autoimmunity

There are several ways to detect whether someone has had an infection and to search for abnormalities in the immune system that might make someone vulnerable to an infection or that indicate an autoimmune response. In fact, nearly 100 years ago, investigators found higher levels of white blood cells (a key component of immunity) in schizophrenia patients. While white blood cell levels are a crude measure that can be affected by stress and other factors, later studies have looked at more specific measures of immune cells and reported many different abnormalities in both the number and function of circulating lymphocytes (key cells involved in the immune response). Recently, sophisticated techniques to identify very specific subgroups of lymphocytes have shown that schizophrenia patients have increased numbers of a particular type of cell that is thought to be closely linked to autoimmunity.

In addition to studies of blood cells involved in the immune system, there has been research regarding the antibody response in schizophrenia patients. Antibodies are produced by immune cells in response to an infection. In some cases, autoantibodies that attack the body's own tissue are incorrectly produced by immune cells. Some researchers have speculated that schizophrenia may result from autoantibodies disrupting normal brain function.

Studies of antibodies against viruses in schizophrenia patients have shown some apparent abnormalities, but the viruses involved are common ones to which most people have been exposed. Thus, it is difficult to prove that infection by the virus had anything to do with the development of schizophrenia. Some studies have shown increased total levels of antibodies in the cerebrospinal fluid of schizophrenia patients—a finding that may more directly reflect infection of the brain and central nervous system. Nevertheless, no specific virus has been proven conclusively to be consistently associated with schizophrenia. Similarly, although some studies have identified what appear to be autoantibodies against brain tissue in schizophrenia patients, these findings have not been consistently replicated.

Other creative approaches have been used in attempts to identify viruses or other infectious particles in schizophrenia patients. Studies have been done in which cerebrospinal fluid from schizophrenia patients or brain tissue samples acquired from autopsies of such patients are injected into various species of laboratory animals and the animals are then observed for neurological or behavioral changes. This technique has been used to prove the presence of infectious particles in other neurological disorders. Once again, the findings of these studies have not yielded conclusive evidence for an infectious agent in schizophrenia. Recently, researchers have used our new understanding of genes and newly developed molecular research techniques to search for genetic material from viruses in brain tissue obtained at autopsy from schizophrenia patients. These techniques are a very sensitive and specific way of identifying viruses in the brain. To date (although only a few viruses have been studied), there has been no conclusive finding of genetic material from a virus in the brain tissue of schizophrenia patients. Nevertheless, it is important to acknowledge that if an infection did cause the brain abnormalities associated with schizophrenia, it might have occurred very early in life. Therefore, it may not be possible to find residual evidence of virus in brain tissue when the patient who died had the illness for many years or even decades after the initial infection.

Conclusions

Many pieces of evidence suggest a possible role for an infection or autoimmune reaction as a causative factor in schizophrenia. As in many other areas of schizophrenia research, the major problem has been the inconsistency of these findings and the difficulty in replicating findings from one study to another. Given the evidence, it does not seem likely that schizophrenia in an adult patient involves any form of active, ongoing infection of the brain. It is possible, however, that early exposure to an infection (even as a fetus) may somehow distort brain development in a way that contributes to later emergence of schizophrenia. Likewise, it remains possible that a subtle autoimmune reaction may affect the brain in ways that contribute to schizophrenia but that may be very difficult to identify using current methods.

One problem in this area of research is that patients are typically studied later in life. Often they have a chronic, difficult-to-treat (refractory) form of schizophrenia. It is increasingly important to study patients earlier in the course of their illness, preferably during their first episode. Similarly, studies of children who are at high risk for developing schizophrenia because of an apparent genetic predisposition running through their families could be very informative as we look for potential involvement of infection or autoimmune reactions in schizophrenia.

A final point must be emphasized most strongly. It seems highly unlikely that schizophrenia (a disorder with many different presentations) has only a single cause. Thus, researchers studying genetics are strongly considering the possibility that there are multiple genes involved in different ways in producing various forms of schizophrenia. These researchers are also careful to point out that some forms of schizophrenia may be wholly nongenetic. Similarly, it is unlikely that a single virus or a single type of autoimmune response causes all cases of schizophrenia. Rather, it is quite likely that various subtypes of schizophrenia exist with different causes, among which are infection or an autoimmune response.

Researchers are continuing to press ahead in studies of infection and autoimmunity in schizophrenia. They have been helped dramatically by the fact that one of the most rapidly advancing areas of science is immunology. Thus, the new scientific tools that have been used to study other infectious and immune disorders (tools that have generated the dramatic advances seen in AIDS research) may also prove to be of great value in the study of schizophrenia.

—Darrell G. Kirch

Neurochemistry and Neuroendocrinology

The search for the etiology of schizophrenia in the scientific era began with studies of neuropathology. The next major line of investigation was clinical neurochemistry. Initial strategies sought to measure the concentrations of neuroactive substances in biological fluids. Later, strategies were devised that focused on indirect measures of neurotransmitter activity which were, to a significant degree, under central nervous system (CNS) regulation. Another indirect approach has used pharmacologic compounds with known biochemical effects to modify neurotransmitter activity and thereby demonstrate an inferential relationship. Despite the passage of many years since the inception of these strategies, they continue to be mainstays of clinical neurochemical studies in schizophrenia. In addition, an enhanced appreciation of the heterogeneous nature of schizophrenia and the potentially confounding effects of antipsychotic drugs have prompted investigators to examine unique and well-characterized clinical subgroups as well as to control for treatment effects by using treatment-naive patients or extended washout periods.

Over the years, an extensive body of investigation has given rise to numerous neurochemical hypotheses of the etiology and pathophysiology of schizophrenia—some fleeting, others more enduring. The dopamine (DA) hypothesis of schizophrenia remains predominant, although there has been increased interest in other neurotransmitters, which are hypothesized to play a role in schizophrenic pathophysiology through their interaction with DA or in their own right.

The DA hypothesis of schizophrenia proposes that schizophrenia is a manifestation of a hyperdopaminergic state. Still, the limitations of both the evidence for and the explanatory power of the DA hypothesis have long been apparent. In recent years there have been relatively few studies of DA in schizophrenia and of the difference between the level of the DA metabolite homovanillic acid (HVA) in the cerebrospinal fluid (CSF) of schizophrenia patients and controls. However, one area in which there has been a proliferation of studies is plasma HVA (pHVA).

Preclinical and subsequent clinical studies have suggested that pHVA concentrations reflect brain DA activity, making pHVA measurement a potentially useful tool for studying the pathophysiology of schizophrenia and the pharmacologic action of antipsychotic drugs. Past studies of pHVA in schizophrenia have reported that the concentration increases with acute neuroleptic treatment, decreases with chronic treatment, increases with neuroleptic discontinuation, and is correlated with psychopathology. The initial increase and subsequent decrease of pHVA with neuroleptics have been associated with clinical response, and several studies have found that pHVA measurement can differentiate between responders and nonresponders and has prognostic significance. Some studies have also found positive correlations between psychopathology and baseline pHVA or the change in pHVA with treatment, while others have not.

Next to DA, serotonin (5-hydroxytryptamine [5-HT]), and norepinephrine (NE) have historically been the neurotransmitters most often implicated in schizophrenia. Serotonin receptors are distributed in brain regions (including frontal cortex) believed to be important in mediating behavioral functions. Moreover, antipsychotic drugs bind to

$5\text{-}HT_2$ receptors. Renewed interest in the 5-HT system has been stimulated recently by the development of a specific class of atypical antipsychotic drugs that have potent activity at 5-HT receptors. There have also been several reports of behavioral response to m-chlorophenylpiperazine (m-CPP), a selective 5-HT receptor agonist. The cloning of genes that code for 5-HT receptor subtypes provides an important strategy for future investigation of 5-HT.

Several investigators have postulated that NE plays an important role in the pathophysiology of schizophrenia. These claims are based on the relationship of the synthetic pathways of DA and NE, on empirical data on noradrenergic measures in other neuropsychiatric disease, and on experimentally demonstrated interactions between DA and NE systems in the CNS. However, we found relatively few clinical studies that clearly demonstrated abnormal measures of NE activity in patients with schizophrenia. Three reports concluded that CSF levels of NE and 3-methoxy-4-hydroxyphenylglycol (MHPG), in varying degrees, were associated with relapse upon neuroleptic withdrawal and with severity of positive and negative symptoms. Reduction in CSF levels of NE and MHPG by clonidine treatment was associated with better antipsychotic response. Although far from conclusive, these data are consistent with the hypothesized involvement of NE in the pathophysiology of schizophrenia.

As the most abundant inhibitory neurotransmitter in the brain, gamma-amino-butyric acid (GABA) has long been hypothesized to play a role in the pathophysiology of schizophrenia. Moreover, GABA neuronal function is closely linked to DA and glutamatergic systems. However, we could find very few studies of GABA in schizophrenia conducted in the past 5 years, and these were not direct neurochemical investigations. Nevertheless, further investigation of GABA in schizophrenia is warranted.

In the past few years there has been a burgeoning interest in the excitatory amino acids (EAA) and their potential role in schizophrenia. Of specific importance was the understanding of the role of EAA neurotransmission in the induction of long-term potentiation, the physiologic process believed to be central in learning and memory. Moreover, phencyclidine (PCP), a potent psychotogenic drug that causes symptoms similar to those of schizophrenia and led to the development of an etiologic hypothesis of schizophrenia, was found to be a noncompetitive antagonist of neurotransmission mediated by N-methyl-D-aspartic acid (NMDA). Added impetus came from studies that linked EAA-mediated neurotoxicity to various neuropsychiatric disorders.

Surprisingly, however, there has been a dearth of actual data related to EAA activity in schizophrenia. Only one recent study was done, and it found no difference in N-acetyl-L-aspartic acid (NAA) levels, but CSF levels of HVA and MHPG were significantly negatively correlated with NAA in controls but not in patients. These results are at least partially consistent with a hypothesis of decreased glutamatergic inhibition of DA neuronal activity in mesiotemporal and subcortical structures.

Since the discovery of neuropeptides and the demonstration that some may serve as neurotransmitters, cotransmitters, and neuromodulators, attempts have been made to explore the significance of these compounds in the pathophysiology of schizophrenia. Clinical neurochemical studies of peptides have largely consisted of measurements of CSF concentrations of different neuropeptides and have yielded conflicting results. Research into the interaction between DA and cholecystokinin (CCK) so far indicates that CCK and DA interact at both the pre- and postsynaptic levels in the nucleus accumbens. In clinical studies, basal levels of CCK were reduced in the CSF of drug-free schizophrenia patients compared with controls, and the rapidity of response to haloperidol was inversely related to baseline. On the other hand, another study found increased levels of plasma CCK in neuroleptic-naive drug-free schizophrenia patients compared with controls, and the levels decreased with haloperidol treatment. Earlier studies of schizophrenia patients and control subjects had found increases, decreases, or no difference in levels of CCK in CSF or in postmortem brains.

Another neuropeptide, neurotensin (NT), has been shown to interact with DA in physiological, anatomical, and behavioral studies. Acute and chronic haloperidol treatment increases NT concentrations in the nucleus accumbens and caudate nucleus. Changes in NT concentration appear to be specific to schizophrenia, since no differences in CSF NT concentration have been found in patients with other psychiatric disorders.

Other recently studied neuropeptides include substance P (SP), dynorphin A, neuropeptide Y (NY), peptide YY (PYY), and somatostatin. Chronic treatment with haloperidol, pimozide, or fluphenazine, but not clozapine or sulpiride, decreases SP concentrations in the substantia nigra but not in the striatum or hypothalamus. One study examined CSF levels of NY and PYY in drug-free schizophrenia patients, depressive subjects, and control subjects and found that schizophrenia patients had a normal NY but a low PYY, whereas depressed patients had the reverse.

Somatostatin is distributed abundantly throughout the CNS and stimulates the release of DA from the striatum; in turn, DA stimulates somatostatin release from various regions. Postmortem studies of patients with schizophrenia have found decreased somatostatin concentrations in the hippocampus and frontal cortex. The results of CSF studies of somatostatin have been less consistent. Recent studies of somatostatin in schizophrenia have found that CSF somatostatin was significantly decreased in chronic schizophrenia patients with moderate cognitive impairment. One study found that CSF somatostatin decreased with treatment, and the decrease paralleled the increase in HVA seen with treatment—further evidence for the interaction between DA and somatostatin.

Another study evaluated plasma somatostatin in neuroleptic-treated schizophrenia patients compared with controls and found that not only was plasma somatostatin significantly greater in patients, but it was significantly correlated with positive symptoms. Somatostatin, NT, CCK, and SP have all been reported to interact with DA, and abnormalities of these and other neuropeptides have been found in schizophrenia. Future studies of neuropeptides that may modulate DA neuronal activity are warranted.

Several investigators have previously hypothesized that schizophrenia may involve abnormalities in the composition and structure of neuronal membranes. Early studies of membrane phospholipid pathology in schizophrenia patients found increases in phosphatidyl serine (PS), decreases in phosphatidylcholine (PC) and phosphatidylethanolamine (PE), and altered anisotropy reflecting fluidity of the plasma membrane phospholipid bilayer. Further studies will attempt to replicate these findings.

Phospholipase A_2 (PLA_2), a key enzyme in the metabolism of phospholipids, is concentrated in neuronal membranes and plays an essential role in establishing and maintaining membrane structure. Two recent studies examined PLA_2 activity in schizophrenia patients and produced differing results. In one study, neuroleptic-naive schizophrenia patients, but not nonschizophrenia patients and controls, had increased PLA_2 activity that decreased with treatment. The other study found no difference between schizophrenia patients and controls in PLA_2 activity. A related study examined total phospholipid content and distribution of phospholipid in the platelet membrane of drug-naive and previously treated schizophrenia patients and controls. Lysophosphatidylcholine (LPC), a toxic product of PLA_2-mediated PC metabolism, was significantly greater in schizophrenia patients than in controls and was significantly correlated with duration of illness in neuroleptic-naive but not in previously treated patients.

Other studies of phospholipids have involved the measurement of prostaglandin precursors, essential fatty acids (EFA), and plasma phospholipids. Three studies have found EFA abnormalities in platelets of schizophrenia patients, although the results have not been entirely consistent. Abnormalities have been found in the fatty acid composition of plasma phospholipids in schizophrenia patients, with perhaps the most consistent finding across the studies being a reduced level of linoleic acid.

Another aspect of phospholipid metabolism and function that has been investigated is the platelet phosphoinositide (PI) system. Phosphoinositides are membrane phospholipids that are hydrolyzed to the second messengers. There is also some evidence that D_2 receptor stimulation indirectly suppresses PI hydrolysis. Signal transduction mediated by thrombin-stimulated PI turnover in platelets was examined in three recent studies. Abnormalities were found in schizophrenia patients but not in control subjects, although the studies had different results. Three studies found increased turnover in drug-treated and drug-free patients but not in drug-naive patients, whereas one study found that some acute schizophrenia patients, but not chronic schizophrenia patients or controls, had decreased turnover, and patients with abnormal PI turnover had better outcomes than other acute patients.

The neuroendocrine strategy for research in neuropsychiatric disorders is based on the unique anatomical relationship of the pituitary gland to the hypothalamus and CNS. Pituitary hormone secretion is predominantly regulated by neurochemical mechanisms. Thus, examination of the secretory patterns of pituitary hormones enables investigators to measure indirectly the neurochemical activity of specific brain structures involved in a given hormone's regulation. The specific anatomical level—pituitary, hypothalamic, or suprahypothalamic—can be determined using pharmacologic probes, including releasing factors, neurotransmitter agonists, and antagonists. After this approach was introduced, numerous neuroendocrine studies of schizophrenia were performed. Despite the waning pace of neuroendocrine research, it continues to be an active and potentially fruitful area. Of the various pituitary and peripheral endocrine hormones, prolactin (PRL) and growth hormone (GH) have been the most extensively studied. This is primarily because DA is the major neurotransmitter involved in their regulation.

Various abnormalities in GH secretion have been extensively described in a large number of studies. These abnormalities include differences in schizophrenia patients compared with normal control subjects in basal levels, 24-hour and diurnal secretory pattern, and responses to stimulation with pharmacologic agents. Most studies in schizophrenia have involved hypothalamic-pituitary axis mediated GH responses to pharmacologic probes such as apomorphine, bromocryptine, and methylphenidate. Some abnormalities have been found, including a decrease in GH response to apomorphine over time. In addition, basal GH was found to have prognostic significance, and basal and peak GH response was correlated with psychopathology.

Growth hormone releasing factor (GHRF) stimulates GH release from somatotropin cells and can be used to characterize the anatomic level of GH dysregulation in schizophrenia. There have been three recent reports of GH response to GHRF in schizophrenia. One found that the schizophrenia group had significantly lower GH response than nonschizophrenia and control groups, while the other two studies found that GH response did not differ between patients and controls. Neuroendocrine challenges evaluating GH response have also assessed other neurotransmitter systems in addition to DA in schizophrenia. These results in particular need to be considered preliminary, since there have been few studies and no replications.

Overall, the subtle alterations of basal GH, the normal response to GHRF, and abnormalities of GH response to various agents suggest a suprapituitary abnormality. It seems likely that more than one neurotransmitter system is involved, since GH response to dopaminergic, serotonergic, GABAergic, and nonadrenergic agents has been abnormal and/or has been correlated with psychopathology or treatment response.

PRL has also been examined in schizophrenia. One study measured the 24-hour secretory patterns of PRL in drug-free schizophrenia patients and healthy subjects and found the secretory amplitude of PRL was markedly increased immediately before and following sleep onset. In addition, the schizophrenia group had more PRL pulses throughout the 24-hour period. Another study measured the responses of PRL to fenfluramine and found that PRL response was blunted in the schizophrenia patients. A recent study measured PRL response to thyroid-releasing hormone (TRH) in schizophrenia, schizoaffective disorder (SAD), major depressive disorder (MDD) patients, and healthy subjects and found blunted PRL only in the MDD patients. This evidence suggested that SAD was distinct from the major affective disorders and was more closely related to schizophrenia. Other studies have shown that PRL level could be used to predict global outcome, and lower peak PRL responses to intravenous haloperidol were associated with an increased risk of relapse.

Five other recent studies have used the TRH test to detect neuroendocrine disturbances in schizophrenia. No significant differences in basal or peak thyroid-stimulating hormone (TSH) were found between schizophrenia patients and control subjects. Two studies compared schizophrenia patients (some with postpsychotic depression) with MDD patients and found significant differences in basal or peak TSH levels between the two, groups. On the other hand, a study that compared schizoaffective mania, schizophrenia, and mania patients found that those with schizophrenia had significantly less blunting of their TSH response. Studies that examined correlations between clinical variables and psychopathology did not find any association with abnormalities on the TRH test.

The extensive body of data produced by clinical neurochemical and neuroendocrine studies of schizophrenia can only be described as fragmentary. At present, these data do not provide clear or convincing support for any specific etiologic hypothesis, and the patterns of results of neurochemical and endocrine studies are modest in magnitude and consistency. At the same time, however, it is also clear that schizophrenia patients as a population have distinct neurochemical and endocrine differences from the general population. Given the biological heterogeneity of the general population and within the syndrome of schizophrenia, and the potential confounding effects of drug treatment and environmental factors, the background noise against which the pathophysiologic feature must be detected is considerable. This may be an even greater problem for neurochemical and endocrine variables, since they are such indirect measures. Viewed in this context, it may be no surprise that a consensus on robust neurochemical abnormalities has not yet been achieved.

At this point it seems unlikely that traditional methods of clinical neurochemistry will find the "single bullet"—the biologic substrate responsible for the pathogenesis of schizophrenia. However, through the use of more precise patient sampling, comprehensive clinical characterization, and longitudinal repeated-measures assessments of patients in different stages of their illness, the clinical and prognostic correlates of neurochemical and endocrine measures can be determined.

—Jeffrey A. Lieberman
and Amy R. Koreen

Neuropathology

In the first half of the century, schizophrenia was the subject of some 200 neuropathologic studies, which in general did not find specific brain abnormalities associated with this disease. After several decades of relative neglect, the neuropathology of schizophrenia has reemerged as one of the major challenges of current biological psychiatric research.

A new era of neuroanatomical schizophrenia research started about 20 years ago, receiving strong impetus from modern neuroimaging methods. Since that time, about 50 neuroanatomical postmortem studies in schizophrenia have been published. The majority of these studies demonstrated various types of subtle anomalies in limbic structures (i.e., hippocampal formation, parahippocampal and cingulate gyrus, entorhinal cortex, amygdala, and septum). These structures play a crucial role in the functions that are now thought to be disturbed in schizophrenia, including the coordination of cognitive and emotional activities, the higher cortical integration and association of different sensory modalities, representation and analysis of environmental contexts, sensory gating, and the neuronal generation and control of basic drives and emotions. Therefore, a broad spectrum of schizophrenic symptoms might be related to structural and functional disturbances of limbic brain regions.

The findings in the limbic system comprise (1) reduced volumes and cross-sectional areas of the hippocampus, parahippocampal gyrus, and amygdala; (2) enlargement of adjoining parts of the ventricular system (temporal horn), especially in the left hemisphere; (3) reduced cell numbers and cell size in the hippocampus, parahippocampal gyrus, and entorhinal cortex; (4) reductions in white matter that contains myelinated fibers from and to the hippocampus, parahippocampal gyrus, and entorhinal cortex; (5) disturbed cytoarchitecture and fiber architecture as well as abnormal cell arrangements in the hippocampus, cingulate gyrus, and entorhinal cortex; (6) deficits in small (probably inhibitory) interneurons in the cingulate gyrus; and (7) an increased incidence of a cavum in the septum pellucidum.

The type and extent of the reported changes vary, however, and some of the findings could not be replicated by all research groups. While there does not seem to be a homogeneous pattern of limbic pathology in schizophrenia, most researchers working in this field agree that there are subtle changes in limbic brain regions in a significant percentage of schizophrenia subjects. The magnitude of the pathology is far less than that seen in degenerative brain diseases such as Alzheimer's disease and Pick's disease. Limbic tissue volumes, cell numbers, and cell size differ by some 10 to 30 percent between schizophrenia patients and control subjects, and there is considerable overlap between patients and controls. Only about one-quarter of the patients have values outside the normal range.

Additional evidence linking temporolimbic pathology to schizophrenic symptoms was provided by brain imaging studies using computed tomography, magnetic resonance imaging, and positron emission tomography. According to these studies, there is an especially strong association between left temporolimbic pathology and the so-called positive symptoms of schizophrenia.

There are also reports of changes in brain regions outside the limbic system. Some researchers found anatomic abnormalities in the neurotransmitter systems of the basal ganglia, thalamus, cortex, corpus callosum, and brainstem. These findings, however, are less consistent than those in the limbic system. There are reports of increased and decreased volumes or cross-sectional areas in the basal ganglia and corpus callosum, respectively. Many of the studies are based on small sample sizes and therefore must be regarded as preliminary.

Studies of psychopathological syndromes associated with organic lesions of different brain regions suggest that basal ganglia pathology in schizophrenia may be related to catatonic symptoms (which are characterized by abnormal movements), while thalamic or prefrontal cortical pathology may be related to negative symptoms.

There is still no evidence of a specific and consistent anatomic abnormality in the brains of all patients diagnosed as having schizophrenia. One possible explanation for the present lack of homogeneous brain pathology in schizophrenia is that unlike well-defined organic brain disease, schizophrenia is not considered to be a specific disease entity, but rather a diagnostic construct that may include a heterogeneous mix of diseases. Even if schizophrenic symptoms are similar, different causes and types of neuropathology could account for them. Alternatively, it is possible that the brains of many patients suffering from schizophrenia are structurally normal, but patients may decompensate because of functional disturbances of neurotransmitter or other biochemical systems.

Neuropathological strategies to study potential causes of schizophrenia include (1) investigations of glial cells, (2) examination of the cortical architecture, and (3) studies of cerebral asymmetries.

The majority of glial cell studies in brains of schizophrenia patients seem to indicate that the anatomic abnormalities described in the mesiotemporal structures, cingulate gyrus, and thalamus are not associated with gliosis and, therefore, might reflect a disorder of brain development. There might, however, also be a subgroup of patients with a reactive gliosis around the third ventricle, possibly caused by a subtle brain lesion acquired later.

The findings of abnormal architectonic features of single nerve cells, cell clusters, cortical layers, and myelinated fibers in limbic structures (as well the increased incidence of a cavum septi) in schizophrenia subjects are strong indicators of disturbed early brain development. These reported cytoarchitectural abnormalities are subtle, however, compared with several severe and well-known disorders of cortical development. There is a substantial overlap between brain findings in schizophrenia and similar developmental irregularities in normal controls.

Additional support for the assumption of abnormal prenatal brain development in schizophrenia comes from recent postmortem studies showing an absence of normal structural asymmetry of the Sylvian fissure and cortical structures in a significant proportion of the patients. These asymmetries develop as genetically programmed in the second and third trimesters of pregnancy and are present at birth.

Several theories attempt to explain the long latency between early disturbances of brain development in schizophrenia and the later onset of typical clinical symptoms. Common to all these theories is that they regard the structural abnormalities in brains of schizophrenia patients as vulnerabilities that predispose the brain to decompensate under stress and the influence of additional factors related to the typical age of onset of schizophrenia.

—*Bernhard Bogerts*

Part Three

Mood Disorders

Chapter 10

Depression

Up to one in eight individuals may require treatment for depression during their lifetimes. According to data based on a 1980 population base, the total number of cases of major depressive disorder among those 18 or older in a 6-month period is 4.8 million; in addition, over 60 percent of suicides can be attributed to major depressive disorder. The direct costs of treatment for major depressive disorder combined with the indirect costs from lost productivity are significant, accounting for approximately $16 billion per year in 1980 dollars. Regrettably, only one-third to one-half of those with major depressive disorder are properly recognized by practitioners.

There are many places to get the help [for depression].

- Call your family physician or other health care provider.

- Call your local health department, community mental health center, hospital, or clinic. They can help you or tell you where else you can go for help.

- Contact a local university medical center (many have special programs for the treatment of depression).

This chapter consists of excerpts from *Depression in Primary Care: Volume 1. Detection and Diagnosis*, NIH Pub. No. 93-0550; *Depression in Primary Care: Volume 2. Treatment of Major Depression* NIH Pub. No. 93-0551; and *Depression is a Treatable Illness*, NIH Pub. No. 93-0553. To assist the reader, subheads have been added.

- Contact one of the national health groups listed below. They can refer you to a health professional where you live. They can also give you more information about depression, provide you with books and pamphlets, and tell you about support groups.

National Alliance for the Mentally Ill (NAMI)
2101 Wilson Blvd, Suite 302
Arlington, VA 22201
Toll free: 800-950-6264

National Depressive and Manic Depressive Association (NDMDA)
730 N. Franklin St., Suite 501
Chicago, IL 60610
Toll free: 800-82-NDMDA

National Foundation for Depressive Illness, Inc. (NFDI)
P.O. Box 2257
New York, NY 10116-2257
Toll free: 800-248-4344

National Mental Health Association (NMHA)
National Mental Health Information Center
1021 Prince Street
Alexandria, VA 23314-2971
Toll free: 800-969-6642

What Is a Clinical Depression?

A clinical depression or a mood disorder is a syndrome (i.e., a constellation of signs and symptoms) that is not a normal reaction to life's difficulties. Depressive and other mood disorders involve disturbances in emotional, cognitive, behavioral, and somatic regulation. Depressive disorders should not be confused with the depressed or sad mood that is a normal response to specific life experiences—particularly losses or disappointments. These responses are transient and are not associated with significant functional impairment. A sad or depressed mood is only one of the many signs and symptoms of clinical depression. In fact, the mood disturbance may include apathy, anxiety, or irritability rather than or in addition to sadness; further, the patient's interest or capacity for pleasure or enjoyment may be markedly reduced.

By definition, major depressive episodes last at least 2 weeks (typically much longer) in both major depressive and bipolar disorders. A sad mood or a significant loss of interest is required, along with several associated signs and symptoms, to warrant a diagnosis of a major depressive episode. A major depressive episode can occur as part of a primary mood disorder (e.g., major depressive or bipolar disorder), as part of other nonmood psychiatric conditions (e.g., eating, panic, or obsessive-compulsive disorders), in association with drug or alcohol intoxication or withdrawal, as a biologic consequence of various general medical conditions (secondary mood disorders), or as a consequence of selected prescribed medications.

Major depressive disorder may begin at any age, but it most commonly begins in the 20s to 30s. Symptoms develop over days to weeks. Some persons have only a single episode, with a full return to premorbid functioning. However, more than 50 percent of those who initially suffer a single major depressive episode eventually develop another. In these cases, the diagnosis is revised to recurrent major depressive disorder.

The course of recurrent major depressive disorder is variable. In some patients, the episodes are separated by many years of normal functioning without symptoms. For others, the episodes become increasingly frequent with greater age. Major depressive episodes nearly always reduce social, occupational, and interpersonal functioning to some degree, but functioning usually returns to the premorbid level between episodes if they remit completely. Major depressive episodes may end completely or only partially.

Signs and Symptoms of Depression

People who have major depressive disorder have a number of symptoms nearly every day, all day, for at least 2 weeks. These always include at least one of the following:

- Loss of interest in things you used to enjoy.
- Feeling sad, blue, or down in the dumps.

[Symptoms also include] at least three of the following:

- Feeling slowed down or restless and unable to sit still.

149

- Feeling worthless or guilty.
- Increase or decrease in appetite or weight.
- Thoughts of death or suicide.
- Problems concentrating, thinking, remembering, or making decisions.
- Trouble sleeping or sleeping too much.
- Loss of energy or feeling tired all of the time.

With depression, there are often other physical or psychological symptoms, including:

- Headaches.
- Other aches and pains.
- Digestive problems.
- Sexual problems.
- Feeling pessimistic or hopeless.
- Being anxious or worried.

Treatment of Depression

Once identified, depression can almost always be treated successfully, either with medication, psychotherapy, or a combination of both. Not all patients respond to the same therapy, but a patient who fails to respond to the first treatment attempted is highly likely to respond to a different treatment.

Effective treatment rests on accurate diagnosis. The practitioner must first distinguish clinical depression, which is sufficiently severe and disabling to require intervention, from sadness or distress that is a normal part of the human experience. A formal mood syndrome should be treated. Treatments with established efficacy are preferred initially over less well tested or untested interventions.

In selecting an appropriate treatment, the clinician weighs the certainty of treatment response against the likelihood and severity of potential adverse treatment effects. The optimal treatment is highly acceptable to patients, predictably effective, and associated with minimal adverse effects. It results in complete removal of symptoms and restoration of psychosocial and occupational functioning. Treatment proceeds in three phases: acute treatment, continuation treatment, and maintenance treatment.

Acute Treatment

Acute treatment aims to remove all signs and symptoms of the current episode of depression and to restore psychosocial and occupational functioning (a remission). A remission (absence of symptoms) may occur either spontaneously or with treatment. If the patient improves significantly, but does not fully remit with treatment, a response is declared. If the symptoms return and are severe enough to meet syndromal criteria within 6 months following remission, a relapse (return of symptoms of the current episode) is declared.

Continuation and Maintenance Treatment

Continuation treatment is intended to prevent this relapse. Once the patient has been asymptomatic for at least 4 to 9 months following an episode, recovery from the episode is declared. At recovery, continuation treatment may be stopped. For those with recurrent depressions, however, a new episode (recurrence) may occur months or years later. Maintenance treatment is aimed at preventing a new episode of depression and may be prescribed for 1 year to a lifetime, depending on the likelihood of recurrences.

Types of Treatments

Formal treatments for major depressive disorder fall into five broad domains: medication, psychotherapy, the combination of medication and psychotherapy, electroconvulsive therapy (ECT), and light therapy. Each domain has benefits and risks, which must be weighed carefully in selecting a treatment option for a given patient. Once selected, the initial treatment should be applied for a sufficient length of time to permit a reasonable assessment of the patient's response (or lack of response). If the treatment is going to be effective, a 4- to 6-week trial of medication or a 6- to 8-week trial of psychotherapy usually results in at least a partial symptomatic response; a 10- to 12-week trial usually results in a symptomatic remission, though full recovery of psychosocial function appears to take longer. The selection of the first and subsequent treatments should, whenever possible, be a collaborative decision between practitioner and patient. Such shared decision making is likely to increase patient adherence and, therefore, treatment effectiveness.

If the patient shows a partial response to treatment by 4 to 6 weeks, the same treatment should be continued for 4 or 6 more weeks. If the patient does not respond at all by 6 weeks or responds only partially by 10 to 12 weeks, other treatment options should be considered. If the initial treatment is the administration of an antidepressant medication, available evidence suggests that both partial responders and nonresponders will benefit from either switching to a different medication class or adding a second medication to the first. If psychotherapy alone is the initial treatment and it produces no response at all by 6 weeks or only a partial response by 12 weeks, clinical experience and logic suggest a trial of medication, given the strong evidence for the specific efficacy of medication. If the initial acute treatment is combined treatment and it produces no response by 6 weeks, switching to another medication is a strong consideration. For some patients, especially those who have had previous medication trials, medication augmentation rather than switching may be preferred.

Medications

Medications have been shown to be effective in all forms of major depressive disorder. Given the evidence to date, it is appropriate to treat patients with moderate to severe major depressive disorder with medication whether or not formal psychotherapy is also used. Medication is administered in dosages shown to alleviate symptoms. No one antidepressant medication is clearly more effective than another, and no single medication results in remission for all patients. The specific medication choice is based on side-effect profiles, patient's history of prior response, family history of response, and type of depression. Some patients respond well to one antidepressant medication, while others respond to a different medication. If the patient has previously responded well to and has had minimal side effects with a particular drug, that agent is preferred. Similarly, if the patient has previously failed to respond to an adequate trial of or could not tolerate the side effects of a particular compound, that agent should generally be avoided.

In general, of the tricyclics, the secondary amines (e.g., desipramine, nortriptyline) have equal efficacy, but fewer side effects, than do the parent tertiary amines (e.g., imipramine, amitriptyline). The newer antidepressants (e.g., bupropion, fluoxetine, paroxetine, sertraline, trazodone) are associated with fewer long-term side effects, such as weight gain, than are the older tricyclic medications. Patients whose disorder has atypical features appear to fare better on monoamine oxidase inhibitors (MAOIs) or selective serotonin reuptake inhibitors (SSRIs) than on tricyclic antidepressants (TCAs).

A history of failure to respond to a truly adequate trial of a drug in one class strongly suggests that it would be appropriate to try a medication from a different class rather than another drug from the same class. If the patient has not responded at all or has only a modest symptomatic response to medication by 6 weeks, the practitioner is advised to reevaluate the accuracy of diagnosis and the adequacy of treatment. Options for further treatment include continuing the current medication at a corrected dosage, discontinuing the first medication and beginning a second, augmenting the first medication with a second, adding psychotherapy to the initial medication, or obtaining a consultation/referral.

Psychotherapy

Patients with milder forms of major depressive disorder may be unwilling to tolerate medication side effects, and those with certain coexisting medical conditions may be physically unable to tolerate these drugs. Psychotherapy alone to reduce the symptoms of major depressive disorder may be considered a first-line treatment if (1) the depression is mild to moderate, nonpsychotic, not chronic, and not highly recurrent and (2) the patient desires psychotherapy as the first-line therapy. Preferred psychotherapy approaches are those shown to benefit patients in research trials, such as interpersonal psychotherapy, cognitive therapy, behavioral therapy, and marital therapy. The therapies that target depressive symptoms (i.e., cognitive or behavioral therapies) or specific interpersonal or current psychosocial problems related to the depression (i.e., interpersonal psychotherapy) are more similar than different in efficacy.

The efficacy of long-term psychotherapies for the acute phase treatment of major depressive disorder is not known; therefore, these therapies are not recommended for first-line treatment. The psychotherapy should generally be time-limited, focused on current problems, and aimed at symptom resolution rather than personality change. The therapist should be experienced and trained in the use of the therapy with patients who have major depressive disorder. Regular visits once or twice a week are typical.

Combination of Medication and Psychotherapy

If the patient being treated with psychotherapy fails to show any improvement in depressive symptoms by 6 weeks or only partial response by 12 weeks, a reevaluation and potential switch to, or addition of, medication are indicated. Medication is almost always recommended for those who do not respond to therapy at all. Given the evidence for the efficacy of medication and the lack of information regarding the efficacy of formal psychotherapy alone, the [Depression Guideline] panel does not advise practitioners to treat severe and/or psychotic major depressive disorders with psychotherapy alone.

Combined treatment with both medication and psychotherapy may have an advantage for patients who have responded partially to either treatment alone or who have a history of chronic episodes or poor inter-episode recovery, a history of chronic psychosocial problems (both in and out of episodes of major depression), and/or a history of treatment adherence difficulties. However, combined treatment may provide no unique advantage for patients with uncomplicated, nonchronic major depressive disorder. The possibility that these patients need adjunctive psychotherapy may be better gauged once the depressive syndrome has largely resolved with medication, since medication that induces a symptomatic remission also, as a consequence, improves psychosocial difficulties in many patients. The condition of patients given the combination of medication and psychotherapy who have not responded at all by week 6 or only partially by week 12 should be reevaluated to ensure that an alternative cause of symptoms has not been overlooked.

Electroconvulsive Therapy

Electroconvulsive therapy is not recommended as first-line therapy for uncomplicated, nonpsychotic cases of major depressive disorder in primary care, as effective treatments that are less invasive and less expensive are available. It is a first-line option for patients suffering from severe or psychotic forms of major depressive disorder, whose symptoms are intense, prolonged, and associated with neurovegetative symptoms and/or marked functional impairment, especially if these patients have failed to respond fully to several adequate trials of medication. Electroconvulsive therapy may also be considered for patients who do not respond to other therapies, those at imminent risk of suicide or complications, and those with medical conditions precluding the use of medications. Very few patients will be sufficiently ill to require ECT. However, when ECT is indicated, it must be provided by a specialist.

Light Therapy

Light therapy—a relatively new treatment option—is a consideration only for well-documented mild to moderately severe seasonal, nonpsychotic, winter depressive episodes in patients with recurrent major depressive or bipolar II disorders. Training in the administration and potential risks of light therapy is requisite to its use. Medication may also be effective for seasonal depression.

Depressive Features, Subtypes, and Onsets

Psychotic Features

Psychotic features refer to the presence of delusions or hallucinations. They occur in 15 percent of patients with major depressive disorders.

In psychotic depressions, psychotic features are never present without concurrent mood symptoms. Psychotic depressions must be distinguished from schizoaffective disorder. In the latter only, there are periods of at least 2 weeks during which delusions or hallucinations are present without mood disturbances.

The content of the hallucinations or delusions in psychotic depressions is usually logically consistent with the predominant sad mood (mood-congruent). For example, there may be a delusion that the patient has sinned in an unforgivable way. Less commonly, the hallucinations or delusions have no obvious relationship to sadness (mood-incongruent); for example, there may be persecutory delusions, for which the person has no explanation. Studies to date suggest that mood-incongruent symptoms are associated with a worse prognosis; evolve into schizophreniform or schizoaffective disorders; involve a less episodic, more chronic course; and require more assiduous, longer maintenance treatment(s).

The psychotic features of psychotic major depressive disorder usually recur in subsequent episodes, should such episodes occur. Some studies suggest that psychotic depressive episodes are familial.

For psychotic depressions, TCAs [tricyclic antidepressants] plus a neuroleptic or electroconvulsive therapy (ECT) are each superior to TCAs alone in treating the illness. Given the markedly disabling nature of psychotic depression, maintenance treatments are strongly indicated when the disorder is recurrent. However, the relative efficacy of maintenance treatment compared to placebo; the value of including both a neuroleptic and an antidepressant in maintenance treatment; and the acute and maintenance phase efficacy of non-TCA medications, lithium, or selected anticonvulsants have not been studied in randomized controlled trials.

Melancholic Features

The key melancholic features of major depressive disorder are:

- Psychomotor retardation or agitation.
- Loss of interest or pleasure.
- Lack of reactivity to usually pleasant stimuli.
- Worse depression in the morning.
- Early morning awakening.

Melancholic symptom features appear to repeat from episode to episode in individuals with recurrent, severe major depressive disorder. They are more commonly present in older depressed patients. Melancholic features are not uniquely associated with a family history of depression. They are associated with reduced rapid eye movement latency and/or dexamethasone nonsuppression.

Severely symptomatic patients whose depression has melancholic features are likely to respond to treatment with TCAs or to ECT. Melancholic features do not predict which antidepressants will be effective, though their presence indicates that anxiolytics will not be effective. The presence of melancholic symptom features, especially in the severely ill, should sharply increase the practitioner's tendency to treat with antidepressants and should provoke a thorough questioning for the presence of psychotic symptom features. If medications fail, ECT should be strongly considered for these patients.

Atypical Features

The groups studying atypical features define the features differently. Two types, vegetative and anxious, have been proposed in the literature. Vegetative features include:

- Overeating.
- Oversleeping.
- Weight gain.
- A mood that still responds to events (reactive mood).
- Extreme sensitivity to interpersonal rejection.
- A feeling of heaviness in the arms and legs.

Anxious features include:

- Marked anxiety.
- Difficulty in falling asleep.
- Phobic symptoms.
- Symptoms of sympathetic arousal.

Atypical features of either type are associated with a younger age at onset of illness. Whether these symptoms run in families, repeat across episodes, or are associated with an identifiable or unique biology is not known. However, rapid eye movement latency is not characteristically reduced in this type of mood disorder. The relationship between atypical and melancholic symptom features remains to be clarified. Some data suggest that atypical symptoms may be more likely earlier in the course of major depressive disorder, while melancholic features are more likely to appear later.

Several randomized controlled trials indicate that, when atypical features (those in the vegetative group above) are present, monoamine oxidase inhibitors (MAOIs) are more effective than TCAs, although the latter are still more effective than placebo. Case reports and clinical experience suggest that those depressions with atypical features may respond better to selective serotonin reuptake inhibitors (SSRIs) than to TCAs.

Seasonal Pattern

The *Diagnostic and Statistical Manual of Mental disorders, Third Edition, Revised (DSM-III-R)* indicates that a seasonal pattern for major depressive disorder can be diagnosed only if:

- Episodes are recurrent (at least two episodes by some criteria, three by other criteria).

- There has been a regular temporal relationship between the onset of the major depressive episodes and a particular period of the year (such as regular onset of depression in fall and offset in spring).

- Seasonal episodes substantially outnumber nonseasonal episodes. Most often depressive symptoms remit fully between seasonal episodes.

The first systematic evidence of the prevalence of seasonal affective disorder was an estimate of 6 percent from a study in the New York area. Subsequently extended to various east coast latitudes, this study showed less than 2 percent prevalence in Florida and nearly 10 percent prevalence in New Hampshire. There are two to three times as many people personally troubled by the winter recurrence of seasonal mood symptoms than there are those with manifestations severe enough to warrant clinical diagnosis.

Preliminary evidence suggests that light therapy is effective in the short-term treatment of outpatients with mild to moderate seasonal major depressive disorder. Further research is required before such a claim can be made for subsyndromal seasonal affective disorder. To date, no hazard has been encountered with short-term light therapy using standard fluorescent lighting apparatus (designed to produce 2,500 to 10,000 lux stimulation and low levels of ultraviolet emission). Exposure extending beyond 2 weeks has not been fully evaluated. Clinical reports suggest that medications may also be effective for some seasonal mood disorders.

Postpartum Onset

Postpartum mood symptoms are divided into three categories, based on severity: blues, psychosis, and depression. Postpartum blues are brief episodes (1 to 4 days) of labile [unstable] mood/tearfulness that normally occur in 50 to 80 percent of women within 1 to 5 days of delivery. Treatment consists of reassurance and time to resolve this normal response.

Postpartum psychoses can be divided into depressed and manic types. Patients with the depressed type show more psychotic, disoriented, agitated, and emotionally labile features, as well as more psychomotor retardation, than do nonpostpartum matched depressed controls. Most of these cases are associated with signs of organic impairment. Features of the manic type are similar to features of a classic mania. The incidence of postpartum psychosis is low (0.5 to 2.0 per 1,000 deliveries), as shown in eight studies. Many early cases were mistaken for toxic/infectious states.

The symptoms of postpartum psychosis develop rapidly (over 24 to 72 hours), typically beginning 2 to 3 days after delivery. The period of risk for developing postpartum psychosis is within the first month following delivery. For acute postpartum psychosis, the prognosis is generally good. However, many patients have previously had or subsequently develop a bipolar disorder. The risk of postpartum psychosis is higher for those with episodes at prior deliveries. The recurrence rate is from 33 to 51 percent.

Nonpsychotic postpartum depressions (major or minor depressive disorders) have also been identified. These conditions may occur from 2 weeks to 12 months postpartum, but typically occur within 6 months. The prevalence of nonpsychotic depressions is 10 to 15 percent within the first 3 to 6 months after childbirth, which is somewhat higher than are the rates (5 to 7 percent) in nonchildbearing matched controls. However, the risk for nonpsychotic postpartum depression is higher for persons with a psychiatric history.

No randomized controlled treatment trials for any of the postpartum mood conditions are available. Logic and clinical experience suggest that prophylactic lithium be given as soon as possible after delivery to prevent a postpartum precipitation in patients with a history of bipolar disorder. Likewise, given the high likelihood of recurrence, other previously effective psychotropic medications should be considered in those with a history of psychotic postpartum mood episodes immediately after giving birth.

Grief and Adjustment Reactions

DSM-III-R indicates that, if depressive symptoms begin within 2 to 3 weeks of a loved one's death, the diagnosis is uncomplicated bereavement, which is not viewed as a disorder but as a normal, relatively benign state that resolves spontaneously without treatment. While uncomplicated bereavement and major depressive episodes share many symptoms, active suicidal thoughts, psychotic symptoms, and profound guilt are rare in bereavement. However, if a major depressive episode is still present 2 months following the loss, the episode is likely to be prolonged and associated with substantial morbidity. Clinically, the diagnosis of major depressive disorder may be made during the period of "grief" in those who meet the criteria for a major depressive episode 2 months following the loss.

Grief reactions are equally common in women and men. Over the course of the first year of bereavement, [one study] found that 35 percent of 109 widows and widowers met the criteria for a major depressive episode at 1 month, 25 percent at 7 months, 17 percent at 13 months, and 46 percent were depressed some time during the first year following the loss of a spouse.

[Another research effort] studied 350 widows and widowers 2 and 13 months after their spouses' deaths. Twenty-four percent met the *DSM-III-R* criteria for a major depressive episode at 2 months. Since the deaths had occurred only recently, the condition of these subjects was diagnosed as uncomplicated bereavement rather than major depressive disorder. Those meeting the criteria for major depressive disorder early in the period of grief were more likely to have personal or family histories of major depressive episodes (not in response to the death of a loved one), current treatment with antidepressant medications, suicidal ideation, poor health, and poor current job satisfaction. Most important, they were likely to be in a major depressive episode 1 year following the loss. Given the anticipated prolonged suffering and disability, it is logical to consider treating these patients for the major depressive disorder, though randomized controlled trials of any treatment are lacking in this population.

Depression Not Otherwise Specified

Depression not otherwise specified (DNOS) identifies mood conditions with depressive symptoms that do not meet either severity or duration criteria for dysthymic, major depressive, or bipolar disorders. It is a heterogeneous category.

Examples of DNOS include minor depression, recurrent brief depressive disorder, and mixed anxiety/depression. Whether these three groupings are true disorders is under investigation. Currently, they are not formally recognized diagnoses.

Minor depressive disorder is symptomatically similar to major depressive disorder, but with fewer symptoms and less disability; symptoms come and go, but are present for at least 2 weeks at a time.

Minor depressive disorder does not have the chronic/pervasive, multiyear pattern of dysthymic disorder.

Recurrent brief depressive disorder features brief (3 to 7 days) episodes that return 6 to 10 times per year and meet the symptomatic threshold and clinical features of a major depressive episode, but not the 2-week duration criterion. It occurs somewhat more often in women than in men, and the age of onset is late adolescence to mid-20s. The likelihood of a positive history in first-degree relatives of patients with recurrent brief depressive disorder is 12 to 20 percent for major depressive disorder and 1 to 3 percent for bipolar disorder.

Studies have begun to suggest the existence of a disorder involving symptoms of both anxiety and depression. [In one study], 4.1 percent of a sample of 1,055 primary care patients had mixed anxiety/depression, defined as concurrent anxious and depressive symptoms, neither of which was of sufficient frequency or duration to meet criteria for a formal anxiety or mood disorder.

Causes of Depression

Major depressive disorder is not caused by any one factor. It is probably caused by a combination of biological, genetic, psychological, and other factors. Certain life conditions (such as extreme stress or grief) may bring out a natural psychological or biological tendency toward depression. In some people, depression occurs even when life is going well.

Both recognition and diagnosis of depression rest on an awareness of the risk factors for depression, as well as elicitation of the key signs, symptoms, and history of illness. The risk factors include:

- Prior episodes of depression.
- Family history of depressive disorder.
- Prior suicide attempts.
- Female gender.
- Age of onset under 40.
- Postpartum period.
- Medical co-morbidity.
- Lack of social support.
- Stressful life events.
- Current substance abuse.

Depression Co-Occurring with Other General Medical Disorders

Many general medical conditions are risk factors for major depression. Major depressive disorder, when present, should be viewed as an independent condition and specifically treated. Treatment may include (a) optimizing the treatment of the general medical disorder and/or (b) providing specific treatment for the depression.

Clinically significant depressive symptoms are detectable in approximately 12 to 36 percent of patients with another nonpsychiatric, general medical condition. Rates in patients with specific medical disorders may be even higher. These figures far exceed the approximate 4 percent prevalence of diagnosable depression in large community samples. On the other hand, *most* patients with a general medical condition do not have a mood disorder. Therefore, the mood disorder, when present, should be viewed as an independent condition (perhaps precipitated by the biologic or psychological vulnerability of the individual) that should be specifically treated.

Stroke. The association between cerebral infarction and depression has long been recognized. However, systematic studies have found only a weak relationship between depression severity and physical/cognitive impairment following stroke. Case reports indicate that post-stroke patients who are also depressed, especially those with major depressive disorder, are less compliant with treatment, are more irritable and demanding, and have an apparent personality change.

Dementia. Distinguishing depressive disorders from early dementing disorders (from known or unknown causes) is a complex clinical problem. Apathy, impaired concentration, or memory loss may occur in primary major depressive episodes in the elderly, as well as early in the course of dementing disorders with or without depression. The term *pseudodementia* refers to the clinical presentation of cognitive impairment due to depression in the elderly. The co-occurrence of depression and dementia is by far the more frequent clinical problem. In some patients with symptoms of both depression and dementia, a personal or family history of depression suggests a depressive condition as the primary diagnosis.

Parkinson's disease is associated with mild dementia in approximately 38 percent of patients, while 46 percent suffer severe dementia in the end stages of the disease. Approximately 50 percent of Parkinson's patients with dementing symptoms have major depressive disorder sometime during the course of the illness. Unlike primary degenerative dementia, Parkinson's dementia is considered a subcortical dementia; it is association with physiologic changes in the subcortical regions. In those with subcortical dementia (e.g. patients with Parkinson's or Huntington's disease), cognitive symptoms appear to improve with improvement of mood, so assessment for and treatment of the depression may be particularly helpful to these patients.

Approximately 30 to 40 percent of Alzheimer's disease patients demonstrate formal depressive mood syndromes and/or psychotic symptoms sometime during their illness. The exact relationship between the two disorders is not clear. The earlier or concurrent presence of depression does not alter either the progression or dementia *per se* or its neuropsychological features. Some suggest that depression may occur during the early stages of dementia and that treatment of the depression may reduce some of the cognitive difficulties. However, long-term followup shows that many older patients presenting with both depression and cognitive difficulties go on to develop primary degenerative dementia without depressive features.

Diabetes. A variety of metabolic and endocrinologic diseases are associated with depressive symptoms/syndromes. One such condition [is diabetes].

Numerous recent studies that have estimated the prevalence of depression in treated samples of diabetic adults suggest that major depressive syndrome is approximately three times more common in patients with diabetes than in the general population. The prevalence of major depression in patients with insulin-dependent diabetes mellitus is similar to that in patients with non-insulin-dependent diabetes mellitus.

Coronary Artery Disease. The prevalence of various forms of depression in patients who have had a myocardial infarction is estimated at 40 to 65 percent. High prevalence rates have also been found in patients undergoing coronary artery or heart transplant surgery. The prevalence of minor and major depressive disorders combined has been reported to be as high as 40 percent in patients who have coronary heart disease and 45 percent in those who recently experienced a myocardial infarction.

163

Cancer. The diagnosis of cancer can be a catastrophic event to which many individuals initially react with shock and denial. This early reaction is often followed by emotional turmoil accompanied by anxiety, depressed mood, poor concentration, and cessation of daily activities. This response is normal. Dysphoria and sadness are parts of this normal reaction. These symptoms usually abate within a week or two with support from caregivers, family, and friends. Patients return to normal adaptation over the ensuring weeks to months.

Physicians must be able to differentiate between this normal reaction and a psychiatric disorder. Considerable evidence indicates that, for patients with cancer, a depressive disorder leads to greater distress; decreased physical, social, and occupational functioning; and decreased ability to adhere to medical recommendations. Therefore, diagnosis and effective management of the depressive disorder in patients with cancer are potentially very important.

Chronic Fatigue Syndrome. Nearly all depressed patients complain of fatigue and low energy. This symptom is associated with a 46 to 75 percent lifetime rate of major depressive disorder. Complaints of chronic fatigue must be differentiated from the formal chronic fatigue syndrome.

Only a small minority of patients with complaints of chronic fatigue meet the Centers for Disease Control (CDC) criteria for chronic fatigue syndrome. When the patient meets criteria for major depression, dysthymia, or other formal mood syndromes, the mood syndrome is diagnosed. The complaint of chronic fatigue per se is insufficient for the diagnosis of chronic fatigue syndrome. The symptom of chronic fatigue (not the syndrome) is the seventh most common complaint among adult patients in primary care settings and may be a significant problem in as many as 20 to 25 percent of these patients. Studies of patients with chronic fatigue symptoms reveal lifetime rates of psychiatric disorders in the 50 to 77 percent range, based on structured psychiatric interviews. In all studies, major depressive disorder was the most commonly reported illness (lifetime rates ranging from 46 to 75 percent). These studies also found that various anxiety disorders and somatization disorder occurred in 15 to 40 percent of patients with chronic fatigue symptoms.

Most studies that examined the temporal sequence of chronic fatigue symptoms found a 50 to 90 percent onset rate of psychiatric illness (most commonly, major depressive disorder) prior to the onset of chronic fatigue symptoms.

While the central feature of chronic fatigue syndrome is persistent, excessive fatiguability, it must be accompanied by various other somatic and psychological symptoms, including aching muscles and joints, headache, sore throat, painful lymph nodes, muscle weakness, sleep disturbance, mental fatigue, difficulty in concentrating, emotional lability, and sadness. In chronic fatigue syndrome, the somatic and fatigue complaints are out of proportion to physical and laboratory findings. According to the CDC criteria, the presence of a diagnosable formal psychiatric disorder, such as major depressive or dysthymic disorder, excludes the diagnosis of chronic fatigue syndrome. That is, patients who present with the formal symptomatic CDC criteria for chronic fatigue syndrome and who also meet the criteria for a formal mood disorder are treated for the mood disorder. Whether this mood disorder is etiologically connected to the chronic fatigue syndrome or whether it is an independent illness is unclear.

Fibromyalgia. As with other medical conditions, patients with fibromyalgia may or may not have clinical depression. If present, it should be diagnosed and treated as a separate entity.

Fibromyalgia (fibrositis) is a syndrome of diffuse, aching, musculoskeletal pain associated with chronic insomnia, daytime tiredness, morning stiffness, dysesthesia [impairment of the sense of touch] in the hands, and symptoms of irritable bowel type.

Two studies have compared fibromyalgia and rheumatoid arthritis patients in structured psychiatric interviews. In one, patients with fibromyalgia had significantly higher rates of lifetime major depressive disorder than did rheumatoid arthritis patients (71 versus 14 percent), and they had significantly more first-degree relatives with mood and anxiety disorders. The second study also found higher rates of mood disorders in patients with fibromyalgia than in those with rheumatoid arthritis (20 versus 8.7 percent). Statistical significance was not attained, probably because of the small sample size.

Depression Associated with Medications

Various medications have long been reported to cause or to be associated with mood symptoms or formal disorders as side effects.

It is essential to recognize that idiosyncratic reactions to medications do occur. Even without data to suggest a causal relationship between a drug and mood symptoms, good clinical judgment dictates that it should be stopped or changed if a patient develops depression after beginning use. However, such an event does not suggest that the particular medication should not be used in other patients who appropriately require it, but may have either a depression or a propensity for depression. That is, the reaction should be regarded as truly idiosyncratic and should not form the basis for a general conclusion about the medication in all patients.

Antihypertensives. Various blood pressure medications have been linked to depressive symptomatology, although much of the evidence for the association has been weak or equivocal.

[One study] found a 5 to 20 percent risk of depression in patients treated with reserpine. Depression was related to the dosage; more severe depressions were reported in patients receiving more than 0.5 mg per day. A history of depression was associated with a higher incidence of depressive symptoms and a higher incidence of severe depression. These data suggest that, if reserpine is used, the dosage should not exceed 0.5 mg per day, and the drug should be avoided in patients with a history of mood disorders.

Beta-adrenergic blocking agents have been associated with depressive symptomatology, with lethargy being the main symptom reported. In one study, depression was found to be no greater, and perhaps less, in the beta-blocker group than in controls. Another study evaluated various beta-blockers at varying dosages. The treated group experienced a 21 percent incidence of depression, but the control group of hypertensive patients on other medications had a 33 percent incidence of depression. [Another study] compared hypertensive patients on various medications and a control group of medically ill (nonhypertensive) patients. [The study] found a "high" prevalence of depression in both groups, but no preponderance in the hypertensive patients. Hypertensive patients with a personal or family history of psychiatric illness had a higher level of depression. The Veterans Administration Cooperative Study used patient symptom questionnaires and reported only a 1 percent incidence of depression with propranolol, which is consistent with that found in the general population. On the other hand, patients with a personal or family history of depression may be prone to develop depression when treated with propranolol. Data are not available to recommend avoiding propranolol in such patients, but the clinician should be alert to the possibility of depressive reactions in patients beginning this treatment. There is no clear-cut contraindication for its use in any particular patient group.

Studies reviewed fail to show a causal relationship between alphamethyldopa given in typical dosages and depression. While alphamethyldopa can be used in patients with a history of depression, they appear to be at greater risk for depression while they are taking it.

A review of 44 studies evaluating the use of clonidine for hypertension found a 1.5 percent incidence of depression. This finding indicates that clonidine is rarely associated with depression.

The psychiatric side effects of calcium-channel blockers have been reported to include depression. While most of the data are from case reports, some comprehensive, double-blind, crossover studies have evaluated the potential use of verapamil in the treatment of bipolar disorder. Since there are no controlled reports of depressive disorders associated with calcium-channel blockers, they can be used in depressed patients. At present, there is no evidence that angiotensin I converting enzyme (ACE) inhibitors are associated with depression.

Hormones. Glucocorticoids are well known to cause depression or psychosis. [One study] found that 5 percent of steroid-treated patients experienced severe psychiatric reactions (mostly mood disorders), which usually occurred early in the course. Risk factors were female gender, a diagnosis of systemic lupus erythematosus, and high doses of prednisone.

Anabolic steroids used for athletic enhancement deserve comment. [The results of one study suggest] that 22 percent of young bodybuilders who returned their questionnaires suffered from a full mood syndrome, 12 percent had psychotic symptoms, and 12 percent suffered depression when cycled off the drug. The greatest use of these drugs seems to be among young men and women focused on enhancing their physiques. Practitioners should be aware of these drugs and ask about them in all who present with a mood syndrome.

Case reports of depression associated with the use of oral contraceptives are available, but many of the better documented studies found little relationship.

Histamine-2 Receptor Blockers. Multiple case reports have linked histamine-2 receptor blockers (cimetidine and ranitidine) to depressive, manic, and psychotic behaviors. When closely evaluated, however, these cases occur in patients who are otherwise severely ill with multiple system failure or renal or hepatic insufficiency.

Anticonvulsants. Numerous investigators have evaluated the depressant effects of phenobarbital and carbamazepine. Many, however, do not define depression in standard ways. "Depression" is usually attributed to the generalized psychomotor slowing and sedation noted in association with these drugs. In a carefully documented study of patients on phenobarbital and carbamazepine using depression criteria, 40 percent of 64 patients on anticonvulsant drugs had clinical major depression (34 percent with a family history of mood disorder). Patients on phenobarbital were more depressed than those on carbamazepine. There are no comparative controlled studies.

Levodopa. Another therapeutic agent long associated with mood symptoms is levodopa (L-dopa). Most of the studies reviewed did not use currently accepted criteria for diagnosis of depression and employed variable assessment scales. There is no clear evidence that L-dopa increases the incidence of depression in these patients when there is no history of depression.

Antibiotics. Mood disorders associated with antibiotics have largely been noted in case reports, without controlled studies. Dapsone has been reported to cause depression and anger. In these cases, symptoms have resolved within days of discontinuing the drug, and the symptoms have recurred on rechallenge. Isoniazid is reported to be related to psychotic syndromes and delirium. Amphotericin B shows a dose-related delirium and electroencephalograph changes when injected intrathecally. By and large, antibiotic use should be based on medical indications rather than on concern about mood disorders.

Antiarrhythmics. Digoxin has been studied only with regard to its toxicity and the related delirium. There are no reports of mood disorders per se related to digoxin. Procainamide has been linked in several case reports to mania.

Possible Co-existing Mental Health Problems

Patients with depressive symptoms or in a major depressive episode may also be suffering from another, nonmood psychiatric disorder. When the formal major depressive syndrome is associated with another psychiatric condition, the decision of which to treat first rests on the nature of the nonmood disorder. If the nonmood disorder is causing the mood symptoms, then it should usually be treated first. If it is an eating or obsessive-compulsive disorder, that is usually the initial treatment target. If the nonmood disorder is generalized anxiety or personality disorder, the major depressive disorder is the first treatment target, because patients with one of these two nonmood conditions are not typically excluded from randomized controlled treatment trials for major depressive disorder. If the associated nonmood condition is panic disorder, the practitioner must decide which is primary by considering the patient's personal and family history, as well as by gauging which of the two conditions is causing the greater impairment.

Alcoholism

Although alcoholics do become depressed over time, alcoholism is rarely a consequence of depression. Rather, alcoholism and major depressive disorder are distinct clinical entities. They are not different expressions of the same underlying condition. Overall, the prevalence of alcoholism in patients with primary depression is probably no higher than in the general population.

Somatization Disorder

Somatization is defined as the presentation of somatic symptoms [complaints of bodily dysfunction such as pain complaints and gastrointestinal disturbances] by patients with underlying psychiatric illness or psychosocial distress. These somatic symptoms are not accounted for by an underlying general medical disorder. Somatization may well be the main reason for the misdiagnosis of mental illness by primary care physicians. In primary care settings, many depressed and nondepressed patients complain of medically unexplained symptoms, particularly pain. The condition of most patients with such complaints does not meet the formal criteria for somatization disorder, which in *DSM-III-R* requires the presence of 13 or more medically unexplained symptoms. While many depressed patients have medically unexplained somatic complaints, their symptoms are rarely of sufficient intensity or frequency to meet the threshold for somatization disorder.

Chapter 11

Dysthymia

Dysthymia is a chronic form of depression that affects up to ten million Americans or about 5.4 percent of the population. Among adults, the disorder is more common in females, affecting about two to three times more women than men. Dysthymic individuals suffer from a joyless mood, low self-esteem, guilt-ridden thoughts, a pessimistic outlook, sleep problems, including sleeping too much, lethargy, social withdrawal, and thoughts of suicide. Persons are diagnosed as dysthymic when they have suffered from these symptoms for more than two years, without a break in depressive symptoms for more than two months (*DSM-III-R*).

Dysthymia often begins in childhood and adolescence and tends to last for many years, sometimes for a lifetime. Although the intensity of symptoms of dysthymia is less severe than that of acute, major depression, the fact that its duration is very long accounts for the great suffering it causes individuals and their loved ones. Disruption of the dysthymic person's ability to enjoy life and feelings of constant gloominess often cause longstanding marital conflicts and may even drive some to suicide.

Dysthymia often coexists with other psychiatric and medical conditions. As many as 50 percent of persons suffering from dysthymia will later develop more severe or major depressive episodes, further reducing their ability to cope. When a person has an episode of major depression in addition to dysthymia, that is called "double depression."

NIMH Pub. No. 00-0025.

171

People with dysthymia may suffer from additional potentially disabling conditions such as social phobias, other anxiety disorders, borderline personality disorder, and abuse of alcohol or other psychoactive substances. Adolescents in particular may resort to substance abuse as a form of self-treatment.

Dysthymia is more common among patients seeking primary care than in the general population. The disorder is also at increased prevalence in people with chronic fatigue, hypothyroidism, sleep disorders, or somatoform disorders (conditions in which a person complains of medical symptoms that have no detectable physical basis).

Children and adolescents with dysthymia often suffer from attention-deficit hyperactivity disorder, conduct disorder, anxiety disorders, or mental retardation. Because some of these children also may develop major depression, manic-depressive (bipolar) disorder, substance abuse, or school failure, it is especially important that young persons with dysthymia receive proper treatment.

Studies in the 1980's demonstrated abnormalities in the sleep of dysthymics that provided the rationale for the pharmacological treatment of the disorder. Today many antidepressants, including serotonin reuptake inhibitors, are known to be effective in treating dysthymia. Because studies have also shown certain psychological disturbances in dysthymic individuals, interpersonal psychotherapy and cognitive/behavioral psychotherapy also have been helpful in these patients.

The National Institute of Mental Health (NIMH) funds research studies on the diagnosis, treatment, and prognosis of dysthymia. Genetic studies of families, investigations into the association of other conditions with the disorder, and studies of children and adolescents with dysthymia hold promise for improving the quality of life for people with this disorder.

Chapter 12

Helping the Depressed Person Get Treatment

Preface

The National Institute of Mental Health is sponsoring a nation-wide prevention education program about depressive disorders called Depression Awareness, Recognition, and Treatment (D/ART). The program is designed to reduce unnecessary suffering by helping people with depressive illnesses recognize that their symptoms are treatable. To this end, D/ART has produced public education materials that describe the symptoms and treatments for the various depressive disorders. These can be obtained by writing to the D/ART Program, National Institute of Mental Health, Room 15C-05, 5600 Fishers Lane, Rockville, MD 20857.

This text addresses an issue that is particularly important to family, friends, and others who care about a depressed individual—helping the depressed person get treatment. The sad truth is that almost 10 million American adults have a depressive disorder, but only one-third seek treatment. One reason for this phenomenon is that people with depressive illnesses often *need help to get help.*

The very symptoms of depression—feelings of exhaustion, helplessness, and worthlessness—may keep depressed people from seeking treatment. Further, some people do not recognize that they have a disorder and believe that their symptoms are a sign of personal weakness. Others know they are ill, but are afraid to be labeled as "men-

DHHS Pub. No. (ADM) 90-1675.

tally" ill. Children are dependent on adults who often do not understand that children get depressed.

The terrible irony is that much of the suffering caused by depressive illnesses is avoidable. With appropriate diagnosis and treatment, more than 80 percent of those with a depressive illness could have their symptoms alleviated.

There is no single tried-and-true method for helping depressed people get treatment. In fact, it can be quite challenging, particularly when they refuse treatment. Nevertheless, many depressed people do seek help, and many have assistance in doing so. Some adults merely need encouragement from a caring person; others respond to the advice of a respected doctor or clergyman. In some cases, pressure from a supervisor may be needed. Friends and relatives can play critical roles, but the depressed person may be most obstinate with those who are closest.

In the absence of scientific literature on how to encourage help-seeking, we turned to several people who have, as part of their professional or personal experiences, helped others get treatment for depression. We asked them how they did it, and the following information is based on conversations with them. Included are case histories. The names are fictitious and the situations represent a synthesis of those described by interviewees. Some of their experiences may sound familiar. Others may not. Every situation is somewhat different, influenced by such factors as the depressed person's age, sex, type of depressive disorder, severity of symptoms, and relationship to the helper. While this text could not possibly address every situation, you might find something in it to help you help the depressed person you care about.

Helping the Depressed Child

The first step in helping the depressed child is to recognize that the child is, in fact, depressed. This can be challenging. For one thing, it is difficult for adults to accept that young children—even infants— can suffer from depression. Childhood is supposed to be a happy, carefree time of life. Only in recent years has scientific evidence convinced most mental health specialists that childhood depression exists.

Recognizing the symptoms of childhood depression can also be difficult. While some children display the classic symptoms—sadness, anxiety, restlessness, eating, and sleeping problems—others express their depression through physical problems—various aches and pains that do not respond to treatment. Still others hide their feelings of hopelessness and worthlessness under a cover of irritability, aggression, hyperactivity, and misbehavior.

Complicating the recognition of depression are the developmental stages that children pass through on the way to adulthood. Negativism, clinginess, or rebellion may be normal and temporary expressions of a particular stage. In addition, children go through temporary depressed moods just as adults do. Careful observation of a child for several weeks may be required to determine if there is a problem. When symptoms of possible depression seem severe or continue for more than a few weeks, an evaluation by the child's pediatrician to rule out a physical illness would be a good first step. A next step, if deemed necessary, would be consultation with a mental health professional who specializes in treating children.

While parents typically assume prime responsibility for getting treatment for their depressed child, other people—relatives, teachers, friends—can play a role. In the following case, school personnel were instrumental in getting help for a child.

Scott

Scott was not doing at all well in school. He was alternately disruptive and unresponsive in class. His third-grade teacher sought help from the school counselor, who observed Scott on and off for several weeks. She soon shared his teacher's concern. Scott was not learning. He seemed unable to follow instructions. Withdrawn for the most part, he also regularly lashed out at the other children, either physically or verbally.

The counselor's efforts to win Scott's confidence failed and her invitations to his mother brought no response. She, therefore, turned to Scott's sixth-grade brother for help. He explained that his parents were divorced and that all three children lived with their mother, who worked long hours outside the home. He commented that his mother seemed tired and stressed most of the time and that Scott was a special problem, causing her a great deal more trouble than did the other children.

The counselor reported the situation to a team of school officials—psychologist, principal, caseworker, teacher—who regularly met to address problems such as Scott's. They recommended followup by the school caseworker, who met with Scott's father and arranged for Scott to receive psychological and physical evaluations. The evaluations indicated that Scott was physically all right, but quite depressed, angry, and emotionally confused. He missed his father very much, but was angry with him for leaving. He loved his mother, but blamed her for his father's absence. Deep down he blamed himself for his parents' divorce.

The clinician who evaluated Scott recommended that he receive treatment for depression. It was also clear that Scott wanted and needed more contact with his father. His mother also needed some relief from the burdens she had been shouldering. Scott's parents worked out an agreement to increase his father's visits with his children and to cover the cost of Scott's treatment with his father's health insurance.

While Scott was helped through the intervention of school staff, the important role played by his parents cannot be emphasized enough. Parents not only procure their child's treatment, it often is necessary for them to participate in it. Sometimes a parent may reap some personal benefit from a child's treatment. Scott's mother, for instance, improved her own abilities to handle stress while she was learning how to help her son.

The major objectives of treatment, however, are to alleviate the child's depression and strengthen the child's coping and adaptive skills, possibly preventing future psychological problems. This is not to say that early treatment is the total answer. Some problems are not readily resolved and some reemerge later in life.

Helping the Depressed Adolescent

Depression may be even harder to recognize in an adolescent than in a younger child. Feelings of sadness, loneliness, anxiety, and hopelessness associated with depression may be perceived as the normal emotional stresses of growing up. Some depressed youngsters act out their distress, becoming inappropriately angry or aggressive, running away, or becoming delinquent. Such behaviors, too often dismissed as typical adolescent storminess, are signs of problems and sometimes cries for help or attention.

For example, bipolar disorder (also called manic-depressive illness) often emerges during adolescence. It is manifested by episodes of impulsivity, irritability, and loss of control, sometimes alternating with periods of withdrawal. This behavior also can be confused with the emotional ups and downs of adolescence.

The clue to depressive disorder in an adolescent is persistent signs of change or withdrawal. Has the once outgoing youngster become withdrawn and antisocial? Is the former good student failing subjects or skipping classes? Has the happy-go-lucky kid been moping around for weeks? Is the usually easy-going teenager inappropriately irritable? If the answer to any of these questions is "yes," it is time to ask more questions. Is the youngster feeling unable to cope, demoralized, friendless, possibly suicidal?

If so, it is important—vital, in fact—to get the youngster help. A depressed adolescent may or may not be willing to see a mental health professional. Often youngsters have mixed feelings about getting help and may resist treatment if they sense similar ambivalence in their parents. Or they may play on parental guilt. They seem to have an uncanny ability to know what makes parents feel guilty and are particularly adept at pushing "guilt buttons." It is all too easy for loving parents to give in to strong resistance, but this only does the youngster a disservice. Sometimes, it is wise for parents to seek advice on how best to help their depressed child. If the youngster is destructive of self or others, it is essential to get help. Leesha is a case in point.

Leesha

Once a happy child and good student, Leesha became withdrawn, listless, and disinterested in school during her junior high years. She could no longer summon the energy and enthusiasm she once took for granted. Her pervasive sadness discouraged friendship, and she found herself socially isolated. She began to skip classes and then to avoid her mother's "nagging," started staying away from home until late in the evening.

Leesha's mother became increasingly upset and eventually confided her concerns to her pastor, who had a doctorate in family counseling. After his invitation to Leesha and her father to meet with him was turned down he encouraged Leesha's mother to seek help for herself, and she decided to accept his counseling. With his help, she learned much about herself and her relationship with her family. The pastor also convinced her that Leesha had an illness—probably a form of depression—that required appropriate treatment. She then begged Leesha to see a psychiatrist recommended by the pastor. Leesha wanted help, but feared her father's disapproval. He believed that only "crazy" people needed psychiatrists, that getting help was a sign of weakness and, besides, that Leesha was just going through a phase.

The tension between her parents mounted. Her father often stayed out late and came home drunk. One day, her parents received a call from the local hospital. Leesha had attempted suicide.

On the advice of the treating physician, Leesha's parents admitted her to a psychiatric hospital. As part of that hospital's program, they were expected to join families of other patients in group counseling. Leesha's father, more frightened by his daughters suicide attempt than the prospect of joining a therapy group, reluctantly participated. He was relieved to find that his problems were not unique, but shared by others in the group. Also, the help and understanding he received from the group enabled him to give Leesha needed love and support during her treatment and after her recovery.

Leesha and her parents were lucky that she survived her suicide attempt. Perhaps, if both parents had strongly insisted she get treatment earlier, a good deal of guilt and pain could have been avoided. However, some teenagers resist treatment no matter what. This is when mental health professionals advise parents to get tough, particularly if the child is using alcohol or drugs, running away, getting into trouble, or is suicidal.

Getting tough does not mean physically or verbally abusing children or putting them on the street. In fact, if a youngster runs away, efforts to find the child should begin as soon as possible. Sometimes parents are tempted to "teach the runaway a lesson" by not looking for the youngster for a day or two. This is not wise. If youngsters manage to avoid danger, they will not avoid feeling rejected, an emotion that only exacerbates depression.

Getting tough with youngsters means seeing to it that they get appropriate treatment. Such treatment may be provided on an outpatient basis while the child lives at home or with a relative. Or the youngster may be better off in a psychiatric hospital, drug rehabilitation program, behavior modification program, or a residential treatment center. Sometimes, various treatments have to be tried to find the one that works best.

Finding the right treatment is usually predicated upon a complete psychiatric and physical diagnostic assessment. A depressive disorder is not a passing bad mood, but rather an illness that should and can be treated. For information about treatment programs, see Helping Resources.

Helping the Depressed Young Adult

When does parental responsibility end? In most States, when children reach 18, they are considered legally independent adults who are responsible for their own welfare. In reality, many children require parental assistance beyond age 18. Depressed children, regardless of age, often need a helping hand, but there are limits to what parents can and, at times, should do.

Parents can help their grown children recognize that they are depressed by familiarizing them with the symptoms. They can encourage treatment and provide information about available resources. Parents can also help their child fight the isolation often associated with depression by calling, visiting, and extending invitations to dinner, to a movie, or to spend a night or weekend. If the depression is interfering with the young adult's ability to function, parents can provide transportation to treatment and offer shelter, food, and money until the symptoms subside.

If the young adult refuses treatment, parents have even fewer options. They can ask individuals whom the depressed person trusts and respects to intercede. Friends are often more influential than parents. Sometimes, it takes a combination of several persons and the right strategy—actually recommending or taking the depressed person to a therapist—to get the individual's illness evaluated and appropriately treated.

Some people learn to live with depression. They can get up, go to work, and do their chores. They do not know there is a better way to feel and are not motivated to get treatment. Without treatment, however, they can spend a lifetime feeling miserable and making those around them feel almost as bad. Parents (or others) who have a depressed adult living with them who refuses to get treatment will find it useful to consult with a mental health specialist on how best to deal with this situation.

If the depressed child is suicidal, stops eating, or becomes psychotic (loses touch with reality, has delusions or hallucinations), parents can best show their love and concern by hospitalizing their child, even if involuntarily, as was the case with Marta's parents.

Marta

Marta was in her early 20s the first time her parents hospitalized her some 5 years ago. She was diagnosed as having bipolar disorder (also known as manic-depressive illness). At that time, she was placed on lithium by the hospital psychiatrist. Much to her parent's relief, the medication controlled Marta's extreme mood changes, her frightening ups and downs.

However, Marta would not stay on the lithium. She didn't want to give up the "highs" that made her feel unbelievably elated, energetic, and invincible. In reality, the extreme things she did during these periods—uncontrolled spending, nonstop talking, nighttime wanderings, and sexual promiscuity—caused serious problems. She lost a husband, friends, and several jobs.

Even more frightening were the terrible lows that alternated with the highs. During these periods, Marta felt worthless, helpless, and hopeless to such an extent that she attempted suicide on several occasions. Each suicide attempt was followed by hospitalization and a return to lithium, but she seemed unable to stay on the medication.

Marta's emotional roller coaster was shared by her parents. Each time Marta went back on lithium, their hopes were raised that she would lead a stable, predictable life, and each time she went off the medication, their hopes were dashed. They also lived with uncertainty and fear, never knowing if Marta might turn up on their doorstep, in jail, or in the morgue.

Following one of Marta's suicide attempts, her parents confessed to a hospital social worker that they were so emotionally and physically drained that they no longer wanted contact with their daughter. Although sympathetic, the social worker encouraged them to take a different and less drastic approach to alleviating their situation. Parents, she explained, often find it hard to differentiate between caring about and taking care of a child, even a gown child.

"Tell Marta that you love her and want her to live, but make it just as clear that you will not and cannot assume responsibility for the way she lives or even whether she lives," the social worker told them. "You can control your behavior—express your wishes and act on them—but you cannot control Marta's."

Like many parents in this situation, Marta's parents found that actually "giving up" responsibility for Marta was not easy. At the social workers suggestion, they joined a group of parents who discussed problems such as theirs under the team guidance of the social worker and a psychiatrist. In addition, they joined a consumer organization that sponsored mutual support groups and information-sharing seminars.

At the end of the year, Marta was still taking the lithium prescribed during her last hospitalization. She had a new job in another city and was living on her own. She was taking responsibility for her health, regularly seeing a psychiatrist who monitored her medication and helped with any problems she was having.

Marta was not able to take responsibility for her own health and life until it was clear that such responsibility belonged to her and not her parents. But it took 5 years of crises to bring Marta's parents to the point where they could deal realistically with their daughter's illness. This, too, is not uncommon. It often takes crises and time to motivate people to seek and attain the help they need.

Helping Your Spouse

Living with a depressed person is difficult under any circumstances. When the person is your wife or husband, the problems escalate. The role of spouse carries with it expectations of love, companionship, parental partnership, economic support, and all-round helpmate. But depression reduces sexual desire, energy levels, sociability, and productivity. It can destroy a relationship.

Even if the depressed spouse is getting treatment, the situation can be stressful. Depression can cause people to become withdrawn, rejecting, and irritable and to say hurtful things to those they care about. If nondepressed spouses realize that the illness causes these behaviors, they may find it easier not to feel hurt and to respond in a nonrejecting and reality-orienting manner. For instance, if the depressed spouse says something like, "You never loved me," or "I don't love you anymore," the nondepressed spouse might respond, "That's your depression talking. Your illness is hurting both of us, but when you get better, you will feel differently."

Until symptoms are alleviated, depressed people need patience, understanding, encouragement, and assistance; however, they should not be made to feel totally helpless or inadequate. Sometimes it requires walking a rather fine line, and nondepressed spouses may find it useful to get counseling to learn more about depression and how best to help their depressed spouses as well as themselves.

In fact, counseling may be even more useful for the nondepressed spouse if the depressed spouse refuses treatment. For one thing, counseling can help the nondepressed spouse avoid becoming depressed. It is all too easy to be overcome with feelings of isolation, helplessness, and hopelessness if you are living with a depressed person, particularly one who refuses help. Also, counseling can clarify alternatives, offer solutions, and "stiffen spines"—for it is time to get tough when a depressed spouse refuses treatment.

Although more women than men get depressed, getting tough with a recalcitrant, depressed spouse is more often a wife's problem, because men are often less willing than women to seek treatment for any health problem, including depression. It requires a challenging combination of sensitivity and self-confidence to be caringly forceful with a man—or woman—whose self-esteem has already been undermined by a depressive illness.

Sometimes it pays to ask others to intervene. For example, close relatives or friends, who understand that depression is an illness and not a weakness, can often convince the depressed spouse to seek treatment. A family doctor or religious leader knowledgeable about the symptoms and treatments of depression may also be helpful. Sometimes, if enough people say often enough, "We care about you, but you need professional care to feel better," the message gets through. In some cases, it is most helpful to have several people speak privately to the depressed person, and in others, a group approach is more successful.

If all efforts to get the depressed spouse to seek treatment have failed, nondepressed spouses will need to consider how well they are coping and, if there are children, whether they are being affected. Consultation with a mental health specialist may be particularly useful in this situation.

But depressive illnesses are not always recognized. In fact, it is not unusual for families to be unaware that a loved one is suffering from a depressive illness. They may react inappropriately or suffer unnecessarily as a consequence. Such was the case with Alice and Charles.

Alice and Charles

At first, Alice couldn't believe what was happening. Her once considerate and loving husband had changed dramatically over the past year. She kept expecting him to get over whatever was making him withdrawn, hostile, and antisocial, but on the rare occasions that Charles was willing to discuss his feelings with her, he just kept saying that he was tired of everything and everyone—his job, their kids, and especially her.

Initially, Alice attempted to placate him, but nothing she did made him happy. In fact, the harder she tried, the angrier and more withdrawn he seemed to get. Eventually, she lost patience and returned his anger with her own. Their relationship deteriorated, and Alice contemplated leaving Charles.

Before taking such a desperate step, Alice confided her feelings to a friend, who suggested that Charles might be ill and should see a doctor. Alice then began to take a different approach in dealing with Charles. She spoke to him about her feelings of frustration and concern about their relationship. She told him that she still cared about him very much and was worried about his health. Eventually, she convinced him to visit their family doctor.

The physician listened carefully to Charles, asking him questions about his life and symptoms. Following a complete physical examination and several tests to rule out other explanations for his symptoms, the doctor suggested that Charles might be suffering from depression. He explained that Charles' symptoms were real and not "in his head." Depression, he told Charles, is a disorder that can and should be treated. He referred Charles to a psychiatrist for an evaluation, explaining that it was his practice to send patients to practitioners he thought were expert in a particular area. For instance, if Charles had a heart problem, he would refer him to a cardiologist or if he had a bladder problem to a urologist.

He also reassured Charles that he was not pushing him off onto another doctor, but that he needed a psychiatrist's expert opinion about Charles' condition and whether he needed therapy, antidepressant medication, or both.

Charles' depression was confirmed by the psychiatrist and successfully treated. Within several weeks, he was feeling much better. He also gained insight into some of the problems in his relationship with

Alice. For example, he realized that his behavior was due to his depression rather than her inadequacies. He also realized that, while he could not control the pain of depression, he did not need to accept it either. Best of all, he recognized that his symptoms were not his fault and that he deserved to feel well again.

Charles had a lot going for him. He had a sophisticated family doctor and access to medical insurance that covered mental health treatment. But even if Charles didn't have these advantages, he could have found help. Community mental health clinics and some private clinics and therapists adjust their treatment fees in accordance with a patient's ability to pay. Consumer organizations offer mutual support and assistance. Religious organizations provide social groups and day care, and local governments offer many kinds of help.

Unfortunately, many depressed people lack the energy and motivation to seek the services they need. Here again, friends, family members, religious leaders, and others can help get needed information and provide transportation and encouragement.

Helping the Depressed Older Person

Depression in the elderly is often manifested by memory problems, confusion, social withdrawal, loss of appetite, inability to sleep, irritability, and, in some cases, delusions and hallucinations. Feelings of sadness may or may not be acknowledged or shown. Thus, depression is often mistaken for dementia or the normal aging process and goes untreated.

Regardless of the cause of the depression—and there are many reasons why an elderly person can be depressed—appropriate treatment can alleviate symptoms and suffering. Even Alzheimer's patients, who are often severely depressed during the early stages of the disease, can gain extra years of functioning and pleasure with treatment for depression.

The first step in helping the older person who appears to have symptoms of depression is a complete physical checkup. Depression can be a side effect of a physical illness or of a medication to treat an illness. If patients are confused or withdrawn, it is important that they be accompanied by a person who can give the doctor essential information about their medical history and receive instructions and recommendations. It is particularly important that the examining physician be told of all drugs used by the patient, including over-the-counter, prescribed, and borrowed drugs.

If the cause of the symptoms is not uncovered, the next step is an evaluation by a mental health specialist—preferably one with a geriatric specialty or experience in dealing with older people. Seeking consultations with specialists is a relatively common experience for older patients, who often have multiple clinical problems. Therefore, the need for referral to a mental health expert to gain further diagnostic information can be readily understood by the older patient, particularly if care is taken to explain the interrelationship between physical health and emotional well-being.

A major issue for the older person who has limited energy and financial resources is the length and type of treatment. Patients often believe that all mental health treatments involve many years of analysis, so they need to be told about the medications and relatively short-term psychosocial treatments now used successfully to help depressed adults of all ages. In fact, all aspects of the recommended treatment should be carefully explained by the mental health specialist.

If antidepressant medication is prescribed, the prescribing physician should be fully informed of all other drugs the patient is taking. Since drugs are metabolized more slowly in older people, antidepressants must be carefully prescribed and monitored.

If older depressed people refuse to see a mental health specialist, they may need assurances that treatment will reduce symptoms, improve functioning, and enhance well-being. This message may have to be repeated more than once by several different people. Sometimes close friends, siblings, or a religious leader can have more success in convincing the older depressed person to get help than a spouse or child.

In some cases, the older person who will not or cannot make an office visit may accept a phone call from a mental health specialist, who then might arrange to visit the patient at home, if the patient is willing. Phone contact can introduce and enhance patient/therapist interaction; however, it is not an appropriate substitute for the person-to-person contact needed by a therapist to properly evaluate and treat a patient.

The following vignette illustrates how a phone call from a geriatric psychiatrist laid the groundwork for the treatment that helped Kai overcome his depression.

Kai

Kai had been a devoted family man and a hard worker. He hadn't had time for hobbies or other interests, but he was satisfied with his life. He possessed everything important a man could need—a good job, good health, and a loving family.

Then the first blow came: retirement. He was not ready to stop working when the company vice president suggested, not too subtly, that he should make room for a younger man who needed his job.

The next blow was the heart attack. Fun and relaxation were not what Kai had been used to, and he had tried to avoid his overwhelming feelings of uselessness by compulsively working around the house and yard. His heart attack took that option away. The damage to his heart made him a poor candidate for surgical repair, according to several cardiologists. His life became dependent on the miracle of drugs—many kinds, many times a day. Good health and worthwhile activity, once taken for granted, were replaced by exhaustion, pain, fear, depression, and inactivity.

While still recuperating in the hospital, Kai was told by his doctor about a psychotherapy group organized for heart patients, but Kai did not join. There was nothing wrong with his head, he thought at the time. Later, realizing that he was forgetful and sometimes outright confused, he began to wonder. He knew, however, that he wasn't crazy!

Nevertheless, Kai's bad mood was "driving his wife crazy," or so she said. She begged him to see another doctor, but he couldn't be bothered. Doctors just make you sicker, he proclaimed.

The final blow came from his heart doctor. After a checkup, he threatened to hospitalize Kai because of weight loss and the severe emotional withdrawal described by his wife. The cardiologist said that depression could be complicating Kai's recovery. He gave Kai the name of a psychiatrist who specialized in treating older people and said the psychiatrist would call Kai at home if that was all right. Kai agreed. He didn't want to be hospitalized.

Kai liked what the psychiatrist said when she called. She explained that the body and mind were inseparable, one affecting the other. Heart attacks are often followed by depression and depression affects health she explained. "If a heart attack caused a foot problem which kept you from walking, wouldn't you get your feet treated?" she asked. "Well, the depression is keeping you from walking away from disabling feelings. It's time to treat the depression and get on your feet again," she told Kai.

After the psychiatrist visited Kai at home several times, Kai agreed to continue meeting with her at her office. She also worked with Kai's cardiologist to adjust his medications and to develop an exercise regimen. Kai's memory lapses and confusion abated. Eventually, he and his wife joined a support group for heart patients and their spouses. They found out their experience wasn't really unique.

It took a while for Kai to learn how to accept himself and his "broken" heart and to enjoy life once more. He also learned that lifetime habits do not change overnight. Work is a major force in the lives of many people. More than a source of income and social contact, it serves the ego and fills the days. Without work, people such as Kai, who have not developed other interests, become extremely vulnerable to depression.

Of course, Kai received a double whammy when he had a heart attack. The disability associated with serious illnesses, especially those prevalent among older people, and the medications used to treat them, can also contribute to depression.

Then, too, older people are often dealing with the death of a beloved person or the loss of a familiar home or way of life. Sometimes, there are too many losses, and unrelieved mourning evolves into a depression that is unshakable without treatment.

In many cases, psychiatric treatment will alleviate symptoms of derangement and confusion and thereby contribute to the older person's ability to live at home rather than in a long-term care facility.

While it makes absolute sense for people of all ages to check the credentials of all health practitioners before embarking on treatment, it is particularly important that homebound patients, who have limited access to health care providers, take extra care. Although it is rare, there have been cases of improper and inadequate treatment foisted on the homebound by disreputable practitioners.

Ask for referrals from your doctor, or check with the psychiatric department of a local university hospital or community mental health center, or contact one of the professional or consumer groups listed under Helping Resources. For information about other services devoted to the elderly, call your local and State governments.

Helping the Depressed Employee

Enlightened employers are recognizing that it pays to help depressed employees. They have learned that many depressed people turn to alcohol or drugs in misguided attempts to alleviate their pain. Untreated depression, alcoholism, and drug abuse become very expensive in terms of lost productivity and accidents, so many employers are encouraging workers to get needed help.

In fact, the trend is growing among business, government, and educational organizations to provide onsite employee assistance programs (EAPs) that offer mental health, alcohol, and drug abuse counseling or, when appropriate, referral to outside resources. EAP services are free and convenient, yet many employees do not take advantage of them. Some only need encouragement from a supervisor to seek help; others need pressure. In some cases, EAP counselors help supervisors get help for their depressed employee, as happened in Jane's situation.

Jane

As sometimes happens when you supervise a depressed person, Jane found herself in a difficult position. In her efforts to deal with her employee, she became friend, parent figure, and confidante. Unfortunately, none of this helped get the work done. When she suggested he see an employee counselor, he refused, stating he could solve his own problems. Time did not prove this to be true and eventually, feeling angry, protective, sympathetic, and stressed by turns, Jane sought advice herself.

During several sessions, the EAP counselor helped Jane sort out her emotions and responsibilities from those of her employee. The counselor explained the implications of depression and explored with her the limitations and options she had as a supervisor. Jane became convinced that she could best help her employee recognize that he needed help by clearly demonstrating, through careful recordkeeping, that his work performance had deteriorated.

Jane found the chore of documenting her employee's performance annoying and time consuming. However, as she began to write down what was really happening each day, and sharing her observations with him, the situation became clearer to him as well as to her. He realized that he was not pulling his weight, and she recognized that she was not helping him get well by protecting him. Jane suggested that he come to a counseling session with her. He refused. She then pointed out that she would have no other choice but to take personnel action against him. He then agreed to visit the counselor with her.

Much to his surprise, he found the visit helpful and set up his own future appointments. After several visits, the counselor referred him to a psychiatrist for a complete diagnostic evaluation and then collaborated with the psychiatrist in working out a treatment regime: the psychiatrist prescribed an antidepressant medication and the counselor provided psychotherapy.

He continued to see the counselor regularly for several months and then on an as-needed basis. Within a few months, he was off medication. His symptoms had abated, his work performance had improved dramatically, and he felt much better about himself. He now understands that his lack of energy and inability to concentrate were not personal defects, but rather due to his illness. He told Jane that in the future, if the symptoms recur, he will seek help immediately.

While employee assistance programs are being widely adopted by large companies and government agencies, owners of small businesses who cannot afford their own EAPs can help troubled employees through other mechanisms. They can provide their employees with medical insurance that offers the best available coverage of mental health and substance abuse problems. They also may offer a depressed employee temporary flexible hours or a less demanding job until the symptoms of depression are alleviated. They can provide reassurance and reinforcement for those jobs that are well done or show improvement.

Perhaps most important, employers can encourage and, in fact, pressure employees to seek treatment. It is usually in the employer's interest to help depressed employees get appropriate treatment, for it is rarely cost effective to train a new person or to replace an experienced worker whose performance is temporarily not up to snuff. Helping the depressed employee pays off.

In Brief

Ways to Help a Depressed Person

- Recognize the symptoms.

- Convince the depressed person to get treatment or, in the case of a depressed child or adolescent, help the youngster get treatment.

- Tell the depressed person that he or she is loved, deserves to feel better, and will feel better with appropriate treatment.

- Recommend helping resources.

- If the depressed person is not functioning, accompany him or her to treatment until normal function returns.

- If the depressed person is too young or ill to provide needed information to the therapist, act as a go-between as long as needed.

- If the depressed person is suicidal or having hallucinations or delusions, arrange for hospitalization.

- If the depressed person is functional and refuses treatment, seek the assistance of others—friends, doctor, clergy, relatives—who might convince him or her that treatment is needed and will help.

- Don't give up too soon—the depressed person may have to hear more than once and from several people that he or she deserves to feel better and can, with proper treatment.

- If all efforts to encourage the depressed person to seek treatment have failed, and the depressed person is having a demoralizing impact on those around, further action is needed:

  —A supervisor might threaten personnel action unless the depressed employee gets treatment.

  —A spouse, with the assistance of a mental health specialist, can explore separation from the depressed husband or wife who refuses treatment.

—Parents of a depressed adult can clarify, with the help of a mental health specialist, how much assistance to give their depressed offspring.

—Children, other relatives, friends, or doctors of a depressed older person can assist him or her to get help from a mental health specialist who has geriatric experience and who may be willing to reach out to the older person by telephone and home visits.

It isn't always easy to help the depressed person get treatment, but it can be done, and helping can make you both feel better.

Symptoms of Depression

- Persistent sad, anxious, or "empty" mood
- Decreased energy, fatigue, being "slowed down"
- Loss of interest or pleasure in usual activities, including work or sex
- Sleep disturbances (insomnia, early-morning waking or over-sleeping)
- Appetite and weight changes (either gain or loss)
- Feelings of hopelessness, pessimism
- Feelings of guilt, worthlessness, helplessness
- Thoughts of death or suicide, suicide attempts
- Difficulty concentrating, remembering, making decisions
- Chronic aches or persistent bodily symptoms that are not caused by physical disease

Symptoms of Mania

- Increased energy
- Decreased need for sleep
- Increased risk-taking
- Unrealistic beliefs in own abilities
- Increased talking and physical, social, and sexual activity
- Feelings of great pleasure or irritability
- Aggressive response to frustration
- Racing and disconnected thoughts

If some or all of these symptoms of depression or mania persist for more than 2 weeks, or are causing impairment in usual functioning, treatment is needed.

Facts about Treatment for Depression That You Should Know

- There are different forms of depression and varying types of treatment. A complete diagnostic evaluation is an important first step for determining the type and severity of the illness and which treatment(s) might be most helpful. Such an evaluation should include:

  —a physical and neurological examination and laboratory tests to rule out other medical conditions that might be causing symptoms of depression,

  —a history of patient's symptoms, past treatments, use of alcohol and/or drugs, suicidal thoughts or attempts, and occurrence of depressive illness in other family members, and

  —a mental status examination to check the patient's speaking and thought patterns and memory.

- Based on the evaluation, the treatment of choice may be a form of psychotherapy, antidepressant medication(s), or a combination of psychotherapy and medication. For some severely depressed individuals who are suicidal, or psychotic, or cannot take antidepressants, or who have not responded to other treatments, electroconvulsive therapy (ECT) can be extraordinarily helpful and even lifesaving.

- There are many types of psychotherapy, including short-term, 16-week therapies, that have proven useful for some depressive episodes.

- There is also a wide choice of medications. It may be necessary for the patient to try several different medications to find the one most effective for him or her. Since most antidepressants take several weeks to begin working, patients may need encouragement to stick with the treatment.

- If the patient doesn't start to feel better after several months of treatment (regardless of which treatment), a different treatment should be considered.

- As with any form of health treatment, the credentials of the treating clinician should be checked. Ask for referrals from your doctor or check with the psychiatric department of a local university or hospital or with a community mental health center. Or contact one of the professional or consumer organizations listed in Helping Resources.

- For further information about the different forms of depressive illnesses and their treatments, refer to *Depressive Illnesses: Treatments Bring New Hope, Useful Information on Medications for Mental Illness,* and *A Consumer's Guide to Mental Health Services,* which can be obtained by writing to Public Inquiries, NIMH, Room 15C-05, 5600 Fishers Lane, Rockville, MD 20857.

Helping Resources

General

- Physicians
- Mental health specialists
- Health maintenance organizations
- Community mental health centers
- Hospital departments of psychiatry or outpatient psychiatric clinics
- University or medical school-affiliated programs
- State hospital outpatient clinics
- Family service/social agencies
- Private clinics and facilities
- Employee assistance programs
- Clergy

Professional Organizations

- American Psychiatric Association
- American Psychological Association

- National Association for Social Workers
- American Nurses Association
- American Mental Health Counselors Association
- American Orthopsychiatric Association

Consumer Organizations

- National Mental Health Association
- National Alliance for the Mentally Ill
- National Foundation for Depressive Illness
- National Depressive and Manic Depressive Association

Chapter 13

What to Do When an Employee Is Depressed

Depression Affects the Workplace

As a supervisor, you may notice that some employees seem less productive and reliable than usual—they may often call in sick or arrive late to work, have more accidents, or just seem less interested in work. These individuals may be suffering from a very real and common illness called **clinical depression.** While it is not your job as a supervisor to diagnose depression, it may help to understand more about it.

- Each year, depression affects at least 10 million people, often during their most productive years—between the ages of 25 and 44.

- Untreated clinical depression may become a chronic condition that disrupts work, family, and personal life.

- Depression results in more days in bed than many other ailments (such as ulcers, diabetes, high blood pressure, and arthritis) according to a recent large-scale study published by the Rand Corporation.

DHHS Pub. No. (ADM) 91-1792.

In addition to personal suffering, depression takes its toll at the workplace:

- At any one time, 1 employee in 20 is experiencing depression.

- In 1989, depression cost the Nation an estimated $27 billion, of which more than $17 billion was due to time lost from work. There is no way to estimate the total cost of lost productivity.

"Major Depression and bipolar disorder accounted for 11% of all days lost from work in 1987," reported the medical director of a public utility company. However, there is good news. More than 80% of depressed people can be treated quickly and effectively. The key is to recognize the symptoms of depression early and to receive appropriate treatment. Unfortunately, two out of three people with depression do not receive the treatment they need.

Many companies are helping employees with depression by providing training on depression and other mental disorders for supervisors, employee assistance, and occupational health personnel. Employers are also making appropriate treatment available through employee assistance programs and through company-sponsored health benefits. Such efforts are contributing to significant reductions in lost time and job-related accidents as well as marked increases in productivity.

Depression Is More Than the Blues

Everyone gets the blues or feels sad from time to time. However, if a person experiences these emotions intensely and for long periods of time, it may signal clinical depression, a condition that requires treatment.

Clinical depression affects the total person—body, feelings, thoughts, and behaviors—and comes in various forms. Some people have a single bout of depression; others suffer recurrent episodes. Still others experience the severe mood swings of bipolar disorder—sometimes called manic-depressive illness—with moods alternating between depressive lows and manic highs.

Symptoms of Depression Include

- Persistent sad or "empty" mood
- Loss of interest or pleasure in ordinary activities, including sex
- Decreased energy, fatigue, being "slowed down"
- Sleep disturbances (insomnia, early-morning waking, or over-sleeping)
- Eating disturbances (loss of appetite and weight, or weight gain)
- Difficulty concentrating, remembering, making decisions
- Feelings of hopelessness, pessimism
- Feelings of guilt, worthlessness, helplessness
- Thoughts of death or suicide, suicide attempts
- Irritability
- Excessive crying
- Chronic aches and pains that don't respond to treatment

Symptoms of Mania Include

- Inappropriate elation
- Irritability
- Decreased need for sleep
- Increased energy and activity
- Increased talking, moving, and sexual activity
- Racing thoughts
- Disturbed ability to make decisions
- Grandiose notions
- Being easily distracted

In the Workplace, Symptoms of Depression Often May Be Recognized by

- Decreased productivity
- Morale problems
- Lack of cooperation
- Safety risks, accidents
- Absenteeism
- Frequent statements about being tired all the time
- Complaints of unexplained aches and pains
- Alcohol and drug abuse

Get an Accurate Diagnosis

If four or more of the symptoms of depression or mania persist for more than two weeks, or are interfering with work or family life, a thorough diagnosis is needed. This should include a complete physical checkup and history of family health problems as well as an evaluation of possible symptoms of depression.

Depression Affects Your Employees

> *John had been feeling depressed for weeks though he didn't know why. He had lost his appetite and felt tired all the time. It wasn't until he couldn't get out of bed and move that his wife took him to a mental health professional for treatment. He soon showed improvement and was able to return to work.*

Depression can affect your workers' productivity, judgment, ability to work with others, and overall job performance. The inability to concentrate fully or make decisions may lead to costly mistakes or accidents. In addition, it has been shown that depressed individuals have high rates of absenteeism and are more likely to abuse alcohol and drugs, resulting in other problems on and off the job.

Unfortunately, many depressed people suffer needlessly because they feel embarrassed, fear being perceived as weak, or do not recognize depression as a treatable illness.

Treatments Are Effective

> *Mary couldn't sleep at night and had trouble staying awake and concentrating during the day. After visiting the doctor and being put on medication for depression, she found that her symptoms disappeared and her work and social life improved.*

More than 80% of people with depression can be treated effectively, generally without missing much time from work or needing costly hospitalization.

There is a choice of treatments available, including medications, psychological treatments, or a combination of both. These treatments usually relieve the symptoms of depression in a matter of weeks.

What Can a Supervisor Do?

As a supervisor, you can:

- Learn about depression and the sources of help. Reading this text is a good first step. Familiarize yourself with your company's health benefits. Find out if your company has an employee assistance program (EAP) that can provide on-site consultation or refer employees to local resources.

- Recognize when an employee shows signs of a problem affecting performance which may be depression-related and refer appropriately.

As a supervisor, you cannot diagnose depression. You can, however, note changes in work performance and listen to employee concerns. If your company does have an EAP, ask a counselor for suggestions on how best to approach an employee who you suspect is experiencing work problems that may be related to depression.

When a previously productive employee begins to be absent or tardy frequently, or is unusually forgetful and error-prone, he/she may be experiencing a significant personal or health problem.

- Discuss changes in work performance with the employee. You may suggest that the employee seek consultation if there is a personal problem. Confidentiality of any discussion with the employee is critical.

If an employee voluntarily talks with you about health problems, including feeling depressed or down all the time, keep these points in mind:

- Do not try to diagnose the problem yourself.

- Recommend that any employee experiencing symptoms of depression seek professional consultation from an EAP counselor or other health or mental health professional.

- Recognize that a depressed employee may need a flexible work schedule during treatment. Find out about your company's approach by contacting your human resources specialist.

- Remember that severe depression may be life threatening to the employee, but rarely to others. If an employee makes comments like "life is not worth living" or "people would be better off without me," take the threats seriously. Immediately call an EAP counselor or other specialist and seek advice on how to handle the situation.

What Can a Supervisor Say to a Depressed Person?

"I'm concerned that you've been late to work recently and aren't meeting you performance objectives...I'd like to see you get back on track. I don't know whether this is the case for you, but if you have a personal problem you can speak confidentially to one of our employee assistance counselors. The service was set up to help employees who are experiencing personal problems. Our conversation today and your appointment with the counselor are confidential. Whether a not you contact this service, you will still be expected to meet your performance goals."

Professional Help Is Available from:

- Physicians
- Mental health specialists
- Employee assistance programs
- Health maintenance organizations
- Community mental health centers
- Hospital departments of psychiatry of outpatient psychiatric clinics
- University of medical school affiliated programs
- State hospital outpatient clinics
- Family service/social agencies
- Private clinics and facilities

Additional Information about D/ART

"*What To Do When An Employee Is Depressed: A Guide for Supervisors*" is published by the National Worksite Program organized by D/

ART—DEPRESSION Awareness, Recognition and Treatment. Sponsored by the National Institute of Mental Health, an agency of the Federal Government, D/ART is a national science-based program to educate the public, primary care providers, and mental health specialists about depressive illnesses—their symptoms, diagnosis, and treatments. D/ART's goals include early identification and effective treatment of depressive disorders that affect millions of Americans each year.

D/ART has three major components: The Public Education Campaign, Professional Training Program, and National Worksite Program.

- The **Pubic Education Campaign** seeks to change attitudes and help-seeking behavior of the citizenry-at-large through media activities; distribution of print information; and joint activities with public and private advocacy, service, professional, and business organizations as well as with D/ART Community Partners.

- The **Professional Training Program** provides up-to-date information on the diagnosis and treatment of depressive disorders to health and mental health providers through grants to universities and medical schools and collaborations with professional associations.

- The **National Worksite Program** aims to reduce direct and indirect costs of depression in the workplace by educating corporate executives, managers, health/mental health professionals, employees and families about symptoms of depression and about effective, available treatments. This component of the D/ART Program was developed collaboratively with private employers and Washington Business Group on Health.

For further information about the National Worksite Program or D/ART contact:

D/ART
5600 Fishers Lane, Room 14C-02
Rockville, MD 20857
(301) 443-4140

For a free brochure about depression, call 1-800-421-4211.

Chapter 14

Depression Awareness, Recognition and Treatment (D/ART)

What Is D/ART?

D/ART is a national program to educate the public, primary care providers, and mental health specialists about depressive illnesses—their symptoms, diagnosis, and treatments. Sponsored by the National Institute of Mental Health (NIMH) and based on 40 years of scientific research, D/ART is a major private/public enterprise to benefit the mental health of the American public.

Why Is D/ART Needed?

Serious depression is an important public health problem. More than 11 million people in the United States will suffer a depressive illness this year, and many will be incapacitated for weeks or months. The estimated cost to the Nation in 1989 was more than $27 billion, of which over $17 billion was due to time lost from work. The suffering of depressed people and their families is immeasurable.

Available medications and psychological treatment alone or in combination, can help 80 percent of those who experience depression. With adequate treatment, future episodes may be prevented or reduced in severity. Yet, current scientific evidence indicates that many depressed people suffer needlessly since only one out of three people with a depressive illness seeks treatment.

DHHS Pub. No. (ADM) 92-1680.

203

D/ART Goals

D/ART's primary goal is to alleviate suffering due to depressive illnesses by:

- Helping the public recognize the symptoms of depression and where to go for accurate diagnosis and professional treatment.
- Encouraging changes in help-seeking behaviors and more appropriate use of the health and mental health care systems.
- Providing health and mental health specialists with the most up-to-date knowledge about effective treatments for depressive illnesses.

D/ART Messages

The D/ART Program has three primary messages:

- Clinical depression is a common illness that usually is unrecognized. When identified, it can be treated.
- There are effective medications and psychological treatments which often are used in combination.
- The large majority of clinical depressions, including the most serious, improve with treatment usually in a matter of weeks.

D/ART Organization and Accomplishments

The NIMH and D/ART have worked with scientists, health care providers, professional organizations, advocacy and consumer groups, and industry to develop major components of the D/ART Program: professional education, public education, and a worksite program.

Professional Training Programs (initiated in 1986) utilize a variety of approaches to make accurate scientific information about the diagnosis and treatment of depressive illnesses available to practitioners. These approaches include:

- Training grants to universities and medical schools.
- Continuing education courses at professional meetings.
- Seminars and courses provided by NIMH staff and consultants.

- Collaboration with professional organizations.
- Consultation with universities to incorporate the newest knowledge about depression into curricula.
- Development of television satellite network courses.

The Public Education Campaign "Depression: Define it. Defeat it." (launched in 1988) also emphasizes additional messages that depression is:

- More than the blues.
- Not a personal weakness.
- A treatable illness.
- A major public health concern.
- A national economic issue.

Campaign materials are produced in English and Spanish:

- Fact sheets, flyers, and brochures for the general public.
- Media materials such as print "ads" and television and radio public service announcements (PSAs).

Educational programs are organized in cooperation with national advocacy and mutual support organizations.

A Community Partnership Program develops networks of public and private organizations at the local and State levels to:

- Conduct educational outreach activities and media campaigns.
- Implement collaborative programs with businesses, schools, and other community groups.
- Provide community-based training for health and mental health professionals.

A Worksite Program initiated among major national corporations promotes worksite education for managers and other employees about depressive illnesses. This education encourages early diagnosis and treatment for depression in order to:

- Improve productivity.
- Reduce time lost from work.

- Avoid costs of prolonged treatment or expensive hospitalization.
- Reduce health care costs for treatment of other physical and mental disorders resulting from untreated depression.

How You Can Help

D/ART needs your assistance to help people learn more about depressive illnesses and effective, available treatments. You can:

- Reproduce and distribute D/ART materials through media, schools, unions, and businesses or through a variety of health, volunteer, professional, community, and religious organizations.

- Sponsor or encourage local organizations to sponsor public education programs.

- Contact local radio and television stations and encourage the public service directors to air D/ART public service announcements.

- Help a depressed person get treatment.

- Join a D/ART Community Partnership.

- Work with groups such as the Alliance for the Mentally Ill, Depressive and Manic-Depressive Association, or the Mental Health Association to organize mutual support groups for depressed people.

How to Recognize Depressive Illnesses

Clinical depression is a "whole body" disorder that affects body, feelings, thoughts, and behaviors. Depressive illnesses come in various forms. Some people have a single episode of depression; others suffer recurrent episodes. Still others experience the severe mood swings of bipolar disorder, sometimes called manic-depressive illness, alternating between depressive lows and manic highs. Others have ongoing, chronic symptoms.

When four or more of the symptoms for depression or mania persist for more than two weeks, an accurate diagnosis and professional treatment should be sought.

Symptoms of Depression

- A persistent sad, "empty," or anxious mood
- Loss of interest or pleasure in ordinary activities, including sex
- Decreased energy, fatigue, being "slowed down"
- Sleep disturbances (insomnia, early-morning waking, or over-sleeping)
- Eating disturbances (loss of appetite and weight, or weight gain)
- Difficulty concentrating, remembering, making decisions
- Feelings of hopelessness, pessimism
- Feelings of guilt, worthlessness, helplessness
- Thoughts of death or suicide, suicide attempts
- Irritability
- Excessive crying
- Chronic aches and pains that don't respond to treatment

Symptoms of Mania

In this condition, symptoms may range from moderate to severe. Symptoms of a manic episode might include any of the following:

- Inappropriate elation or irritability
- Decreased need for sleep
- Increased energy
- Increased talking, moving, and sexual activity
- Racing thoughts
- Disturbed ability to make decisions
- Grandiose notions

Where to Get Diagnosis and Treatment for Depression

- Physicians
- Mental health specialists
- Employee assistance programs (EAPs)

- Health maintenance organizations
- Community mental health centers
- Hospital departments of psychiatry or outpatient psychiatric clinics
- University or medical school affiliated programs
- State hospital outpatient clinics
- Family service/social agencies
- Private clinics and facilities

In addition to professional help, many people find mutual and family support groups useful.

For a free brochure about depression, call 1-800-421-4211.

For additional information about depression and the D/ART program, write:

D/ART Program, NIMH
5600 Fishers Lane
Room 10-85,
Rockville, MD 20857

Depression: Treat it. Defeat it.

For more Information about depression or where to get an evaluation or treatment, please contact the D/ART Community Partner nearest you. D/ART Partners are networks of public and private organizations that make referrals to local services as well as conduct depression education and training activities for the community, the media, and health and mental health practitioners.

State D/ART Community Partners

AL Mental Health Association in Madison County, Huntsville, AL (205) 536-9441

AK Alaska Mental Health Association, Anchorage, AK (907) 563-0880

AZ Mental Health Association of Greater Tucson, Tucson, AZ
(602) 882-8512

CA Mental Health Association of Napa County, Napa, CA (707)
224-9033

Family Service Agency of Shasta County, Redding, CA (916)
243-2024

Mental Health Association Sacramento/Placer Counties,
Sacramento, CA (916) 368-3100

Mental Health Association of San Francisco, San Francisco,
CA (415) 921-4401

Patient Care Services, Langley Porter Psychiatric Hospital,
San Francisco, CA (415) 476-7307

CO Mental Health Association of Colorado, Denver, CO (303)
595-3500

DC Mental Health Association-DC, Washington, DC (202) 265-
6363

FL Mental Health Association of Central Florida, Orlando, FL
(407) 843-1564

GA Mental Health Association of Georgia, Atlanta, GA (404)
875-7081

IN Mental Health Association of Indiana, Indianapolis, IN
(317) 638-3501

IA Alliance for the Mentally Ill of Iowa, Johnston, IA (515) 254-
0417

KS Mental Health Association of Johnson County, Lenexa, KS
(913) 888-5863

MD Mental Health Association of Montgomery County,
Rockville, MD (301) 424-0656

MD Mental Health Association of Prince George's County, Largo, MD (301) 499-2107

MI Mental Health Association in Michigan, Southfield, Ml (313) 557-6777

MN Mental Health Association of Minnesota, Minneapolis, MN (612) 331-6840

MO Mental Health Association of the Ozarks, Springfield, MO (417) 882-4677

NJ Mental Health Association of Southwestern New Jersey, Camden, NJ (609) 966-6767

NY Mental Health Association in New York State, Albany, NY (518) 434-0439

ND Mental Health Association in North Dakota, Bismarck, ND (701) 255-3692

OH Mental Health Association in Ohio, Columbus, OH (614) 221-5383

Office of Prevention, Ohio Department of Mental Health, Columbus, Ohio (614) 466-1195

OK Mental Health Association in Tulsa, Tulsa, OK (918) 585-1213

PA United Mental Health, Inc., Pittsburgh, PA (412) 391-3820

TN Mental Health Association of Knox County, Knoxville, TN (615) 584-9125

TX Mental Health Association of Houston and Harris County, Houston, TX (713) 523-8963

Mental Health Association of Tarrant County, Ft. Worth, TX (817) 335-5405

UT Mental Health Association of Utah, Salt Lake City, UT (801) 531-8996

VA Mental Health Association of Alexandria, Alexandria, VA (703) 548-0010

Mental Health Association of Northern Virginia, Annandale, VA (703) 642-0800

Mental Health Association of Roanoke Valley, Roanoke, VA (703) 344-0931

WA Alliance for the Mentally Ill of Washington State, Lacey, WA (206) 438-0211

Washington Advocates for the Mentally Ill, Seattle, WA (206) 789-7722

State D/ART Professional Partners

CA University of California at San Diego School of Medicine, LaJolla, CA (619) 552-8585 ext. 2096

Bio-Behavioral Medical Clinics, Inc. Fresno, CA (209) 226-7748

Chapter 15

Seasonal Affective Disorder

Seasonal Affective Disorder (SAD), Sub-Syndromal SAD (S/SAD), or the Winter Blues

- SAD is a cyclical illness, characterized by depressed periods in fall and winter (beginning in October/November and subsiding in March/April) which alternate with less depressed, nondepressed or even elevated moods in spring and summer.

- Ten million (6%) and 25 million (14%) Americans are estimated to suffer from SAD and S/SAD respectively.

- Four times as many, (about 80%) of those suffering from SAD are women, with symptoms typically appearing in the third decade of life and premenstrual mood changes often worsening in winter months.

- Most children affected by SAD have a parent or a first degree relative with SAD or another psychiatric condition.

- Light therapy can be effective in treating SAD as can medications and other forms of treatments.

- Light therapy can work within days, but may take a few weeks.

NIH Pub. No. 00-0009.

Symptoms

In Adults

- Decreased energy in the fall and winter
- Tiredness and fatigue
- Appetite changes (usually increased appetite)
- Weight gain
- Carbohydrate craving
- Difficulty concentrating and getting tasks accomplished
- Sadness or anxiety
- Withdrawal from friends and family

In Children

- Irritability
- Difficulty getting out of bed
- School problems in fall and winter

Causes of SAD

- SAD is caused by response to changes in environmental light.
- Researchers have targeted specific hormones and neurotrans-mitter that vary with daily as well as seasonal patterns of sunlight.

Recommended Treatments

- Light therapy usually involves exposing SAD patients to lev-els of artificial light 5-20 times brighter than ordinary indoor lighting. Studies show that anywhere from 30 minutes to a few hours of light therapy in the morning, per day, relieves symptoms within days to 2 weeks in about 75% of SAD suffer-ers.

- Light entering via the eye is thought to modify brain chemis-try and physiology to correct the abnormalities resulting from light deficiency in vulnerable individuals.

- Alterations in lifestyle including: indoor lighting environment, exposure to natural sun light, winter vacations, stress management and dietary approaches are helpful in relieving the symptoms of SAD.

- Medications, psychotherapy or a combination of both are also helpful in relieving the symptoms of SAD.

Side Effects of Light Therapy

- eyestrain
- headaches
- insomnia
- hypermanic symptoms

Recommended Action

- Consult your physician or a mental health professional for diagnosis and treatment.
- Call 1-800-421-4211 D/ART (Depression Awareness, Recognition, Treatment) for free print information on depression.

Information from NIMH Concerning Seasonal Affective Disorder (SAD) and Light Therapy.

We have been working in these two areas in the Intramural Research Program of the National Institute of Mental Health since the early 1980's, when we recognized and described the syndrome of SAD and began our first treatment studies with artificial light. Since then the condition of SAD has been recognized by the standard manual for psychiatric diagnoses in the U.S., called the *DSM-III-R*, where it is termed "seasonal pattern." Since our early work in the field of light therapy, many groups in the United States, Europe and Japan have reported that light treatment improves the symptoms of SAD.

In addition, researchers at various centers have found that light therapy may also be helpful for other conditions, including depression that is not seasonal in nature, delayed sleep phase syndrome (a condition in which people have a hard time getting to sleep and waking up at conventional times), premenstrual syndrome, shift work and jet lag. The work in these areas is still preliminary and the benefits of light are not as well established yet for these conditions as they are for SAD.

Specific questions are best referred to your local physician or mental health professional.

Suitable light fixtures can be obtained from several sources, including:

The SunBox Company
1927 Orbit Dr.
Gaithersburg, MD 20850
(301) 762-1786

Medic-Light, Inc.
Yacht Club Drive
Lake Hopatcong, NJ 07849
(800) 544-4825.

Apollo Light Systems, Inc.
352 West 1060 South,
Orem, UT 84058
(801) 226-2370

We do not at this time have a complete list of light companies. The above-mentioned represents the larger companies in the United States. The NIMH is not officially endorsing any particular light company and it is quite possible that another company would work out better for your particular purposes.

A portable light visor is currently being tested. More information about it can be obtained from:

Bio-Brite
7315 Wisconsin Avenue
Suite 900E
Bethesda, MD 20814
(800) 621-5483

A "dawn simulator" is also currently being tested. More information about it can be obtained from:

Pi Square, Incorporated
12305 9th Avenue S.W.
Seattle, WA 98146
(800) 786-3296

We would like to emphasize the following points:

1. We strongly recommend that this and indeed any treatment for mood problems be supervised by a qualified psychiatrist or therapist.

2. Although we have documented no visual problems in the ten years during which we have used light treatment, we cannot rule out the possibility of visual problems following long term usage of lights in some people. People with any history of eye problems might be at special risk in this regard.

3. The information in this letter in no way constitutes a recommendation for or an endorsement of light treatment for any individual we have not evaluated, and the National Institute of Mental Health cannot take responsibility for any adverse effects which may result from the use of light treatment.

If you are interested in participating in the Clinical Research Program at the National Institute of Mental Health, please contact Ron Barnett or Todd Hardin at (301) 496-0500. In general, we only accept subjects from the Washington Metropolitan area though in some instances we have included people from other regions. In these cases, the cost of travel has been assumed by the participant.

We hope this information will be of some help to you.

Norman E. Rosenthal, M.D.
Chief, Section on Environmental Psychiatry
Clinical Psychobiology Branch

Thomas A. Wehr, M.D.
Chief, Clinical Psychobiology Branch

National Institute of Mental Health
Room 4S-239, Building 10
9000 Rockville Pike
Bethesda, MD 20892
(301) 496-0500
(301) 496-5439 fax

Chapter 16

Bipolar Disorder

Today, lithium and other medicines are largely successful in treating bipolar disorder, which the National Institute of Mental Health (NIMH) estimates afflicts more than 2 million Americans. Also suffering, not always silently, are family members and sometimes friends and business acquaintances who must endure the extravagant ups and melancholy downs of the bipolar disorder patient.

Bipolar disorder, also known as manic-depressive illness and mood swing, is an inherited ailment that most often remains latent until young adulthood. In fact, some who have the aberrant gene never develop the disorder. The chance that a child who inherits the predisposition to bipolar disorder from one parent will eventually develop the illness is about one in seven; twice that if the gene is received from both parents.

For those who eventually do develop the disease, symptoms may first appear without any apparent "trigger." In others, they may begin during or after a period of stress or personal crisis (sometimes in women following childbirth). For whatever reason bipolar disorder begins, the patient's biological clock then executes its own rhythm, controlling the frequency and duration of later episodes.

In its most common form, bipolar disorder consists of a period of mania, or "high," and then depression, or "low." These two-sided episodes can last for days, weeks, or even months, if not treated. After

---

"Calming the Roller Coaster Ride of Mood Swings," *FDA Consumer,* November 1988.

each episode, some patients return to normal, even without treatment, but most will have subsequent episodes. And for some—20 percent to 35 percent—there's no return to normal; their disorder becomes chronic, repeating the florid behavior of mania and the devastation of depression without reprieve.

Bipolar disorder should not be confused with the other main mood disorder, unipolar depression, which is two or three times more prevalent. Essentially, unipolar depression is depression without mania. The average bout of unipolar depression usually lasts six months or more, while the depressed phase of bipolar depression is usually much shorter.

Milder Mania

Bipolar disorder occurs in several forms or patterns, and different ones may afflict the same person over time. In the most common form, a cycle consists of an episode of mania followed by one of depression (or the depressed phase may come first). Some patients may experience a volatile or erratic mixture of symptoms occurring together or following each other rapidly over a period of weeks, days, even hours. Others may have milder episodes, especially of mania.

In fact, there is a less serious form of bipolar disorder, called cyclothymia, that consists of periods of hypomania (a mild form of mania not severe enough to impair work or social functioning or require hospitalization) alternating with mild depression. Cyclothymic patients, however, often develop the more severe forms of bipolar disorder.

It is during this milder form of mania—with its elevated mood, euphoria, and seemingly boundless energy—that some talented persons have created notable works of art in painting, literature, and music, or consummated complex business deals, political triumphs, and the like, sometimes working tirelessly for days at a time without sleep.

But in the full-blown manic phase, bipolar disorder is generally severe enough to impair work and relationships, and may even require hospitalization for the patient's own protection, according to the *Diagnostic and Statistical Manual of Mental Disorders* of the American Psychiatric Association (APA). Symptoms can include:

- inflated self-esteem or grandiose ideas,
- reduced need for sleep,
- talkativeness,

- flight of ideas and racing thoughts,
- easy distractibility,
- unrestrained involvement in group activities such as those involving work, politics, religion (or sex),
- looking up old acquaintances,
- calling friends at all hours of the night,
- wearing showy clothes or heavy makeup,
- distributing money or advice to strangers,
- engaging excessively in pleasurable activities, such as buying sprees or sexual indiscretions, and
- making foolish business investments.

Common complications include abuse of mood-altering drugs (such as stimulants or psychedelics) and the consequences of poor judgment, such as financial losses and trouble with the law.

The most severe manic episodes can require supervision most of the time to prevent the patient from getting hurt or hurting others. They may even include psychotic features: delusions, hallucinations, stupor, loss of feeling, or muscular rigidity.

Symptoms of Depression

A major depressive episode, according to the APA manual, consists of either a depressed mood or loss of interest or pleasure in most activities, plus at least three of these seven symptoms:

- significant weight gain or loss and increased or decreased appetite,

- sleeplessness or excessive sleepiness

- psychomotor agitation (such as floor pacing, inability to sit still, hand wringing, or pulling of hair, skin or clothing) or psychomotor retardation (such as slowed speech, muteness, or slowed body movements),

- fatigue or loss of energy,

- feelings of worthlessness or undeserved guilt, at times amounting to delusions,

- reduced ability to think or make decisions, or

- concern with death or suicide, or attempts at suicide.

Some associated features include tearfulness, anxiety, irritability, brooding or obsessive pondering, concern with physical health, panic attacks, and phobias.

A depressed patient may "self-treat" with sedatives and alcohol, which may only worsen the depression.

Degrees of depression range from the mildest, with only a minor effect on work and social and personal relationships, to the most severe, which, like manic episodes, may include psychotic features, such as delusions or hallucinations about personal inadequacy, guilt, disease, persecution or death.

Bipolar disorder occurs equally in men and women (unlike unipolar depression, where women victims outnumber men 2 to 1). The average age of onset of bipolar disorder is the late 20s. It is more prevalent among wealthier and more educated people. There is no difference in rates between blacks and whites, but there is a greater prevalence in certain ethnic groups, such as Ashkenazic Jews, whose roots are in Eastern and Northern Europe.

At least since 1921, when Emil Kraepelin gave a name to manic-depressive illness and delineated its features, psychiatrists have believed the disorder is inherited.

Bipolar patients tend to have first-degree relatives (parents, brothers and sisters) with bipolar or unipolar disorders. If one identical twin has bipolar disorder, the chance that the other will have it is between 40 percent and 71 percent. (The percentages apply whether the twins are raised together or not.) This strongly suggests that what's inherited is only a predisposition, with differences in actual occurrence attributable to environmental factors.

Amish Genes

A genetic origin finally was confirmed in 1987, following a major study of a close-knit population in Pennsylvania known as the Old Order Amish.

The study, which began in 1976, was published in *Nature*, a British scientific journal, in February 1987. It was conducted by researchers from the University of Miami, Massachusetts Institute of

Technology, and Yale University, and was supported by NIMH.

The Amish group constituted a homogeneous population whose ancestors were easy to trace genealogically because of their common descent from 30 Europeans who emigrated to America in the 18th century. The descendants married only among themselves. Further, the group tended to have large families with complete genealogical records.

Of the 12,000 descendants, one family with 81 living members was selected for study from among 32 families with bipolar disorder victims. This family had 19 members with mood disorders, of which 14 had some form of bipolar illness. The 62 others were psychiatrically well, according to the report.

The researchers analyzed the DNA—the genetic material—of cells from blood samples from the 81 family members. They found that those with bipolar disorder tended to have certain variations on one pair of chromosomes. The correlation was so strong, in fact, that the odds of it being due to chance were less than one in 1,000.

Shortly after publication of the Amish findings, the results of another study, also published in *Nature*, showed a genetic connection for bipolar disorder, but on a different pair of chromosomes. That study, also supported in part by NIMH, covered 161 people from five large families in the Jerusalem area of Israel. These families, from Iran, Iraq, Turkey and Yemen, belonged to the Sephardic Jews, whose roots are in Africa and the Mediterranean area. Of the 161 family members, 47 had bipolar illness or related mood disorders.

The results supported speculation that aberrant genes carrying a bipolar disorder trait probably occur in more than one chromosome location. It appears that more than one genetic cause is involved in the basic features of bipolar disorder.

Researchers believe bipolar (and unipolar) mood disorders result from imbalances of certain chemicals in the brain that facilitate thinking and behavior and ensure normal mental and psychological functioning. Some of these chemicals are called neurotransmitters because they aid transmission of internal messages by means of electrical impulses across neurons, or nerve cells.

Balancing Brain Chemicals

The neurotransmitters of main concern in bipolar disorder are norepinephrine, serotonin and dopamine. Researchers have found that certain drugs can affect the balance of these brain chemicals. Lithium, for instance, is thought to stabilize mood by affecting certain neurotransmitters.

In fact, lithium is the most effective medicine yet discovered for bipolar disorder. It can bring remission of symptoms in 70 percent of manic bipolar patients in 4 to 10 days. Although lithium is not the drug of first choice for depressed bipolar episodes, it sometimes works when antidepressants don't. One principal use of lithium is as a "maintenance" drug, used indefinitely (usually with psychotherapy) to prevent the return of symptoms or at least soften future occurrences. Other drugs may be used with lithium in patients not adequately helped by lithium alone. Mental health researchers are not certain if maintenance therapy—either lithium alone or with an antidepressant drug—actually reduces the number of episodes or simply dampens the intensity of the highs and lows. Most think it depends on the individual.

Lithium is toxic in large amounts, so the minimum effective dosage must be carefully established and the amount of the drug circulating in the blood checked periodically to prevent toxic buildup. (Lithium had been marketed as a salt substitute in the late 1940s, and several people died before its toxicity was discovered and the product was removed from the market. FDA approved it as a drug in 1969 after safe doses had been established.)

Reduction in sodium or loss of fluids from the body can leave a toxic concentration of lithium, so patients taking the drug who have low salt intake, heavy sweating, fever, vomiting, or diarrhea should replace both sodium and fluids quickly. Lithium also can be especially risky for patients with kidney or heart disorders, so its directions carry warnings for especially careful monitoring and low dosages in such cases.

For the past several years the drug carbamazepine (brand name Tegretol), approved by FDA for use as an anticonvulsant, has been used experimentally, alone and with other drugs, in treating bipolar disorder. Early in 1988, Robert Post, M.D., chief of NIMH's biological psychiatry branch, reviewed the test use of carbamazepine and other therapies for treating bipolar patients who show only partial improvement with lithium, or who are treated for mania with antipsychotic drugs and for depression with monoamine oxidase (MAO) inhibitors or heterocyclic antidepressants (formerly known as tricyclic antidepressants until the advent of other chemical forms of these drugs).

Lithium-Carbamazepine

Post found evidence that the use of antipsychotic drugs for the manic phase and heterocyclics and MAO inhibitors for the depressed phase increases the likelihood of a rapid onset of the next opposite episode, or of an especially severe episode. He also found various reports from studies at NIMH and elsewhere that a combination of lithium and carbamazepine is substantially effective in treating episodes of mania and depression. He said that the lithium-carbamazepine combination is also better than either drug used alone for maintenance treatment of patients who aren't helped by other treatments.

In addition to carbamazepine, valproate, clonazepam and a few other anticonvulsants are being used experimentally in specific problems of bipolar disorder.

The heterocyclic antidepressants and MAO inhibitors sometimes used to treat the depressed phase of bipolar disorder have their drawbacks. According to a report by Thomas A. Wehr, chief of NIMH's clinical psychobiology branch, and Frederick K. Goodwin, NIMH's director of research, these drugs can "switch" bipolar patients from depression to mania or hypomania. They can also cause more rapid cycling, mainly in women.

MAO inhibitors are believed to be most effective against so-called atypical, or neurotic, depression, in which some of the symptoms are excessive sleepiness, overeating, anxiety, or extreme sensitivity to criticism or rejection. But these drugs, too can "switch" bipolar depressed patients to the manic phase of their illness. Further, patients taking MAO inhibitors must avoid certain foods and medications or risk a pounding headache, sudden high blood pressure, and possible stroke. Prescribing physicians customarily hand the patient a list of foods and drugs to avoid or be cautious about.

Electroconvulsive therapy (ECT, also known as electroshock therapy) is used to treat depression and has also been used to treat mania, according to an NIMH study by Dr. Matthew V. Rudorfer and colleague Markku Linnoila. ECT consists of electric shocks to the brain that induce a seizure whose convulsive activity has beneficial effect against the disorder. Unlike drugs, ECT produces beneficial results immediately. This is a clear advantage when a depressed patient is suicidal or when a patient cannot take drugs for one reason or another, such as a high risk of side effects. But ECT can cause temporary loss of memory of the immediate past.

Mania in the Wee Hours

Some researchers have looked into the importance of the body's "biological clock"—its own internal mechanism for regulating not only mood but other bodily functions—in guiding the course of this illness. For instance, NIMH researchers studying the biological rhythms of depressed bipolar patients found that 9 of 12 patients were switched temporarily to mania or hypomania when kept awake all night. NIMH's Wehr said sleep deprivation during the second part of the night (after 1 or 2 a.m.) is more effective against depression—but is more likely to induce mania or hypomania—than such deprivation in the first part of the night. He notes that most people have more of a stage of sleep called REM (rapid eye movement) in the late part of the night, and that depriving a patient of REM sleep during that period is more likely to have antidepressant effects.

Wehr hypothesizes that many unexplained mania onsets in bipolar patients may have been triggered by something that kept them awake in the early morning hours. Mania might be prevented, he believes, by educating known or suspected bipolar patients and their families about the mania-inducing effects of sleep disruptions and by intervening when patients are being deprived of sleep or experiencing insomnia.

Today, most bipolar victims can be restored to normal functioning, and many can be kept that way. Successful treatment can bring relief not only to patients but also to their families, who share in the suffering from the melodramatic crises, domestic disruption, dereliction of responsibility, and financial disaster that may attend the erratic ways of a mania-driven bipolar patient, who has little control over his or her behavior and who sometimes, when depressed, becomes suicidal.

Even though effective treatment is available for most bipolar patients, NIMH believes that about half of those who have the illness—a million or more individuals—are unidentified and thus untreated. Further, even after diagnosis, persuading the person to accept help can be almost impossible. Many, especially when manic, deny anything is wrong. Even among patients undergoing treatment, at least half will slyly or negligently stop taking their medication, or take it incorrectly, unless there's somebody to enforce "drug compliance." Bipolar patients are not long in discovering that the medicine brings them down to earth when many would rather be flying—on a manic high.

The task of getting a patient with bipolar disorder to treatment falls most often on the family. Firm resolve is needed, but also tact and sympathy, especially when a bipolar patient is depressed and possibly suicidal. The family doctor can help determine if psychiatric attention is needed and can support the family's efforts to that end.

Manic-depressive illness has long awaited a treatment that restores the victim to normal, or near normal. That treatment is now available. Although modern medicine cannot cure bipolar disorder, it can remove most of its sting.

—by Harold Hopkins

Harold Hopkins is a free-lance writer in Gaithersburg, Md.

Chapter 17

Mood Disorders: Pharmacologic Prevention of Recurrences

Introduction

Mood disorders, also called affective illnesses, are common and serious conditions. It is estimated that at any given time 3 to 4 percent of the nation's population will be suffering from a major depressive or manic episode. Recurrences are frequent. During the past decade, clinical and research interest in mood disorders has expanded beyond the treatment of acute episodes to include consideration of long-term maintenance treatment aimed at preventing or reducing the frequency and intensity of further attacks. This broadening of focus has occurred in the context of improved approaches to the description and classification of these disorders and newer epidemiologic studies. Recent evidence has demonstrated the recurrent and chronic nature of these illnesses and the extent to which they represent a continual source of distress and dysfunction for affected individuals and their families, as well as a substantial burden to society. Interest in preventive maintenance treatment has been stimulated further by results from recent long-term trials involving antidepressant drugs and lithium.

The need to consider the longitudinal nature of affective disorders in treatment planning has raised many issues of concern about whether, when, and how to use psychopharmacologic agents to protect

Concensus Develoment Conference Consensus Statement, Volume 5, Number 4; OM-00-4015.

patients against recurring episodes of depression or mania. In an effort to resolve questions surrounding these issues, the National Institutes of Health in conjunction with the National Institute of Mental Health convened a Consensus Development Conference on Mood Disorders: Pharmacologic Prevention of Recurrences on April 24-26, 1984. After a day and a half of presentations by experts in the field, a consensus panel including representatives of psychiatry, psychology, pharmacology, epidemiology, internal medicine, and the general public considered the scientific evidence and agreed on answers to the following key questions:

1. How common are recurrent mood disorders, and what are the variations in the course of these illnesses?

2. What groups of patients with mood disorders should be considered for preventive maintenance medication?

3. How effective are these medications in modifying the course of recurrent affective illness?

4. What principles guide selection of specific therapeutic agents for these groups?

5. What are the treatment strategies for using these medications on a long-term basis? What additional or alternative strategies are available for breakthrough episodes, treatment failures, or aspects of the illness unresponsive to medication?

6. What are the long-term risks and complications of maintenance therapy? How should these be assessed and managed?

7. What research areas need further development?

Panel's Conclusions

Recurrent mood disorders have high prevalence and serious consequences but are currently underdiagnosed and undertreated. There are groups of patients with recurrent mood disorders for whom treatments are available which effectively reduce the frequency and intensity of subsequent episodes. Complete evaluation and careful differential diagnosis are required before initiating long-term preventive treatment. For patients with bipolar disorders, who are particularly likely to suffer recurrences, extensive studies have supported the efficacy of lithium in preventing recurrences.

While unipolar disorder [depression] is associated with a reduced rate of recurrence, both lithium and the tricyclic antidepressants have been shown to be effective as long-term preventive treatments for recurrent unipolar disorder.

Although the long-term use of these agents poses certain risks, they are not appreciably different from their use in acute situations. Applying appropriate strategies to the management and use of these drugs will enhance the likelihood of compliance and consequent prevention of recurrences with a minimum of bothersome side effects. Such strategies must be used within the context of an ongoing, supportive relationship among the doctor, the patient, and the family.

Research priorities should be placed on basic research aimed at elucidating the etiology and pathogenesis of major mood disorders and the development of more effective treatments.

1. How common are recurrent mood disorders, and what are the variations in the course of these illnesses?

Recurrent major mood (affective) disorders are highly prevalent and have serious consequences. These conditions often are not accurately identified by either patients or clinicians and even when correctly diagnosed are often undertreated or not treated at all. Precision in differential diagnosis using explicit inclusion and exclusion criteria is essential to the identification and optimal treatment of these disorders.

"Depression" can refer either to a normal mood or to an illness requiring treatment. The normal mood, which consists of those transitory feelings of sadness or discouragement that everyone experiences during difficult times of life, is not what is being discussed in this report but rather the specific clinical syndromes of depression and mania. Within this clinical context, the symptoms of depression are many and varied. They may include loss of interest or pleasure in almost all usual activities; poor appetite or weight loss or increased appetite or weight gain; insomnia or hypersomnia; psychomotor agitation or retardation, decrease in sexual drive; loss of energy; fatigue; feelings of worthlessness, self-reproach, or excessive or inappropriate guilt; difficulty thinking or concentrating; and, most serious, suicidal thinking or attempts. Some individuals with manic syndromes may be euphoric, overconfident, and optimistic. However, their mood is typically brittle and deteriorates rapidly into irritability. Others may only be angry or irritable. These individuals may become more active, restless, and talkative; feel that their thoughts are racing; have an inflated sense of self-esteem; be distracted easily; and engage impulsively in activities that could have severe consequences, such as buying sprees, sexual indiscretions, violent behaviors, or foolish business investments. As a result, mania can be devastating to personal relationships and careers.

For the purposes of this report, a major recurrent mood disorder represents a full-blown syndrome of depression or mania, as defined by criteria set forth in the *Diagnostic and Statistical Manual of Mental Disorders, Third Edition (DSM-III)*. Other affective disorders, such as single episodes of depression, chronic milder depression of at least 2 years' duration (dysthymic disorder), and mild depressive or hypomanic syndromes, are discussed only when they occur in patients who also have a recurrent major mood disorder. These other affective disorders also should be recognized as important causes of emotional impairment and often will benefit from treatment, but they are beyond the scope of this consensus statement. Depressive and manic states caused by medical disorders (e.g., hypothyroidism) or exogenous agents (e.g., amphetamines) also are not considered.

The division of major mood disorders into *unipolar* and *bipolar* subtypes is clinically useful. Patients with unipolar disorder have episodes of depression only; patients with bipolar disorder have either episodes of mania or hypomania and depression or episodes of mania alone. Unipolar disorder is reported to be considerably more prevalent than bipolar disorder. Family and genetic (twin, adoption, and pedigree) studies provide compelling support for strong heritability of these disorders, especially bipolar disorder.

The rates of recurrence, variations in course of illness, and the results of clinical trials in this report are based on studies involving patients who sought treatment at inpatient and outpatient units affiliated with university medical centers. It is premature to generalize from these data on course and outcome for the entire population of persons with recurrent mood disorders, which presumably includes a substantial number whose conditions remit spontaneously, who never seek treatment, or who are treated in other settings. However, the treatment recommendations derived from these studies are applicable to patients who suffer major recurrent mood disorders regardless of the setting in which they are seen.

Variations in Patterns of Course of Illness

Relapse refers to the exacerbation of an ongoing episode after an initial suppression of symptoms. Recurrence refers to a new episode that follows a complete recovery that has lasted for at least several months. Treatment for preventing a relapse is called continuation therapy and is distinguished from longer term efforts to prevent completely or reduce the intensity and frequency of recurrence (preventive treatment). Thus, the sequence of treatment may be: (a) an acute phase to control disabling symptoms (may be measured in weeks), (b) a continuation phase to avoid relapses of a single episode (may be measured in months), and (c) a preventive phase to avoid recurrences of new episodes over time (may be measured in years). This report addresses only the third item in the sequence—the preventive treatment of recurrent episodes of affective disorders.

Most of the information presented in this section on course of illness is based on the study of patients whose treatment was not under the control of research investigators, and a substantial proportion of these patients received other minimal or no treatment.

Most patients who have a manic episode go on to have a course marked by multiple recurrences of major depressive and manic episodes. The course of unipolar depression is more variable and less well established. Studies suggest that between 50 and 85 percent of patients with a major depressive episode who seek treatment at university medical centers will have at least one subsequent episode of depression in their lifetime. Between 10 and 15 percent of unipolar patients will have subsequent episodes that will involve manic or hypomanic symptoms, at which point they are reclassified as having a bipolar disorder. This reclassification occurs less frequently as patients become older and have an increased number of depressive episodes.

Although there are fewer studies of affective disorder in children and adolescents than in adult populations, emerging evidence suggests that these disorders do occur in childhood and, when present, may have a chronic, recurring course. It is reported that the lifetime incidence of major depression is as high as 30 percent by late adolescence in children who have at least one parent with a major affective illness.

Once mood disorders become recurrent, they have a course marked by high rates of relapse and recurrence and significant morbidity in subsequent episodes and in the intervals between episodes.

Fifteen to 20 percent of patients with a recurrent unipolar disorder do not recover fully from any given episode and have persistent symptoms for at least 2 years. Recently, similar rates have been reported for patients with bipolar disorder who formerly were believed to have much higher rates of full recovery between episodes.

As many as 50 percent of patients with recurrent unipolar disorders who recover from a given episode are reported to have a recurrence within the first 2 years after recovery. The likelihood of recurrence is greatest in the 4 to 6 months following initial symptomatic recovery; this risk levels off markedly between 6 and 12 months and is still lower after the patient has been well for 18 months. Some evidence suggests that the length of well intervals between episodes decreases for the first few episodes and then remains steady, while the duration of episodes remains fairly constant. The rate of recurrence in bipolar patients is greater than in unipolar conditions and does not decrease over time.

Some recurrent affective disorders have courses of illness marked by discrete episodes with minimal or no symptoms or impairment in social functioning in the intervals between episodes. Other patients have more insidious onsets of episodes, as well as less complete symptomatic recovery and more impairment in social functioning in the intervals between episodes. The proportion of patients in each of these groups is unknown. Patients who have either of these patterns also may have antecedent or concurrent nonaffective mental disorders.

Factors That Increase Risk of Recurrence

A substantial proportion of patients with recurrent mood disorders also suffer from a dysthymic disorder. If dysthymic symptoms persist after recovery from the major depressive syndrome, the risk of developing new episodes of major depression is especially high. The presence of a nonaffective psychiatric disorder such as alcoholism, drug dependence, or anxiety disorder and an older age of onset also substantially increase the risk of recurrence in unipolar or bipolar recurrent disorders. In addition, the greater the number of previous episodes, the higher the risk of recurrence.

Health and Social Consequences

Complications of affective disorders include attempted and completed suicide, increase in deaths from non-psychiatric medical causes and accidents, impaired social functioning, impaired occupational functioning, impaired parenting, and marital discord. The rates of these events and their severity are substantial.

2. What groups of patients with mood disorders should be considered for preventive maintenance medication?

Before preventive medication is begun, the patient should have a careful medical evaluation to search for organic cause(s) of the affective syndrome or conditions that would contraindicate the use of one or another of the proposed treatments. A comprehensive medical history, physical examination, and appropriate laboratory tests are indicated. This evaluation should include an assessment by, or consultation with, a clinician skilled in the differential diagnosis of mental disorders.

Bipolar Disorder

Patients who have a manic episode are at high risk for recurrences. Manic episodes themselves are very disruptive. The likelihood of becoming psychotic (i.e., having delusions or hallucinations) when manic or depressed is great, and suicide risk is high. Therefore, the occurrence of a manic episode should always raise the question of preventive therapy.

Patients who have not had a full-blown manic episode, but have had a hypomanic and a depressive episode, are also at high risk for recurrence and are more likely to become psychotic when depressed than are patients with unipolar disorder. Therefore, careful consideration should be given to implementing preventive therapy in these patients. Other factors in this patient group that indicate a need to consider preventive therapy include number and recency of prior episodes of depression, family history of bipolar disorder, past suicide attempts, past psychotic episodes, past functional incapacity associated with episodes, and level of social functioning or affective symptoms between episodes. Each of these factors tends either to increase the likelihood of recurrence or to be associated with considerable disability and risk should a new episode occur.

Unipolar Disorder

This condition is less frequently recurrent than the bipolar disorders, and the efficacy of the preventive treatments is less clearly established. Therefore, the decision of whether and when to initiate preventive therapy is more highly individualized for patients with unipolar disorders. It depends on identifying those unipolar patients with a high risk of recurrence. The presence of another mental disorder, a chronic medical disorder, or chronic affective symptoms each increases the rate of recurrence, as does older age at the onset of the first depressive episode. Psychotic features, serious suicide attempts, or serious functional impairment during recent episodes all predict increased severity in subsequent episodes. A family history of suicide, bipolar disorder, or psychotic affective episodes also is predictive of increased severity.

Additional Considerations

Additional factors also play a role in the timing and decision to begin preventive therapy in patients who have never had a manic episode. A slow or incomplete response to treatment for a prior episode of depression would lead one to consider preventive therapy more closely. A rapid therapeutic response in a patient with long intervals between episodes argues against the initiation of preventive therapy. The potentially irreparable disruption that a depressive episode may exact on a patient's work, family, and social relationships also would increase the need for preventive therapy. The decision to use preventive treatment is complicated in women who are, or may become, pregnant. Special consideration is also needed for patients who find the presence of side effects disruptive or highly unpleasant. For such patients the decision involves the careful weighing of the potential benefits and risks of preventive treatment.

3. How effective are these medications in modifying the course of recurrent affective illness?

In a summary of 14 studies of bipolar disorder, the percentage of patients having a recurrent episode of either mania or depression during 1 year after the start of treatment was greatly reduced by lithium maintenance in contrast to placebo. In most of the studies, the number of recurrences was reduced by 50 percent compared to placebo, and the recurrences were less severe. However, rapidly cycling bipolar patients, i.e., those who have three or more episodes a year, often respond poorly.

Preventive treatment with lithium is equally effective against both manic and depressive recurrences in male and female bipolar patients of all ages from early adulthood to old age, but few data are available for children and adolescents and for the elderly.

The preventive effect of lithium may not develop fully for several months. An early recurrence of bipolar illness following initiation of treatment should not necessarily lead to its abandonment. Antidepressants have not been shown to be effective in preventing recurrence of manic episodes in bipolar disorder.

Unipolar Disorder

Many controlled studies have shown that preventive treatment with lithium or antidepressants (imipramine and amitriptyline) can substantially prevent recurrent episodes of unipolar depression. In most patients, lithium and tricyclics decrease the frequency and/or intensity of recurrences. In six studies with follow-up periods ranging from 5 months to 3 years, the percentages of patients who relapsed or had a recurrence on placebo were significantly greater than the percentages of patients who relapsed or had a recurrence on lithium. In a similar manner, a significant difference between tricyclic antidepressants and placebo was found in several studies. Most studies, however, find lithium and tricyclics to be equally effective or lithium to be somewhat superior.

Individual patients may respond better to either lithium or tricyclics. One multi-center study suggests that patients whose last episode was severe have a better response to imipramine and that patients whose last episode was of only moderate intensity respond equally well to lithium and tricyclics. Research to date has not produced clear-cut guidelines for choosing one over the other when all other factors are equal, nor has it supported the combination of the two as superior to either alone.

Tricyclic antidepressants and lithium prevent recurrences of unipolar depression in both men and women of all ages from early adulthood to old age; however, few data are available for children and adolescents and for the elderly.

Successful prevention of recurrence may involve other important gains, including increased stability of mood during intervals between episodes, regained self-esteem, renewed hope for the future, improved social relations, enhanced vocational abilities, and increased enjoyment of recreational activities.

Because the preventive treatment of recurrent mood disorders is clearly effective for large numbers of persons suffering from these conditions, and because a substantial proportion do not now seek treatment or are not accurately diagnosed, systematic efforts should be made to bring about a greater awareness and understanding by both health professionals and the public of the nature and effective treatment of these illnesses.

4. What principles guide selection of specific therapeutic agents for these groups?

Decision to Initiate Preventive Treatment

Repeated and candid discussions with the patient and the patient's spouse or other relatives are mandatory to ensure full understanding of potential advantages and risks of preventive treatment as well as of no treatment. These discussions should begin as early as possible after an acute episode is under control. The clinician should have complete information regarding the illness from the patient's and the family's perspective, and it is essential that patients and their families share in the decision-making process. The possible salutary effects on family and job stability should be explained thoroughly, and the known serious and troublesome side effects of each drug under consideration should be made clear. The necessity and importance of long-term monitoring, including required laboratory tests, should be understood fully. Compliance during treatment is improved greatly when all parties understand the therapeutic goals.

Choice of Drugs

Lithium is the drug of choice for preventing recurrences of bipolar disorder. In treating unipolar disorders, both lithium and tricyclic antidepressants have been shown to be effective for prevention. Since most patients will have been treated previously with tricyclic drugs for their depressive episodes, it is usually most appropriate to continue with the same drug, provided it has been effective and is well tolerated. Tricyclic antidepressants also may be preferable in older patients in whom renal function shows a normal decline with age. In addition, elderly individuals are more likely to be using other drugs to treat concurrent illnesses. Either these other agents or the illnesses themselves could interfere with lithium excretion and, thereby, predispose to toxicity. On the other hand, some older patients may be more vulnerable to certain side effects of the tricyclic antidepressants, such as urinary retention, cardiac arrhythmias, and increased intra-ocular pressure. Some clinicians recommend that lithium be used in both bipolar and unipolar cases to minimize the risk of an unexpected manic episode in a patient considered to be unipolar. In particular, lithium may be preferable for patients who have first degree relatives with a history of bipolar illness or whose psychiatric history is uncertain, since some previously diagnosed unipolar depressions ultimately may prove to be bipolar. The consequences of an unexpected manic episode, which lithium is likely to prevent, are generally serious.

Only a few tricyclic antidepressants have been used in controlled studies of the preventive effect of these agents. It is likely, however, that all standard tricyclic drugs are equally effective, although the question has not been studied empirically. On the other hand, some patients seem to respond to one tricyclic antidepressant after receiving no benefit from another, and side effects will differ from patient to patient and agent to agent. Thus, close monitoring is required, and some sequential courses of treatment with different antidepressants may be indicated.

239

5. What are the treatment strategies for using these medications on a long-term basis? What additional or alternative strategies are available for breakthrough episodes, treatment failures, or aspects of the illness unresponsive to medication?

Use of Lithium and Tricyclic Antidepressants

Specific clinical guidelines for the use of lithium and tricyclic antidepressants are available in various pharmacologic and psychiatric textbooks as well as articles in professional journals. Unfortunately, despite the interest in various biological tests for the diagnosis and treatment of mood disorders (dexamethasone suppression test, thyrotropin releasing hormone test, thyroid stimulating hormone test, measurement of 3-methoxy-4-hydroxy-phenethyleneglycol), no clear-cut guidelines for their use in the treatment of recurrent mood disorders have been established. What follows is only a brief outline of the use of these drugs as preventive agents.

Preventive doses of tricyclic antidepressants have not been adequately defined and, thus, physicians must be flexible in seeking to achieve optimal control. In general, doses similar to or somewhat lower than those used in treating the acute episode have been found effective. Studies of long-term preventive maintenance treatment with tricyclics have not adequately evaluated the effectiveness of dosages greater than 150 mg/day. Lithium in conventional forms is satisfactory. The goal in lithium treatment is to achieve serum concentrations between 0.6 and 0.8 mEq/L in most patients. While some patients may require higher concentrations, in general the physician is advised to maintain the patient on the lowest dose that prevents the return of symptoms since these lower concentrations are associated with fewer side effects.

Duration of Treatment

Duration of treatment must be determined on an individual basis, depending on the previous pattern of episodes, degree of impairment produced, the adverse consequences of a new recurrence, and the patient's ability to tolerate the drug. Data concerning the optimal duration of treatment are lacking. Most clinicians, as well as patients, would be loath to embark on a lifetime course of treatment. If the patient remains free of recurrences during a period equivalent to several of the previous cycle lengths, a decision may be reached to discontinue treatment, provided that a family member or friend of the patient is available to alert the patient and, if necessary, the physician to symptoms of recurrence. In general, the stronger the indications for initiating preventive treatment, the longer its duration should be.

When tricyclics are discontinued after long-term exposure to the drug, the process should be gradual to avoid symptoms that sometimes occur after sudden cessation. Thus, decreases in doses may be spread over weeks or months, with larger decrements early in the withdrawal phase and smaller decrements once the daily dose becomes 50 mg or less. Discontinuation of lithium can be done abruptly or spread out over a couple of weeks. The latter is probably advisable for patients receiving relatively high doses. Neither drug is addictive or prone to abuse.

Breakthrough Episodes

Breakthrough episodes during preventive treatment are manifested by the emergence of clinically significant signs and symptoms of either mania or depression. Purely symptomatic treatment (e.g., sedative, hypnotics or anxiolytics) should be delayed at this stage since close assessment over several weeks is desirable to be sure that a clinically significant recurrence of symptoms has occurred. When such breakthroughs occur during lithium treatment, the first step is to check serum lithium levels either to assure compliance or to justify an increased dose. The second step is to check the thyroid status, since hypothyroidism may mimic depression. The third step would be to add to the lithium an antipsychotic for manic breakthroughs or on antidepressant for depressive breakthroughs. These agents, however, should be used only temporarily for relief of the acute symptoms and should be withdrawn when these symptoms abate.

Treatment Failures

If the aforementioned measures fail, other treatments should be tried. Although many alternatives have been suggested, none has been extensively tested. Several reasonable alternatives are the replacement of lithium with carbamazepine, the addition of carbamazepine to lithium, or the replacement of tricyclic antidepressants with monoamine oxidase inhibitors for depressive treatment failures. Electroconvulsive therapy may also be considered for either manic or depressive treatment failures, particularly where suicidal risks seem high.

Some patients, usually those who have frequent and severe recurrences of depression that require large doses of tricyclic antidepressants, may experience more frequent episodes after use of these agents. When such a pattern is recognized, the minimal effective doses of tricyclic should be used. In some cases, allowing a depressive episode to run its course without antidepressant treatment will break the cycle.

Psychological Management of Patients in Preventive Therapy

The problem of patient compliance, especially with lithium, has been well documented in several studies. Medication side effects as well as patient and family attitudes toward these illnesses and their treatment may each contribute to noncompliance. It is believed that the treating physician can make a considerable impact on treatment efficacy by counseling patients who are on preventive therapy, interviewing carefully, asking directly about particular side effects, eliciting patients' concerns, treating side effects as indicated, and providing information to ensure optimal adherence.

More specific psychotherapies or brief counseling sessions may be helpful in reducing the secondary consequences of chronic conditions that are often associated with recurrent major affective illness (e.g., occupational or marital disruptions). This treatment may be provided either by the treating physician or by another professional skilled in such services.

Three types of psychotherapy (cognitive, interpersonal, and behavioral) have been found helpful in alleviating depressive symptoms. Whether these specific psychotherapies or others also play an adjunctive role with pharmacotherapy in preventing recurrence has not been firmly established. Based on our present state of knowledge, for nearly all patients suffering from major recurrent mood disorders, psychotherapy should be used in combination with, not as a substitute for, pharmacotherapy for long-term preventive treatment.

6. What are the long-term risks and complications of preventive therapy? How should these be assessed and managed?

Adverse Effects of Preventive Treatment

The risks of preventive therapy with lithium or tricyclic antidepressants do not appear to differ appreciably from the adverse reactions to these drugs for treatment of acute episodes of mood disorders, with the exception of impaired thyroid function, which may increase in frequency over time on preventive lithium therapy. Because lower doses are frequently successful for prevention, side effects may, in fact, be less of a problem. The earlier fears of irreversible renal damage now seem to be unwarranted. Except during the first trimester of pregnancy, there are few significant permanent risks with either lithium or tricyclic therapy. There may be minor renal tubular defects and hypothyroidism brought on by long-term lithium therapy, and a few patients may be at minimal risk for arrhythmias with extended treatment with tricyclic antidepressants. Tricyclics may lead to weight gain, orthostatic hypotension, subtle confusional states, and exacerbation of mania. Lithium may create symptoms of thirst, polyuria, tremor, diarrhea, weight gain, or, less commonly, hypothyroidism. Memory problems, tiredness, and a dulling of senses have been reported as additional complications of lithium that may contribute to noncompliance. Separation of these possible side effects from symptoms of the illness needs to be explored. A carefully supervised reduction in dose, reevaluation of thyroid status or a therapeutic trial of antidepressants are ways in which the distinction may be achieved. Because patients with mania and depression are at high risk for suicide, supplies of medication should be limited. Adverse consequences of lithium on the fetus and nursing newborn should be made known to women who may become pregnant. Preventive use of lithium and tricyclic antidepressants in children and adolescents must be based on clinical judgment as risks and benefits have yet to be firmly established. Preliminary studies suggest that the potential problems are similar to those seen in adults.

Monitoring for Adverse Effects

Follow-up visits at regular intervals provide an opportunity to assess changes in clinical status resolve compliance issues institute appropriate medical interventions and establish a basis for treatment during breakthrough episodes. More frequent contact is clearly necessary during periods of potential recurrence or change in clinical status. Clinical observation and laboratory tests provide useful benchmarks in the event of complications during long-term treatment. Current practice during treatment with lithium is to monitor serum lithium levels of intervals of 1 to 3 months and to assess serum creatinine values and thyroid stimulating hormone (TSH) values every 6 to 12 months. Additional studies such as EKGs may be needed to elucidate other adverse effects.

Lithium intoxication is less likely in patients on low doses and with low serum concentrations as recommended here for preventive treatment. Patients should be advised always to keep well hydrated and to report immediately intercurrent illnesses that cause vomiting, diarrhea, or fever, or treatment with or use of new drugs.

7. What research areas need further development?

There are many deficiencies in our knowledge of how best to prevent recurrent mood disorders.

The fundamental questions that underlie these deficiencies and need to be investigated are:

1. Why do some patients develop severe recurrent illnesses while others do not?

2. Why do some patients respond well to preventive treatment while others do not?

3. Why do some patients lose benefits after an initial response to treatment?

Answers to these questions will require information from therapeutic, epidemiologic, neurobiologic and genetic studies. The results of such studies should elucidate basic mechanisms of the disorders themselves.

Some research strategies would include, for example, studies of high-risk populations (e.g., children of a parent with a mood disorder) the development and testing of new therapeutic approaches and identification of clinical and biochemical predictors of recurrence. The panel feels that priority should be given to the search for new knowledge about the pathogenesis of mood disorders. Such knowledge might then lead to new and more effective therapies for their treatment.

Part Four

Anxiety Disorders

Chapter 18

Understanding Panic Disorder

Fear...heart palpitations...terror, a sense of impending doom...dizziness...fear of fear. The words used to describe panic disorder are often frightening. But there is great hope: Treatment can benefit virtually everyone who has this condition. It is extremely important for the person who has panic disorder to learn about the problem and the availability of effective treatments and to seek help.

The encouraging progress in the treatment of panic disorder reflects recent, rapid advances in scientific understanding of the brain. In fact, the President and the U.S. Congress have declared the 1990s the Decade of the Brain. In addition to supporting intensified research on brain disorders, the Federal Government is working to bring information about these conditions to the people who need it.

The National Institute of Mental Health (NIMH), the Federal agency responsible for conducting and supporting research related to mental disorders, mental health, and the brain, is conducting a nationwide education program on panic disorder. The program's purpose is to educate the public and health care professionals about the disorder and encourage people with it to obtain effective treatments.

What Is Panic Disorder?

In panic disorder, brief episodes of intense fear are accompanied by multiple physical symptoms (such as heart palpitations and dizzi-

NIH Pub. No. 93-3509.

ness) that occur repeatedly and unexpectedly in the absence of any external threat. These "panic attacks," which are the hallmark of panic disorder, are believed to occur when the brain's normal mechanism for reacting to a threat—the so-called "fight or flight" response—becomes inappropriately aroused. Most people with panic disorder also feel anxious about the possibility of having another panic attack and avoid situations in which they believe these attacks are likely to occur. Anxiety about another attack, and the avoidance it causes, can lead to disability in panic disorder.

Who Has Panic Disorder?

In the United States, 1.6 percent of the adult population, or more than 3 million people, will have panic disorder at some time in their lives. The disorder typically begins in young adulthood, but older people and children can be affected. Women are affected twice as frequently as men. While people of all races and social classes can have panic disorder, there appear to be cultural differences in how individual symptoms are expressed.

Symptoms and Course of Panic Disorder

Panic Attack Symptoms

During a panic attack, some or all of the following symptoms occur:

- Terror—a sense that something unimaginably horrible is about to happen and one is powerless to prevent it
- Racing or pounding heartbeat
- Chest pains
- Dizziness, lightheadedness, nausea
- Difficulty breathing
- Tingling or numbness in the hands
- Flushes or chills
- Sense of unreality
- Fear of losing control, going "crazy," or doing something embarrassing
- Fear of dying

Initial Panic Attack

Typically, a first panic attack seems to come "out of the blue," occurring while a person is engaged in some ordinary activity like driving a car or walking to work. Suddenly, the person is struck by a barrage of frightening and uncomfortable symptoms. These symptoms often include terror, a sense of unreality, or a fear of losing control.

This barrage of symptoms usually lasts several seconds, but may continue for several minutes. The symptoms gradually fade over the course of about an hour. People who have experienced a panic attack can attest to the extreme discomfort they felt and to their fear that they had been stricken with some terrible, life-threatening disease or were "going crazy." Often people who are having a panic attack seek help at a hospital emergency room.

Initial panic attacks may occur when people are under considerable stress, from an overload of work, for example, or from the loss of a family member or close friend. The attacks may also follow surgery, a serious accident, illness, or childbirth. Excessive consumption of caffeine or use of cocaine or other stimulant drugs or medicines, such as the stimulants used in treating asthma, can also trigger panic attacks.

Nevertheless panic attacks usually take a person completely by surprise. This unpredictability is one reason they are so devastating.

Sometimes people who have never had a panic attack assume that panic is just a matter of feeling nervous or anxious—the sort of feelings that everyone is familiar with. In fact, even though people who have panic attacks may not show any outward signs of discomfort, the feelings they experience are so overwhelming and terrifying that they really believe they are going to die, lose their minds, or be totally humiliated. These disastrous consequences don't occur, but they seem quite likely to the person who is suffering a panic attack.

Some people who have one panic attack, or an occasional attack, never develop a problem serious enough to affect their lives. For others, however, the attacks continue and cause much suffering.

Panic Disorder

In panic disorder, panic attacks recur and the person develops an intense apprehension of having another attack. As noted earlier, this fear—called *anticipatory anxiety* or *fear of fear*—can be present most of the time and seriously interfere with the person's life even when a panic attack is not in progress. In addition, the person may develop irrational fears called phobias about situations where a panic attack has occurred. For example, someone who has had a panic attack while driving may be afraid to get behind the wheel again, even to drive to the grocery store.

People who develop these panic-induced phobias will tend to avoid situations that they fear will trigger a panic attack, and their lives may be increasingly limited as a result. Their work may suffer because they can't travel or get to work on time. Relationships may be strained or marred by conflict as panic attacks, or the fear of them, rule the affected person and those close to them.

Also, sleep may be disturbed because of panic attacks that occur at night, causing the person to awaken in a state of terror. The experience is so harrowing that some people who have nocturnal panic attacks become afraid to go to sleep and suffer from exhaustion. Also, even if there are no nocturnal panic attacks, sleep may be disturbed because of chronic, panic-related anxiety.

Many people with panic disorder remain intensely concerned about their symptoms even after an initial visit to a physician yields no indication of a life-threatening condition. They may visit a succession of doctors seeking medical treatment for what they believe is heart disease or a respiratory problem. Or their symptoms may make them think they have a neurological disorder or some serious gastrointestinal condition. Some patients see as many as 10 doctors and undergo a succession of expensive and unnecessary tests in the effort to find out what is causing their symptoms.

This search for medical help may continue a long time, because physicians who see these patients frequently fail to diagnose panic disorder. When doctors do recognize the condition, they sometimes explain it in terms that suggest it is of no importance or not treatable. For example, the doctor may say, "There's nothing to worry about, you're just having a panic attack," or "It's just nerves." Although meant to be reassuring, such words can be dispiriting to the worried patient whose symptoms keep recurring. The patient needs to know that the doctor acknowledges the disabling nature of panic disorder and that it can be treated effectively.

Agoraphobia

Panic disorder may progress to a more advanced stage in which the person becomes afraid of being in any place or situation where escape might be difficult or help unavailable in the event of a panic attack. This condition is called *agoraphobia*. It affects about a third of all people with panic disorder.

Typically, people with agoraphobia fear being in crowds, standing in line, entering shopping malls, and riding in cars or public transportation. Often, these people restrict themselves to a "zone of safety" that may include only the home or the immediate neighborhood. Any movement beyond the edges of this zone creates mounting anxiety. Sometimes a person with agoraphobia is unable to leave home alone, but can travel if accompanied by a particular family member or friend. Even when they restrict themselves to "safe" situations, most people with agoraphobia continue to have panic attacks at least a few times a month.

People with agoraphobia can be seriously disabled by their condition. Some are unable to work, and they may need to rely heavily on other family members, who must do the shopping and run all the household errands, as well as accompany the affected person on rare excursions outside the "safety zone." Thus the person with agoraphobia typically leads a life of extreme dependency as well as great discomfort.

Treatment for Panic Disorder

Treatment can bring significant relief to 70 to 90 percent of people with panic disorder, and early treatment can help keep the disease from progressing to the later stages where agoraphobia develops.

Before undergoing any treatment for panic disorder, a person should undergo a thorough medical examination to rule out other possible causes of the distressing symptoms. This is necessary because a number of other conditions, such as excessive levels of thyroid hormone, certain types of epilepsy, or cardiac arrhythmias, which are disturbances in the rhythm of the heartbeat, can cause symptoms resembling those of panic disorder.

Several effective treatments have been developed for panic disorder and agoraphobia. In 1991, a conference held at the National Institutes of Health (NIH) under the sponsorship of the National Institute of Mental Health and the Office of Medical Applications of Research, surveyed the available information on panic disorder and its treatment. The conferees concluded that a form of psychotherapy called cognitive-behavioral therapy and medications are both effective for panic disorder. A treatment should be selected according to the individual needs and preferences of the patient, the panel said, and any treatment that fails to produce an effect within 6 to 8 weeks should be reassessed.

Cognitive-Behavioral Therapy

This is a combination of *cognitive therapy*, which can modify or eliminate thought patterns contributing to the patient's symptoms, and *behavioral therapy*, which aims to help the patient to change his or her behavior.

Typically the patient undergoing cognitive-behavioral therapy meets with a therapist for 1 to 3 hours a week. In the cognitive portion of the therapy, the therapist usually conducts a careful search for the thoughts and feelings that accompany the panic attacks. These mental events are discussed in terms of the "cognitive model" of panic attacks.

The cognitive model states that individuals with panic disorder often have distortions in their thinking, of which they may be unaware, and these may give rise to a cycle of fear. The cycle is believed to operate this way: First the individual feels a potentially worrisome sensation such as an increasing heart rate, tightened chest muscles, or a queasy stomach. This sensation may be triggered by some worry, an unpleasant mental image, a minor illness, or even exercise. The person with panic disorder responds to the sensation by becoming anxious. The initial anxiety triggers still more unpleasant sensations, which in turn heighten anxiety, giving rise to catastrophic thoughts. The person thinks "I am having a heart attack" or "I am going insane," or some similar thought. As the vicious cycle continues, a panic attack results. The whole cycle might take only a few seconds, and the individual may not be aware of the initial sensations or thoughts.

Proponents of this theory point out that, with the help of a skilled therapist, people with panic disorder often can learn to recognize the earliest thoughts and feelings in this sequence and modify their responses to them. Patients are taught that typical thoughts such as "That terrible feeling is getting worse!" or "I'm going to have a panic attack" or "I'm going to have a heart attack" can be replaced with substitutes such as "It's only uneasiness—it will pass" that help to reduce anxiety and ward off a panic attack. Specific procedures for accomplishing this are taught. By modifying thought patterns in this way, the patient gains more control over the problem.

Often the therapist will provide the patient with simple guidelines to follow when he or she can feel that a panic attack is approaching.

In cognitive therapy, discussions between the patient and the therapist are not usually focused on the patient's past, as is the case with some forms of psychotherapy. Instead, conversations focus on the difficulties and successes the patient is having at the present time, and on skills the patient needs to learn.

The behavioral portion of cognitive-behavioral therapy may involve systematic training in relaxation techniques. By learning to relax, the patient may acquire the ability to reduce generalized anxiety and stress that often sets the stage for panic attacks.

Breathing exercises are often included in the behavioral therapy. The patient learns to control his or her breathing and avoid *hyperventilation*—a pattern of rapid, shallow breathing that can trigger or exacerbate some people's panic attacks.

Another important aspect of behavioral therapy is exposure to internal sensations called *interoceptive exposure*. During interoceptive exposure the therapist will do an individual assessment of internal sensations associated with panic. Depending on the assessment, the therapist may then encourage the patient to bring on some of the sensations of a panic attack by, for example, exercising to increase heart rate, breathing rapidly to trigger lightheadedness and respiratory symptoms, or spinning around to trigger dizziness. Exercises to produce feelings of unreality may also be used. Then the therapist teaches the patient to cope effectively with these sensations and to replace alarmist thoughts such as "I am going to die," with more appropriate ones, such as "It's just a little dizziness—I can handle it."

Another important aspect of behavioral therapy is *"in vivo"* or *real-life exposure*. The therapist and the patient determine whether the patient has been avoiding particular places and situations, and which patterns of avoidance are causing the patient problems. They agree to work on the avoidance behaviors that are most seriously interfering with the patient's life. For example, fear of driving may be of paramount importance for one patient, while inability to go to the grocery store may be most handicapping for another.

Some therapists will go to an agoraphobic patient's home to conduct the initial sessions. Often therapists take their patients on excursions to shopping malls and other places the patients have been avoiding. Or they may accompany their patients who are trying to overcome fear of driving a car.

The patient approaches a feared situation gradually, attempting to stay in spite of rising levels of anxiety. In this way the patient sees that as frightening as the feelings are, they are not dangerous, and they do pass. On each attempt, the patient faces as much fear as he or she can stand. Patients find that with this step-by-step approach, aided by encouragement and skilled advice from the therapist, they can gradually master their fears and enter situations that had seemed unapproachable.

Many therapists assign the patient "homework" to do between sessions. Sometimes patients spend only a few sessions in one-on-one contact with a therapist and continue to work on their own with the aid of a printed manual.

Often the patient will join a therapy group with others striving to overcome panic disorder or phobias, meeting with them weekly to discuss progress, exchange encouragement, and receive guidance from the therapist.

Cognitive-behavioral therapy generally requires at least 8 to 12 weeks. Some people may need a longer time in treatment to learn and implement the skills. This kind of therapy, which is reported to have a low relapse rate, is effective in eliminating panic attacks or reducing their frequency. It also reduces anticipatory anxiety and the avoidance of feared situations.

Treatment with Medications

In this treatment approach, which is also called *pharmaco-therapy*, a prescription medication is used both to prevent panic attacks or reduce their frequency and severity, and to decrease the associated anticipatory anxiety. When patients find that their panic attacks are less frequent and severe, they are increasingly able to venture into situations that had been off-limits to them. In this way, they benefit from exposure to previously feared situations as well as from the medication.

The three groups of medications most commonly used are the *tricyclic antidepressants*, the *high-potency benzodiazepines*, and the *monoamine oxidase inhibitors* (MAOIs). Determination of which drug to use is based on considerations of safety, efficacy, and the personal needs and preferences of the patient. Some information about each of the classes of drugs follows.

The tricyclic antidepressants were the first medications shown to have a beneficial effect against panic disorder. Imipramine is the tricyclic most commonly used for this condition. When imipramine is prescribed, the patient usually starts with small daily doses that are increased every few days until an effective dosage is reached. The slow introduction of imipramine helps minimize side effects such as dry mouth, constipation, and blurred vision. People with panic disorder, who are inclined to be hypervigilant about physical sensations, often find these side effects disturbing at the outset. Side effects usually fade after the patient has been on the medication a few weeks.

It usually takes several weeks for imipramine to have a beneficial effect on panic disorder. Most patients treated with imipramine will be panic-free within a few weeks or months. Treatment generally lasts from 6 to 12 months. Treatment for a shorter period of time is possible, but there is substantial risk that when imipramine is stopped, panic attacks will recur. Extending the period of treatment to 6 months to a year may reduce this risk of a relapse. When the treatment period is complete, the dosage of imipramine is tapered over a period of several weeks.

The high-potency benzodiazepines are a class of medications that effectively reduce anxiety. Alprazolam, clonazepam, and lorazepam are medications that belong to this class. They take effect rapidly, have few bothersome side-effects, and are well tolerated by the majority of patients. However, some patients, especially those who have had problems with alcohol or drug dependency, may become dependent on benzodiazepines.

Generally, the physician prescribing one of these drugs starts the patient on a low dose and gradually raises it until panic attacks cease. This procedure minimizes side effects.

Treatment with high-potency benzodiazepines is usually continued for 6 months to a year. One drawback of these medications is that patients may experience withdrawal symptoms—malaise, weakness, and other unpleasant effects—when the treatment is discontinued. Reducing the dose gradually generally minimizes these problems. There may also be a recurrence of panic attacks after the medication is withdrawn.

Of the MAOIs, a class of antidepressants which have been shown to be effective against panic disorder, phenelzine is the most commonly used. Treatment with phenelzine usually starts with a relatively low daily dosage that is increased gradually until panic attacks cease or the patient reaches a maximum dosage of about 100 milligrams a day.

Use of phenelzine or any other MAOI requires the patient to observe exacting dietary restrictions, because there are foods and prescription drugs and certain substances of abuse that can interact with the MAOI to cause a sudden, dangerous rise in blood pressure. All patients who are taking MAOIs should obtain their physician's guidance concerning dietary restrictions and should consult with their physician before using any over-the-counter or prescription medications.

As in the case of the high-potency benzodiazepines and imipramine, treatment with phenelzine or another MAOI generally lasts 6 months to a year. At the conclusion of the treatment period, the medication is gradually tapered.

Newly available antidepressants such as fluoxetine (one of a class of new agents called serotonin reuptake inhibitors), appear to be effective in selected cases of panic disorder. As with other anti-panic medications, it is important to start with very small doses and gradually raise the dosage.

Scientists supported by NIMH are seeking ways to improve drug treatment for panic disorder. Studies are underway to determine the optimal duration of treatment with medications, who they are most likely to help, and how to moderate problems associated with withdrawal.

Combination Treatments

Many believe that a combination of medication and cognitive-behavioral therapy represents the best alternative for the treatment of panic disorder. The combined approach is said to offer rapid relief, high effectiveness, and a low relapse rate. However, there is a need for more research studies to determine whether this is in fact the case.

Comparing medications and psychological treatments, and determining how well they work in combination, is the goal of several NIMH-supported studies. The largest of these is a 4-year clinical trial that will include 480 patients and involve four centers at the State University of New York at Albany, Cornell University, Hillside Hospital/Columbia University, and Yale University. This study is designed to determine how treatment with imipramine compares with a cognitive-behavioral approach, and whether combining the two yields benefits over either method alone.

Psychodynamic Treatment

This is a form of "talk therapy" in which the therapist and the patient, working together, seek to uncover emotional conflicts that may underlie the patient's problems. By talking about these conflicts and gaining a better understanding of them, the patient is helped to overcome the problems. Often, psychodynamic treatment focuses on events of the past and making the patient aware of the ramifications of long-buried problems.

Although psychodynamic approaches may help to relieve the stress that contributes to panic attacks, they do not seem to stop the attacks directly. In fact, there is no scientific evidence that this form of therapy by itself is effective in helping people to overcome panic disorder or agoraphobia. However, if a patient's panic disorder occurs along with some broader and pre-existing emotional disturbance, psychodynamic treatment may be a helpful addition to the overall treatment program.

When Panic Recurs

Panic disorder is often a chronic, relapsing illness. For many people, it gets better at some times and worse at others. If a person gets treatment, and appears to have largely overcome the problem, it can still worsen later for no apparent reason. These recurrences should not cause a person to despair or consider himself or herself a "treatment failure." Recurrences can be treated effectively, just like an initial episode.

In fact, the skills that a person learns in dealing with the initial episode can be helpful in coping with any setbacks. Many people who have overcome panic disorder once or a few times find that, although they still have an occasional panic attack, they are now much better able to deal with the problem. Even though it is not fully cured, it no longer dominates their lives, or the lives of those around them.

Coexisting Conditions

At the NIH conference on panic disorder, the panel recommended that patients be carefully evaluated for other conditions that may be present along with panic disorder. These may influence the choice of treatment, the panel noted. Among the conditions that are frequently found to coexist with panic disorder are:

Simple Phobias. People with panic disorder often develop irrational fears of specific events or situations that they associate with the possibility of having a panic attack. Fear of heights and fear of crossing bridges are examples of simple phobias. Generally, these fears can be resolved through repeated exposure to the dreaded situations, while practicing specific cognitive-behavioral techniques to become less sensitive to them.

Social Phobia. This is a persistent dread of situations in which the person is exposed to possible scrutiny by others and fears acting in a way that will be embarrassing or humiliating. Social phobia can be treated effectively with cognitive-behavioral therapy or medications, or both.

Depression. About half of panic disorder patients will have an episode of clinical depression sometime during their lives. Major depression is marked by persistent sadness or feelings of emptiness, a sense of hopelessness, and other symptoms.

When major depression occurs, it can be treated effectively with one of several antidepressant drugs, or, depending on its severity, by cognitive-behavioral therapies. [See Chapter 10 for more information about depression].

Obsessive-Compulsive Disorder (OCD). In OCD, a person becomes trapped in a pattern of repetitive thoughts and behaviors that are senseless and distressing but extremely difficult to overcome. Such rituals as counting, prolonged handwashing, and repeatedly checking for danger may occupy much of the person's time and interfere with other activities. Today, OCD can be treated effectively with medications or cognitive-behavioral therapies.

Alcohol Abuse. About 30 percent of people with panic disorder abuse alcohol. A person who has alcoholism in addition to panic disorder needs specialized care for the alcoholism along with treatment for the panic disorder. Often the alcoholism will be treated first.

Drug Abuse. As in the case of alcoholism, drug abuse is more common in people with panic disorder than in the population at large. In fact, about 17 percent of people with panic disorder abuse drugs. The drug problems often need to be addressed prior to treatment for panic disorder.

Suicidal Tendencies. Recent studies in the general population have suggested that suicide attempts are more common among people who have panic attacks than among those who do not have a mental disorder. Also, it appears that people who have both panic disorder and depression are at elevated risk for suicide. (However, anxiety disorder experts who have treated many patients emphasize that it is extremely unlikely that anyone would attempt to harm himself or herself during a panic attack.)

Anyone who is considering suicide needs immediate attention from a mental health professional or from a school counselor, physician, or member of the clergy. With appropriate help and treatment, it is possible to overcome suicidal tendencies.

There are also certain physical conditions that are often associated with panic disorder:

Irritable Bowel Syndrome. The person with this syndrome experiences intermittent bouts of gastrointestinal cramps and diarrhea or constipation, often occurring during a period of stress. Because the symptoms are so pronounced, panic disorder is often not diagnosed when it occurs in a person with irritable bowel syndrome.

Mitral Valve Prolapse. This condition involves a defect in the mitral valve, which separates the two chambers on the left side of the heart. Each time the heart muscle contracts in people with this condition, tissue in the mitral valve is pushed for an instant into the wrong chamber. The person with the disorder may experience chest pain, rapid heartbeat, breathing difficulties, and headache. People with mitral valve prolapse may be at higher than usual risk of having panic disorder, but many experts are not convinced this apparent association is real.

Causes of Panic Disorder

The National Institute of Mental Health supports a sizable and multifaceted research program on panic disorder—its causes, diagnosis, treatment, and prevention. This research involves studies of panic disorder in human subjects and investigations of the biological basis for anxiety and related phenomena in animals. It is part of a massive effort to overcome the major mental disorders, an effort that is taking place during the 1990s—the Decade of the Brain. Here is a description of some of the most important new research on panic disorder and its causes.

Genetics

Panic disorder runs in families. One study has shown that if one twin in a genetically identical pair has panic disorder, it is likely that the other twin will also. Fraternal, or non-identical, twin pairs do not show this high degree of "concordance" with respect to panic disorder. Thus, it appears that some genetic factor, in combination with environment, may be responsible for vulnerability to this condition.

NIMH-supported scientists are studying families in which several individuals have panic disorder. The aim of these studies is to identify the specific gene or genes involved in the condition. Identification of these genes may lead to new approaches for diagnosing and treating panic disorder.

Brain and Biochemical Abnormalities

One line of evidence suggests that panic disorder may be associated with increased activity in the hippocampus and locus ceruleus, portions of the brain that monitor external and internal stimuli and control the brain's responses to them. Also, it has been shown that panic disorder patients have increased activity in a portion of the nervous system called the adrenergic system, which regulates such physiological functions as heart rate and body temperature. However, it is not clear whether these increases reflect the anxiety symptoms or whether they cause them.

Another group of studies suggests that people with panic disorder may have abnormalities in their benzodiazepine receptors, brain components that react with anxiety-reducing substances within the brain.

In conducting their research, scientists can use several different techniques to provoke panic attacks in people who have panic disorder. The best known method is intravenous administration of sodium lactate, the same chemical that normally builds up in the muscles during heavy exercise. Other substances that can trigger panic attacks in susceptible people include caffeine (generally 5 or more cups of coffee are required). Hyperventilation and breathing air with a higher-than-usual level of carbon dioxide can also trigger panic attacks in people with panic disorder.

Because these provocations generally do *not* trigger panic attacks in people who do *not* have panic disorder, scientists have inferred that individuals who have panic disorder are biologically different in some way from people who do not. However, it is also true that when the people prone to panic attacks are told in advance about the sensations these provocations will cause, they are much less likely to panic. This suggests that there is a strong psychological component, as well as a biological one, to panic disorder.

NIMH-supported investigators are examining specific parts of the brain and central nervous system to learn which ones play a role in panic disorder, and how they may interact to give rise to this condition. Other studies funded by the Institute are under way to determine what happens during "provoked" panic attacks, and to investigate the role of breathing irregularities in anxiety and panic attacks.

Animal Studies

Studies of anxiety in animals are providing NIMH-sponsored researchers with clues to the underlying causes of this phenomenon. One series of studies involves an inbred line of pointer dogs that exhibit extreme, abnormal fearfulness when approached by humans or startled by loud noises. In contrast with normal pointers, these nervous dogs have been found to react more strongly to caffeine and to have brain tissue that is richer in receptors for adenosine, a naturally occurring sedative that normally exerts a calming effect within the brain. Further study of these animals is expected to reveal how a genetic predisposition toward anxiety is expressed in the brain.

Other animal studies involve macaque monkeys. Some of these animals exhibit anxiety when challenged with an infusion of lactate, much like people with panic disorder. Other macaques do not exhibit this response. NIMH-supported scientists are attempting to determine how the brains of the responsive and non-responsive monkeys differ. This research should provide additional information on the causes of panic disorder.

In addition, research with rats is exploring the effect of various medications on the parts of the brain involved in anxiety. The aim is to develop a clearer picture of which components of the brain are responsible for anxiety, and to learn how their actions can be brought under better control.

Cognitive Factors

Scientists funded by NIMH are investigating the basic thought processes and emotions that come into play during a panic attack and those that contribute to the development and persistence of agoraphobia. The Institute also supports research evaluating the impact of various versions of cognitive-behavioral therapy to determine which variants of the procedure are effective for which people. The NIMH panic disorder research program will also explore the effects of interpersonal stress such as marital conflict on panic disorder with agoraphobia and determine if including spouses in the cognitive-behavioral treatment of the condition improves outcome.

Finding Help for Panic Disorder

Often the person with panic disorder must undertake a strenuous search to find a therapist who is familiar with the most effective treatments for the condition. A list of places to start follows. The Anxiety Disorders Association of America can provide a list of professionals in your area who specialize in the treatment of panic disorder and other anxiety disorders.

Self-help and *support groups* are the least expensive approach to managing panic disorder, and are helpful for some people. A group of about 5 to 10 people meet weekly and share their experiences, encouraging each other to venture into feared situations and cope effectively with panic attacks. Group members are in charge of the sessions. Often family members are invited to attend these groups, and at times a therapist or other panic disorder expert may be brought in to share insights with group members. Information on self-help groups in specific areas of the country can be obtained from the Anxiety Disorders Association of America.

Sources of Referral to Professional Help for Panic Disorder

Here are the types of people and places that will make a referral to, or provide, diagnostic and treatment services for a person with symptoms resembling those described in this text. Also check the Yellow Pages under "mental health," "health," "anxiety," "suicide prevention," "hospitals," "physicians," "psychiatrists," "psychologists," or "social workers" for phone numbers and addresses.

- Family doctors
- Mental health specialists, such as psychiatrists, psychologists, social workers, or mental health counselors
- Health maintenance organizations
- Community mental health centers
- Hospital psychiatry departments and outpatient clinics
- University- or medical school-affiliated programs and clinics
- State hospital outpatient clinics
- Family service/social agencies
- Private clinics and facilities
- Employee assistance programs
- Local medical, psychiatric, or psychological societies

Help for the Family

When one member of a family has panic disorder, the entire family is affected by the condition. Family members may be frustrated in their attempts to help the affected member cope with the disorder, overburdened by taking on additional responsibilities, and socially isolated. Family members must encourage the person with panic disorder to seek the help of a qualified mental health professional. Also, it is often helpful for family members to attend an occasional treatment or self-help session or seek the guidance of the therapist in dealing with their feelings about the disorder.

Certain strategies, such as encouraging the person with panic disorder to go at least partway toward a place or situation that is feared, can be helpful. By their skilled and caring efforts to help, family members can aid the person with panic disorder in making a recovery.

Also, it may be valuable for family members to join or form a support group to share information and offer mutual encouragement.

Acknowledgments

[The preceding text] was written by Mary Lynn Hendrix, science writer in the Office of Scientific Information, National Institute of Mental Health.

Panic Disorder Resource List

[The following lists were compiled from documents produced by the National Institute of Mental Health.] Please consult the appropriate organization listed to obtain copies of these materials. Further information on panic disorder can be found at libraries and book stores.

Books

Anxiety Disorders Association of America. *National Professional Membership Directory*. 1992.

Babior, S., and Goldman, C. *Overcoming Panic Attacks: Strategies to Free Yourself from the Anxiety Trap*. Duluth, MN: Pfeifer-Hamilton Publishers/Whole Person Associates, 1990.

Barlow, D.H., and Craske, M.G. *Mastery of Your Anxiety and Panic*. (A workbook) Albany, NY: Graywind Publications, 1988.

Beck, A.T., and Emery, G. *Anxiety Disorders and Phobias: A Cognitive Perspective*. New York: Basic Books, 1985.

Beckfield, D.F. *Master Your Panic... and Take Back Your Life!* San Luis Obispo, CA: Impact Publishers, 1994.

Bourne, E.J. *The Anxiety and Phobia Workbook*. Oakland, CA: New Harbinger, 1991.

Gold, M.S. *The Good News About Panic, Anxiety, and Phobias*. New York: Bantam Books, 1989.

Greist, J.H., and Jefferson, J.W. *Panic Disorder and Agoraphobia: A Guide*. Madison, WI: Anxiety Disorders Center and Information Centers, University of Wisconsin, 1992.

Hecker, J.E., and Thorpe, G.L. *Agoraphobia and Panic: A Guide to Psychological Treatment*. Needham Heights, MA: Allyn and Bacon, 1992.

Kernodle, W.D. *Panic Disorder: What You Don't Know May Be Dangerous to Your Health*. 2d ed. Richmond, VA: William Byrd Press, 1993.

Mathews, A.M.; Gelder, M.G.; and Johnston, D.W. *Agoraphobia: Nature and Treatment*. New York and London: Guilford Press, 1981.

Penzer, W.N., and Goodman, B. *You Have Choices: Recovering from Anxiety, Panic, Phobia*. Plantation, FL: Esperance Publishing Company, 1991.

Peurifoy, R.Z. *Anxiety, Phobias, and Panic*. (A workbook) Citrus Heights, CA: Lifeskills, 1992.

Sheehan, D.V. *The Anxiety Disease*. New York: Bantam, 1986.

Ross, J. *Triumph Over Fear: A Book of Help and Hope for People with Anxeity, Panic Attacks and Phobias*. New York: Bantam, 1994.

Wilson, R.R. *Don't Panic: Taking Control of Anxiety Attacks*. New York: Perennial Library (Division of Harper and Row), 1986.

Pamphlets and Other Publications

American Counseling Association. *Seeking Help for Life's Challenges. What is Counseling?*

American Psychiatric Association. *Let's Talk Facts About Panic Disorder*.

American Psychological Association. *How Do I Know if I Have a Panic Disorder?*; *How to Choose a Psychotherapist*.

Anxiety Disorders Association of America. *Panic and Agoraphobia*; *Phobias*; *Social Phobia*; *Breaking the Panic Cycle*.

Association for the Advancement of Behavior Therapy. *Guidelines for Choosing a Behavior Therapist*.

National Alliance for the Mentally Ill. *Panic Disorder*.

National Anxiety Foundation. *Panic Disorder: A Highly Treatable Disorder*.

National Institute of Mental Health. *Panic Disorder*; *Understanding Panic Disorder*; *Getting Treatment for Panic Disorder: Information for Patients, Families, and Friends*; *A Consumer's Guide to Mental Health Services*; *Medications*; *You Are Not Alone: Facts About Mental Health and Mental Illness*; and *NIH / NIMH Consensus Development Conference Statement, Vol. 9, No. 2, Treatment of Panic Disorder*, September 1991. For information on depression, which often co-occurs with panic disorder, call 1-800-421-4211.

National Mental Health Association. *Fact Sheets on Panic.*
The National Panic/Anxiety Disorder Newsletter.
Pathway Systems. *Panic Attack: What It Is and How to Handle It.*

Videotapes

American Academy of Family Physicians. "Managing Anxiety Disorders."

American Psychiatric Association. "Panic Disorder: Diagnosis, Treatment, and Management"; and "Anxiety Disorders in Primary Care: A New Approach to Diagnosis and Management." And for lay audiences, "The Panic Prison," a 28 1/2-minute videotape that is part of a series of APA "Let's Talk About Mental Illness" public awareness film packages.

National Institute of Mental Health. "Panic Disorder: Stories of Hope." For professional and lay audiences. This 20-minute video, introduced by Willard Scott, profiles three people with panic disorder and their journeys to recovery. The video can be purchased from Modern Talking Picture Service, Inc., 5000 Park Street, North, St. Petersburg, FL 33709; (813) 541-7571. Cost is $14.50. Residents of CA, FL, IL, NY, and Washington, DC, must add state and local taxes.

Science and Medicine. "Anxiety Profiles: New Perspectives for Diagnosis and Treatment."

Organizations to Contact for More Information about Panic Disorder and Related Conditions, Referrals, and Self-Help Groups

A.I. M. (Agoraphobics in Motion)
1729 Crooks St.
Royal Oak, MI 48067-1306
(810) 547-0400

American Academy of Child and Adolescent Psychiatry
3615 Wisconsin Ave., N.W.
Washington, DC 20016
(202) 966-7300

American Academy of Family Physicians
8880 Ward Parkway
Kansas City, MO 64114
(816) 333-9700

American Counseling Association
5999 Stevenson Ave.
Alexandria, VA 22304
(703) 823-9800

American Psychiatric Association
1400 K St., N.W.
Washington, D.C. 20005
(202) 682-6220

American Psychological Association
750 First St., NE
Washington, D.C. 20002
(202) 336-5500

American Self-Help Clearinghouse
St. Clares-Riverside Medical Center
25 Pocono Rd.
Denville, NJ 07834
(800) 367-6274 (in NJ)
(201) 625-9565 (outside NJ)

Anxiety Disorders Association of America
6000 Executive Blvd., Suite 513
Rockville, MD 208524004
(301) 231-8368

Association for the Advancement of Behavior Therapy
305 Seventh Ave.
New York, NY 10001
(212) 647-1890

Freedom from Fear
308 Seaview Ave.
Staten Island, NY 10305
(718) 351-1717

National Alliance for the Mentally Ill
2101 Wilson Blvd., Suite 302
Arlington, VA 22201
(800) 950-NAMI

National Anxiety Foundation
3135 Custer Drive
Lexington, KY 40517-4001
(800) 755-1576

National Association of Social Workers (NASW)
Clinical Registrar Office
750 First St., N.E., Suite 700
Washington.,DC 20002-4241
(800) 638-8799

National Depressive and Manic Depressive Association (NDMDA)
53 West Jackson Builevard, Suite 618
Chicago, IL 60601
(800) 82N-DMDA

National Institute of Mental Health (NIMH)
5600 Fishers Lane
Rockville, MD 20857
(301) 443-4513
(800) 64-PANIC

National Mental Health Association (NMHA)
1021 Prince St.
Alexandria, VA 22314-2971
(703) 684-7722
(800) 969-NMHA

National Mental Health Consumers' Self-Help Clearinghouse
311 South Juniper St., Suite 1000
Philadelphia, PA 19107
(800) 553-4539 or
(215) 735-6082

National Panic/Anxiety Disorder Newsletter
1718 Burgandy Place
Santa Rosa, CA 95403
(707) 527-5738

Pathway Systems
P.O. Box 269
Chapel Hill, NC 27514
(800) 394-2299

Phobics Anonymous
P.O. Box 1180
Palm Springs, CA 92263
(619) 322-COPE

Recovery, Inc.
802 N. Dearborn St.
Chicago, IL 60610
(312) 337-5661

Science and Medicine
79 Madison Ave.
New York, NY 10016-7880
(212) 213-7144

Chapter 19

Obsessive-Compulsive Disorder

What Is OCD?

Obsessive-compulsive disorder (OCD), one of the anxiety disorders, is a potentially disabling condition that can persist throughout a person's life. The individual who suffers from OCD becomes trapped in a pattern of repetitive thoughts and behaviors that are senseless and distressing but extremely difficult to overcome. OCD occurs in a spectrum from mild to severe, but if severe and left untreated, can destroy a person's capacity to function at work, at school, or even in the home.

How Common Is OCD?

For many years, mental health professionals thought of OCD as a rare disease because only a small minority of their patients had the condition. The disorder often went unrecognized because many of those afflicted with OCD, in efforts to keep their repetitive thoughts and behaviors secret, failed to seek treatment. This led to underestimates of the number of people with the illness. However, a survey conducted in the early 1980s by the National Institute of Mental Health (NIMH)—the Federal agency that supports research nationwide on the brain, mental illnesses, and mental health—provided new knowledge about the prevalence of OCD. The NIMH survey showed that OCD affects more than 2 percent of the population, meaning that

NIH Pub. No. 94-3755.

OCD is more common than such severe mental illnesses as schizophrenia, bipolar disorder, or panic disorder. OCD strikes people of all ethnic groups. Males and females are equally affected. The social and economic costs of OCD were estimated to be $8.4 billion in 1990 (DuPont et al, 1994).

Although OCD symptoms typically begin during the teenage years or early adulthood, recent research shows that some children develop the illness at earlier ages, even during the preschool years. Studies indicate that at least one-third of cases of OCD in adults began in childhood. Suffering from OCD during early stages of a child's development can cause severe problems for the child. It is important that the child receive evaluation and treatment by a knowledgeable clinician to prevent the child from missing important opportunities because of this disorder.

Key Features of OCD

Obsessions

These are unwanted ideas or impulses that repeatedly well up in the mind of the person with OCD. Persistent fears that harm may come to self or a loved one, an unreasonable belief that one has a terrible illness, or an excessive need to do things correctly or perfectly, are common. Again and again, the individual experiences a disturbing thought, such as, "My hands may be contaminated—I must wash them"; "I may have left the gas on"; or "I am going to injure my child." These thoughts are intrusive, unpleasant, and produce a high degree of anxiety. Often the obsessions are of a violent or a sexual nature, or concern illness.

Compulsions

In response to their obsessions, most people with OCD resort to repetitive behaviors called compulsions. The most common of these are washing and checking. Other compulsive behaviors include counting (often while performing another compulsive action such as hand washing), repeating, hoarding, and endlessly rearranging objects in an effort to keep them in precise alignment with each other. These behaviors generally are intended to ward off harm to the person with OCD or others. Some people with OCD have regimented rituals while others have rituals that are complex and changing. Performing rituals may give the person with OCD some relief from anxiety, but it is only temporary.

Insight

People with OCD usually have considerable insight into their own problems. Most of the time, they know that their obsessive thoughts are senseless or exaggerated, and that their compulsive behaviors are not really necessary. However, this knowledge is not sufficient to enable them to stop obsessing or the carrying out of rituals.

Resistance

Most people with OCD struggle to banish their unwanted, obsessive thoughts and to prevent themselves from engaging in compulsive behaviors. Many are able to keep their obsessive-compulsive symptoms under control during the hours when they are at work or attending school. But over the months or years, resistance may weaken, and when this happens, OCD may become so severe that time-consuming rituals take over the sufferers' lives, making it impossible for them to continue activities outside the home.

Shame and Secrecy

OCD sufferers often attempt to hide their disorder rather than seek help. Often they are successful in concealing their obsessive-compulsive symptoms from friends and coworkers. An unfortunate consequence of this secrecy is that people with OCD usually do not receive professional help until years after the onset of their disease. By that time, they may have learned to work their lives—and family members' lives—around the rituals.

Long-lasting Symptoms

OCD tends to last for years, even decades. The symptoms may become less severe from time to time, and there may be long intervals when the symptoms are mild, but for most individuals with OCD, the symptoms are chronic.

What Causes OCD?

The old belief that OCD was the result of life experiences has given way before the growing evidence that biological factors are a primary contributor to the disorder. The fact that OCD patients respond well to specific medications that affect the neurotransmitter serotonin suggests the disorder has a neurobiological basis. For that reason, OCD is no longer attributed to attitudes a patient learned in childhood—for example, an inordinate emphasis on cleanliness, or a belief that certain thoughts are dangerous or unacceptable. Instead, the search for causes now focuses on the interaction of neurobiological factors and environmental influences.

OCD is sometimes accompanied by depression, eating disorders, substance abuse disorder, a personality disorder, attention deficit disorder, or another of the anxiety disorders. Co-existing disorders can make OCD more difficult both to diagnose and to treat.

In an effort to identify specific biological factors that may be important in the onset or persistence of OCD, NIMH-supported investigators have used a device called the positron emission tomography (PET) scanner to study the brains of patients with OCD. Several groups of investigators have obtained findings from PET scans suggesting that OCD patients have patterns of brain activity that differ from those of people without mental illness or with some other mental illness. Brain-imaging studies of OCD showing abnormal neurochemical activity in regions known to play a role in certain neurological disorders suggest that these areas may be crucial in the origins of OCD. There is also evidence that medications and cognitive/behavior therapy induce changes in the brain coincident with clinical improvement.

Symptoms of OCD are seen in association with some other neurological disorders. There is an increased rate of OCD in people with Tourette's syndrome, an illness characterized by involuntary movements and vocalizations. Investigators are currently studying the hypothesis that a genetic relationship exists between OCD and the tic disorders. Another illness that may be linked to OCD is trichotillomania (the repeated urge to pull out scalp hair, eyelashes, or eyebrows). Genetic studies of OCD and other related conditions may enable scientists to pinpoint the molecular basis of these disorders.

Do I Have OCD?

A person with OCD has obsessive and compulsive behaviors that are extreme enough to interfere with everyday life. People with OCD should not be confused with a much larger group of individuals who are sometimes called "compulsive" because they hold themselves to a high standard of performance and are perfectionistic and very organized in their work and even in recreational activities. This type of "compulsiveness" often serves a valuable purpose, contributing to a person's self-esteem and success on the job. In that respect, it differs from the life-wrecking obsessions and rituals of the person with OCD.

Treatment of OCD; Progress Through Research

Clinical and animal research sponsored by NIMH and other scientific organizations has provided information leading to both pharmacologic and behavioral treatments that can benefit the person with OCD. A combination of the two therapies is often an effective method of treatment for most patients. Some individuals respond best to one therapy, some to another.

Pharmacotherapy

Clinical trials in recent years have shown that drugs that affect the neurotransmitter serotonin can significantly decrease the symptoms of OCD. Two serotonin reuptake inhibitors (SRIs), clomipramine (Anafranil®) and fluoxetine (Prozac®), have been approved by the Food and Drug Administration for the treatment of OCD. Other SRIs that have been studied in controlled clinical trials include sertraline (Zoloft®) and fluvoxamine (Luvox®). Paroxetine (Paxil®) is also being used. All these SRIs have proved effective in treatment of OCD. If a patient does not respond well to one SRI, another SRI may give a better response. For patients who are only partially responsive to these medications, research is being conducted on the use of an SRI as the primary medication and one of a variety of medications as an additional drug (an augmenter). Medications are of great help in controlling the symptoms of OCD, but often, if the medication is discontinued, relapse will follow. Most patients can benefit from a combination of medication and behavioral therapy.

Behavior Therapy

Traditional psychotherapy, aimed at helping the patient develop insight into his or her problem, is generally not helpful for OCD. However, a specific behavior therapy approach called "exposure and response prevention" is effective for many people with OCD. In this approach, the patient is deliberately and voluntarily exposed to the feared object or idea, either directly or by imagination, and then is discouraged or prevented from carrying out the usual compulsive response. For example, a compulsive hand washer may be urged to touch an object believed to be contaminated, and then may be denied the opportunity to wash for several hours. When the treatment works well, the patient gradually experiences less anxiety from the obsessive thoughts and becomes able to do without the compulsive actions for extended periods of time.

Studies of behavior therapy for OCD have found it to produce long-lasting benefits. To achieve the best results, a combination of factors is necessary: The therapist should be well trained in the specific method developed; the patient must be highly motivated; and the patient's family must be cooperative. In addition to visits to the therapist, the patient must be faithful in fulfilling "homework assignments." For those patients who complete the course of treatment, the improvements can be significant.

With a combination of pharmacotherapy and behavioral therapy, the majority of OCD patients will be able to function well in both their work and social lives. The ongoing search for causes, together with research on treatment, promises to yield even more hope for people with OCD and their families.

How to Get Help for OCD

If you think that you have OCD, you should seek the help of a mental health professional. Family physicians, clinics, and health maintenance organizations usually can provide treatment or make referrals to mental health centers and specialists. Also, the department of psychiatry at a major medical center or the department of psychology at a university may have specialists who are knowledgeable about the treatment of OCD and are able to provide therapy or recommend another doctor in the area.

What the Family Can Do to Help

OCD affects not only the sufferer but the whole family. The family often has a difficult time accepting the fact that the person with OCD cannot stop the distressing behavior. Family members may show their anger and resentment, resulting in an increase in the OCD behavior. Or, to keep the peace, they may assist in the rituals or give constant reassurance.

Education about OCD is important for the family. Families can learn specific ways to encourage the person with OCD by supporting the medication regime and the behavior therapy. Self-help books are often a good source of information. Some families seek the help of a family therapist who is trained in the field. Also, in the past few years, many families have joined one of the educational support groups that have been organized throughout the country.

If You Have Special Needs

Individuals with OCD are protected under the Americans with Disabilities Act (ADA). Among organizations that offer information related to the ADA are the ADA Information Line at the U.S. Department of Justice, (202) 514-0301, and the Job Accommodation Network (JAN), part of the President's Committee on the Employment of People with Disabilities in the U.S. Department of Labor. JAN is located at West Virginia University, 809 Allen Hall, P.O. Box 6122, Morgantown, WV 26506, telephone (800) 526-7234 (voice or TDD), (800) 526-4698 (in West Virginia).

The Pharmaceutical Manufacturers Association publishes a directory of indigent programs for those who cannot afford medications. Physicians can request a copy of the guide by calling (800) PMA-INFO.

For Further Information

For further information on OCD, its treatment, and how to get help, you may wish to contact the following organizations:

Anxiety Disorders Association of America
6000 Executive Blvd., Suite 513
Rockville, MD 20852
(301) 231-9350

The Anxiety Disorders Association of America makes referrals to professional members and to support groups. Has a catalog of available brochures, books, and audiovisuals.

Association for Advancement of Behavior Therapy
305 Seventh Ave.
New York, NY 10001
(212) 647-1890

Membership listing of mental health professionals focusing in behavior therapy.

Dean Foundation
Obsessive Compulsive Information Center
8000 Excelsior Dr., Suite 302
Madison, WI 53717-1914
(608) 836-8070

Computer data base of over 4,000 references updated daily. Computer searches done for nominal fee. No charge for quick reference questions. Maintains physician referral and support group lists.

Obsessive Compulsive Foundation
P.O. Box 70
Milford, CT 06460
(203) 878-5669

Offers free or at minimal cost brochures for individuals with the disorder and their families. In addition, videotapes and books are available. A bimonthly newsletter goes to members who pay an annual membership fee of $30.00. Has over 250 support groups nationwide.

Tourette Syndrome Association, Inc.
42-40 Bell Boulevard
New York, NY 11361-2874
(718) 224-2999

Publications, videotapes, and films available at minimal cost. Newsletter goes to members who pay an annual fee of $35.00.

Books Suggested for Further Reading

Baer L. *Getting Control. Overcoming Your Obsessions and Compulsions*. Boston: Little, Brown & Co., 1991.

Foster, CH. *Polly's Magic Games: A Child's View of Obsessive-Compulsive Disorder*. Ellsworth, ME: Dilligaf Publishing, 1994.

Greist JH. *Obsessive Compulsive Disorder: A Guide*. Madison, WI: Obsessive Compulsive Disorder Information Center, rev. ed., 1992. (Thorough discussion of pharmacotherapy and behavior therapy)

Johnston HF. *Obsessive Compulsive Disorder in Children and Adolescents: A Guide*. Madison, WI: Child Psychopharmacology Information Center, 1993.

Livingston B. *Learning to Live with Obsessive Compulsive Disorder*. Milford, CT: OCD Foundation, 1989. (Written for the families of those with OCD)

Rapoport JL. *The Boy Who Couldn't Stop Washing: The Experience and Treatment of Obsessive-Compulsive Disorder*. New York: E. P. Dutton, 1989.

Videotape

The Touching Tree. Jim Callner, writer/director, Awareness films. Distributed by the O.C. Foundation, Inc., Milford, CT. (about a child with OCD)

References

DuPont RL, Rice DP, Shiraki S, Rowland C. Economic Costs of Obsessive Compulsive Disorder. Unpublished, 1994.

Jenike MA. Obsessive-Compulsive Disorder: Efficacy of Specific Treatments as Assessed by Controlled Trials. *Psychopharmacology Bulletin* 29:4:487-499, 1993.

Jenike MA. Managing the Patient with Treatment-Resistant Obsessive Compulsive Disorder: Current Strategies. *Journal of Clinical Psychiatry* 55:3 (suppl):11-17, 1994.

Leonard HL, Swedo SE, Lenane MC, Rettew DC, Hamburger SD, Bartko JJ, Rapoport JL. A 2- to 7-Year Follow-up Study of 54 Obsessive-Compulsive Children and Adolescents. *Archives of General Psychiatry* 50:429-439, 1993.

March JS, Mulle K, Herbel B. Behavioral Psychotherapy for Children and Adolescents with Obsessive-Compulsive Disorder: An Open Trial of a New Protocol-Driven Treatment Package. *Journal of the American Academy of Child and Adolescent Psychiatry* 33:3:333-341, 1994.

Pato MT, Zohar-Kadouch R, Zohar J, and Murphy DL. Return of Symptoms after Discontinuation of Clomipramine in Patients with Obsessive Compulsive Disorder. *American Journal of Psychiatry* 145:1521-1525, 1988.

Swedo SE and Leonard HL. Childhood Movement Disorders and Obsessive Compulsive Disorder. *Journal of Clinical Psychiatry* 55:3 (suppl):32-37, 1994.

Chapter 20

Generalized Anxiety Disorder

Anxiety and worry are a normal part of life. Whether the stakes are a job or the outcome of a sporting event, most people will worry at least a little bit about how things will turn out. Not only is anxiety a common human emotion, but moderate amounts of anxiety can be helpful by motivating people to prepare for an exam, complete a work assignment or deliver an energized speech.

But excessive anxiety can disrupt people's lives, interfere with performance, and trigger physical discomforts. When persistent and unrealistic worry becomes a habitual way of approaching situations, an individual may be suffering from generalized anxiety disorder.

Generalized Anxiety Disorder (GAD)

The key element of generalized anxiety disorder is persistent worry that is unrelated to another mental or physical illness. GAD is marked by excessive or unrealistic worry, lasting six months or more, about two distinct life experiences such as health, money, and career prospects. Realistic anxiety, such as financial concerns after losing a job, is not a sign of GAD. But chronic and excessive worry about events that are unlikely to occur is cause for concern.

Individuals with GAD also experience a number of other physical and emotional difficulties including trembling, muscular aches or soreness, restlessness, fatigue, shortness of breath, heart palpitations, insomnia, sweating, abdominal upsets, dizziness, concentration problems, edginess, and irritability.

The precise symptoms will vary with the individual, but at least six must be present for a diagnosis of GAD.

GAD Worry

People with GAD worry more frequently and with greater intensity than most people would in the same circumstance. The anxiety is difficult or impossible to turn off and can disrupt an individual's ability to concentrate on other tasks.

GAD can cause memory problems because so much energy is diverted to worrying that it undermines the individual's ability to process unrelated information.

Difficult Diagnosis

GAD can be hard to diagnose. It lacks the dramatic and obvious symptoms, such as unprovoked panic attacks, that characterize some other anxiety disorders. It is not traceable to a specific traumatic experience like post-traumatic stress disorder, nor is the anxiety a response to a specific stimulus, as is generally true of phobias.

Its physical symptoms are typical of many other mental and physical disorders. Patients with GAD often suffer from other ailments such as panic disorder, depression, and alcoholism.

If GAD coexists with other psychological disorders, the therapist will have to decide which deserves primary attention. In many cases, GAD disappears once coexisting ailments are under control. In other instances, GAD is the primary problem that must be treated first. It is, therefore, critical that the therapist obtain a detailed patient history before proceeding with treatment.

Who Gets GAD?

Researchers have not identified the cause of GAD, but the best evidence suggests that biological factors, family background, and life experiences are important contributors to this disorder. It appears that some individuals are genetically predisposed to react more emotionally than others to the same event. In addition, people who grew up with anxious role models may have learned to view the world as an uncontrollable and dangerous place. These people appear more likely to suffer from GAD. The disorder tends to manifest itself in the early 20s, but it can begin in childhood, and some people report their first battle with GAD only after they reach their 30s.

Increased stress often appears to trigger the disorder. Many GAD victims report an increase in stressful events such as a death in the family, illness, job loss, or divorce in the months or years immediately prior to the onset of the disorder. Stress from positive events such as marriage, a new baby, or a new job can also trigger GAD. But mental health professionals say stress is only a catalyst and does not cause GAD. Stress seems to contribute to GAD in people who are already experiencing chronic anxiety.

Treatment

Fortunately, mental health professionals have developed a variety of treatment approaches that have proven successful against this disorder.

Successful treatment regimens often include behavioral-cognitive therapies that seek to alter the way GAD victims think about and respond to troubling situations. For some people, relaxation techniques and physical exercise by themselves can greatly diminish anxiety. Medication has also proven effective in relieving anxiety symptoms.

There is no single correct treatment for GAD. Therapy programs must be tailored to the individual. In many cases, the therapist will use a combination of treatment approaches. Modifying habits that support GAD is key to all treatments.

Anxiety-Management Techniques

Some individuals with GAD report they have regained control of their lives without medication or extensive psychological counseling by learning anxiety management techniques.

Systematic tensing and relaxing of muscle groups, a technique known as progressive muscle relaxation, has helped a large percentage of GAD victims. Some patients report that physical exercise programs, perhaps requiring no more than 30 minutes a day and no more strenuous than brisk walking, provide relief from GAD. Meditation, yoga, massage, and biofeedback are other relaxation tools that may be beneficial for some people. Controlled breathing and refocusing one's thoughts on the present may also reduce anxiety.

These techniques do not provide instant relief. As a rule they take effect gradually, and they must be practiced regularly for lasting benefit.

Cognitive Therapy

Understanding their own thought processes and how they evaluate disturbing situations helps some people control their anxieties. Cognitive therapy is designed to reduce anxiety by giving individuals the skills to assess situations more realistically.

Patients may be trained to identify anxious and unrealistic thoughts and develop techniques to change their responses. Cognitive therapy may be supported by instruction in altering behavior or by lifestyle changes designed to cut down on stress.

Medication

Medication can be extremely beneficial in the treatment of GAD, particularly in providing fast relief from acute anxiety and allowing other therapy to go forward.

Medication is generally used in combination with other therapies. It may take tests of different medications and dosages to identify the proper prescription for each patient. Ideally, dosages are reduced over time. In some cases, the drugs will be administered only on an as-needed basis and may ultimately be discontinued completely. In other cases, longer-term drug therapy may be necessary.

The therapist has a wide variety of anti-anxiety medications to choose from. He or she will base the selection on individual circumstances including the severity of the anxiety disorder, potential side effects, and the patient's ability to follow instructions.

Drug therapy generally lasts several months and some patients may require medication for a year or more. The doctor's decision about which medication to prescribe may be based, in part, on how long the treatment is expected to last.

Finding Treatment

Any qualified psychiatrist, psychologist, social worker, or other mental health professional should be able to recognize GAD and either treat it or arrange a referral to someone who can. In many cases, a specialist or a support group can be located.

The Anxiety Disorders Association of America (ADAA) publishes a treatment guide to help people find assistance in their home area. The ADAA also operates a self-help network that may be able to put individuals in touch with a local support group.

Anxiety Disorders Association of America
6000 Executive Boulevard, Suite 513
Rockville, Maryland 20852-3801
(301) 231-9350

Chapter 21

Anxiety Disorders in the Elderly

Growing up, most of us probably remember elderly neighbors or relatives who seemed to worry about everything. We may have joked about them or vowed never to be that way ourselves.

But as we grew older, we realized that the anxieties of senior citizens usually have real causes such as failing health, loneliness, and stress.

For many elderly people, anxiety seems to be a part of growing old. It can be a symptom associated with many physical ailments, a realistic response to life circumstances such as loss of a mate, or a sign of a mental health problem.

Whatever the cause, management and treatment of anxiety in the elderly are often complicated by such factors as diagnostic difficulties, the infirmities of age, and memory problems.

Do Older People Have Anxiety Disorders?

While anxiety itself is common among the elderly, senior citizens appear less likely than younger people to suffer from specific anxiety disorders. When an older person does have one of the anxiety disorders, the disorder is usually developed earlier in life. Anxiety disorders typically make their first appearance in the late teens or twenties; it is unusual for an elderly person to develop one in late adult life.

Simple phobia—anxiety caused by a specific object or circumstance such as fear of heights, fear of driving, or fear of flying—is the most common anxiety disorder for both young and old.

Agoraphobia, a fear of being in public places from which escape appears difficult, is the second most common anxiety disorder in the elderly. In extreme cases, people with agoraphobia may refuse to leave their homes.

Although agoraphobia often appears in tandem with panic disorder, in which patients suffer unprovoked panic attacks, panic disorder by itself is rare in older people. Obsessive-compulsive disorder is also relatively uncommon in the elderly.

Some researchers think the traditional definitions of anxiety disorders are inappropriate for the elderly. These professionals believe that older people react differently to stress than younger people, and the symptoms of anxiety disorders may also be different in the elderly. In addition, new situations such as living alone, failing health, and issues of safety and security may trigger realistic anxiety among older citizens.

Difficult Diagnosis

Diagnosis of an anxiety disorder can be difficult at any age, but particularly in the elderly patient. Many of the signs of an anxiety disorder are identical to the symptoms of physical illness. Some anxiety disorder symptoms may also be characteristics of old age or side effects of medication.

For example, shortness of breath, trembling, sleep problems, and muscular aches may indicate the presence of an anxiety disorder. They are also typical complications of old age and, possibly, depression.

Anxiety may, itself, be a symptom of a physical disease. It is sometimes a side effect of medication—a special problem in the elderly because many older people require drugs for physical illnesses. Anxiety symptoms may indicate depression, which is common among older people in response to declining health or the death of loved ones.

Avoiding Help

Anxiety disorders are highly responsive to treatment, but only a small percentage of elderly patients seek help from a mental health professional. In fact, just 25 percent of anxiety disorder victims of all ages ever get proper care.

For a variety of reasons senior citizens tend to avoid treatment by mental health professionals.

- Many older people with mental health problems fail to recognize the nature of their difficulties and seek help for physical ailments instead. They often attribute problems to old age.

- The elderly tend to view mental health problems as an embarrassment. They are likely to blame themselves and feel ashamed of needing help.

- Misunderstanding about mental health care causes many older people to fear they will be institutionalized if they seek help.

- The low level of Medicare and insurance coverage for mental health treatments also discourages the elderly from seeking help.

These problems are not unique to the elderly population, but they seem to be more prevalent among older people.

Medication and the Older Patient

Medications have proven effective in reducing or eliminating many of the symptoms of anxiety and anxiety disorders and tend to be many therapists' treatment of choice for the elderly. But the physician has several unique considerations that must be weighed when prescribing drugs for older patients.

Metabolism, kidney and liver function, and the workings of the central nervous system tend to become less efficient with age, making the elderly more sensitive to some of the medications used in the treatment of anxiety and anxiety disorders.

Physicians have to consider the possible interaction of anxiety medications with other drugs, including over-the-counter medications. Other illnesses, particularly those involving the central nervous system such as stroke, may also affect the body's tolerance of certain drugs. The likelihood of other illnesses or an existing drug regimen that might interfere with anxiety medications increases substantially in older patients. For that reason, the doctor must be provided with a detailed medical history before prescribing medication.

Memory tends to decline with age. That can be a concern in prescribing for the elderly because forgetfulness may make it hard for some older people to follow their prescribed dosage schedule. Some physicians insist that another member of the household take responsibility for monitoring the elderly patient's adherence to the medication schedule and any adverse reaction to the drug.

Other Treatment

Many mental health specialists report success in treating elderly patients with phobias. "Exposure" therapy, in which the patient is gradually exposed to the feared circumstance to demonstrate that it can be confronted without danger, is one type of approach commonly used.

But some therapists believe the traditional approaches may not work as well in the elderly. They argue, for example, that the levels of arousal triggered by exposure may be beneficial in a younger person, but may overwhelm many older patients. These specialists believe a better treatment approach for the elderly may focus on ways to manage and control fear. Relaxation techniques may be a key element of programs that stress fear management.

Flexibility Is Important

The precise treatment approach will be determined by the therapist on the basis of individual circumstances, but whatever approach is used, treating a senior citizen is likely to require flexibility on the part of the therapist.

For example, many mental health care professionals think it is wise to adopt more limited goals in treating the elderly because the older patient may lack both the physical and emotional stamina and the economic resources for open-ended therapy.

The therapist may have to be flexible about treatment locations as well. Phone calls may, at times, substitute for office visits, and it may be necessary to visit the homes or hospital rooms of patients with physical illnesses to avoid a break in the treatment program.

Finding Treatment

Any qualified psychiatrist, psychologist, social worker, or other mental health professional should be able to recognize an anxiety disorder and either treat it or arrange a referral to someone who can. In many cases, a specialist or a support group can be located.

The Anxiety Disorders Association of America (ADAA) publishes a treatment guide to help people find assistance in their home area. The ADAA also operates a self-help network that may be able to put individuals in touch with a local support group.

Anxiety Disorders Association of America
6000 Executive Boulevard, Suite 513
Rockville, Maryland 20852-3801
(301) 231-9350

Chapter 22

Anxiety Disorders: Helping a Family Member

Illnesses happen to individuals, but one person's disease can exact a toll on everyone in the patient's life. If one member of the family becomes sick, the routine of the entire household can be disrupted. If the illness is shortlived, the family can return to its normal activities quickly and without lasting impact. But a chronic illness or one that is disabling may permanently affect the way family members interact with one another and with the world.

Anxiety disorders and other mental illnesses can be equally or more disruptive than physical ailments. Many normal family activities may become difficult or impossible. Economic loss may occur if the anxiety disorder limits a person's ability to work. Anxiety disorders may exact a significant emotional toll on all members of the family because the individual with the disorder may be reluctant to participate in typical social activities.

Missing Out

There are times when every parent disappoints a child or when a spouse lets down a mate. But those instances usually involve choices and, hopefully, the disappointments are infrequent.

For some people with an anxiety disorder, however, letting down their family becomes a way of life. Because of their disorder, some people are simply unable to take part in activities that others take for granted.

"Do you know what it's like when your children ask you to take them to the store or to a birthday party and you can't? It is a living nightmare that I hope and pray I will be able to overcome," one victim of agoraphobia wrote in a letter to the Anxiety Disorders Association of America (ADAA).

Hiding the Problem

Relationships can be further complicated by the failure of family members to honestly confront the existence of an anxiety disorder.

Individuals with a phobia or obsessive-compulsive disorder (OCD) may be too ashamed or embarrassed to ask for help. They may try to hide their anxieties and, at the same time, expect members of the household to be sensitive to their needs and concerns.

Other family members, not aware that their loved one has an emotional problem, may feel rejection or anger over behavior caused by the disorder.

In one documented case, a woman who was afraid of driving in thunderstorms hid her phobia from her children and suffered pain and guilt because she never picked them up at school during storms. Years later, the woman's grown-up daughter recalled her confusion and rejection when her mother made excuses for not picking her up and arranged for someone else to bring her home.

What's a Family To Do?

Families find a variety of ways to deal with anxiety disorders and other health problems of family members. Some rearrange their lives and activities to accommodate the afflicted person. For example, the family of a person with OCD who worries about contamination might try to keep peace by agreeing to extra cleaning.

Some family members attempt to maintain their normal routines. While offering assurances of emotional support and understanding, they schedule activities even though the patient might not be able to take part. Others respond with hostility and either ignore or criticize their relative's behavior.

While these strategies may provide structure and short-term stability, they rarely produce a satisfactory family life, and they do not address the fundamental problem of how to treat the disorder.

Providing Support

The family can play a major supporting role in combatting one member's anxiety disorder. Although ultimate responsibility lies with the patient, family members can help by taking part in the treatment program. With training they can accompany the troubled person into anxiety-producing situations, offer support and encouragement, and create an environment that promotes healing.

At a minimum, family members should learn as much as they can about their relative's disorder and avoid blame. Family members must also adapt to changes that may occur as recovery takes place.

Family members should recognize and praise small accomplishments; modify expectations during stressful periods; measure progress on the basis of individual improvement, not against some absolute standard; be flexible and try to maintain a normal routine.

Family Members Can Help

Family members can often play an active role in anxiety disorder treatment. The precise nature of the assistance will vary depending on the disorder and the family member's relationship with the patient.

In addition to providing psychological therapy and medication, mental health professionals are increasingly recommending treatment programs that include family members. As a rule, the more severe the disorder the more likely that family and/or marital issues will need to be addressed by the therapy program.

In one common approach to family therapy, mental health professionals enlist a spouse or other family member as a co-therapist. Making the family member part of the treatment team tends to reduce the possibility of tension concerning the therapy program. Involving a family member diminishes the chance he or she will feel neglected or harbor suspicions about being blamed for their mate's problem. By promoting understanding, bringing family members into the treatment process also reduces the chance that the relative will think the patient's behavior is just a bid for attention. Reading educational materials also promotes understanding.

Family members who are excluded from the treatment process sometimes undermine the therapy, either intentionally or by accident, because they do not understand what is going on.

Family Support

Typically, the patient will be interviewed privately by the therapist to help assemble a history of the disorder and devise a treatment plan. The patient, relatives, and therapist may then hold one or more joint sessions in an effort to arrive at treatment goals.

One key part of the therapy is to discover and alter attitudes and behavior of both the patient and family member that directly or indirectly perpetuate the disorder.

Family members can play an extremely valuable supportive role by assisting the patient in "homework" that has been agreed upon in consultation with the therapist. Most typically, at home assignments for patients with phobias involve controlled exposure to situations that trigger anxiety. Another type of homework, frequently adopted for patients with obsessive-compulsive disorder, is the implementation of "behavior contracts" limiting how often the patient may indulge in ritual activities.

Helping the Patient with Homework

Exposure therapy works by gradually exposing patients to a feared object or situation to teach them that they can face their anxieties without harm.

Family members can supplement the exposure sessions involving the therapist by accompanying the patient into the feared circumstance on other occasions.

These sessions seem to work best if specific goals are set at the outset and the patient is given a clearly defined way out of the situation if desired. Knowing there is a way out is generally a major source of reassurance. Achievement and progress, no matter how small, should be acknowledged. The patient, using anxiety reduction techniques taught by the therapist, should be encouraged to remain in the situation even when anxiety increases. But the patient should not be forced or humiliated into staying.

For example, OCD patients, who tend to respond to anxiety by performing rituals or routines, will be exposed to distressing circumstances and—according to a prearranged plan—be discouraged by family members from repeatedly performing their typical calming ritual. The behavior contract may establish rewards for achieving prescribed goals.

All goals and rewards should be clearly spelled out and agreed upon before the home practice sessions get underway.

Changing Roles

Families and patients must recognize that the recovery process can itself become a source of tension by changing existing relationships. Family structures that have consciously or subconsciously been built to cope with one member's anxiety disorder will inevitably be altered.

Patients' emotional needs may change during treatment. They may become more assertive or independent, causing distress and confusion for other members of the household who may begin to wonder where they fit in.

Working through such changes will require patience and understanding by all members of the family, but they should ultimately lead to more stable and more satisfactory lives for all.

Finding Treatment

Any qualified psychiatrist, psychologist, social worker, or other mental health professional should be able to recognize an anxiety disorder and either treat it or arrange a referral to someone who can. In many cases, a specialist or a support group can be located.

The Anxiety Disorders Association of America (ADAA) publishes a treatment guide to help people find assistance in their home area. The ADAA also operates a self-help network that may be able to put individuals in touch with a local support group.

Anxiety Disorders Association of America
6000 Executive Boulevard, Suite 513
Rockville, MD 20852-3801
(301) 231-9350

Chapter 23

Phobias

Everybody has fears or situations they would rather avoid. Some people are frightened by job interviews. Others are uncomfortable to be home alone at night. Most people manage to control their fears and go about their normal activities. Sometimes they develop coping strategies such as turning on the television or radio to keep them company in an empty house. Other times they merely grit their teeth and go forward.

But some people's lives are consumed by inappropriate and involuntary fears. Normal coping mechanisms don't work and the need to avoid the objects or situations that cause anxiety can be so intense that normal living becomes impossible. These people are suffering from a phobia.

Phobias

Phobias are divided into three broad categories—simple phobia, social phobia, and agoraphobia—depending on what triggers the fear and how the individual reacts to the dreaded object or situation. Typically, people with phobias do whatever they can to avoid the feared object or situation. If the source of the anxiety is rarely encountered the phobia may be little more than an annoyance. But in many cases the feared circumstance is encountered so often or the anxiety is so intense that normal life is disrupted.

The fear of a panic attack, including such symptoms as faintness, trembling, rapid heartbeat, fear of death or losing control, and shortness of breath, is generally one of the main factors in keeping the phobia alive. Some people spend so much time worrying about a possible panic attack that the anticipation itself becomes crippling.

Individuals with phobias recognize that their fears are unreasonable, but they are unable to control them. They experience extreme anxiety and panic when exposed to certain objects or situations that they logically know are not dangerous.

Simple or Single Phobia

People with simple phobia suffer from an illogical, but real and intense, fear of a specific object such as dogs or insects or a situation such as flying or deep water. Fear of certain types of animals is the most common simple phobia. Other typical simple phobias include fear of flying (aerophobia), fear of closed spaces (claustrophobia), and fear of heights (acrophobia). One of the most crippling phobias for children is school phobia, which makes it difficult or impossible for them to attend school.

Many simple phobias, such as fear of animals, begin in childhood and may disappear with age. In some cases, phobias may have started after real encounters with danger. More commonly, they seem to come out of the blue. Simple phobias that first appear in adulthood rarely go away without treatment.

Social Phobia

Social phobia is an intense anxiety of being judged by others and publicly behaving in a way that could lead to embarrassment or ridicule. Probably the most common social phobia is fear of public speaking. Individuals with social phobia may also be terrified of such routine activities as writing in public, casual conversation, parties, or using a public restroom.

People with social phobia have no problem performing these activities in private, but worry that they may perform them poorly in a situation where they could be observed and/or evaluated.

The anxiety may become self-fulfilling by hampering an individual's performance and making the fear seem appropriate. This, in turn, can increase the worry about doing things in public and heighten the desire to avoid the feared situation.

Agoraphobia

People with agoraphobia (Greek for fear of the marketplace) are frightened by the possibility of being "trapped" in a public place. Some agoraphobics are also afraid of being alone. This ailment tends to occur in combination with panic disorder. The overriding concern of most people with agoraphobia is that they may have a panic attack where public embarrassment would occur or where immediate help or escape is not available.

In severe cases of agoraphobia, individuals may refuse to leave their home or may do so only when accompanied by a trusted friend or relative. Some individuals with agoraphobia become "territory bound" and are able to travel only by a fixed route or within a safe territory, such as the route between their home and work. Others may only avoid specific activities such as riding a bus or visiting a shopping mall.

Who Gets Phobias?

Phobias are the most common of a set of ailments known as anxiety disorders, which are themselves the most common mental health problem. It is estimated that up to 12 percent of adult Americans, perhaps 20 million people, will suffer from a phobia during their lifetime.

Most of these disorders tend to begin during the teen years, although simple phobias are common among younger children. Women are more likely than men to suffer from simple phobias and agoraphobia, but men and women are equally likely to experience social phobias.

The causes of phobias are a matter of debate. Some researchers think phobias can be traced to genetic tendencies, chemical disturbances in the brain, or other biological or psychological factors. Others say a traumatic event such as being publicly humiliated or being assaulted by a dog can condition people to phobias.

Related Problems

The suffering caused by phobias extends far beyond the immediate frustration of the disorder. Large numbers of people with social phobia and agoraphobia turn to alcohol or illegal drugs for comfort. Studies indicate that about 20 percent of people with these disorders drink too much and about half of individuals with social phobia or agoraphobia suffer from depression.

Phobias also can disrupt family life, reduce self-esteem, and limit work efficiency.

Help is Available

The good news is that researchers and therapists have developed treatment programs that bring about significant improvement and enable the vast majority of individuals with phobias to regain control of their lives.

There are a number of standard approaches used by therapists to try to block panic attacks and modify the actions and thought patterns of people suffering from phobias.

Unfortunately, about three-quarters of individuals with phobias never get help. Many people with phobias are reluctant to seek assistance because of embarrassment. Others don't understand what they have or where to find help, and some fear the treatment itself.

Treatment Approaches

A key component of most treatments is **behavior therapy** designed to alter the way a person acts. Behavior therapy typically involves gradual exposure of the patient to the feared situation.

Behavior techniques are often combined with **cognitive therapy** that aims to change the way people view themselves and their fears. Rather than thinking "I'm frightened and might have a panic attack," the individual is encouraged to assess the situation in a more positive way, perhaps thinking "I'm frightened, but I'm not in danger." The patient is trained to analyze his feelings and separate realistic from unrealistic assumptions.

Medication has proven to be increasingly useful in controlling panic and other symptoms. It is most effective in combination with behavioral and cognitive therapy.

Exposure

Exposure therapy works by gradually exposing the individual to the feared object or situation. Facing the feared situation helps the patient see that he can cope successfully and that flight is unnecessary. Over time, the individual gains greater control over his anxiety. Ultimately, he can face the threatening situation or object with little or no fear.

In social phobia, the exposure is almost always done in group therapy because a key element of this disorder is the fear of performing an activity in front of others. Treatment for agoraphobia or simple phobia can be conducted individually or in a group.

There are a number of variations in exposure therapy. The degree of exposure will vary depending on the therapist's assessment of the patient. The feared situation, such as giving a speech, may be simulated, or the person with the disorder may be placed in a real situation that he fears, such as driving over a bridge.

Finding Treatment

A qualified psychiatrist, psychologist, social worker or other mental health professional should be able to recognize a phobia and either treat it or arrange a referral to someone who can. In many cases, a specialist center or support groups can be located.

The Anxiety Disorders Association of America publishes a list of therapists to help people find a specialist in their home area. The ADAA also operates a self-help network that may be able to put you in touch with a local support group.

Anxiety Disorders Association of America
6000 Executive Boulevard, Suite 513
Rockville, Maryland 20852-3801
(301) 231-9350

Chapter 24

Agoraphobia

Panic disorder frequently occurs in combination with agoraphobia. People with agoraphobia are afraid of being in public places from which they think escape would be difficult. Paradoxically, some are frightened of being alone.

Some agoraphobics stop using public transportation or visiting shopping malls. Others refuse to leave their homes, often for years at a time. Some will leave home only when accompanied by a trusted companion. In another variation, individuals become "territory-bound" and are able to move only in a fixed route between home and work. These people cannot venture outside their "safe" territory without anxiety and they will rarely deviate from the home-to-work routine.

Fear of the Fear

Some agoraphobics never have panic attacks and many people with panic disorder do not develop agoraphobia. But large numbers suffer from both disorders. Their chief concern is having a panic attack in public or in a place where they think help or safety is not immediately available.

Worry about future panic attacks becomes a preoccupation for people with agoraphobia and each new episode reinforces the fear. In most cases, fear of another attack causes as much anxiety as the attack itself.

Excerpted from "Panic and Agoraphobia," © ADAA 1991, reprinted with permission.

Life may become dominated by efforts to avoid situations the ago-raphobic believes might trigger a panic attack. Typically, that means staying away from places or circumstances where previous episodes have taken place. People with agoraphobia are also likely to avoid places where escape or immediate help would not be available. Such behavior tends to make normal life impossible.

Who Gets Panic Disorder and Agoraphobia?

There is no such thing as a typical victim of panic disorder or ago-raphobia. The ailments cut across social, ethnic, and economic lines. But a variety of studies suggest as many as 3 million Americans may suffer from panic disorder at some point in their lives and that a still larger number have agoraphobia. At one time, researchers believed panic disorder was due primarily to psychological problems. But there is increasing evidence that genetic factors or changes in body chemis-try, in combination with stressful circumstances or events, play a piv-otal role. The disorder appears to run in families and is two or three times more common in women than in men.

Panic disorder typically begins in the late teen years or early-to-mid twenties. The first attack is often, but not always, preceded by a stressful event such as the death of a parent, a move to a new city, or the breakup of a marriage.

Other Problems

Panic disorder is often compounded by depression and/or sub-stance abuse problems. Some studies show that 30 percent or more of people with panic disorder also suffer from depression serious enough to benefit from treatment.

Many individuals with panic disorder or agoraphobia try to smother their anxieties by drinking or taking drugs. The National In-stitute of Mental Health estimates that 36 percent of people with panic disorder also have substance abuse problems.

Help Is Available

Fortunately, panic disorder and agoraphobia are highly treatable once diagnosed. As many as 90 percent of those who seek treatment for these disorders will resume normal activities. Recovery may occur in a matter of months, but can take longer depending on individual circumstances.

The most successful treatment regimens include a combination of **behavioral therapy**, **cognitive therapy** and **medication**. Behavioral therapy usually includes **relaxation techniques** and **exposure therapy**. Support groups may also be extremely useful because many individuals need the reassurance that they are not alone.

A successful treatment program must address all of an individual's problems including any depression or substance abuse that might accompany the underlying emotional disorder.

Treatment

Behavior therapy works by trying to change the way an individual acts. Specifically, the therapist seeks to develop the patient's anxiety reduction skills and teach new ways to express emotions. Relaxation techniques, such as controlled breathing, are a typical feature of behavior therapy.

Exposure therapy is the most common treatment for people whose lives are dominated by avoiding feared situations. As the name suggests, the patient is gradually exposed to the feared situation and taught that he can cope. Cognitive therapy attempts to alter the way a person thinks about certain circumstances. The patient will be taught to reexamine the thoughts and feelings that trigger his fears. This therapy is intended to change the thought patterns that cause and maintain anxiety.

There are a number of anti-anxiety and antidepressant medications that are effective in controlling panic disorder. The medication regimen may last just a few weeks, but in many cases this therapy will be required for a year or longer. The medication should be accompanied by other therapy, however, because the majority of patients treated only with drugs tend to relapse once the medication is discontinued.

Finding Treatment

A qualified psychiatrist, psychologist, social worker, or other mental health professional should be able to recognize panic disorder and either treat it or arrange referral to someone who can. In many cases, a specialist center or a support group can be located.

The Anxiety Disorders Association of America publishes a list of therapists to help people find specialists in their home area. The ADAA also operates a self-help network that may be able to put you in touch with a local support group.

Anxiety Disorders Association of America
6000 Executive Boulevard
Rockville, Maryland 20852
(301) 231-9350

Chapter 25

Social Phobia

Most of us become nervous before certain social events. Dinner out with the boss, a high school reunion, or meeting future in-laws can all be worrisome. Some people will fuss for hours wondering what to wear or what to talk about on such occasions. Anyone who has ever given a speech or a business presentation has probably experienced some butterflies before stepping up to the microphone.

But for many people these types of social engagements bring feelings that go well beyond simple nervousness. Some people become so anxious over the possibility of embarrassing themselves in public that normal life is disrupted. These people are suffering from **social phobia** and, for some, avoiding certain situations becomes the dominant goal in their lives.

Social Phobia

The key element of social phobia is extreme anxiety about being judged by others or behaving in a way that might cause embarrassment or ridicule. The person with social phobia believes that all eyes are on him. The anxiety can lead to panic-like attacks including such symptoms as heart palpitations, faintness, shortness of breath, and profuse sweating. Whether or not they have panic reactions, people with social phobia generally expend considerable energy avoiding feared situations.

Social phobia is selective. A person may have an intense fear of a single circumstance such as public speaking, but be perfectly comfortable in all other social settings. Others may have several social phobias and become anxious about a variety of situations in which their performance might be observed.

Fear of Embarrassment

In social phobia, the central fear is embarrassment over the way one might act and the anxiety is generally triggered by specific social circumstances. The most common social phobia is anxiety over public speaking. Other specific social phobias include such routine activities as writing in public, casual conversation, parties, eating in a restaurant, or using a public restroom.

Individuals with social phobia do not have a general fear of being trapped in a public place or having a panic attack. Nor is social phobia the same as shyness. Shy individuals may be extremely self-conscious, but they do not display the anticipatory anxiety or avoidance behavior of those with social phobia.

The Social Phobia Cycle

People with social phobia tend to underestimate their social skills. They are acutely aware of physical signs of their nervousness such as blushing or sweating and assume these cues are obvious to others. They may also overestimate others' social ability and comfort level.

The advance anxiety over public behavior may become self-fulfilling because extreme nervousness may result in poor performance. That bad performance, in turn, may intensify future worry about embarrassing oneself in public.

The Effect of Social Phobia

The impact of social phobia varies with the individual. A phobia about public speaking may bar career advancement in some executive positions or for a sales representative, but have only limited impact on a construction worker. On the other hand, a phobia about eating in restaurants or using public restrooms can severely restrict any person's life.

The amount of energy devoted to avoiding feared circumstances also differs with the individual. For some people with social phobia, so-called avoidance behavior may dominate their life. Other individuals go ahead with the threatening activity, but suffer extreme anxiety before, during, and after the event.

Social phobia may occur as a complication of panic disorder as individuals seek to avoid specific activities or circumstances where a panic attack has occurred.

Who Gets Social Phobia?

The precise number of Americans with social phobia is not known, but the best evidence is that two percent of the U.S. population, or more than four million people, may be afflicted in a six-month period. While women are more likely than men to experience panic disorder or agoraphobia (a fear of being trapped in a public place), men and women are equally likely to suffer from social phobia.

There are different opinions about what causes social phobia. Some researchers believe biological or genetic factors play the crucial role. Others blame unpleasant or frightening social experiences, particularly in childhood and the teen years.

Whatever the cause, the disorder tends to make its first appearance in the mid- to late-teens and grow worse over time. It seems to take hold more gradually than other anxiety disorders, some of which literally appear overnight.

Treatment

Most people with social phobia can be helped by a therapy program. Although results vary, it appears that as many as 80 percent of those who enter treatment programs report significant improvement and say they are able to get their social phobia under control.

The most common treatment option for social phobia is **behavior therapy**, typically in a group setting, in which the individual is exposed to the circumstance that triggers his fear. Other behavioral methods such as relaxation techniques may also be used to help people gain better control of their actions and reactions.

The effort to modify behavior may be combined with **cognitive therapy**, which is designed to help people change the way they think about the feared social situation.

Medications are also effective in the treatment of social phobia and are often used in conjunction with behavior and cognitive therapy. Some individuals benefit from training in specific social skills.

Exposure Therapy

Treatment for social phobia generally centers around a type of behavior therapy called **exposure** in which people gradually confront the situation that brings on their anxiety. Repeated exposure, combined with practice in coping with the dreaded situation, is designed to show people they can perform satisfactorily without embarrassing themselves.

Exposure therapy for some disorders may be administered in one-on-one sessions with the therapist. In social phobia, the treatment almost always takes place in a group setting because the key feature of this disorder is that anxiety is only triggered by an activity performed in front of others. Additionally, group members may benefit by observing simulations and borrowing others' coping techniques.

Most treatment programs include homework in which the patient initiates his own exposure sessions according to plans made in the group session. A report is then made at the next group meeting.

Other Treatment Techniques

For some people, exposure therapy alone is not sufficient to help them control their anxiety. In these cases, behavior therapy may be supplemented by cognitive therapy designed to alter their thinking about themselves and their social abilities.

Cognitive therapy examines people's expectations of social situations and their perceptions of their own performance. Typically, the individual with social phobia exaggerates others' competence and expectations, while belittling his own. This therapy is intended to help the individual with social phobia learn to separate realistic from unrealistic assumptions. Training in social skills may support cognitive therapy and exposure by boosting confidence levels.

Medication is useful in easing the core symptoms of social phobias. Individuals whose anxiety is triggered by just a few predictable situations may be helped by taking medication about an hour before a feared event. Those with more pervasive or less predictable anxiety may do better with medication that is administered daily.

Finding Help

A qualified psychiatrist, psychologist, social worker, or other mental health professional should be able to recognize and treat social phobia. In many cases, referral to a specialist center can be arranged and support groups can be located.

The Anxiety Disorders Association of America publishes a list of therapists to help individuals locate specialists in their home area. The ADAA also operates a self-help network that may be able to put you in touch with a local support group.

Anxiety Disorders Association of America
6000 Executive oulevard
Rockville, Maryland 20852
(301) 231-9350

Chapter 26

Post Traumatic Stress Disorder

Everyone looks backwards at times. Sometimes we recollect a happy memory because it makes us feel good. Other times, we recall something we didn't handle so well and wish we could have a second chance. Following a death or other personal trauma, we may brood and ask, "why?" Eventually, we put the past aside and get on with our lives. But, for some people, moving forward is not so easy. Some individuals who survive a traumatic event become so preoccupied with the experience that they are unable to live a normal life.

Post-Traumatic Stress Disorder (PTSD)

When a traumatic experience begins to interfere with normal activities, a person may be suffering from post-traumatic stress disorder or PTSD. This disorder may follow an unusually distressing experience such as rape, war, a fire, a flood, sexual abuse, a car or plane crash, a traumatic death, or captivity. For some people, merely witnessing a violent or tragic event is sufficient to cause PTSD, which is part of a larger group of mental health difficulties known as anxiety disorders.

Symptoms can range from constantly reliving the trauma to general emotional numbness. Individuals with PTSD may be unable to concentrate on routine tasks. In most cases, people with PTSD recover

---

© ADAA 1991, reprinted with permission.

without treatment—often in a matter of months. But other victims will be troubled by PTSD for months or years and will not get better unless treated by a mental health specialist.

Who Gets PTSD?

Women tend to get PTSD more often than men and it seems to be somewhat less common in the elderly. The disorder has been familiar to soldiers over the years as "shell shock" or "battle fatigue." It has been estimated that between 15 and 30 percent of the 3.5 million men and women who served in Vietnam have suffered from PTSD.

But it can affect anybody at any age and recent studies show it is far more common among children than previously believed. The disorder tends to be more severe if the trauma was unanticipated. Estimates of the disorder's frequency vary widely. Some studies say 2 percent of the population has had a bout with PTSD, while others say as many as 9 percent have been afflicted.

What are the Symptoms of PTSD?

PTSD has a wide variety of symptoms. The specific symptoms, their number, and their intensity will vary with each individual, so it is possible for two people with PTSD to be affected in much different ways. The symptoms are divided into three different categories and a diagnosis of PTSD will rarely be made unless an individual has at least one element from each group. Symptoms must be recurring and distressing for this disorder to exist.

Nightmares and Flashbacks

People with PTSD have frequent episodes in which they relive the traumatic event. This experience can manifest itself as a nightmare, a flashback, or simply a sudden flood of emotions or images related to the trauma.

A person having a flashback may think he is actually experiencing or seeing the traumatic event again. Sometimes a flashback can be so severe that the individual unconsciously begins acting as he did at the time of the trauma and may appear to be sleepwalking. A war veteran, for example, may take cover as if under bombardment.

Nightmares may be so intense that an individual will wake up screaming. They can be so terrifying that an individual may develop insomnia to avoid the dreams. Sudden memories of the distressing event, coming without warning, may be powerful enough to bring tears.

Withdrawing from Family and Friends

A second category of symptoms is characterized by an effort to avoid any situation or activity that might revive memories of the trauma. This avoidance behavior may include withdrawal from friends and family. People with PTSD often have trouble feeling and displaying emotions, particularly to those closest to them. This can strain personal relationships by causing others to feel rejected or ignored.

The avoidance behavior may interfere with routine activities. An individual caught in a bank holdup, for example, may refuse to go to a bank. Someone with PTSD may become so wary of certain situations that avoiding them becomes the dominant element in his or her life.

Others with this disorder may avoid responsibility, lose interest in favorite activities, or feel hopeless about the future. Such attitudes can lead to poor work performance and cause family problems.

Sudden Anger and Other Reactions

The third group of symptoms includes unprovoked anger, jumpiness, an extreme sense of being "on guard," problems with concentration, insomnia, and physical distress such as sweating and rapid heart beat when reminded of the trauma.

Somebody who has been in a war situation may overreact to noises such as fireworks or a car backfire that are similar to the sounds of battle. Sometimes individuals with PTSD have panic attacks, with such symptoms as chest pain, dizziness, rapid breathing, and the feeling they are dying or losing control.

When Do Symptoms Appear?

Symptoms typically appear within a few weeks of the trauma, but on rare occasions there can be a long gap between the triggering event and the beginning of PTSD. Some individuals may go months or years before having any PTSD symptoms.

The diagnosis of PTSD may be difficult because the patient and the therapist may overlook a distant episode. Often, a patient has forgotten the incident or simply fails to tell the therapist about it in the belief it is not important. It is essential that a person seeking help for an emotional problem inform the therapist about any traumatic experience. This enables the therapist to consider whether that event may be related to the patient's difficulties.

Related Problems

It is not unusual for individuals with a mental health disorder to have more than one problem at the same time. Individuals with PTSD or other emotional problems frequently turn to drugs and alcohol for comfort. One recent study by the National Institute of Mental Health found that half of the drug or alcohol abusers in the United States have a mental illness. Sometimes, the problems associated with substance abuse mask the symptoms of PTSD.

In other instances, the most significant symptoms may also be characteristic of ailments other than PTSD. Temper tantrums, tension headaches, and despair are common characteristics of many disorders. An individual with PTSD may also suffer from depression or other emotional ailments.

Getting Help

Fortunately, PTSD can be effectively treated. **Behavior therapy** can play a useful role by helping modify the way the patient acts and reducing avoidance behavior. Behavior therapy is often combined with **cognitive therapy**, which is intended to change underlying thought patterns. These approaches may be used in a group or individual setting.

Medication can be a valuable complement to other treatment by relieving many of the most debilitating symptoms and enabling other therapy to go forward. It is particularly helpful in controlling anger, jumpiness, insomnia, nightmares, flashbacks and depression.

The use of medication may be required for only a few weeks, but in severe cases it may be needed for several years.

Supplemental Therapy

Family therapy can help close relatives understand and cope with the illness. Through such counseling, family members can learn that any apparent rejection by a relative with PTSD is the result of the disorder. Family counseling can repair communications and help restore normal interaction.

Support groups of individuals who have experienced PTSD can show victims that their reactions to trauma are shared by many. By discussing common experiences and emotions groups of survivors can help each other rebuild confidence.

Finding Treatment

A qualified psychiatrist, psychologist, social worker, or other mental health professional should be able to recognize and treat PTSD. In many cases, referral to a specialist center can be arranged and support groups can be located.

The Anxiety Disorders Association of America publishes a list of therapists to help individuals locate specialists in their home area.

Anxiety Disorders Association of America
6000 Executive Boulevard, Suite 513
Rockville, Maryland 20852-3801
(301) 231-9350

Treatment of PTSD can generally be arranged on an outpatient basis. But some severe cases may require hospitalization, particularly if there are complications like suicidal depression or excessive use of drugs or alcohol.

Part Five

Other Mental Health Disorders

Chapter 27

Useful Information on Paranoia

Paranoia—The Word

Paranoia is a term used by mental health specialists to describe suspiciousness (or mistrust) that is either highly exaggerated or not warranted at all. The word is often used in everyday conversation, often in anger, often incorrectly. Simple suspiciousness is not paranoia—not if it is based on past experience or expectations learned from the experience of others.

Paranoia can be mild and the affected person may function fairly well in society, or it can be so severe that the individual is incapacitated. Because many psychiatric disorders are accompanied by some paranoid features, diagnosis is sometimes difficult. Paranoias can be classified into three main categories—*paranoid personality disorder*, *delusional (paranoid) disorder*, and *paranoid schizophrenia*.

Paranoid Personality Disorder

Derek worked in a large office as a computer programmer. When another programmer received a promotion, Derek felt that the supervisor "had it in for him" and would never recognize his worth. He was sure that his coworkers were subtly downgrading him. Often he watched as others took coffee breaks together and imagined they spent

DHHS Pub. No. (ADM) 89-1495.

this time talking about him. If he saw a group of people laughing, he knew they were laughing at him. He spent so much time brooding about the mistreatment he received that his work suffered and his supervisor told him he must improve or receive a poor performance rating. This action reinforced all Derek's suspicions, and he looked for and found a position in another large company. After a few weeks on his new job, he began to feel that others in the office didn't like him, excluded him from all conversations, made fun of him behind his back, and eroded his position. Derek has changed jobs six times in the last seven years. Derek has paranoid personality disorder.

Some people regularly become suspicious without cause—so much so that their paranoid thoughts disrupt their work and family life. Such people are said to have a *paranoid personality*. They are:

Suspicious

An unmistakable sign of paranoia is continual mistrust. People with paranoid personality disorder are constantly on their guard because they see the world as a threatening place. They tend to confirm their expectations by latching on to any speck of evidence that supports their suspicions and ignore or misinterpret any evidence to the contrary. They are ever watchful and may look around for signs of a threat.

Anyone in a new situation—beginning a job or starting a relationship, for example—is cautious and somewhat guarded until he or she learns that the fears are groundless. People suffering from paranoia cannot abandon their fears. They continue to expect trickery and to doubt the loyalty of others. In a personal relationship or marriage, this suspiciousness may take the form of pathological, unrealistic jealousy.

Hypersensitive

Because persons with paranoid personality disorder are hyperalert, they notice any slight and may take offense where none is intended. As a result, they tend to be defensive and antagonistic. When they are at fault, they cannot accept blame, not even mild criticism. Yet they are highly critical of others. Other people may say that these individuals make "mountains out of molehills."

Cold and Aloof

In addition to being argumentative and uncompromising, the people with paranoid personality disorder are often emotionally cut off from other people. They appear cold and, in fact, often avoid becoming intimate with others. They pride themselves on their rationality and objectivity. People with a paranoid outlook on life rarely come to the attention of clinicians—it is not in their nature to seek help. Many presumably function competently in society. They may seek out social niches in which a moralistic and punitive style is acceptable, or at least tolerated to a certain degree.

Delusional (Paranoid) Disorder

Psychiatrists make a distinction between the milder paranoid personality disorder described above and the more debilitating delusional (paranoid) disorder. The hallmark of this disorder is the presence of a persistent, nonbizarre delusion without symptoms of any other mental disorder.

Delusions are firmly held beliefs that are untrue, not shared by others in the culture, and not easily modifiable. Five delusional themes are frequently seen in delusional disorder. In some individuals, more than one of them is present.

Ruth is a clerk typist who is efficient and helpful. Her employers and co-workers value her contribution to the office. But Ruth spends her evenings writing letters to State and Federal officials. She feels that God has opened her mind and given her the cure for cancer. She wants some leading treatment center to use her cure on all its patients so that the world can see she is right. Many of her letters go unanswered, or she receives noncommittal replies that only make her feel that no one understands that she can save all cancer patients if only given the chance. When one of her letters is answered by an employee of the official to whom she wrote, she is sure that the official is being deliberately kept unaware of her knowledge and power. Sometimes she despairs that the world will ever know how wonderful she is, but she doesn't give up. She just keeps writing. Ruth suffers from one of the delusional disorders, grandiose delusion.

The most common delusion in delusional disorder is that of *persecution*. While persons with paranoid personality might suspect their colleagues of joking at their expense, persons with delusional disorder may suspect others of participating in elaborate master plots to persecute them. They believe that they are being poisoned, drugged, spied upon, or are the targets of conspiracies to ruin their reputations or even to kill them. They sometimes engage in litigation in an attempt to redress imagined injustices.

Another theme seen frequently is that of *delusional jealousy*. Any sign—even a meaningless spot on clothing, or a short delay in arriving home—is summoned up as evidence that a spouse is being unfaithful.

Erotic delusions are based on the belief that one is romantically loved by another, usually someone of higher status or a well-known public figure. Individuals with erotic delusions often harass famous persons through numerous letters, telephone calls, visits, and stealthy surveillance.

Persons with *grandiose delusions* often feel that they have been endowed with special powers and that, if allowed to exercise these powers, they could cure diseases, banish poverty, ensure world peace, or perform other extraordinary feats.

Individuals with *somatic delusions* are convinced that there is something very wrong with their bodies—that they emit foul odors, have bugs crawling in or on their bodies, or are misshapen and ugly. Because of these delusions, they tend to avoid the society of other people and spend much time consulting physicians for their imagined condition.

Whether or not persons with delusional disorder are dangerous to others has not been systematically investigated, but clinical experience suggests that such persons are rarely homicidal. Delusional patients are commonly angry people, and thus they are perceived as threatening. In the rare instances when individuals with delusional disorder do become violent, their victims are usually people who unwittingly fit into their delusional scheme. The person in most danger from an individual with delusional disorder is a spouse or lover.

Paranoid Schizophrenia

Steven had not liked high school very much and was glad to graduate and get a job. But when he realized he needed more education to reach his goals, he applied for admission into a nearby college. He rented a house with several other young men and did well in his stud-

ies. Near the end of his second year, Steven stopped eating with the others and ate only food directly out of a can so he could be sure it wasn't poisoned. When he crossed the campus, he tried to avoid girls as he felt they shot poisoned webs at him that encompassed his body like a giant spider web. When he began to feel that his housemates had put poisoned gas in his room, he dropped out of school and returned home. He cleaned up his room at home and put a lock on the door so his parents could not enter it and contaminate it. He bought a small electric hot plate and prepared all his own food. If his mother urged him to eat a meal with the family, he accused her of wanting to poison him. His parents finally were able to convince him to see a psychiatrist who diagnosed "schizophrenia, subtype paranoia." With medication, individual and group therapy, Steven has improved enough to work in an office under the supervision of an understanding and supportive employer.

Paranoid thinking and behavior are hallmarks of the form of schizophrenia called "paranoid schizophrenia." Individuals with paranoid schizophrenia commonly have extremely bizarre delusions or hallucinations, almost always on a specific theme. Sometimes they hear voices that others cannot hear or believe that their thoughts are being controlled or broadcast aloud. Also, their performance at home and on the job deteriorates, often with a much diminished degree of emotional expressiveness.

In contrast, people with relatively milder paranoid disorders may have such symptoms as delusions of persecution or delusional jealousy, but not the prominent hallucinations or impossible, bizarre delusions of paranoid schizophrenia. Those with milder paranoid disorders are customarily able to work, and their emotional expression and behavior are appropriate to their delusional belief. Apart from their delusions, their thinking remains clear and orderly. On the other hand, those with paranoid schizophrenia are often intellectually disorganized and confused.

Causes of Paranoia

Genetic Contribution

Little research has been done on the role of heredity in causing paranoia. Scientists have found that the families of paranoid patients do not have higher than normal rates of either schizophrenia or depression. However, there is some evidence that paranoid symptoms in schizophrenia may be genetically influenced. Some studies have shown that when one twin of a pair of identical twins with schizophrenia has paranoid symptoms, the other twin usually does also. And, recent research has suggested that paranoid disorders are significantly more common in relatives of persons with schizophrenia than in the general population. Whether paranoid disorder—or a predisposition to it—is inherited is not yet known.

Biochemistry

The discovery that psychosis (a state in which the individual is out of touch with reality) is treatable with antipsychotic drugs has led scientists to look for the origins of severe mental disorders in abnormal brain chemistry. The search has become very complex, as more and more of the chemical substances that carry messages from one nerve cell to another—the neurotransmitters—have been discovered. So far, no clear-cut answers have been found. As with the genetic studies, biochemical studies have not examined paranoia except as a subtype of schizophrenia. There is, however, limited evidence that paranoid schizophrenia is biochemically distinct from nonparanoid forms of the disorder.

Abuse of drugs such as amphetamines, cocaine, marijuana, PCP, LSD, or other stimulants or "psychedelic" compounds may lead to symptoms of paranoid thinking or behavior. Patients with major mental disorders like paranoid schizophrenia may have their symptoms become worse under the influence of these drugs. Scientists are studying the biochemical actions of such drugs to determine how they produce their behavioral effects. This may help us to learn more about the neurochemistry of paranoid disorders, which is poorly understood at this time.

Stress

Some scientists believe paranoia may be a reaction to high levels of life stress. Lending support to this opinion is the evidence that paranoia is more prevalent among immigrants, prisoners of war, and others undergoing severe stress. Sometimes, when thrust into a new and highly stressful situation, people suffer an acute form—called "acute paranoia"—in which delusions develop over a short period of time and last only a few months.

Some studies indicate that paranoia has become more prevalent in the twentieth century. The connection between stress and paranoia does not, of course, rule out other contributing factors. A genetic defect, a brain abnormality, an information-processing disability—or all three—could predispose a person to paranoia; stress may merely act as a trigger.

Treatment of Paranoia

Paranoid people's mistrustfulness makes treatment of the condition difficult. Rarely will they talk casually in an interview. They are suspicious of the kind of open-ended questions many therapists rely on to learn about the patient's history (for example, "Tell me about your relationships with your coworkers."). They may try to avoid hospitalization and drugs, fearing a loss of control or other real or imagined dangers.

Drug Treatment

Treatment with appropriate antipsychotic drugs may help the paranoid patient overcome some symptoms. Although the patient's functioning may be improved, the paranoid symptoms often remain intact. Some studies indicate that symptoms improve following drug treatment, but the same results sometimes occur among patients who receive a placebo, a "sugar pill" without active ingredients. This finding suggests that in some cases the paranoia diminishes for psychological reasons rather than because of the drug's action. Paranoid patients receiving medication must be closely monitored. Their fearfulness and persecutory delusions often lead them to refuse or sabotage treatment—for example, by holding the drug in their cheek until they are alone and then spitting it out.

Psychotherapy

Reports on individual cases suggest that the regular opportunity to express suspicions and self-doubts afforded by psychotherapy can help the paranoid patient function in the community. Although paranoid ideas do seem to persist, they may be less disruptive. Other types of psychotherapy that have reportedly led to improved social functioning without appreciably diminishing paranoid delusions are art therapy, family therapy, and group therapy.

Outlook for Paranoid Patients

In spite of the treatment difficulties, patients with a paranoid disorder may function quite well. Even though their paranoid views are apparently unshakable, various treatments appear effective in improving social functioning, so that they do not often require lengthy hospitalization. The symptoms are less bizarre than those associated with paranoid schizophrenia. Also, the paranoid disorders seem to cause less disorganization of the personality and disruptions in social and family life. Unlike schizophrenia, which can become progressively worse, paranoid disorder seems to reach a certain level of severity and stay there.

For Further Information

Schizophrenia Bulletin, Volume 7, Issue Number 4, 1981 (available in most medical libraries).

Kendler, Kenneth S., Spitzer, Robert L., and Williams, Janet B.W. Psychotic disorders in DSM-III-R. *The American Journal of Psychiatry*, 1989, 146:953-962.

Munro, Alistair. Delusional (paranoid) disorders. *Canadian Journal of Psychiatry*, 1988, Vol. 33(5):399-404.

Opjordsmoen, Stein. Long-term course and outcome in delusional disorder. *Acta Psychiatrica Scandinavica*, 1988, Vol 78(5):576-586.

Sorenson, Donna J., Paul, Gordon L., Mariotto, Marco J. Inconsistencies in paranoid functioning, premorbid adjustment, and chronicity: Question of diagnostic criteria. *Schizophrenia Bulletin*, 1988, Vol. 14(2):323-336.

Williams, Janice G. Cognitive intervention for a paranoid personality disorder. *Psychotherapy*, 1988, Vol. 25(4):570-575.

Chapter 28

Multiple Personality Disorder

Multiple personality disorder (MPD) is a dissociative disorder involving a disturbance of identity in which two or more separate and distinct personalities control the individual's behavior at different times. When under the control of one personality, the person is usually unable to remember some of the events that occurred while other personalities were in control. The different personalities, referred to as alters, may exhibit differences in speech, mannerisms, attitudes, thoughts, and gender orientation. The personalities may even differ in "physical" properties such as allergies, right-or-left handedness, or the need for eyeglass prescriptions. These differences between alters are often quite striking.

The person with MPD may have as few as two alters, or as many as 100. The average number is about 10. Often alters are stable over time, continuing to play specific roles in the person's life for years. Some alters may harbor aggressive tendencies, directed toward individuals in the person's environment, or toward other alters within the person.

At the time that a person with MPD first seeks professional help, he or she is usually not aware of the condition. A very common complaint in people with MPD is episodes of amnesia, or time loss. These individuals may be unable to remember events in all or part of a preceding time period. They may repeatedly encounter unfamiliar people

Excerpted from NIMH Pkt. No. 00-0018.

who claim to know them, find themselves somewhere without knowing how they got there, or find items that they don't remember purchasing among their possessions.

Often people with MPD are depressed or even suicidal, and self-mutilation is common in this group. Approximately one-third of patients complain of auditory or visual hallucinations. It is common for these patients to complain that they hear voices within their head.

Treatment for MPD consists primarily of psychotherapy with hypnosis. The therapist seeks to make contact with as many alters as possible and to understand their roles and functions in the patient's life. In particular, the therapist seeks to form an effective relationship with any personalities that are responsible for violent or self-destructive behavior, and to curb this behavior. The therapist seeks to establish communication among the personalities and to find ones that have memories of traumatic events in the patient's past. The goal of the therapist is to enable the patient to achieve breakdown of the patient's separate personalities and their unification into a single personality.

Retrieving and dealing with memories of trauma is important for the person with MPD, because this disorder is believed to be caused by physical or sexual abuse in childhood. Young children have a pronounced ability to dissociate, and it is believed that those who are abused may learn to use dissociation as a defense. In effect, the child slips into a state of mind in which it seems that the abuse is not really occurring to him or her, but to somebody else. In time, such a child may begin to split off alter personalities. Research has shown that the average age for the initial development of alters is 5.9 years.

Children with MPD have a great variety of symptoms, including depressive tendencies, anxiety, conduct problems, episodes of amnesia, difficulty paying attention in school, and hallucinations. Often these children are misdiagnosed as schizophrenic. By the time the child reaches adolescence, it is less difficult for a mental health professional to recognize the symptoms and make a diagnosis of MPD.

The National Institute of Mental Health, the U.S. Government agency with responsibility for conducting and supporting research on brain and mental disorders, is conducting and supporting studies of MPD. The aim is to achieve a better understanding of the disorder— its causes, its diagnosis and treatment, and its underlying mechanisms. This research will benefit people with MPD and those who care about them.

Chapter 29

Borderline Personality Disorder

Borderline personality disorder (BPD) is a diagnostic term used to describe a somewhat controversial disorder. The fundamental characteristics are 1) unstable mood, including angry outbursts and a tendency to develop acute depressions or "dysphorias" in response to some event such as an apparent rejection, often superimposed on a chronic sense of depression or emptiness; 2) unstable behavior, including repeated episodes of impulsive behavior, self-injury, suicide gestures/attempts, or violence; and 3) enduring problems with self-image, self-esteem, and identity. Sometimes, individuals with BPD experience brief psychotic episodes or dissociative episodes (such as feelings of unreality or out-of-body experiences). These features lead to significant problems in relationships with others.

The term "borderline" is likely to be somewhat puzzling or misleading to the average reader. This disorder was originally thought to be closely related to ("border on") schizophrenia. More recent research suggests that this is not true of most BPD. In fact, BPD is more likely to be related to classical depression, or in some cases to neurological disorders or residual attention deficit disorder.

There are conflicting theories about the origin of this disorder. Some emphasize problems in psychological development during childhood, possibly associated with neglect, abuse, or inconsistent parenting, which lead to maladaptive ways of dealing with the world, problems with identity, and difficulties managing impulses. Others

Excerpted from NIMH Pkt. No. 00-0013.

emphasize biological underpinnings or predisposing factors leading to mood instability or problems with controlling impulses, which in turn contribute to troubled relationships. Further research should help clarify the relative contributions of biology and experience to the development of this disorder.

One of the critical issues in the evaluation of an individual thought to have BPD is establishing whether there are other disorders present as well. For example, about 50% of individuals with BPD also experience classical episodes of major depression, during which the "usual" depression becomes more intense and more steady, sleep and appetite disturbances may occur or become worse, and demoralization may become more marked. Such episodes may indicate a need to treat the depressive episode itself, as part of the comprehensive treatment of BPD. A smaller number of patients may have a form of bipolar disorder and benefit from appropriate treatment. In some patients, a neurological evaluation may be indicated. Eating disorders and drug or alcohol abuse frequently occur as part of the clinical problem.

This disorder is not easy to treat. Many of the problems which occur in everyday life, including mistrust or marked dependency, hostility, manipulations, impulsive behavior, and a tendency to see people and events as "all good" or "all bad" occur in therapy as well. Long-standing patterns of perceiving and responding to events are not rapidly changed. Long-term outpatient psychotherapy is frequently needed and can be effective, but periods of both improvement and worsening, satisfaction and dissatisfaction often continue for a significant period of time. During periods of particular stress, impulsive behavior, or substance abuse, short-term inpatient hospitalization may be needed to help bring the immediate situation under some degree of control. Group therapy is sometimes beneficial, but the patient must be carefully matched to the group.

Research has demonstrated that medication can play a useful role in treatment, but it is unlikely to have magical effects. Except in rare instances in which the effect is dramatic, medication is most useful as an adjunct to psychotherapy, helping to control the most disruptive symptoms and facilitating the work of psychotherapy. Research has shown several medications which are of benefit, at least in the short term and for at least some patients: neuroleptics, tricyclic antidepressants, MAO inhibitor antidepressants, and anticonvulsants. However, deciding whether to use medication and identifying the best medication for an individual patient requires a collaborative effort between patient and physician.

Research into biological factors in BPD is also underway at several research centers, using pharmacologic challenges to identify possible abnormalities in neurotransmitter or endogenous opiate systems and using brain imaging techniques to identify possible structural or functional abnormalities in the brain.

Although the course of treatment may be rocky and prolonged, individuals with BPD can often be helped both to feel better and to function better.

—Description written by Rex William Cowdry, M.D.

For information on NIMH research programs for borderline personality disorder, please contact:

Kathleen M. Oleary, M.S.W.
Room 562
Clinical and Research Services Branch
National Institute of Mental Health
Neuroscience Center at St. Elizabeths
Washington, DC 20032
(202) 373-6068

Chapter 30

Eating Disorders

Each year millions of people in the United States are affected by serious and sometimes life-threatening eating disorders. The vast majority—more than 90 percent—of those afflicted with eating disorders are adolescent and young adult women. One reason that women in this age group are particularly vulnerable to eating disorders is their tendency to go on strict diets to achieve an "ideal" figure. Researchers have found that such stringent dieting can play a key role in triggering eating disorders.

Approximately 1 percent of adolescent girls develop *anorexia nervosa*, a dangerous condition in which they can literally starve themselves to death. Another 2 to 3 percent of young women develop *bulimia nervosa*, a destructive pattern of excessive overeating followed by vomiting or other "purging" behaviors to control their weight. These eating disorders also occur in men and older women, but much less frequently.

The consequences of eating disorders can be severe. For example, one in ten cases of anorexia nervosa leads to death from starvation, cardiac arrest, other medical complications, or suicide. Fortunately, increasing awareness of the dangers of eating disorders—sparked by medical studies and extensive media coverage of the illness—has led many people to seek help. Nevertheless, some people with eating disorders refuse to admit that they have a problem and do not get treat-

NIH Pub. No. 94-3477.

ment. Family members and friends can help recognize the problem and encourage the person to seek treatment.

This text provides valuable information to individuals suffering from eating disorders, as well as to family members and friends trying to help someone cope with the illness. The text describes the symptoms of eating disorders, possible causes, treatment options, and how to take the first steps toward recovery.

Scientists funded by the National Institute of Mental Health (NIMH) are actively studying ways to treat and understand eating disorders. In NIMH-supported research, scientists have found that people with eating disorders who get early treatment have a better chance of full recovery than those who wait years before getting help.

Anorexia Nervosa

People who intentionally starve themselves suffer from an eating disorder called *anorexia nervosa*. The disorder, which usually begins in young people around the time of puberty, involves extreme weight loss—at least 15 percent below the individual's normal body weight. Many people with the disorder look emaciated but are convinced they are overweight. Sometimes they must be hospitalized to prevent starvation.

Deborah developed anorexia nervosa when she was 16. A rather shy, studious teenager, she tried hard to please everyone. She had an attractive appearance, but was slightly overweight. Like many teenage girls, she was interested in boys but concerned that she wasn't pretty enough to get their attention. When her father jokingly remarked that she would never get a date if she didn't take off some weight, she took him seriously and began to diet relentlessly—never believing she was thin enough even when she became extremely underweight.

Soon after the pounds started dropping off, Deborah's menstrual periods stopped. As anorexia tightened its grip, she became obsessed with dieting and food, and developed strange eating rituals. Every day she weighed all the food she would eat on a kitchen scale, cutting solids into minuscule pieces and precisely measuring liquids. She would then put her daily ration in small containers, lining them up in neat rows. She also exercised compulsively, even after she weakened and became faint. She never took an elevator if she could walk up steps.

No one was able to convince Deborah that she was in danger. Finally, her doctor insisted that she be hospitalized and carefully monitored for treatment of her illness. While in the hospital, she secretly continued her exercise regimen in the bathroom, doing strenuous routines of sit-ups and knee-bends. It took several hospitalizations and a good deal of individual and family outpatient therapy for Deborah to face and solve her problems.

Deborah's case in not unusual. People with anorexia typically starve themselves, even though they suffer terribly from hunger pains. One of the most frightening aspects of the disorder is that people with anorexia continue to think they are overweight even when they are bone-thin. For reasons not yet understood, they become terrified of gaining any weight.

Food and weight become obsessions. For some, the compulsiveness shows up in strange eating rituals or the refusal to eat in front of others. It is not uncommon for people with anorexia to collect recipes and prepare gourmet feasts for family and friends, but not partake in the meals themselves. Like Deborah, they may adhere to strict exercise routines to keep off weight. Loss of monthly menstrual periods is typical in women with the disorder. Men with anorexia often become impotent.

Bulimia Nervosa

People with *bulimia nervosa* consume large amounts of food and then rid their bodies of the excess calories by vomiting, abusing laxatives or diuretics, taking enemas, or exercising obsessively. Some use a combination of all these forms of purging. Because many individuals with bulimia "binge and purge" in secret and maintain normal or above normal body weight, they can often successfully hide their problem from others for years.

Lisa developed bulimia nervosa at 18. Like Deborah, her strange eating behavior began when she started to diet. She too dieted and exercised to lose weight, but unlike Deborah, she regularly ate huge amounts of food and maintained her normal weight by forcing herself to vomit. Lisa often felt like an emotional powder keg—angry, frightened, and depressed.

Unable to understand her own behavior, she thought no one else would either. She felt isolated and lonely. Typically, when things were not going well, she would be overcome with an uncontrollable desire for sweets. She would eat pounds of candy and cake at a time, and often not stop until she was exhausted or in severe pain. Then, overwhelmed with guilt and disgust, she would make herself vomit.

Her eating habits so embarrassed her that she kept them secret until, depressed by her mounting problems, she attempted suicide. Fortunately, she didn't succeed. While recuperating in the hospital, she was referred to an eating disorders clinic where she became involved in group therapy. There she received medications to treat the illness and the understanding and help she so desperately needed from others who had the same problem.

Family, friends, and physicians may have difficulty detecting bulimia in someone they know. Many individuals with the disorder remain at normal body weight or above because of their frequent binges and purges, which can range from once or twice a week to several times a day. Dieting heavily between episodes of binging and purging is also common. Eventually, half of those with anorexia will develop bulimia.

As with anorexia, bulimia typically begins during adolescence. The condition occurs most often in women but is also found in men. Many individuals with bulimia, ashamed of their strange habits, do not seek help until they reach their thirties or forties. By this time, their eating behavior is deeply ingrained and more difficult to change.

Binge Eating Disorder

An illness that resembles bulimia nervosa is *binge eating disorder*. Like bulimia, the disorder is characterized by episodes of uncontrolled eating or binging. However, binge eating disorder differs from bulimia because its sufferers do not purge their bodies of excess food.

Individuals with binge eating disorder feel that they lose control of themselves when eating. They eat large quantities of food and do not stop until they are uncomfortably full. Usually, they have more difficulty losing weight and keeping it off than do people with other serious weight problems. Most people with the disorder are obese and have a history of weight fluctuations. Binge eating disorder is found in about 2 percent of the general population—more often in women than men. Recent research shows that binge eating disorder occurs in about 30 percent of people participating in medically supervised weight control programs.

Medical Complications

Medical complications can frequently be a result of eating disorders. Individuals with eating disorders who use drugs to stimulate vomiting, bowel movements, or urination may be in considerable danger, as this practice increases the risk of heart failure.

In patients with anorexia, starvation can damage vital organs such as the heart and brain. To protect itself, the body shifts into "slow gear": monthly menstrual periods stop, breathing, pulse, and blood pressure rates drop, and thyroid function slows. Nails and hair become brittle; the skin dries, yellows, and becomes covered with soft hair called lanugo. Excessive thirst and frequent urination may occur. Dehydration contributes to constipation, and reduced body fat leads to lowered body temperature and the inability to withstand cold.

Mild anemia, swollen joints, reduced muscle mass, and light-headedness also commonly occur in anorexia. If the disorder becomes severe, patients may lose calcium from their bones, making them brittle and prone to breakage. They may also experience irregular heart rhythms and heart failure. In some patients, the brain shrinks, causing personality changes. Fortunately, this condition can be reversed when normal weight is reestablished.

In NIMH-supported research, scientists have found that many patients with anorexia also suffer from other psychiatric illnesses. While the majority have co-occurring clinical depression, others suffer from anxiety, personality or substance abuse disorders, and many are at risk for suicide. Obsessive-compulsive disorder (OCD), an illness characterized by repetitive thoughts and behaviors, can also accompany anorexia. Individuals with anorexia are typically compliant in personality but may have sudden outbursts of hostility and anger or become socially withdrawn.

Bulimia nervosa patients—even those of normal weight—can severely damage their bodies by frequent binge eating and purging. In rare instances, binge eating causes the stomach to rupture; purging may result in heart failure due to loss of vital minerals, such as potassium. Vomiting causes other less deadly, but serious, problems—the acid in vomit wears down the outer layer of the teeth and can cause scarring on the backs of hands when fingers are pushed down the throat to induce vomiting. Further, the esophagus becomes inflamed and the glands near the cheeks become swollen. As in anorexia, bulimia may lead to irregular menstrual periods. Interest in sex may also diminish.

Some individuals with bulimia struggle with addictions, including abuse of drugs and alcohol, and compulsive stealing. Like individuals with anorexia, many people with bulimia suffer from clinical depression, anxiety, OCD, and other psychiatric illnesses. These problems, combined with their impulsive tendencies, place them at increased risk for suicidal behavior.

People with binge eating disorder are usually overweight, so they are prone to the serious medical problems associated with obesity, such as high cholesterol, high blood pressure, and diabetes. Obese individuals also have a higher risk for gallbladder disease, heart disease, and some types of cancer. Research at NIMH and elsewhere has shown that individuals with binge eating disorder have high rates of co-occurring psychiatric illnesses—especially depression.

Causes of Eating Disorders

In trying to understand the causes of eating disorders, scientists have studied the personalities, genetics, environments, and biochemistry of people with these illnesses. As is often the case, the more that is learned, the more complex the roots of eating disorders appear.

Personalities

Most people with eating disorders share certain personality traits: low self-esteem, feelings of helplessness, and a fear of becoming fat. In anorexia, bulimia, and binge eating disorder, eating behaviors seem to develop as a way of handling stress and anxieties.

People with anorexia tend to be "too good to be true." They rarely disobey, keep their feelings to themselves, and tend to be perfectionists, good students, and excellent athletes. Some researchers believe that people with anorexia restrict food— particularly carbohydrates— to gain a sense of control in some area of their lives. Having followed the wishes of others for the most part, they have not learned how to cope with the problems typical of adolescence, growing up, and becoming independent. Controlling their weight appears to offer two advantages, at least initially: they can take control of their bodies and gain approval from others. However, it eventually becomes clear to others that they are out-of-control and dangerously thin.

People who develop bulimia and binge eating disorder typically consume huge amounts of food—often junk food—to reduce stress and relieve anxiety. With binge eating, however, comes guilt and depression. Purging can bring relief, but it is only temporary. Individuals with bulimia are also impulsive and more likely to engage in risky behavior such as abuse of alcohol and drugs.

Genetic and Environmental Factors

Eating disorders appear to run in families—with female relatives most often affected. This finding suggests that genetic factors may predispose some people to eating disorders; however, other influences—both behavioral and environmental—may also play a role. One recent study found that mothers who are overly concerned about their daughters' weight and physical attractiveness may put the girls at increased risk of developing an eating disorder. In addition, girls with eating disorders often have fathers and brothers who are overly critical of their weight.

Although most victims of anorexia and bulimia are adolescent and young adult women, these illnesses can also strike men and older women. Anorexia and bulimia are found most often in Caucasians, but these illnesses also affect African Americans and other racial ethnic groups. People pursuing professions or activities that emphasize thinness—like modeling, dancing, gymnastics, wrestling, and long-distance running—are more susceptible to the problem. In contrast to other eating disorders, one-third to one-fourth of all patients with binge eating disorder are men. Preliminary studies also show that the condition occurs equally among African Americans and Caucasians.

Biochemistry

In an attempt to understand eating disorders, scientists have studied the biochemical functions of people with the illnesses. They have focused recently on the neuroendocrine system—a combination of the central nervous and hormonal systems. Through complex but carefully balanced feedback mechanisms, the neuroendocrine system regulates sexual function, physical growth and development, appetite and digestion, sleep, heart and kidney function, emotions, thinking, and memory—in other words, multiple functions of the mind and body. Many of these regulatory mechanisms are seriously disturbed in people with eating disorders.

In the central nervous system—particularly the brain—key chemical messengers known as neurotransmitters control hormone production. Scientists have found that the neurotransmitters *serotonin* and *norepinephrine* function abnormally in people affected by depression. Recently, researchers funded by NIMH have learned that these neurotransmitters are also decreased in acutely ill anorexia and bulimia patients and long-term recovered anorexia patients. Because many people with eating disorders also appear to suffer from depression, some scientists believe that there may be a link between these two disorders. This link is supported by studies showing that antidepressants can be used successfully to treat some people with eating disorders. In fact, new research has suggested that some patients with anorexia may respond well to the antidepressant medication fluoxetine, which affects serotonin function in the body.

People with either anorexia or certain forms of depression also tend to have higher than normal levels of *cortisol*, a brain hormone released in response to stress. Scientists have been able to show that the excess levels of cortisol in both anorexia and depression are caused by a problem that occurs in or near a region of the brain called the hypothalamus.

In addition to connections between depression and eating disorders, scientists have found biochemical similarities between people with eating disorders and obsessive-compulsive disorder (OCD). Just as serotonin levels are known to be abnormal in people with depression and eating disorders, they are also abnormal in patients with OCD. Recently, NIMH researchers have found that many patients with bulimia have obsessive-compulsive behavior as severe as that seen in patients actually diagnosed with OCD. Conversely, patients with OCD frequently have abnormal eating behaviors.

The hormone *vasopressin* is another brain chemical found to be abnormal in people with eating disorders and OCD. NIMH researchers have shown that levels of this hormone are elevated in patients with OCD, anorexia, and bulimia. Normally released in response to physical and possibly emotional stress, vasopressin may contribute to the obsessive behavior seen in some patients with eating disorders.

NIMH-supported investigators are also exploring the role of other brain chemicals in eating behavior. Many are conducting studies in animals to shed some light on human disorders.

For example, scientists have found that levels of *neuropeptide Y* and *peptide YY*, recently shown to be elevated in patients with anorexia and bulimia, stimulate eating behavior in laboratory animals. Other investigators have found that *cholecystokinin* (CCK), a hormone known to be low in some women with bulimia, causes laboratory animals to feel full and stop eating. This finding may possibly explain why women with bulimia do not feel satisfied after eating and continue to binge.

Treatment

Eating disorders are most successfully treated when diagnosed early. Unfortunately, even when family members confront the ill person about his or her behavior, or physicians make a diagnosis, individuals with eating disorders may deny that they have a problem. Thus, people with anorexia may not receive medical or psychological attention until they have already become dangerously thin and malnourished. People with bulimia are often normal weight and are able to hide their illness from others for years. Eating disorders in males may be overlooked because anorexia and bulimia are relatively rare in boys and men. Consequently, getting—and keeping—people with these disorders into treatment can be extremely difficult.

In any case, it cannot be overemphasized how important treatment is—the sooner, the better. The longer abnormal eating behaviors persist, the more difficult it is to overcome the disorder and its effects on the body. In some cases, long-term treatment may be required. Families and friends offering support and encouragement can play an important role in the success of the treatment program.

If an eating disorder is suspected, particularly if it involves weight loss, the first step is a complete physical examination to rule out any other illnesses. Once an eating disorder is diagnosed, the clinician must determine whether the patient is in immediate medical danger and requires hospitalization. While most patients can be treated as outpatients, some need hospital care. Conditions warranting hospitalization include excessive and rapid weight loss, serious metabolic disturbances, clinical depression or risk of suicide, severe binge eating and purging, or psychosis.

The complex interaction of emotional and physiological problems in eating disorders calls for a comprehensive treatment plan, involving a variety of experts and approaches. Ideally, the treatment team includes an internist, a nutritionist, an individual psychotherapist, a group and family psychotherapist, and a psychopharmacologist—someone who is knowledgeable about psychoactive medications useful in treating these disorders.

To help those with eating disorders deal with their illness and underlying emotional issues, some form of psychotherapy is usually needed. A psychiatrist, psychologist, or other mental health professional meets with the patient individually and provides ongoing emotional support, while the patient begins to understand and cope with the illness. Group therapy, in which people share their experiences with others who have similar problems, has been especially effective for individuals with bulimia.

Use of individual psychotherapy, family therapy, and cognitive-behavioral therapy—a form of psychotherapy that teaches patients how to change abnormal thoughts and behavior—is often the most productive. Cognitive-behavior therapists focus on changing eating behaviors, usually by rewarding or modeling wanted behavior. These therapists also help patients work to change the distorted and rigid thinking patterns associated with eating disorders.

NIMH-supported scientists have examined the effectiveness of combining psychotherapy and medications. In a recent study of bulimia, researchers found that both intensive group therapy and anti-depressant medications, combined or alone, benefited patients. In another study of bulimia, the combined use of cognitive-behavioral therapy and antidepressant medications was most beneficial. The combination treatment was particularly effective in preventing relapse once medications were discontinued. For patients with binge eating disorder, cognitive-behavioral therapy and antidepressant medications may also prove to be useful.

Antidepressant medications commonly used to treat bulimia include desipramine, imipramine, and fluoxetine. For anorexia, preliminary evidence shows that some antidepressant medications may be effective when combined with other forms of treatment. Fluoxetine has also been useful in treating some patients with binge eating disorder. These antidepressants may also treat any co-occurring depression.

The efforts of mental health professionals need to be combined with those of other health professionals to obtain the best treatment. Physicians treat any medical complications, and nutritionists advise on diet and eating regimens. The challenge of treating eating disorders is made more difficult by the metabolic changes associated with them. Just to maintain a stable weight, individuals with anorexia may actually have to consume more calories than someone of similar weight and age without an eating disorder.

This information is important for patients and the clinicians who treat them. Consuming calories is exactly what the person with anorexia wishes to avoid, yet must do to regain the weight necessary for recovery. In contrast, some normal weight people with bulimia may gain excess weight if they consume the number of calories required to maintain normal weight in others of similar size and age.

Helping the Person With an Eating Disorder

Treatment can save the life of someone with an eating disorder. Friends, relatives, teachers, and physicians all play an important role in helping the ill person start and stay with a treatment program. Encouragement, caring, and persistence, as well as information about eating disorders and their dangers, may be needed to convince the ill person to get help, stick with treatment, or try again.

Family members and friends can call local hospitals or university medical centers to find out about eating disorder clinics and clinicians experienced in treating these illnesses. For college students, treatment programs may be available in school counseling centers.

Family members and friends should read as much as possible about eating disorders, so they can help the person with the illness understand his or her problem. Many local mental health organizations and the self-help groups listed at the end of this chapter provide free literature on eating disorders. Some of these groups also provide treatment program referrals and information on local self-help groups. Once the person gets help, he or she will continue to need lots of understanding and encouragement to stay in treatment.

NIMH continues its search for new and better treatments for eating disorders. Congress has designated the 1990s as the Decade of the Brain, making the prevention, diagnosis, and treatment of all brain and mental disorders a national research priority. This research promises to yield even more hope for patients and their families by providing a greater understanding of the causes and complexities of eating disorders.

For Further Information

For additional information on eating disorders, check local hospitals or university medical centers for an eating disorders clinic, or contact:

National Association of Anorexia Nervosa and Associated Disorders (ANAD)
P.O. Box 7
Highland Park, IL 60035
(708) 831-3438

Anorexia Nervosa and Related Eating Disorders, Inc. (ANRED)
P.O. Box 5102
Eugene, OR 97405
(503) 344-1144

American Anorexia/Bulimia Association, Inc. (AABA)
425 East 61st Street, 6th Floor
New York, NY 10021
(212) 891-8686

Center for the Study of Anorexia and Bulimia
1 West 91st Street
New York, NY 10024
(212) 595-3449

National Eating Disorder Organization
445 East Grandille Road
Worthington, OH 43085
(614) 436-1112

Foundation for Education about Eating Disorders (FEED)
P.O. Box 16375
Baltimore, MD 21210
(410) 467-0603

For information on Eating Disorders Awareness Week, contact:

Eating Disorders Awareness & Prevention Inc.
603 Stewart Street, Suite 803
Seattle, WA 98101
(206) 382-3587

For information on other mental disorders, contact:

Information Resources and Inquiries Branch
National Institute of Mental Health
5600 Fishers Lane, Room 7C-02
Rockville, MD 20857

—by Lee Hoffman
Office of Scientific Information
National institute of Mental Health

Chapter 31

Sleep Disorders

Introduction

One-third of all adult Americans—about 50 million people—complain about their sleep. Some sleep too little, some fitfully, and some too much. Although one-third of our lives is spent asleep, most of us don't know much about sleep, not even our own. We don't even know exactly why we sleep, other than—like an overnight battery recharge—sleep promotes daytime alertness. Sleep problems profoundly disturb both sleeping and waking life. What is the significance of these problems and what can be done about them? Recent scientific research is beginning to provide some of the answers.

The Balm of the Bard

Sleep was, for Shakespeare, the "balm of hurt minds, great nature's second course, chief nourisher in life's feast." For centuries, science knew little more: sleep was a magical phenomenon. Not until the 1930s was it shown to possess a secret life. Only then did investigators, using the electroencephalogram (EEG), measure the brain's electrical activity in sleeping subjects. On rivers of graph paper, they could watch the rhythm of activity in the brain during sleep. They discovered that these biological rhythms naturally fall into different

DHHS Pub. No. (ADM) 87-1541, and "Melatonin: A Chemical Slumber Switch," *NCRR Reporter*, July/August 1994.

states, stages, and cycles. Instead of being a quiet and peaceful period of rest and recuperation, as most of us think of it, sleep is a very complex, dynamic activity. Your body may be the picture of tranquility while you sleep. But, in fact, numerous biochemical, physiological, and psychological events are constantly taking place.

How Long to Sleep

Most adults sleep between 7 and 8 hours. But no one really knows how much sleep we need. Sleep duration varies widely. A natural "short sleeper" may sleep for only 3 or 4 hours, and actually function worse with more sleep. A "long sleeper," on the other hand, may need more than 10 hours. "Variable sleepers" seem to need more sleep at times of stress and less during peaceful times. Changes with age also contribute to changes in the ability to sleep continuously and soundly. A newborn infant may sleep 16 hours a day, an adolescent may sleep very deeply for 9 or 10 hours straight, while an elderly person may take daytime naps and then sleep only 5 hours a night. With advancing age, some people switch to shorter days and some to longer ones. Such a switch may be simply a normal condition of aging. Or, it may result from shifts in daily patterns, retirement, or changes in the person's physical or mental health.

In general, sleep is helped by two factors—being tired at bedtime and being in tune with your own internal clock. Sleep may be difficult or less satisfying if it occurs at a time when the biological clock says, "It's time to be awake."

To find out how much sleep you need, try to determine your own sleep pattern. You should feel sleepy about the same time every evening. If you frequently have trouble staying awake in the daytime, you may not be sleeping long enough. Or perhaps you are not sleeping well enough. Both the quantity and quality of sleep and wakefulness are important. You are sleeping as much as you need if, during your waking hours, you are alert and have a sense of well-being.

Insomnia: A Symptom, Not an Illness

Insomnia, the most common sleep complaint, is the feeling that you have not slept well or long enough. It occurs in many different forms. Most often it is characterized by difficulty falling asleep (taking more than 30 to 45 minutes), awakening frequently during the night, or waking up early and being unable to get back to sleep.

With rare exceptions, insomnia is a *symptom* of a problem, and not the problem itself. Good sleep is a sign of health. Poor sleep is often a sign of some malfunctioning and may signal either minor or serious medical or psychiatric disorders. Insomnia can begin at any age. And, it can last for a few days (transient insomnia), a few weeks (short-term insomnia), or indefinitely (long-term insomnia).

Causes of Insomnia

Transient insomnia may be triggered by stress—say, a hospitalization for surgery, a final exam, a cold, headache, toothache, bruised muscles, backache, indigestion, or itchy rash. It can also be caused by jet travel that involves rapid time-zone change.

Short-term insomnia, lasting up to 3 weeks, may result from anxiety, nervousness, and physical and mental tension. Typical are worries about money, the death of a loved one, marital problems, divorce, looking for or losing a job, weight loss, excessive concern about health, or plain boredom, social isolation, or physical confinement.

Long-lasting distress over lack of sleep is sometimes caused by the environment, such as living near an airport or on a noisy street. Working a night shift can also cause problems: sleeping during the day may be difficult on weekdays, especially when the person sleeps at night on weekends. But more often, long-term insomnia stems from such medical conditions as heart disease, arthritis, diabetes, asthma, chronic sinusitis, epilepsy, or ulcers. Long-term impaired sleep can also be brought on by chronic drug or alcohol use, as well as by excessive use of beverages containing caffeine and abuse of sleeping pills.

Sometimes (as we shall see), long-term sleep difficulty can result from a number of other directly sleep-related medical ailments that are more directly related to sleep. Some examples are sleep apnea, nocturnal myoclonus, or "restless legs" syndrome.

Many patients with long-term insomnia may be suffering from an underlying psychiatric condition, such as depression or schizophrenia. Depression, in particular, is often accompanied by sleep problems (which usually disappear when the depression is treated). People with phobias, anxiety, obsessions, or compulsions are often awakened by their fears and worries, sometimes by nightmares and feelings of sadness, conflict, and guilt.

Sleep Hygiene: A First Move Against Insomnia

Insomnia is a complex problem, not given to simple solutions. Most experts agree that treatment should start with assessing and correcting sleep hygiene and habits.

Exercise

Regular exercise tends to benefit sleep, but not right at bedtime. Vigorous exercise, especially just before sleep, can cause arousal and delay sleep. You cannot force sleep on a given night by exercising excessively during the day. Exercise in the morning also has little beneficial effect on sleep. The best time to exercise is in the afternoon or early evening. But, even then, it probably won't help you sleep unless you exercise on a regular schedule.

Trying Too Hard

Trouble falling asleep, the most common form of sleep disturbance, may be brought on simply by going to bed too early. Sleep cannot be forced. You should not go to sleep until you are sleepy. If you turn in too early—even if you do fall asleep—you could experience a disturbed night's rest or could wake early without feeling refreshed. If you go to bed when you feel sleepy but find that you can't fall asleep, don't stay in bed brooding about being awake. It is best to get out of bed. Leave the bedroom. Read, sew, watch TV, take a warm bath, or find some other way to relax before slipping between the sheets once more.

Naps

Laboratory tests have shown that daytime naps disrupt normal nighttime sleep. Although many people feel like napping between 2 and 4 p.m. (siesta time), most sleep better if they don't nap during the day. Naps should not be used as a substitute for poor sleep at night. However, there are exceptions to this general rule. Many older people, in particular, do sleep better at night when they take daytime naps. But if you are a napper who sleeps poorly at night, your nighttime sleep might improve if you skip the naps.

Bedtime Snacks

If hunger keeps you awake, a light snack might help you sleep, unless it causes problems with digestion. Avoid heavy meals, alcohol, and caffeine-containing coffee, tea, and cola. For those who can tolerate milk, that old, time-tested remedy may work best.

Smoking at Bedtime

Nicotine stimulates the nervous system and can interfere with sleep. In one sleep laboratory study, smokers experienced greater difficulty than nonsmokers. Sleep patterns also improved significantly among chronic smokers when they abstained from smoking.

Alcohol

The effect of alcohol is deceiving. It may induce sleep, but chances are it will be a fragmented sleep. The sleeper will probably wake up in the middle of the night when the alcohol's relaxing effect wears off.

Regular Bedtime

The best way to sleep better is to keep a regular schedule for sleeping. Go to bed at about the same time every night, but only when you are tired. Set your alarm clock to awaken you about the same time every morning—including weekends and regardless of the amount of sleep you have had. If you have a poor night's sleep, don't linger in bed or oversleep the next day. If you awaken before it is time to rise, get out of bed and start your day. Most insomniacs stay in bed too long and get up too late in the morning. By establishing a regular wakeup time you help solidify the biological rhythms that establish your periods of peak efficiency during the 24-hour day.

Sleeping Pills: A Temporary Solution

According to the latest evidence, the medical profession is becoming increasingly conservative in prescribing sleep-promoting medications. Over the past decade, prescriptions filled in drugstores have dropped from 42 to 21 million. Only about 10 percent of people with insomnia receive prescribed sleeping pills. Another 5 percent buy over-the-counter sleep compounds that don't require a prescription. Still others use drugs intended for other purposes—for example, daytime sedatives, antihistamines, anticholinergic drugs, and tranquilizers.

None of these drugs should be used without consulting a physician first. Their misuse or outright abuse poses a danger. All sleeping medications should be used sparingly, for the shortest possible time, and in the smallest effective dose.

Prescribed Sleeping Pills

All brands of prescribed sleeping pills are hypnotics—that is, drugs that depress the central nervous system and put users to sleep. A variety of hypnotics are now on the market, including barbiturates, benzodiazepines, and several classes of drugs generally referred to as the nonbarbiturates/nonbenzodiazepines.

The barbiturates usually lose their effectiveness within 2 or 3 weeks of daily use. Doctors today tend not to prescribe the barbiturates. Most prefer to treat their patients with one of the benzodiazepines or a variant class of drug, which are considered less addictive and safer in overdose than barbiturates. The benzodiazepines are still very toxic, however, when taken in combination with alcohol, or when overdoses are taken by persons with respiratory disorders. Benzodiazepine drugs sometimes can aid sleep for up to 30 days. The benzodiazepines are not all alike, though. Some work faster than others, some produce effects that last longer, and some are eliminated from the body sooner.

Which type of sleeping pill is prescribed depends on a person's particular problem and needs. One pill might be right for problems in falling asleep and another for problems in maintaining sleep or insomnia associated with anxiety.

Do Sleeping Pills Help?

When taken for a brief period and under a doctor's guidance, prescription sleeping pills may help you sleep better. But insomnia cannot be corrected with pills. At best, sleeping pills have only limited usefulness. They provide a temporary solution to insomnia. Thus, only when a person's health, safety, and well-being are threatened should sleep-promoting drugs be considered—and then only after the doctor takes a medical history and does a physical examination. He or she might identify conditions that should not be treated with sleeping pills and weigh other risks of drug treatment.

Hazards

Although temporarily helpful, sleep-promoting medications can eventually cause disturbed sleep, side effects, a sleep "hangover" during the day, and dependence on the drug. Furthermore, once the drugs are stopped, sleep problems return, at least temporarily, and may be even more severe than they were before the medication was first taken. Clearly, the regular, long-term use of sleeping pills should usually be avoided.

Sleeping pills can be fatal when taken in combination with alcohol or other drugs. Even when not fatal, combining drugs and alcohol can be perilous to driving and the use of other machinery. Long-acting sleeping pills, by themselves, may also impair driving performance the day after they are taken. People who are taking sleeping pills should *never* drink for a couple of days afterward.

Sleeping Pills for the Elderly

Many people over 60 are dissatisfied with their sleep. While they make up about 14 percent of the population, they consume about 20 to 45 percent of all sleep medications.

Toxic (poisonous) drug reactions occur more frequently in the elderly than in the young. In addition to their frequent use of sleeping pills, many older people also take other medications prescribed by their doctors. Combining sleeping pills and other drugs poses an increased hazard for the elderly because of changes in bodily functioning that accompany aging. The elderly tend to absorb and excrete all medications more slowly than younger people and usually require smaller doses. Their nervous systems may also be more sensitive, which, in turn, may increase the effects of combining drugs.

Sleeping pills may cause older people to stumble or fall, feel groggy or hung-over, or appear forgetful and senile. Before turning to sleep medications, older people (like people of any age) should consult their doctor and first seek help to the underlying cause of the sleep problem.

Sleeping Pills and Pregnant Women

Pregnant women should be aware that sleeping pills may be harmful to their infants. If a woman is pregnant or intends to become pregnant, she should ask her physician whether it is safe or advisable to use any drug. She also should learn about the effects of every drug, including cigarettes and alcohol, on her and her unborn baby.

Sleep Disorders: A National Health Problem

Sleep disturbances place an uncalculated, but enormous, burden on the American public. Many industrial and automobile accidents are related to undiagnosed and untreated disorders of sleep. School and job performance, and even everyday social relationships, are also affected. Most sleep disorders, whether caused by physical or mental factors, can be treated or managed effectively once they are properly diagnosed.

Anxiety, Depression, and Sleep

In a recent national survey, 47 percent of those reporting severe insomnia reported a high level of emotional distress. Psychological factors, such as fears, phobias, and compulsions, can so occupy the mind that sleep is delayed, disturbed, or shortened. Chronically tense people are frequently so restless, hyperactive, and apprehensive that they expect not to sleep when they go to bed.

In depressed people, an overwhelming feeling of sadness, hopelessness, worthlessness, or guilt can be associated with abnormal sleep patterns. Often, the depressed person awakens early and cannot return to sleep. Yet, sometimes, just the opposite is true. Some depressed people find relief in sleeping, denying or escaping from the problems of living by sleeping. The loss of a sense of purpose in life may be associated with an overwhelming urge to sleep, a constant feeling of tiredness, or nighttime sleep marked by an irregular sleep/wake pattern.

Many depressed people complain of insomnia without recognizing they are depressed. If you have lost interest in activities you used to enjoy, or if you have feelings of hopelessness or suicidal thoughts, you may be one of them. You should discuss the problem with your physician, who may recommend psychiatric consultation. While the complaint may be insomnia, the underlying depression, not the insomnia, must be treated. Antidepressant medications and/or psychotherapy can produce remarkable improvement, both in mood and sleep patterns.

Snoring

Snoring is a sign of impaired breathing during sleep. The older you get, the more apt you are to snore. Almost 60 percent of males in their 60s and 45 percent of females are habitual snorers—in all, one in eight Americans. Light snoring may be no more than a nuisance. But, snoring that is loud, disruptive, and accompanied by extreme daytime sleepiness or sleep attacks should be taken very seriously. Such snoring may be a sign that a person is suffering from the life-threatening condition called sleep apnea—a blockage of breathing during sleep.

Sleep Apnea

Discovered only recently, sleep apnea is believed to affect at least 1 out of every 200 Americans—70 to 90 percent of them men, mostly middle-aged, and usually overweight. But the condition can afflict both men or women at any age.

People with this disorder actually may stop breathing while asleep—even hundreds of times—without being aware of the problem. During an apnea attack, the snorer may seem to gasp for breath, and the oxygen level in the blood may become abnormally low. In severe cases, a sleep apnea victim may actually spend more time not breathing than breathing and may be at risk for death.

In the most common form of the condition, obstructive apnea (also called upper airway apnea), air stops flowing through the nose and mouth, but throat and abdominal breathing efforts are uninterrupted. The snoring that results is produced when the upper rear of the mouth (the soft palate and the cone-shaped tissue—the uvula—that descends from it) relaxes and vibrates as air passes in and out. This sets up an air current between the palate and the base of the tongue, resulting in snoring. Typically, the individual will wake up, emit a vigorous snort or grunt while gasping for air, then immediately fall back to sleep, only to repeat the cycle.

In another form of the disorder, central apnea, both oral breathing and throat and abdominal breathing efforts are simultaneously interrupted. In a third type of apnea, mixed apnea, a brief period of central apnea is followed by a longer period of obstructive apnea.

Sleep apnea can be recognized by a number of symptoms. As mentioned, loud and intermittent snoring is one warning signal. The person who has sleep apnea may experience a choking sensation, early-morning headaches, or extreme daytime sleepiness, as well. His bed partner or roommate might comment on his excessive body movements or his snorting or gasping for breath during sleep.

If the condition is suspected, it should be reported to a physician, who may recommend evaluation by a specialist in sleep disorders. Since sleeping pills may be harmful for people with sleep apnea, they should not be taken if the condition is suspected.

Many people with such conditions as obesity, deviated nasal septum, polyps, enlarged tonsils, large adenoids, or a host of other problems may be particularly likely to develop sleep apnea. Doctors can reliably diagnose the disorder only by monitoring oxygen intake, breathing, and other physical functions while the patient is sleeping.

In mild cases, sleep apnea often responds to medication. Or, in the case of overweight middle-aged males, losing weight may lessen the problem. Another procedure, known as continuous positive air pressure, involves the use of a machine that blows air into the nose during the night, opening the air passages in the throat. Patients with severe sleep apnea may require surgery. One procedure widens the throat. In another, a tracheostomy, which is used in very severe cases, a small hole is made at the base of the neck, below and in front of the Adam's apple. At night, a valve on a hollow tube in the hole is opened so that air can flow directly to the lungs, bypassing the sleep-induced upper airway blockage. During the day, the valve is closed, allowing the patient to breathe and speak normally.

Narcolepsy—Sleep Attacks

A sleepy feeling during the day could be caused by insufficient, inadequate, or fragmented sleep, by insomnia, or by boredom, social isolation, physical confinement, or depression. But, if you continually experience excessive daily daytime sleepiness—sometimes expressed as tiredness, lack of energy, and/or irresistible sleepiness—you could be suffering from another little-known, chronic sleep disorder called narcolepsy.

According to the American Narcolepsy Association, 1 out of every 100 Americans is afflicted by this disorder. Yet, between 50 and 80 percent of them remain undiagnosed. People with narcolepsy suffer from sleep apnea more often than the general population, although apnea is not a core feature of the disorder.

During a narcoleptic attack, the person may find it physically impossible to stay awake and sleeps for periods ranging from a few seconds to a half hour. An attack can occur while watching TV, reading, or listening to a lecture. More surprising, these sudden attacks of sleep can also strike while walking, eating, riding a bike, or carrying on a conversation.

Despite modern medical knowledge about narcolepsy, people who have such attacks typically do not seek medical attention for years—an average of 5 to 7 years. Usually, narcolepsy starts in the early teen years, but it can strike anyone at any age. At first, the symptoms are rather mild. Gradually, over a period of years, they increase in severity.

Narcolepsy with Cataplexy. Besides the presence of excessive sleepiness, which usually is the first symptom noted, the person suffering from narcolepsy may experience a sudden weakness of the muscles called cataplexy. A cataplectic attack is usually triggered by such emotions as laughter, anger, elation, or surprise. It may be experienced as partial muscle weakness lasting a few seconds or as almost complete loss of muscle control lasting for 1 to 2 minutes. During this period, the victim may be in a state of nearly total physical collapse, unable to move or speak, but still conscious and at least partially aware of activity in the immediate environment.

Sometimes, narcolepsy is misdiagnosed as epilepsy. But while epilepsy is often accompanied by loss of bladder and bowel control and tongue biting, narcolepsy is not. More often, the symptoms of narcolepsy are attributed to laziness, malingering, or psychiatric disorder. Job and home life usually suffer when narcolepsy goes untreated.

Narcolepsy, believed to be caused by a defect in the central nervous system, has no known cure. However, after proper diagnosis, the disorder can be effectively managed with drugs.

Hazards of Narcolepsy. People who have narcolepsy but don't know it represent a serious safety hazard to themselves and others when they drive. They may doze off while waiting for a traffic signal to change, or they may drive to some destination and be completely unable to recall how they got there. At least one in every 500 drivers is estimated to be suffering from narcolepsy.

Tragically, many of the drivers may not survive to be diagnosed or counted among the sufferers. Yet, narcolepsy is a major traffic safety problem with a low-cost and easy solution: proper diagnosis and medical care. Diagnosed patients who understand their symptoms appear to be very safe drivers, and their driving can be coordinated with the use of medication.

Nocturnal Myoclonus—Unusual Movement During Sleep

Just before some people fall asleep, they experience an uncomfortable, but not always painful, sensation deep in the thigh, calf, or feet. They usually find that vigorous movement eases the discomfort enough to fall asleep, but they complain of sleepiness and fatigue during the day. These people are generally not aware that such episodes of repetitive leg muscle jerks or muscle twitches—nocturnal myoclonus—are followed throughout the night by hundreds of related awakenings. People with nocturnal myoclonus may have involuntary movement in their legs, in addition to twitches, while trying to relax. This condition, known as "restless leg syndrome," usually occurs in people who also have nocturnal myoclonus.

Like many other sleep disorders, nocturnal myoclonus often goes unrecognized by the person who has it. It is most common in middle-aged and older people. And, it may be inherited. Often a bed partner or roommate must call attention to the characteristic twitches—repeated muscle jerks in which the big toe extends, while the ankle, knee, and, occasionally, the hip flex. Upon awakening, some people with nocturnal myoclonus complain of an itching-crawling sensation in their legs, like "current going through them."

In some cases, these disorders have been associated with too little vitamin E, iron, or calcium, and vitamin and mineral supplements have been used as treatment. In other cases, drugs have been found effective, and, in still other, less-severe cases, relief has come from leg exercises.

Sleep Problems of Children

Most childhood sleep disturbances occur only at certain ages, are temporary, and disappear as the child grows older. While annoying or frightening, they usually are not serious. In some cases, however, abnormal sleeping habits can be a sign of more serious problems requiring medical consultation.

Sleepwalking

Sleepwalking (somnambulism) is fairly common, especially among children. An estimated 15 percent of all children between the ages of 5 and 12 have walked in their sleep at least once, and most outgrow the disorder. Typically, the child (or adult) sleepwalker sits up, gets out of bed, and moves about in an uncoordinated-manner. Less frequently, the sleepwalker may dress, open doors, eat, or go to the bathroom without incident and usually will avoid obstacles. But sleepwalkers don't always make their rounds in safety. They sometimes hurt themselves, stumbling against furniture and losing their balance, going through windows, or falling down stairs.

In children, sleepwalking is not believed to be influenced by psychological factors. In adults, it could indicate a personality disturbance.

Usually, it is enough for parents of sleepwalkers to provide their children with emotional support. They should also lock windows and doors and make sure the child does not sleep near stairways and potentially dangerous objects. For severe cases, a doctor may prescribe drugs.

Night Terrors Versus Nightmares

Night terrors (known as *pavor nocturnus* in children) are relatively short nocturnal episodes during which the child sits up in bed, emits a piercing scream or cry, looks frightened and sweats and breathes profusely. Episodes usually occur between the ages of 4 and 12, are more common in boys than girls, and can be expected to disappear as the child grows older. Typically, they occur during the first third of the night. The disorder may progress to sleep walking, but generally that only happens when the child is made to stand up. Later

365

the child will forget the entire episode. Parents should comfort and provide warmth and support to children who experience night terrors. The condition does not indicate any personality disorder.

Nightmares, unlike night terrors, can be recalled afterward and are accompanied by much less anxiety and movement. These frightening dream experiences, which tend to occur at times of insecurity, emotional turmoil, depression, or guilt, can occur in all age groups. They are rarely accompanied by the anguished, terrified scream of the night-terror arousal. A person experiencing a nightmare will usually recount in detail a threat which ultimately led to the awakening. Some people rarely have nightmares, while others seem predisposed to them.

Bedwetting

Bedwetting (enuresis) is a common childhood sleep disorder which, contrary to popular belief, is almost never emotionally or psychologically caused; less than 1 percent of bedwetting has an emotional source. About 5 to 17 percent of children aged 3 to 5 wet their beds; usually the condition will stop by the age of 4 or 5. However, a bedwetting child may feel guilty or ashamed. Waking the child up in the middle of the night or handing out punishments and rewards may only serve to increase the problem.

In most cases, the cause is unknown, but a congenitally small bladder, a bladder infection, or some other physical problem may be responsible. Bedwetting that continues into adolescence or adulthood may be attributed to emotional problems, but neurological disease or diabetes also can be the cause. If the disorder persists, a physician should be consulted. For some children, drugs or time away from home may be prescribed for short periods, such as a week at camp or a weekend with friends or relatives.

Help for Sleep Disorders

If your sleep is continually disrupted and you lack initiative and energy during the day, you should seek professional help. In most cases of sleep disorder, it's best to see your own physician first, in order to sort out the general nature and severity of a sleep problem. The physician may conduct a thorough physical examination, ask you questions about your sleep habits and emotional state, and can often determine whether the sleep difficulty is related to treatable causes. However, if necessary, a referral to a mental health specialist or facility, a sleep clinic, or a sleep disorders center may be made.

The same basic service is provided by both sleep clinics and sleep disorders centers. Generally, sleep clinics are set up as part of hospitals. Sleep disorders centers may be associated with hospitals, medical centers, universities, or psychiatric or neurological institutes. Most clinics or centers primarily treat patients on referral from general practitioners and internists. However, it is possible to obtain information on specific sleep problems directly from a clinic or center or to make an appointment for a consultation.

Specialized sleep facilities usually have on their staffs experts called somnologists with training in a variety of medical and scientific fields. A sleep disorders team will often include a physician, a psychologist, a psychiatrist, and a surgeon.

Patients are typically seen as outpatients. They are interviewed thoroughly, given a battery of psychological tests and, if indicated, have their sleep patterns recorded in the laboratory for one night (sometimes two or three consecutive nights) to determine the cause of the sleep disturbance.

Fees vary, depending on the clinic or center. An entire analysis can range from a few hundred to about a thousand dollars. Insurance companies or Medicare, may cover some of the cost. (This can be determined by consulting the center or your insurance company.)

Special sleep facilities are scattered throughout the country. Your physician or nearest hospital should be able to help you locate the nearest sleep clinic or center. Or, for a complete roster of accredited and provisional sleep disorders centers and clinics, write to:

Association of Professional Sleep Societies
604 2nd St., SW
Rochester, MN 55902

American Narcolepsy Association
P.O. Box 1187
San Carlos, CA 94070

Narcolepsy Network
155 Van Brackle Rd.
Aberdeen, NJ 07747

For Further Information

American Medical Association. *Drugs Used for Anxiety and Sleep Disorders*. Chapter 5. Chicago: AMA, 1986.

Better Sleep Council, Inc. *A Guide to Better Sleep*. Burtonsville, MD: the Council, 1984.

Berger, G. *Addiction: Its Causes, Problems, and Treatment*. New York: Watts, 1982.

Dement, W.C. *Some Must Watch While Some Must Sleep*. Gailfort, CT: Norton, 1978.

Ferber, R. *Solve Your Child's Sleep Problems*. New York: Simon & Schuster, 1985.

Fort, J. *The Addicted Society*. New York: Grove Press, 1981.

Hartmann, E. *The Sleep Book: Understanding and Preventing Sleep Problems in People Over 50*. Glenview, IL: Scot, Furesman, & Co., 1987.

Kales, A.; Kales, J.; and Soldatos, C. Insomnia and other sleep disorders. *Medical Clinics of North America*, 66(5): 971-991, 1982.

Lamberg, L. *The AMA Guide to Better Sleep*. New York: Random House, 1984.

Mendelson, W. B. *The Use and Misuse of Sleeping Pills: A Clinical Guide*. New York: Plenum, 1980.

Nicholi, A.M., Jr:, ed. *The Harvard Guide to Modern Psychiatry*. Cambridge: Harvard U. Press, 1978.

—by Gerald S. Snyder

Melatonin: A Chemical Slumber Switch

When a cup of warm milk or a relaxing bath doesn't do the trick, millions of Americans turn to their medicine cabinet for help in falling asleep. But medicinal assistance comes at a price: common sleep-producing drugs like barbiturates, benzodiazepines, and antihistamines can be addictive, induce tolerance, or cause hangovers. Now scientists at the Massachusetts Institute of Technology (MIT) in Boston report that a tiny dose of a natural hormone, administered orally, rapidly induces fatigue and sleepiness in healthy subjects. Dr. Richard J.

Wurtman and his associates say that this brain hormone, melatonin, is a promising candidate for safe and effective treatment of insomnia, although further evaluation is still needed.

National surveys indicate that each year one in three Americans has trouble falling asleep, and sleep-inducing, or hypnotic, drugs are among the most widely prescribed medicines. Dr. Wurtman, professor of neuroscience and director of MIT's General Clinical Research Center (GCRC), has been exploring the hypnotic potential of melatonin since the mid-1980's, but his interest in this substance goes back even farther. Working with Dr. Julius Axelrod at the National Institute of Mental Health in 1963, Dr. Wurtman and coworkers were the first to recognize that melatonin is a hormone. Back then melatonin was known only to affect the reproductive glands of animals. Scientists have since uncovered a fascinating, but still poorly understood, relationship between melatonin, environmental lighting, and the regulation of the body's biological clock.

Researchers now know that melatonin, secreted by the tiny pinecone-shaped pineal gland near the center of the brain, is generally produced briskly in darkness and sluggishly in light. By the mid-1970's Dr. Wurtman and other researchers discovered that melatonin levels in human adults ebb and flow each day, falling as low as 10 picograms per milliliter during the day and increasing about tenfold at night. "We showed that the rhythm is not really caused by light and darkness, since the cycle persists even when subjects are in constant darkness, but it's normally locked into place by light and darkness," says Dr. Wurtman. "The relationship between melatonin and sleep became an obvious possibility to explore," he says.

Ten years ago, in a trial at MIT's GCRC, Dr. Wurtman and his colleagues administered megadoses (240 mg in three doses of 80 mg, given an hour apart) of melatonin to healthy subjects and noted a rapid induction of sleep compared to volunteers who took placebos. But the hormone pills raised blood melatonin levels to 1,000 to 10,000 times their normal values. "The megadoses made people sleepy, but they also gave people a hangover and made them dysphoric and nasty," says Dr. Wurtman.

In their most recent study, designed to measure the effects of smaller doses of the hormone, the MIT researchers administered melatonin or placebo capsules to 20 healthy male volunteers at midday. For the next 6 hours the volunteers participated in a battery of tests to measure their physiological status, mood, sleepiness, and ability to perform tasks. Each volunteer was tested on five separate occasions, each time with a different dose of the hormone (0, 0.1, 0.3, 1, or 10 mg).

Forty-five minutes after taking the pills, volunteers were asked to close their eyes and squeeze a bar in each hand while relaxing in a quiet, dark room for half an hour. All doses of the hormone significantly shortened the time to sleep onset, as measured when a subject loosened his grip on the bar. A 0.3-mg dose of melatonin put volunteers to sleep about 9 minutes sooner, and a 1-mg dose about 11 minutes sooner, than did placebo. The 0.3-mg dose raised participants' melatonin levels to about 100 picograms per milliliter of blood, which is the normal nighttime concentration of the hormone. "This suggests that the natural rise in melatonin each evening induces sleep," Dr. Wurtman says.

All doses of melatonin significantly increased sleep duration and volunteers' self-reported feelings of fatigue and sleepiness during the course of the test. In addition, melatonin significantly reduced participants' body temperature and their performance on a vigilance test.

The Boston researchers note that melatonin's hypnotic effects are similar to those produced by benzodiazepine sleeping pills like Halcion. "Repeated use of benzodiazepines, however, can lead to habituation or tolerance," Dr. Wurtman says. "I'm optimistic that we won't see those effects with melatonin, since blood levels normally go from 10 to 100 picograms per milliliter every day and this rise doesn't induce tolerance. All we have to do is raise blood levels to their normal nighttime range to produce sleep." He adds that larger clinical trials are needed to confirm melatonin's hypnotic effects and safety.

Melatonin tablets can be purchased in some health food stores, but Dr. Wurtman advises against their use. "These pills are being sold without certification by the Food and Drug Administration, and this worries me terribly," he says, noting that melatonin is chemically similar to the amino acid tryptophan. Several years ago dozens of people died after ingesting impure L-tryptophan tablets purchased by mail order or at health food stores. "We've purchased melatonin from some health food stores and checked the purity. These tablets are not pure. People should not take melatonin for the time being except under controlled research conditions," Dr. Wurtman warns.

In a more recent study, which has been submitted for publication, Dr. Wurtman and his associate Dr. Irina Zhdanova discovered that melatonin's hypnotic effects are enhanced when the pills are given in the evening, closer to the subjects' regular bedtime. Moreover, the sleep-inducing effect of melatonin is readily demonstrable using electroencephalograms (EEG)—rather than the squeeze-bar technique—to measure sleep onset. The squeeze method was simple and "surprisingly good," says Dr. Wurtman, but it did have its drawbacks. For instance one volunteer, after lying in the darkened room for several minutes, maintained a strong grip on the bar even as he snored loudly. EEG, a more accurate indicator of mental arousal, has since confirmed that low doses of melatonin do indeed induce true, stage 2 sleep more rapidly than does placebo, says Dr. Wurtman.

"People have been looking for a sleep hormone for years," he says. "Maybe this is it."

—by Victoria L. Contie

Additional Reading

1. Dollins, A. B., Zhdanova, I. V., Wurtman, R. J., et al., Effect of inducing nocturnal serum melatonin concentrations in daytime on sleep, mood, body temperature, and performance. *Proceedings of the National Academy of Sciences USA* 91:18241828, 1994.

2. Dollins, A. B., Lynch, H. J., Wurtman, R. J., et al., Effect of pharmacological daytime doses of melatonin on human mood and performance. *Psychopharmacology* 112:490-496, 1993.

This research was supported by the General Clinical Research Centers Program of the National Center for Research Resources, the National Institute of Mental Health, the U.S. Air Force, and the National Aeronautics and Space Administration.

Chapter 32

The Trauma of Sexual Abuse

Sexual abuse is a painful reality. Millions of children have suffered the shame, humiliation, anger and sadness that sexual abuse often causes. Fortunately, as we become better able to recognize the signs of sexual abuse and help children understand that it's safe to tell someone about it, more people are getting the help they need.

What Is Sexual Abuse

Sometimes it is difficult to decide whether or not sexual abuse has occurred. Clearly, if an adult has sexual intercourse with a child, the child has been sexually abused. But this is certainly not the only sexual act that is classified as abuse. Even seemingly less serious sexual behaviors are damaging to children and are considered abusive. For instance:

- Fondling or kissing a child in a sexual manner
- Making a child watch pornographic movies or observe sexual activities
- Exhibiting one's sexual organs to a child or making the child display his or her own genitals
- Taking sexually explicit photographs of a child

"The Trauma of Sexual Abuse," is taken from the *Learn to Understand Mental Illness* program, produced by the Psychiatric Institute of Washington, DC; reprinted with permission.

• Talking with a child in a sexual or seductive manner

Regardless of the severity, any form of sexual abuse is detrimental to the victim's well-being and requires serious attention.

Who Is Sexually Abused?

Confronting sexual abuse, your own or a child's, is often very difficult. It is not unusual to deny or try to cover up sexual abuse. Sometimes this is because the perpetrator, or abuser, has threatened harm if the abuse is disclosed. Other times it is because of the victim's feelings of shame, guilt, or embarrassment. Telling someone about the abuse can be especially difficult if the abuser is a trusted family member or family friend. In fact, over one-third of individuals who are sexually abused never reveal the abuse. Adults who have kept the secret of sexual abuse locked away for many years may find it too painful to re-open these wounds and acknowledge the abuse. For these reasons, it is difficult to determine how many people have actually been sexually abused. However, recent studies have found that:

• Up to two-thirds of females and one-third of males may be sexually abused at some time in their lives.
• Sexual abuse is present in all classes, races and religions.
• Females are two to three times more likely than males to be sexually abused.
• The majority of sexual abuse begins when children are under 6 years old.

Who Are the Sexual Abusers?

Sexual abuse can occur both within and outside the family. However, almost all sexual abuse victims know their abusers and oftentimes it is a male relative, such as a stepfather, uncle, grandfather or brother. Although less common, there are incidents in which the abuser is female.

It is difficult to understand what drives an individual to sexually abuse a child; it is even more difficult to understand when the abuser is a family member or someone you love. Although little is known about the characteristics of sexual abusers, we do know that many perpetrators, or abusers, have themselves been sexually abused as children. Also, many of these individuals suffer from alcoholism, drug abuse problems or a variety of other psychiatric disturbances. It is important that the perpetrators of sexual abuse seek help. Often, psychiatric treatment is beneficial.

Possible Warning Signs of Sexual Abuse

If a child spontaneously reports or suggests sexual abuse, it is crucial to take it seriously; children rarely make false accusations of sexual abuse. Unfortunately, very few children directly report sexual abuse. Because of this, it is helpful to be aware of some of the subtle cues that might indicate abuse is occurring. Below are some of the common symptoms that sexually abused children and adolescents often display.

Indications of Sexual Abuse in Children and Adolescents

Behavioral Signs

- Sexualized behavior, for instance, children engaging in sexual play with dolls, or adolescents engaging in indiscriminate sexual activity.

- Acting-out behaviors such as running away or temper tantrums.

- Regressive behaviors such as thumbsucking, baby talk or curling up in fetal position.

- Poor school performance.

- Drug and/or alcohol abuse.

- Self-mutilating behaviors, cutting self or hurting self in other ways.

- Radical behavior change in any direction. For example, suddenly becoming a model child or suddenly beginning to act rebellious or unruly

- Eating disturbances

- Sleep disturbances, especially nightmares or insomnia

- Difficulty concentrating

Emotional Signs

- Depressed or sad mood

- Feeling anxious in general or having fears of specific settings or circumstances, often related to the abusive situation

- Perfectionism

- Aggression

- Withdrawal

- Low self-esteem

- Guilt, self-blame

- Dissociation which in its mild form may include excessive day-dreaming or a disconnection of feelings and experiences. More severe forms of dissociation, such as multiple personality disorder, may include adopting different and distinct personalities. The presence of multiple personalities is often displayed by rapid changes in mood, lapses in time or memory, and variations in skills and abilities.

Physical Signs

- Abdominal pain
- Genital, urethral or rectal pain, bleeding or abrasions
- Sexually transmitted diseases
- Recurrent urinary tract infections
- Bed-wetting
- Bed-soiling
- Pregnancy

Remember, the presence of any one of these symptoms does not necessarily mean a child has been sexually abused. However, the presence of a combination of these symptoms should alert an adult to the need to investigate the possibility of past or current sexual abuse. If you are concerned, arrange for a diagnostic evaluation with a licensed physician or psychologist.

The Long-Term Effects of Sexual Abuse

Unfortunately, children who have been sexually abused are not always able to tell someone or get help. Although the abuse may have stopped or perhaps was only a single occurrence, failure to recognize or treat a sexually abused child can lead to a variety of emotional problems later in life. Recently, greater attention has been given to the unique difficulties survivors of sexual abuse must confront. Although every person's experience is different, some common long-term effects include:

- Low self-esteem, feelings of self-hatred or shame.

- An inability to trust, often leading to difficulties in establishing relationships.

- Sexual difficulties or a lack of ability to feel sexual with individuals other than those with whom there is no attachment.

- Continuation of the sexual abuse cycle: marrying an abusive partner or abusing one's own children.

- Increase in alcohol or drug use, sometimes leading to substance abuse disorders.

- Chronic abdominal, urinary tract or gynecological problems.

- Repressed anger and hostility.

- Depression and thoughts of suicide.

- Anxiety or panic.

- Eating disorders such as anorexia nervosa, an obsessive concern about food, weight and body image that leads to self-starvation; or bulimia, the destructive cycle of binge eating and purging.

- Dissociative disorders, the most severe form being multiple personality disorder.

The Need for Treatment

If you, or someone you know, has been sexually abused, there are a variety of helpful treatments available. These range from self-help groups to individual or group therapy to a combination of these treatments. Although psychotherapy is the most common form of treatment used to help sexual abuse victims, there are times when medications, such as antidepressants, can be helpful. If psychiatric problems have resulted from the sexual abuse, treatment targeting these difficulties also might be necessary.

Treatment helps reduce the shame and isolation that often follows abuse as well as helps people understand the wide range of conflicting, and often confusing emotional reactions to sexual abuse. Most importantly, treatment can help people realize that the abuse was not their fault or responsibility. The first step toward preventing and treating sexual abuse is accepting the fact that the victim does not provoke sexual abuse.

What Do You Do If You Have Been Abused?

Tell someone. You do not have to suffer the nightmare of sexual abuse alone. There is help available. The pain does not have to continue indefinitely. You may be experiencing one or more of the symptoms we have discussed or other problems that seem unrelated to sexual abuse. Addressing the problems of the abuse is likely to help alleviate many of your emotional difficulties. Do not be ashamed; you are not to blame.

What Do You Do If You Suspect Your Child, Or Another Child, Has Been Sexually Abused

Report it. If the abuse has occurred within your family, contact your local child protection agency. If the abuse has occurred outside of the family, report it to the police. Your first responsibility is to protect the child.

If a child even hints that sexual abuse has occurred, it is important to take it seriously. Allow the child to talk freely and to feel safe talking to you. Disclosing abuse is a frightening experience, especially for a child. Show that you understand and believe the child. Help the child realize that he or she did not cause the abuse and is not to blame for it. Don't let the child suffer alone.

Hope Lies in Learning More

We have developed this text, part of our *Learn to Understand Mental Illness* program, to help you realize that survivors of sexual abuse need and deserve compassionate help. Reading this information may be your first step toward recovery.

If you can recognize the signs and symptoms of sexual abuse it may help you or someone else live a more healthy and fulfilling life.

Chapter 33

Plain Talk about Wife Abuse

"To have and to hold...to love and to cherish..."
"Be it ever so humble, there's no place like home."

These sentiments reflect the feelings of most people toward marriage, home, and family—but not all. The surprising fact is that a lot of violence, bringing fear and pain, is reported among family members.

For example, about one-quarter of all murders in the United States take place within the family. Surveys of American couples show that 20 to 50 percent have suffered violence regularly in their marriages. The records indicate that between two and four million incidents of domestic violence occur every single year. Wife abuse is one kind of family violence that probably occurs far more often than most people imagine. The tragedy is that many women suffer this abuse for years without getting help. This text explores what wife abuse is, who experiences it, some reasons it occurs, the pattern it usually takes, and why women don't get help. Finally, it looks at what women can do if they are abused and how, ultimately, the abuse might be prevented.

What Do We Mean by "Wife Abuse"?

Defining wife abuse or wife battering is not easy. For starters, whom are we thinking of when we use the word "wife"? Actually, any

DHHS Pub. No. (ADM) 85-1265.

woman who maintains an intimate relationship with a man (her husband, ex-husband, boyfriend or lover) could become a battered or abused "wife." The words "abused" or "battered" which are used here do not refer to the normal conflict and stress that occur in all close relationships, but rather to the violence that can cause serious injury and death. In the pamphlet *Assaults on Women: Rape and Wife-beating,* Natalie Jaffe cites a typical description of the kind of physical harm suffered by battered women surveyed in shelters and treatment in California.

> *"Most injuries were to the head and neck and, in addition to bruises, strangle marks, black eyes, and split lips, resulted in eye damage, fractured jaws, broken noses, and permanent hearing loss. Assaults to the trunk of the body were almost as common and produced a broken collarbone, bruised and broken ribs, a fractured tailbone, internal hemorrhaging, and a lacerated liver."*

These are serious consequences of serious assaults. Another serious aspect is that once wife beating occurs, it is likely to happen again and again, with violence getting worse over time.

A Closer Look at How the Abused Woman Feels

A woman who has been abused over a long period of time is afraid. Not only is she afraid that she, herself, will be seriously hurt, but if she has children, she fears for their safety also. Her feelings of fear link her to all other women, from all classes of society, in similar situations.

Fear might be a woman's first and most immediate feeling during or after a beating, but other negative feelings may surface when she is not in physical danger. The abused woman is apt to develop doubts about herself. She might wonder if she is justified in fearing for her life and calling herself an "abused wife." Most likely, however, a woman who thinks or feels she is being abused, probably is.

Or, she may feel guilty, even though she's done nothing wrong. An abused wife may feel responsible for her husband's violence because in some way she may have provoked him. This has her placing the shame and blame on herself—instead of her abuser. The longer she puts up with the abuse and does nothing to avoid or prevent it, the less she likes herself. Along with the feeling of being a failure, both as a woman and in her marriage, may come a real feeling of being trapped and powerless, with no way out.

Why Do Men Abuse Their Wives?

Instances of wife abuse have been on record in the United States since the 1830s, but only every now and then does it arouse public concern. Generally, public opinion supports traditional family relations and male authority. The battering syndrome is both cause and effect of stereotyped roles and the unequal power relations between men and women. No social class is exempt. Wife abuse occurs in wealthy as well as in poor communities—in middle class as well as in working class families. Over the years it has been tolerated by those who govern community affairs, the courts, medicine, psychiatry, police, schools, and the church. History shows that the helping professions often protected patterns of family authority, unwittingly sanctioning wife abuse rather than condemning it.

In present-day society, violence in the movies, on TV, and in the newspapers is familiar and accepted. Many husbands who abuse their wives have learned that violence, especially against women, is okay. They often were abused themselves as children or saw their mothers abused. The battered wife most likely grew up in a similar environment.

There are other psychological reasons. A wife abuser tends to be filled with anger, resentment, suspicion, and tension. He also, underneath all his aggressive behavior, can be insecure and feel like a loser. He may use violence to give vent to the bad feelings he has about himself or his lot in life. Home is one place he can express those feelings without punishment to himself. If he were angry with his boss and struck him, he would pay the price. But all too often he gets away without penalty when he beats his wife. She becomes the target of his vengeance, and he gets the satisfaction he's looking for.

What about the victimized wife? If she accepts her husband's traditional male authority, she may be labeled as immature. If she fights back or if she refuses to sleep with him if he's drunk, she might be accused of being hostile, domineering, and masculine. These are complaints of abused women.

Patterns

Familiar patterns of wife abuse often develop in three phases: the tension-building phase, the explosion or the actual beating phase, and the loving phase.

The tension builds over a series of small occurrences such as a wife's request for money, her refusal to do all the household chores without her husband's help, her serving a meal not pleasing to him, or a similar incident. What follows is inevitable. She may become the object of any or all of the following assaults: punching with fists, choking, kicking, knifing, slamming against a wall, throwing to the floor, or shoving down the stairs. Sometimes even threats with a gun have been reported.

When the beating is over, the couple move into the third phase. The batterer feels guilty about what he has done. He is sorry and may become loving toward her. He assures his wife that he will never do anything violent or hurtful to her again. At that moment, he may believe he will never hurt her again. She wants to believe him, hoping that he will change. However, even with professional help, the tension building and the beatings may continue.

Why Do Women Stay?

Women have learned that it may be their own feelings of fear, guilt, or shame that keep them in a relationship that is physically abusive. Often, social and economic pressures compel a woman to stay. Sometimes she stays for lack of somewhere to go for shelter and advice or because she feels that she loves her husband and lives with the hope that he might change, if only she can "hang in there." Tragically, in most cases, the abuse continues, for in fact her husband's behavior has nothing to do with her actions.

Other reasons for staying with him may seem as compelling. A woman may feel that a divorce is wrong and that she should keep her marriage together at all costs. Perhaps she feels her children need a father. She may be isolated with no outside job and few friends. The friends and relatives she does talk to may give her little support, perhaps because her situation frightens them and they don't want to admit to themselves that such violence could occur. If she confides in a counselor, she may also be encouraged to "save the marriage." And, along with her emotional dependence, she may worry about being able to find a job to support herself and her children. If she has her husband arrested, he may not be able to support her. If she doesn't have him arrested, he may beat her even more severely for trying to leave him. Is there a way out? Most women suffer these attacks for years before they finally find the courage and determination to take steps to keep from being victims of further abuse.

What Can a Battered Woman Do?

The first step for a woman to take is to admit to herself that she is being abused and that she is not being treated fairly. She has the right to feel safe from physical harm, especially in her own home.

Emergency Action

A woman can do a number of things to protect herself. She can hide extra money, car keys, and important documents somewhere safe so that she can get to them in a hurry. The phone number of the police department should be handy. She should have a place to go, such as an emergency shelter, a social service agency, or the home of a trusted friend or relative.

During an actual attack, the woman should defend herself as best she can. As soon as she is able, she should call the police and get their names and badge numbers in case she needs a record of the attack. Most importantly, she should leave the house and take her children with her. She may need medical attention, too, because she might be hurt more severely than she realizes. Having a record of her injuries, including photographs, can protect her legally should she decide to press charges.

Long-Range Plans

A woman needs to talk to people who can help. Good friends can lend support and guidance. Organizations that are devoted to women's concerns and not bound by society's traditions can assist her. They might help her explore her options in new ways. Emergency shelters for women, hotlines, women's organizations, social service agencies, community mental health centers, and hospital emergency rooms are all possible sources of support.

The following organizations have information about State contacts and shelters where a battered woman can go for help:

Center for Women Policy Studies
2000 P Street, NW, No. 508
Washington, DC 20036
(202) 872-1770

National Coalition Against Domestic Violence
1500 Massachusetts Ave., N.W., Suite 35
Washington, DC 20005

Above all, a woman has to determine her own best course of action. Positive measures such as confiding in a relative on whom she can depend, talking seriously with a trusted friend, or consulting with a sympathetic counselor are steps in the right direction. With the help of informal and formal help sources, including individual counseling for the husband as well as herself, a woman may be able to bring an end to the problem.

It has been observed that abused women need to develop better feelings about themselves—that is, change their self-image. In her book *Stopping Wife Abuse*, Jennifer Baker Fleming says the following attitudes are positive and useful:

- I am not to blame for being beaten and abused.
- I am not the cause of another's violent behavior.
- I do not like it or want it.
- I do not have to take it.
- I am an important human being.
- I am a worthwhile woman.
- I deserve to be treated with respect.
- I do have power over my own life.
- I can use my power to take good care of myself.
- I can decide for myself what is best for me.
- I can make changes in my life if I want to.
- I am not alone. I can ask others to help me.
- I am worth working for and changing for.
- I deserve to make my own life safe and happy.

Prevention

Since there is no one cause of wife abuse, there is no easy way to prevent it. Until society rejects its tolerance and acceptance of violence for resolving conflict and expressing anger, meaningful changes in family relationships will not occur. Prevention starts with people changing their attitudes toward violence and women. No one deserves to be beaten or physically threatened, no matter what the excuse. It is a crime to beat anyone—a stranger, a friend, or your wife—and the law should be enforced. The tolerance of family violence as a way of life in one generation encourages family violence in another generation. Since the wife abuser didn't learn to deal with anger appropriately as a child, he handles his frustrations through aggression. He needs to know that it's human to feel anger, but inhuman to release those feelings by beating others. By learning to deal with these emotions through acceptable behavior, he can gain respect for himself and others. It's another positive step toward developing mutual respect in the husband/wife relationship where each sees the other as a worthy human being.

References

About Wife Abuse. South Deerfield, Massachusetts: Channing L. Bete Co., Inc., 1979.

Bowker, Lee H. *Women and Crime in America*. New York: Macmillan Publishing Co., Inc., 1981, Part II: pp. 234-328.

Fleming, Jennifer Baker. *Stopping Wife Abuse: A guide to the Emotional, Psychological, and Legal Implications. . . for the abused woman and those helping her*. New York: Anchor Press/Doubleday, 1979.

Jaffe, Natalie. *Assaults on Women: Rape and Wife Beating*. New York: Public Affairs Committee, Inc. (Public Affairs Pamphlet No. 579). Martin, Del. Battered Wives. San Francisco: Glide Publications, 1976.

Straus, Murray A., Gelles, Richard J., and Steinmetz, Suzanne K. *Behind Closed Doors: Violence in the American Family*. New York: Anchor Books, 1980.

Walker, Lenore. *The Battered Woman*. New York: Harper & Row, 1979.

—by Lenore Gelb, staff writer,
in consultation with NIMH scientists.

Part Six

Mental Health Treatments and Therapies

Chapter 34

A Consumer's Guide to Mental Health Services

A Message from the Center for Mental Health Services

The Center for Mental Health Services was created to help states improve treatment and support services for people with mental illness, their families, and their communities. The Center works with a wide range of partners—from other Federal agencies and state and local mental health systems to mental health professionals, consumers, and family members—to achieve the highest quality and most accessible mental health services possible.

Who needs mental health services? Hundreds of thousands of people. Among them are people with serious and persistent mental illness; America's children and adolescents who have a variety of mental, emotional, and behavioral problems; homeless persons with mental illness; the growing numbers of people with or at risk of HIV/AIDS; underserved residents of rural areas; and survivors of natural disasters such as floods and hurricanes. The Center hopes to respond to their mental health needs through treatment demonstration programs, outreach and case management programs, and support of consumer-run and self help alternative programs. It also provides information about recognizing mental illness, seeking appropriate care, and locating treatment and support services.

NIH Pub. No. 94-3585.

On behalf of the Center, I hope you find *A Consumer's Guide to Mental Health Services* helpful.

Bernard S. Arons, M.D.
Director
Center for Mental Health Services

Message from the National Institute of Mental Health

Research conducted and supported by the National Institute of Mental Health (NIMH) brings hope to millions of people who suffer from mental illness and to their families and friends. In many years of work with animals as well as human subjects, researchers have advanced our understanding of the brain and vastly expanded the capability of mental health professionals to diagnose, treat, and prevent mental and brain disorders.

Today we stand at the threshold of a new era in brain and behavioral sciences. Through research, we are continually learning more about the structure and function of the brain. As our knowledge increases, we will understand more about mental disorders such as depression, bipolar disorder, schizophrenia, panic disorder, and obsessive-compulsive disorder and how they can be effectively treated. We will reach out to individuals in need—to those affected by violence and abuse, to the aged, children, women, minorities, the homeless, and the severely mentally ill.

To achieve the goal of serving those in need, the Institute will work with the Center for Mental Health Services and other professional and advocacy groups to integrate the knowledge gained through clinical research with those of service systems research. We welcome the Center as they join with us in offering this revised edition of *A Consumer's Guide to Mental Health Services*.

Rex William Cowdry, MD.
Acting Director
National Institute of Mental Health

Asking for Help

Twenty percent of adult Americans—or one in five—will have a mental illness during their lifetime that is severe enough to require treatment, and many more have problems that prevent them from enjoying their lives. Often these people live in silence, rather than admit they need help.

Asking for help is not an easy thing for many people to do, but it is a wise move when a person feels that something is wrong. This text offers a guide to finding mental health services.

Many individuals who are looking for help for themselves or a loved one ask the same questions. Following are some of the most commonly asked questions and their answers.

When I need help, where can I go?

For information about resources available in your community, contact your local mental health center or one of the local affiliates of national organizations listed [at the end of this chapter]. These agencies can provide you with information on services designed to meet the needs of people with mental disorders such as depression, schizophrenia, panic disorder, and other anxiety conditions. In addition, they will have information regarding services designed for specific cultural groups, children, the elderly, HIV-infected individuals, and refugees.

I don't have adequate personal finances, medical insurance, or hospitalization coverage—where would I get the money to pay for the services I may need?

In publicly funded mental health centers, such as those funded by State, city or county governments, the cost of many services is calculated according to what you can afford to pay. So, if you have no money, or very little, services are still provided. This is called a sliding-scale or sliding-fee basis of payment.

Many employers make assistance programs available to their employees, often without charge. These programs—usually called Employee Assistance Programs—are designed to provide mental health services, including individual psychotherapy, family counseling, and assistance with problems of drug and alcohol abuse.

Are there other places to go for help?

Yes, there are alternatives. Many mental health programs operate independently. These include local clinics, family service agencies, mental health self-help groups, private psychiatric hospitals, private clinics, and private practitioners. If you go to a private clinic or practitioner, you will pay the full cost of the services, less the amount paid by your insurer or some other payment source.

There are also many self-help organizations that operate drop-in centers and sponsor gatherings for group discussions to deal with problems associated with bereavement, suicide, depression, anxiety, phobias, panic disorder, obsessive-compulsive disorder, schizophrenia, drugs, alcohol, eating disorders (bulimia, anorexia nervosa, obesity), spouse and child abuse, sexual abuse, rape, and coping with the problems of aging parents—to name a few. In addition, there are private practitioners who specialize in treating one or more of these problems. You may contact local chapters of organizations listed [at the end of this chapter] to learn about various services available in your community.

I don't like to bother other people with my problems. Wouldn't it be better just to wait and work things out by myself?

That's like having a toothache and not going to the dentist. The results are the same—you keep on hurting and the problem will probably get worse.

Suppose I decide to go ahead and visit a mental health center. What goes on in one of those places?

A specially trained staff member will talk with you about the things that are worrying you.

Talk? I can talk to a friend for free—why pay someone?

You're quite right. If you have a wise and understanding friend who is willing to listen to your problems, you may not need professional help at all. But often that's not enough. You may need a professionally trained person to help you uncover what's really bothering you. Your friend probably does not have the skills to do this.

How can just talking make problems disappear?

When you're talking to someone who has professional training and has helped many others with problems similar to yours, that person is able to see the patterns in your life that have led to your unhappiness. In therapy, the job is to help you recognize those patterns—and you may try to change them. There may be times, however, when you will need a combination of "talk" therapy and medication.

Are psychiatrists the only ones who can help?

No. A therapist does not have to be a psychiatrist. Many psychologists, social workers, nurses, mental health counselors, and others have been specially trained and licensed to work effectively with people's mental and emotional difficulties. Psychiatrists are medical doctors and can prescribe medication.

Since I work all day, it would be hard to go to a center during regular working hours. Are centers open at night or on weekends?

Often centers offer night or weekend appointments. Just contact the center for an appointment, which may be set up for a time that is convenient for both you and the center.

And how about therapists in private practice—do they sometimes see their patients after working hours?

Many therapists have evening hours to accommodate their patients. Some even see patients very early in the morning.

I feel that I would be helped by going to a mental health center. Actually, I think my spouse could be helped too. But the idea of going to a "mental health center" would seem threatening to my spouse. Could I just pretend that it's something else?

No indeed. It's better to talk your spouse into it than to lie. Don't jeopardize trust by being deceptive. However, you may want to discuss it first with the center. Marital or family therapy is available when a problem exists that involves more than one family member.

If I go to a mental health center, what kind of treatment will I get?

There are many kinds of treatment. A professional at the center will work with you in determining the best form for your needs. Depending on the nature of the illness being treated, psychotherapy and/or treatment with medication may be recommended. Sometimes, joining a group of people who have similar problems is best; at other times, talking individually to a therapist is the answer.

Does talking therapy for mental and emotional problems always work?

Sometimes it does, and sometimes it doesn't. It primarily depends on you and the therapist. It is important to share your concerns in a serious, sincere, and open manner. Only if you are completely honest and open can you expect to receive the best support and advice.

What if I really try, but I still can't feel comfortable with the therapist?

There should be a "fit" between your personality and that of the therapist. Someone else—or some other method—may be more suitable for you. You can ask your therapist for a referral to another mental health professional, or, if you prefer, you can call one of the associations listed in this text for the names of other therapists in your area.

What if I am receiving medication and don't think it is helping?

If there is little or no change in your symptoms after 5 to 6 weeks, a different medication may be tried. Some people respond better to one medication than another. Some people also are helped by combining treatment with medications and another form of therapy.

Does a mental health center provide services for children?

Yes. Children's services are an important part of any center's program. Children usually respond very well to short-term help if, they are not suffering from a severe disorder. Families are often asked to participate and are consulted if the child is found to have a serious disorder—such as autism, childhood depression, obsessive-compulsive disorder, attention deficit hyperactivity disorder, or anorexia nervosa or bulimia—and long-term treatment is needed.

I have an elderly parent who has trouble remembering even close members of the family. He is physically still quite active and has wandered off a number of times. Could someone help with this?

A staff person at a center can advise you about ways you can best care for your parent. You may be referred to a special agency or organization that provides services designed especially to meet the needs of elderly people. The department of public welfare in your county can give you addresses and telephone numbers for both your county and State agencies on aging. These agencies provide information on services and programs for the elderly.

I have a friend who says she could use some professional help, but she is worried about keeping it confidential.

She needn't worry. Confidentiality is basic to therapy, and the patient has the right to control access to information about her treatment. Professional association guidelines plus Federal and State laws underscore the importance of confidentiality in therapist-client relationships and govern the release of records. Some insurance companies require certain information from the therapist as a condition for payment, but that information can be released only if the patient gives written permission. If your friend wants to know exactly who gets information and what kind of information is released, she should ask her insurance provider and discuss it in detail with the therapist.

I have a relative with a severe mental problem. Should I urge this person to go to the hospital?

A person who is mentally ill should be in a hospital only if it is absolutely necessary. In general, most mental health professionals believe that persons with mental illness should live in the community and be treated there. That's why mental health centers and community support and rehabilitation programs stress the importance of having many different services available: day, night, and weekend care, and outpatient treatment through regular visits to an office or clinic.

Do emergency cases wind up as long-term patients in mental hospitals?

Generally no. Mental hospitals are used today for short-term crisis intervention when there are no other community services available or when a person needs extra care to stabilize a drug treatment regimen. Also they serve the small percentage of patients who need long-term, structured, supervised care and treatment in a protective setting.

I have heard people use the term "involuntary commitment." What does this mean?

In an emergency (for example, where a person is considered a danger to self or others), it is possible for someone to be admitted to a hospital for a short period against his or her will. The exact procedures that must be followed vary from one area to another, according to State and local laws. At the end of the emergency commitment period, the State must release the individual, obtain his or her voluntary consent to extend commitment, or file with the court an extended commitment petition to continue to detain the person involuntarily. Most States require an emergency commitment hearing to be held within 2 to 4 days after hospital admission to justify continued involuntary confinement.

Whom can I call if I feel that my rights have been violated or if I want to report suspected violation of rights, abuse, or neglect?

Federal law provides that each State have a Protection and Advocacy (P&A) System. These agencies, partially funded by the Center for Mental Health Services, investigate reports of abuse and neglect in public or private mental health or treatment facilities for current residents or those admitted or discharged during the past 90 days. For the name and the P&A Agency in your State, contact the National Association of Protection and Advocacy Systems at the address listed [at the end of this chapter].

Warning Signals

Many people are not sure how to judge when professional help for mental problems may be needed. There are some behaviors that may be signs of trouble:

1. Is the person acting differently than usual? Could this change be linked to something that has happened recently? Any event, such as the death of a close relative, loss of a job, marital break-up, or even something positive—like a job promotion—can trigger a troublesome emotional reaction.

2. Does the person complain of episodes of extreme, almost un-controllable, anxiety or "nervousness"? One sign of an emotional problem is "free floating" anxiety that is unrelated to a normal concern, such as a child's illness or a backlog of bills.

3. Does the person become aggressive, rude, and abusive over minor incidents or talk about groups or individuals "out to get me"? If such remarks are made in all seriousness, and if violent behavior occurs, it is likely that help is needed and should be sought.

Any of these symptoms, if they persist or become severe, may suggest a need for professional help. Fortunately early identification and treatment of the problems causing this behavior often can make these symptoms disappear.

What to Do in Emergency Situations

If a person becomes violent, gets completely out of control, or tries to commit suicide, there are several things to do:

1. **In a dangerous or violent crisis**, call the police. Often the police are the best equipped, most available resource, especially when violence has occurred or when there is a strong

399

possibility that the person may do physical injury to self or others. Once the emergency situation has been brought under control, if the troubled individual is already in treatment, call his or her therapist.

2. **In a nonviolent crisis,** contacting other resources may be the best choice. For example, if an individual hasn't eaten for a substantial period of time and has become weak and dehydrated, call his or her physician or therapist. If the person doesn't have one, get him or her to a hospital emergency room where doctors are on duty—even if you have to call an ambulance to get there. Look in the Yellow Pages under "Ambulances," or call the fire department or rescue squad. Look under the list of emergency numbers in the front of your phone book, or call the operator if you can't find a number in a hurry.

Emergency room doctors will treat injuries resulting from violence, a suicide attempt, or a drug or alcohol overdose. They also may be able to provide temporary help for an emotional problem, even if they are not mental health specialists. In addition, they will be able to tell you where and how to get further help.

If the person in crisis is a member of a church, synagogue, or temple, you may choose to call the minister, priest, or rabbi. Many members of the clergy are trained to deal with emergencies, or they can refer you to other sources of help.

You may choose to call a mental health or crisis hotline, drug hotline, suicide prevention center, "free clinic," or Alcoholics Anonymous chapter, if your area has such services. Their telephones are often staffed around the clock. Look for a number in the list of emergency or community service numbers in the front of your phone book, or you can find a listing in the white pages under "Suicide," " Mental Health," "Alcoholics Anonymous," or ask the operator for help.

Another option is to call the nearest mental health center. If it's not listed that way in the phone book, look under "Hospitals," "Mental Health Clinics," or "Physicians" in the Yellow Pages. Mental health centers generally provide a wide range of services. Included in these are:

1. **24-hour emergency service**—available at hospitals or other mental health clinics any time of the day or night.

2. **Outpatient care**—a person goes to the center's clinic for treatment that has been set up on a regular appointment basis.

3. **Inpatient service**—a person stays at the hospital where care is provided.

4. **Partial hospitalization**—a person might spend occasional days, nights, or weekends at the hospital center, living at home and going to work as much as possible.

5. **Consultation, education, and prevention services**— assist schools, community organizations, institutions, and businesses in dealing with persons with mental illnesses and in developing programs that help in the understanding and prevention of emotional disorders.

Treatment Methods

The goals of treatment are to reduce symptoms of emotional disorders; improve personal and social functioning; develop and strengthen coping skills; and promote behaviors that make a person's life better. Biomedical therapy, psychotherapy, and behavioral therapy are basic approaches to treatment that may help a person overcome problems. There are many types of therapies that may be used alone or in various combinations.

Biomedical Therapies

Treatment with medications has benefited many patients with emotional, behavioral, and mental disorders and is often combined with other therapy. The medication that a psychiatrist or other physician prescribes depends on the nature of the illness being treated as well as on an assessment of the patient's general medical condition. During the past 35 years, many psychotherapeutic medications have been developed and have made dramatic changes in the treatment of mental disorders. Today there are specific medications to alleviate the symptoms of such mental disorders as schizophrenia, bipolar disorder, major depression, anxiety, panic disorder, and obsessive-compulsive disorder.

Electroconvulsive treatment (ECT) is another biomedical treatment that can help some patients. It is generally reserved for patients with severe mental illnesses who are unresponsive to or unable to tolerate medications or other treatments. While ECT is most commonly indicated in the treatment of major depression, often with psychosis (delusions or hallucinations), it is also used in selected cases of schizophrenia. Severe reduction in food and fluid intake with little physical movement (catatonia), or overwhelming suicidal ideation, where urgency of response is important, are reasons for considering ECT as treatment of choice. Modern methods of administering ECT use low "doses" of electric shock to the brain along with general anesthesia and muscle relaxants to minimize the risk and unpleasantness to patients.

Psychotherapy

Psychotherapy is accomplished through a series of face-to-face discussions in which a therapist helps a person to talk about, define, and resolve personal problems that are troubling. Psychotherapies generally appear to be more effective and appropriate than medications or ECT for less severe forms of emotional distress.

Short-term psychotherapy, lasting for several weeks or months, is used when the problem seems to result from a stressful life event such as a death in the family, divorce, or physical illness. The goal of the therapist is to help the patient resolve the problem as quickly as possible. Often this takes only a few visits. Long-term psychotherapy, lasting from several months to several years, emphasizes the study of underlying problems that started in childhood.

The following is a list of a few types of psychotherapy:

- *Psychodynamic psychotherapy,* which may be either long- or short-term, examines important relationships and experiences from early childhood to the present in an effort to analyze and change unsettling or destructive behaviors and to resolve emotional problems. One form of psychodynamic psychotherapy is *psychoanalysis*, a long-term, intensive therapy that emphasizes how the patient's unconscious motivations and early patterns of resolving issues are important influences in his or her present actions and feelings.

- *Interpersonal therapy* focuses on the patient's current life and relationships within the family social, and work environments.

- *Family therapy* involves discussions and problem-solving sessions with every member of a family—sometimes with the entire group, sometimes with individuals.

- *Couple therapy* aims to develop a more rewarding relationship and minimize problems through understanding how individual conflicts get expressed in the couple's interactions.

- *Group therapy* involves a small group of people with similar problems who, with the guidance of a therapist, discuss individual issues and help each other with problems.

- *Play therapy* is a technique used for establishing communication and resolving problems with young children.

- *Cognitive therapy* aims to identify and correct distorted thinking patterns that can lead to troublesome feelings and behaviors. Cognitive therapy is often combined effectively with behavioral therapy.

Behavioral Therapy

Behavioral therapy uses learning principles to change troublesome thinking patterns and behaviors systematically. The individual can learn specific skills to obtain rewards and satisfaction. Such an approach may involve the cooperation of important persons in the individual's life to give praise and attention to desirable changes. Behavioral therapy includes an array of methods such as stress management, biofeedback, and relaxation training.

Other Treatments

Some treatments, called "adjunctive," are used in combination with other therapies, and sometimes they are used alone. They include occupational, recreational, or creative therapies, as well as some that focus on special education. A mental health professional can help a client find the kind of therapy, or combination of therapies, that is best suited to his or her situation.

Rehabilitation Services—Community Support Programs

Many individuals with severe mental illness find it difficult to work, learn, socialize, and live independently outside a controlled setting. To help in these matters, community support programs offer rehabilitation services, either through freestanding programs that are similar to clubs, or through mental health centers. These agencies offer a variety of activities to assist clients in learning skills that will help them to live and work independently and productively in the community. For information on community support programs, contact your local or State mental health agency.

The Helping Professionals

Helping professionals work in a variety of settings, such as mental health centers, outpatient clinics, private and group practice, general hospitals, psychiatric hospitals, nursing homes, jails, and prisons. They also work in residential treatment centers, partial care organizations, family or social service agencies, and the psychiatric departments of university medical centers or teaching hospitals.

Who They Are—What They Do

Psychiatrists. A psychiatrist is a medical doctor who specializes in mental disorders, is licensed to practice medicine, and has completed a year of internship and 3 years of specialty training. A board-certified psychiatrist has, in addition, practiced for at least 2 years and passed the written and oral examinations of the American Board of Psychiatry and Neurology. Psychiatrists can evaluate and diagnose all types of mental disorders, carry out biomedical treatments and psychotherapy, and work with psychological problems associated with medical disorders. Child psychiatrists specialize in working with children; geriatric psychiatrists concentrate on helping older people.

Psychologists. Psychologists who conduct psychotherapy and work with individuals, groups, or families to resolve problems generally are called clinical psychologists, counseling psychologists, or school psychologists. They work in many settings—for example, mental health centers, hospitals and clinics, schools, employee assistance programs, and private practice. In most States, a licensed clinical psychologist has completed a doctoral degree from a university program with specialized training and experience requirements and has successfully completed a professional licensure examination.

The field of psychology also includes those who specialize in such areas as testing, community organization, industrial relations, and laboratory research.

Psychiatric Nurses. Psychiatric nursing is a specialized area of professional nursing practice that is concerned with prevention, treatment, and rehabilitation of mental health-related problems. These nurses are registered professional nurses who have advanced academic degrees at the master's degree level or above. They conduct individual, family, and group therapy and also work in mental health consultation, education, and administration.

Social Workers. Psychiatric (or clinical) social workers have advanced degrees in social work, have completed a field supervision program, and are licensed/certified. In addition to individual, family, and group counseling and psychotherapy, they are trained in client-centered advocacy. This includes information, referral, direct intervention with governmental and civic agencies, and expansion of community resources.

Mental Health Counselors. A clinical mental health counselor provides professional counseling services that involve psychotherapy, human development, learning theory, and group dynamics to help individuals, couples, and families. The promotion and enhancement of healthy, satisfying lifestyles are the goals of mental health counselors, whether the services are rendered in a mental health center, business, private practice, or other community agency. Clinical mental health counselors have earned at least a master's degree, had supervised experience, and passed a national examination before they can be certified by the National Board for Certified Counselors, Inc. (NBCC).

Case Managers and Outreach Workers. These individuals assist persons with severe mental illness, including some who may be homeless, to obtain the services they need to live in the community.

Most persons with severe mental illness need medical care, social services, and assistance from a variety of agencies, including those dealing with housing, Social Security, vocational rehabilitation, and mental health. Because such services are fragmented in many areas, case managers provide a critical function to monitor a person's needs and assure that appropriate agencies get involved. In many instances they also act as advocates for the client. Case managers can be nurses, social workers, or mental health workers and can be associated with mental health centers, psychosocial rehabilitation programs, or other agencies. Case management and outreach services are frequently provided by teams that may include people who are recovering from a mental illness who function as peer counselors, case management aides, or outreach workers.

Mental Health Research and Services

The core mission of the National Institute of Mental Health is to understand, treat, and prevent mental illness. Research into the kinds of mental health services that will support this mission plays an important role. The Center for Mental Health Services provides national leadership in mental health care delivery and policy development to facilitate accessible, comprehensive, and quality mental health and support services. The Institute and Center, in cooperation with consumer and family groups, professional organizations, and other Federal and State agencies, work to advance the application of scientific findings and practice-based knowledge to improve the range of effective prevention and treatment services.

Information Resources

If you believe that you, or someone you know, might benefit from the services of a mental health professional, mental health center, or one of the organizations described in this text, don't hesitate to take advantage of these useful services.

For referral to a physician, psychiatrist, or psychologist contact your local medical bureau or local department of mental health listed in the telephone book. And remember that your own physician or clergy is usually aware of places in your community to get help.

The following are some excellent information sources:

For Psychiatrists

American Academy of Child and Adolescent Psychiatry
3615 Wisconsin Ave., NW
Washington, DC 20016
(202) 966-7300
(202) 966-2891 FAX

American Medical Association
515 North State St.
Chicago, IL 60610
(312) 464-5000
(312) 464-4184 FAX

American Psychiatric Association
1400 K St. NW, Suite 1101
Washington, DC 20005
(202) 682-6000
(202) 682-6341 FAX

For Psychologists

American Psychological Association
750 First St. NE
Washington, DC 20002-4242
(202) 336-5500
(202) 336-5905 FAX

For Psychiatric Nurses

American Nurses' Association
600 Maryland Ave. SW, Suite 100W
Washington, DC 20024
(202) 651-7000
(202) 561-7001 FAX

American Psychiatric Nurses' Association
1200 19th St., NW, Suite 300
Washington, DC 20036
(202) 857-1133

For Social Workers

National Association of Social Workers
750 First St. NE, Suite 700
Washington, DC 20002-4241
(202) 408-8600; 1-800-638-8799
(202) 336-8310 FAX

For Other Mental Health Practitioners

American Mental Health Counselors Association
P.O. Drawer 22370
Alexandria, VA 22304
(703) 823-9800 ext. 383
(703) 751-1696 FAX

American Association for Marriage and Family Therapy
1100 17th St. NW, 10th Floor
Washington, DC 20036
(202) 452-0109; 1-800-374-2638
(202) 223-2329 FAX

National Board for Certified Counselors, Inc.
3-D Terrace Way
Greensboro, NC 27403
(910) 547-0607
(910) 547-0017 FAX

For Psychosocial Rehabilitation Programs

National Rehabilitation Association
633 S. Washington St.
Alexandria, VA 22314
(703) 836-0850
(703) 836-0848 FAX

International Association of Psychosocial Rehabilitation
10025 Governor Warfield Pkwy., Suite 301
Columbia, MD 21044-3357
(410) 730-7190
(410) 730-5965 FAX

For State Mental Health Centers and Programs

National Association of State Mental Health Program Directors
66 Canal Center Plaza, Suite 302
Alexandria, VA 22314-1591
(703) 739-9333
(703) 548-9517 FAX

For Protection and Advocacy

Judge David L. Bazelon Center for Mental Health Law
1101 Fifteenth St., NW, Suite 1212
Washington, DC 20005
(202) 467-5730
(202) 223-0409 FAX

National Association of Protection and Advocacy Systems
900 2nd St., NE, Suite 211
Washington, DC 20002
(202) 408-9514
(202) 408-9520 FAX

For Outpatient Programs and Mental Health Service Facilities

American Association for Partial Hospitalization, Inc.
901 N. Washington St., Suite 600
Alexandria, VA 22314-1535
(703) 836-2274
(703) 836-0083 FAX

National Association of Psychiatric Health Systems
1319 F St. NW, Suite 1000
Washington, DC 20004
(202) 393-6700
(202) 783-6041 FAX

National Community Mental Healthcare Council
12300 Twinbrook Pkwy., Suite 320
Rockville, MD 20852
(301) 984-6200
(301) 881-7159 FAX

Consumer Advocacy and Support Organizations

There are also a number of consumer advocacy and support organizations. The underlying philosophy of these organizations is that the best helpers are often those who have experienced similar problems. These groups typically provide emotional support and practical help for dealing with problems that their members share.

Organizations that have chapters in many communities, or can provide referrals and/or educational materials, are:

Alzheimer's Association
919 North Michigan Ave., Suite 1000
Chicago, Illinois 60611
(312) 335-8700; 1-800-272-3900
(312) 335-1110 FAX

Anxiety Disorders Association of America
6000 Executive Blvd., Suite 513
Rockville, MD 20852
(301) 231-8368
(301) 231-7392 FAX

Association for Advancement of Behavior Therapy
305 7th Ave.
New York, NY 10001
(212) 647-1890
(212) 647-1865 FAX

Federation of Families for Children's Mental Health
1021 Prince St.
Alexandria, VA 22314-2971
(703) 684-7710
(703) 836-1040 FAX

The National Alliance for the Mentally Ill
2101 Wilson Blvd., Suite 302
Arlington, VA 22201
(703) 524-7600; 1-800-950-NAMI (6264)
(703) 524-9094 FAX

National Anxiety Foundation
3135 Custer Dr.
Lexington, KY 40517-4001
1-800-755-1576

National Depressive and Manic Depressive Association
730 N. Franklin, Suite 501
Chicago, IL 60610
(312) 642-0049; 1-800-826-3632
(312) 642-7243 FAX

National Mental Health Association
1021 Prince St.
Alexandria, VA 22314-2971
(703) 684-7722; 1-800-969-NMHA (6642)
(703) 684-5968 FAX

Pathways to Promise
5247 Fyler Ave.
St. Louis, MO 63139-1494
(314) 644-8400
(314) 644-8834 FAX

Recovery, Inc.
802 North Dearborn St.
Chicago, IL 60610
(312) 337-5661
(312) 337-5756 FAX

Self-Help Groups

There are many self-help or mutual support groups that provide assistance in particular areas such as phobias, panic, bereavement, obsessive-compulsive disorder, anorexia and bulimia, as well as other disorders such as HIV-dementia/AIDS, cancer, multiple sclerosis, Parkinson's, and many others. Due to space limitations, we are unable to list them all here. Information about self-help groups can be obtained from:

411

American Self-Help Clearinghouse
St. Claires-Riverside Medical Center
25 Pocono Rd.
Denville, NJ 07834
(201) 625-7101; 1-800-367-6724 (inside NJ)
(201) 625-8848 FAX
(201) 625-9053 TDD

National Self-Help Clearinghouse
Graduate School and University Center
City University of New York
25 West 43rd St., Room 620
New York, NY 10036
(212) 586-5770
(212) 354-5825
(212) 642-1956 FAX

Self-Help Clearinghouse of the Greater Washington Area
7630 Little River Turnpike, #206
Annandale, VA 22003
(703) 941-5465
(703) 642-0803 FAX

Technical Assistance and Information Sharing

Two organizations engage in a variety of technical assistance and information sharing activities. They area:

National Empowerment Center
20 Ballard Rd.
Lawrence, MA 01843-1018
(508) 685-1518; 1-800-769-3728
(508) 681-6426 FAX

National Mental Health Consumers' Self-Help Clearinghouse
311 South Juniper St., Suite 1000
Philadelphia, PA 19107
(215) 735-6082 ext. 317; 1-800-553-4539
(215) 735-8307 FAX

Other Sources of Information

A list of National Institute of Mental Health publications with information about research into the causes, prevention, and treatment of mental illnesses is available from:

Information Resources and Inquiries Branch
NIMH, Room 7C-02
5600 Fishers Lane
Rockville, MD 20857
(301) 443-4513
(301) 443-4449 TDD

A list of Center for Mental Health Services publications with information about prevention and treatment of mental illnesses is available from:

Office of Consumer
Family and Public Information
CMHS, Room 13-103
5600 Fishers Lane
Rockville, MD 20857

Other helpful information may be obtained from:

National CMHS Clearinghouse
1-800-789-CMHS (2647) CMHS

Electronic Bulletin Board
1-800-790-CMHS (2647)
(301) 443-9006 TDD

Chapter 35

Medications

Special Message

This text is designed to help people understand how and why drugs can be used as part of the treatment of mental health problems. It is important for persons who use mental health services to be well informed about medications for mental illnesses, but this text is *not* a "do-it-yourself" manual. Self-medication can be dangerous. Interpretation of both signs and symptoms of the illness and side effects are jobs for the professional. The prescription and management of medication, in all cases, must be done by a responsible physician working closely with the patient—and sometimes the patient's family or other mental health professionals. This is the only way to ensure that the most effective use of medication is achieved with minimum risk of side effects or complications.

Introduction

Anyone can develop a mental illness—you, a family member, a friend, or the fellow down the block. Some disorders are mild, while others are serious and long-lasting. These conditions can be helped. One way—an important way—is with psychotherapeutic medications. Compared to other types of treatment, these medications are relative

DHHS Pub. No. (ADM) 92-1509.

newcomers in the fight against mental illness. It was only about 35 years ago that the first one, chlorpromazine, was introduced. But considering the short time they've been around, psychotherapeutic medications have made dramatic changes in the treatment of mental disorders. People who, years ago, might have spent many years in mental hospitals because of crippling mental illness may now only go in for brief treatment, or might receive all their treatment at an outpatient clinic.

Psychotherapeutic medications also may make other kinds of treatment more effective. Someone who is too depressed to talk, for instance, can't get much benefit from psychotherapy or counseling; but often, the right medication will improve symptoms so that the person can respond better.

Another benefit from these medications is an increased understanding of the causes of mental illness. Scientists have learned a great deal more about the workings of the brain as a result of their investigations into how psychotherapeutic medications relieve disorders such as psychosis, depression, anxiety, obsessive-compulsive disorder, and panic disorder.

Symptom Relief, Not Cure

Just as aspirin can reduce a fever without clearing up the infection that causes it, psychotherapeutic medications act by controlling symptoms. Like most drugs used in medicine, they correct or compensate for some malfunction in the body. Psychotherapeutic medications do not cure mental illness, but they do lessen its burden. These medications can help a person get on with life despite some continuing mental pain and difficulty coping with problems. For example, drugs like chlorpromazine can turn off the "voices" heard by some people with schizophrenia and help them to perceive reality more accurately. And antidepressants can lift the dark, heavy moods of depression.

How long someone must take a psychotherapeutic medication depends on the disorder. Many depressed and anxious people may need medication for a single period—perhaps for several months—and then never have to take it again. For some conditions, such as schizophrenia or manic-depressive illness, medication may have to be taken indefinitely or, perhaps, intermittently.

Like any other medication, psychotherapeutic medications do not produce the same effect in everyone. Some people may respond better to one medication than another. Some may need larger dosages than others do. Some experience annoying side effects, while others do not. Age, sex, body size, body chemistry, habits, and diet are some of the factors that can influence a medication's effect.

Questions for Your Doctor

To increase the likelihood that a medication will work well, patients and their families must actively participate with the doctor prescribing it. They must tell the doctor about the patient's past medical history, other medications being taken, anticipated life changes—such as planning to have a baby—and, after some experience with a medication, whether it is causing side effects. When a medication is prescribed, the patient or family member should ask the following questions recommended by the U.S. Food and Drug Administration (FDA) and professional organizations:

- What is the name of the medication, and what is it supposed to do?
- How and when do I take it, and when do I stop taking it?
- What foods, drinks, other medications, or activities should I avoid while taking the prescribed medication?
- What are the side effects, and what should I do if they occur?
- Is there any written information available about the medication?

In this text, medications are described by their generic (chemical) names and in italics by their trade names (brand names used by drug companies). They are divided into four large categories based on the symptoms for which they are primarily used—antipsychotic, antimanic, antidepressant, and antianxiety medications. Some are used for more than one purpose; antidepressants, for example, have been found helpful for treating some anxiety disorders.

[Lists at the end of this chapter give the generic and trade names for the most commonly prescribed medications.]

Treatment evaluation studies have established the efficacy of the medications described here; however, much remains to be learned about these medications. The National Institute of Mental Health, other Federal agencies, and private research groups are sponsoring studies of these medications. Scientists are hoping to improve their understanding of how and why these medications work, how to control or eliminate unwanted side effects, and how to make the medications more effective.

Antipsychotic Medications

A person who is psychotic is out of touch with reality. (In the following discussions, "He" is used to refer to both men and women.) He may "hear voices" or have strange and untrue ideas (for example, thinking that others can hear his thoughts, or are trying to harm him, or that he is the President of the United States or some other famous person). He may get excited or angry for no apparent reason, or spend a lot of time off by himself, or in bed, sleeping during the day and staying awake at night. He may neglect his appearance, not bathing or changing clothes, and may become difficult to communicate with—saying things that make no sense, or barely talking at all.

These kinds of behaviors are symptoms of psychotic illness, the principal form of which is schizophrenia. All of the symptoms may not be present when someone is psychotic, but some of them always are. Antipsychotic medications, as their name suggests, act against these symptoms. These medications cannot "cure" the illness, but they can take away many of the symptoms or make them milder. In some cases, they can shorten the course of the illness as well.

There are a number of antipsychotic medications available. They all work; the main differences are in the potency—that is, the dosage (amount) prescribed to produce therapeutic effects—and the side effects. Some people might think that the higher the dose of medication, the more serious the illness, but this is not always true.

A doctor will consider several factors when prescribing an antipsychotic medication, besides how "ill" someone is. These include the patient's age, body weight, and type of medication. Past history is important, too. If a person took a particular medication before and it worked, the doctor is likely to prescribe the same one again. Some less potent drugs, like chlorpromazine (*Thorazine*), are prescribed in higher numbers of milligrams than others of high potency, like haloperidol (*Haldol*).

If a person has to take a large amount of a "high-dose" antipsychotic medication, such as chlorpromazine, to get the same effect as a small amount of a "low-dose" medication such as haloperidol, why doesn't the doctor just prescribe "low-dose" medications? The main reason is the difference in their side effects (actions of the medication other than the one intended for the illness). These medications vary in their side effects, and some people have more trouble with certain side effects than others. A side effect may sometimes be desirable. For instance, the sedative effect of some antipsychotic medications is useful for patients who have trouble sleeping or who become agitated during the day.

Unlike some prescription drugs, which must be taken several times during the day, antipsychotic medications can usually be taken just once a day. Thus, patients can reduce daytime side effects by taking the medications once, before bed. Some antipsychotic medications are available in forms that can be injected once or twice a month, thus assuring that the medicine is being taken reliably.

Most side effects of antipsychotic medications are mild. Many common ones disappear after the first few weeks of treatment. These include drowsiness, rapid heartbeat, and dizziness when changing position.

Some people gain weight while taking antipsychotic medications and may have to change their diet to control their weight. Other side effects that may be caused by some antipsychotic medications include decrease in sexual ability or interest, problems with menstrual periods, sunburn, or skin rashes. If a side effect is especially troublesome, it should be discussed with the doctor who may prescribe a different medication, change the dosage level or schedule, or prescribe an additional medication to control the side effects.

Movement difficulties may occur with the use of antipsychotic medications, although most of them can be controlled with a prophylactic medication. These movement problems include muscle spasms of the neck, eye, back, or other muscles; restlessness and pacing; a general slowing-down of movement and speech; and a shuffling walk. Some of these side effects may look like psychotic or neurologic (Parkinson's disease) symptoms, but aren't. If they are severe, or persist with continued treatment with an antipsychotic, it is important to notify the doctor, who might either change the medication or prescribe an additional one to control the side effects.

Just as people vary in their responses to antipsychotic medications, they also vary in their speed of improvement. Some symptoms diminish in days, while others take weeks or months. For many patients, substantial improvement is seen by the sixth week of treatment, although this is not true in every case. If someone does not seem to be improving, a different type of medication may be tried. Drug treatment for a psychotic illness can continue for up to several months, sometimes even longer.

Even if a person is feeling better or completely well, he should not just stop taking the medication. Continuing to see the doctor while tapering off medication is important. Some people may need to take medication for an extended period of time, or even indefinitely, to remain symptom-free. These people usually have chronic (long-term, continuous) schizophrenic disorders, or have a history of repeated schizophrenic episodes, and are likely to become ill again. Also, in some cases a person who has experienced one or two severe episodes may need medication indefinitely. In these cases, medication may be continued in as low a dosage as possible to maintain control of symptoms. This approach, called maintenance treatment, prevents relapse in many people and removes or reduces symptoms for others.

While maintenance treatment is helpful for many people, a drawback for some is the possibility of developing long-term side effects, particularly a condition called tardive dyskinesia. This condition is characterized by involuntary movements. These abnormal movements most often occur around the mouth, but are sometimes seen in other muscle areas such as the trunk, pelvis, or diaphragm. The disorder may range from mild to severe. For some people, it cannot be reversed, while others recover partially or completely. Tardive dyskinesia is seen most often after long-term treatment with antipsychotic medications. There is a higher incidence in women, with the risk rising with age. There is no way to determine whether someone will develop this condition, and if it develops, whether the patient will recover. At present, there is no effective treatment for tardive dyskinesia. The possible risks of long-term treatment with antipsychotic medications must be weighed against the benefits in each individual case by patient, family, and doctor.

Two approaches that are designed to provide the advantages of medication while reducing the risks of tardive dyskinesia and other possible side effects are sometimes used in long-term treatment. They are a "low-dosage" approach that uses far lower maintenance dosages of antipsychotic medications than have generally been employed, and an "intermittent dosage" treatment that involves stopping the medication when the patient is symptom-free and beginning it again only when symptoms reappear.

In 1990, clozapine (*Clozaril*), an "atypical" antipsychotic drug, was introduced in the United States. In clinical trials, this medication was found to be more effective than traditional antipsychotic medications in individuals with treatment-resistant schizophrenia, and the risk of tardive dyskinesia is lower. However, because of the potential side effect of a serious blood disorder, agranulocytosis, patients who are on clozapine must have a blood test each week. The expense involved in this monitoring, together with the cost of the medication, has made maintenance on clozapine difficult for many persons with schizophrenia.

Antipsychotic medications can also produce unwanted effects when taken in combination with other medications. Therefore, the doctor should be told about all medicine being taken, including over-the-counter preparations, and the extent of the use of alcohol. Some antipsychotic medications interfere with the action of anti-hypertensive medications (taken for high blood pressure), anti-convulsants (taken for epilepsy), and medications used for Parkinson's disease. Some antipsychotic medications add to the effects of alcohol and other central nervous system depressants, such as anti-histamines, antidepressants, barbiturates, some sleeping and pain medications, and narcotics.

Antimanic Medications

Bipolar disorder (manic-depressive illness) is characterized by cycling mood changes: severe highs (mania) and lows (depression). Cycles may be predominantly manic or depressive with normal mood between cycles. Mood swings may follow each other very closely, within hours or days, or may be separated by months to years.

When someone is in a manic "high," he may be overactive, overtalkative, and has a great deal of energy. He will switch quickly from one topic to another, as if he cannot get his thoughts out fast enough; his attention span is often short, and he can easily be distracted. Sometimes, the "high" person is irritable or angry and has false or inflated ideas about his position or importance in the world. He may be very elated, full of grand schemes which might range from business deals to romantic sprees. Often, he shows poor judgment in these ventures. Mania, untreated, may worsen to a psychotic state.

Depression will show in a "low" mood, lack of energy, changes in eating and sleeping patterns, feelings of hopelessness, helplessness, sadness, worthlessness, and guilt, and some times thoughts of suicide.

Lithium

These "highs" and "lows" may vary in intensity and severity. The medication used most often to combat a manic "high" is lithium. It is unusual to find mania without a subsequent or preceding period of depression. Lithium evens out mood swings in both directions, so that it is used not just for acute manic attacks or flare-ups of the illness, but also as an ongoing treatment of bipolar disorder.

Lithium will diminish severe manic symptoms in about 5 to 14 days, but it may be anywhere from days to several months until the condition is fully controlled. Antipsychotic medications are sometimes used in the first several days of treatment to control manic symptoms until the lithium begins to take effect. Likewise, antidepressants may be needed in addition to lithium during the depressive phase of bipolar disorder.

Someone may have one episode of bipolar disorder and never have another, or be free of illness for several years. However, for those who have more than one episode, continuing (maintenance) treatment on lithium is usually given serious consideration.

Some people respond well to maintenance treatment and have no further episodes while others may have moderate mood swings that lessen as treatment continues. Some people may continue to have episodes that are diminished in frequency and severity. Unfortunately, some manic-depressive patients may not be helped at all. Response to treatment with lithium varies, and it cannot be determined beforehand who will or will not respond to treatment.

Regular blood tests are an important part of treatment with lithium. A lithium level must be checked periodically to measure the amount of the drug in the body. If too little is taken, lithium will not be effective. If too much is taken, a variety of side effects may occur. The range between an effective dose and a toxic one is small. A lithium level is routinely checked at the beginning of treatment to determine the best lithium dosage for the patient. Once a person is stable and on maintenance dosage, a lithium level should be checked every few months. How much lithium a person needs to take may vary over time, depending on how ill he is, his body chemistry, and his physical condition.

Anything that lowers the level of sodium (table salt is sodium chloride) in the body may cause a lithium buildup and lead to toxicity. Reduced salt intake, heavy sweating, fever, vomiting, or diarrhea may do this. An unusual amount of exercise or a switch to a low-salt diet are examples. It's important to be aware of conditions that lower sodium and to share this information with the doctor. The lithium dosage may have to be adjusted.

When a person first takes lithium, he may experience side effects, such as drowsiness, weakness, nausea, vomiting, fatigue, hand tremor, or increased thirst and urination. These usually disappear or subside quickly, although hand tremor may persist. Weight gain may also occur. Dieting will help, but crash diets should be avoided because they may affect the lithium level. Drinking low-calorie or no-calorie beverages will help keep weight down. Kidney changes, accompanied by increased thirst and urination, may develop during treatment. These conditions that may occur are generally manageable and are reduced by lowering the dosage. Because lithium may cause the thyroid gland to become underactive (hypothyroidism) or sometimes enlarged (goiter), thyroid function monitoring is a part of the therapy. To restore normal thyroid function, thyroid hormone is given along with lithium.

Because of possible complications, lithium may either not be recommended or may be given with caution when a person has existing thyroid, kidney, or heart disorders, epilepsy, or brain damage. Women of child bearing age should be aware that lithium increases the risk of congenital malformations in babies born to women taking lithium. Special caution should be taken during the first 3 months of pregnancy.

Lithium, when combined with certain other medications, can have unwanted effects. Some diuretics—substances that remove water from the body—increase the level of lithium and can cause toxicity. Other diuretics, like coffee and tea, can lower the level of lithium. Signs of lithium toxicity may include nausea, vomiting, drowsiness, mental dullness, slurred speech, confusion, dizziness, muscle twitching, irregular heart beat, and blurred vision. A serious lithium overdose can be life threatening. Someone who is taking lithium should tell all the doctors—including dentists—he sees about all other medications he is taking.

With regular monitoring, lithium is a safe and effective drug that enables many people, who otherwise would suffer from incapacitating mood swings, to lead normal lives.

Anticonvulsants

Not all patients with symptoms of mania benefit from lithium. Some have been found to respond to another type of medication, the anticonvulsant medications that are usually used to treat epilepsy. Carbamazepine (*Tegretol*) is the anticonvulsant that has been most widely used. Manic-depressive patients who cycle rapidly—that is, they change from mania to depression and back again over the course of hours or days, rather than months—seem to respond particularly well to carbamazepine.

Early side effects of carbamazepine, although generally mild, include drowsiness, dizziness, confusion, disturbed vision, perceptual distortions, memory impairment, and nausea. They are usually transient and often respond to temporary dosage reduction. Another common but generally mild adverse effect is the lowering of the white blood cell count which requires periodic blood tests to monitor against the rare possibility of more serious, even life-threatening, bone marrow depression. Also serious are the skin rashes that can occur in 15 to 20 percent of patients. These rashes are sometimes severe enough to require discontinuation of the medication.

Neither carbamazepine nor any other anticonvulsant has been approved by the Food and Drug Administration for manic-depressive illness. These drugs must undergo further study before they merit FDA approval and general use.

Antidepressant Medications

The kind of depression that will most likely benefit from treatment with medications is more than just "the blues." It's a condition that's prolonged, lasting 2 weeks or more, and interferes with a person's ability to carry on daily tasks and to enjoy activities that previously brought pleasure.

The depressed person will seem sad, or "down," or may show a lack of interest in his surroundings. He may have trouble eating and lose weight (although some people eat more and gain weight when depressed). He may sleep too much or too little, have difficulty going to sleep, sleep restlessly, or awaken very early in the morning. He may speak of feeling guilty, worthless, or hopeless. He may complain that his thinking is slowed down. He may lack energy, feeling "everything's too much," or he might be agitated and jumpy. A person who is depressed may cry. He may think and talk about killing himself and may even make a suicide attempt. Some people who are depressed have psychotic symptoms, such as delusions (false ideas) that are related to their depression. For instance, a psychotically depressed person might imagine that he is already dead, or "in hell," being punished.

Not everyone who is depressed has all these symptoms, but everyone who is depressed has at least some of them. A depression can range in intensity from mild to severe.

Antidepressants are used most widely for serious depressions, but they can also be helpful for some milder depressions. Antidepressants, although they are not "uppers" or stimulants, take away or reduce the symptoms of depression and help the depressed person feel the way he did before he became depressed.

Antidepressants are also used for disorders characterized principally by anxiety. They can block the symptoms of panic, including rapid heartbeat, terror, dizziness, chest pains, nausea, and breathing problems. They can also be used to treat some phobias.

The physician chooses the particular antidepressant to prescribe based on the individual patient's symptoms. When someone begins taking an antidepressant, improvement generally will not begin to show immediately. With most of these medications, it will take from 1 to 3 weeks before changes begin to occur. Some symptoms diminish early in treatment; others, later. For instance, a person's energy level or sleeping or eating patterns may improve before his depressed mood lifts. If there is little or no change in symptoms after 5 to 6 weeks, a different medication may be tried. Some people will respond better to one than another. Since there is no certain way of determining beforehand which medication will be effective, the doctor may have to prescribe first one, then another, until an effective one is found. Treatment is continued for a minimum of several months and may last up to a year or more.

While some people have one episode of depression and then never have another or remain symptom-free for years, others have more frequent episodes or very long-lasting depressions that may go on for years. Some people find that their depressions become more frequent and severe as they get older. For these people, continuing (maintenance) treatment with antidepressants can be an effective way of reducing the frequency and severity of depressions. Those that are commonly used have no known long-term side effects and may be continued indefinitely. The prescribed dosage of the medication may be lowered if side effects become troublesome. Lithium can also be used for maintenance treatment of repeated depressions whether or not there is evidence of a manic or manic-like episode in the past.

Dosage of antidepressants varies, depending on the type of drug, the person's body chemistry, age, and, sometimes, body weight. Dosages are generally started low and raised gradually over time until the desired effect is reached without the appearance of troublesome side effects.

There are a number of antidepressant medications available. They differ in their side effects and, to some extent, in their level of effectiveness. Tricyclic antidepressants (named for their chemical structure) are more commonly used for treatment of major depressions than are monoamine oxidase inhibitors (MAOIs); but MAOIs are often helpful in so-called "atypical" depressions in which there are symptoms like oversleeping, anxiety, panic attacks, and phobias.

A tricyclic antidepressant introduced in 1990, clomipramine (*Anafranil*), is used primarily in the treatment of obsessive-compulsive disorder. A bicyclic antidepressant, fluoxetine (*Prozac*), was approved by the FDA in late 1987 and has been prescribed extensively. Another recently approved antidepressant, bupropion (*Wellbutrin*), is chemically unrelated to the other antidepressants. Some newer antidepressants are currently being studied and may be released in the next few years.

Side Effects of Antidepressant Medications

Tricyclic Antidepressants. There are a number of possible side effects with tricyclic antidepressants that vary, depending on the medication. For example, amitriptyline (*Elavil*) may make people feel drowsy, while protriptyline (*Vivactil*) hardly does this at all and, in some people, may have an opposite effect, producing feelings of anxiety and restlessness. Because of this kind of variation in side effects, one antidepressant might be highly desirable for one person and not

426

recommended for another. Tricyclics on occasion may complicate specific heart problems, and for this reason the physician should be aware of all such difficulties. Other side effects with tricyclics may include blurred vision, dry mouth, constipation, weight gain, dizziness when changing position, increased sweating, difficulty urinating, changes in sexual desire, decrease in sexual ability, muscle twitches, fatigue, and weakness. Not all these medications produce all side effects, and not everybody gets them. Some will disappear quickly, while others may remain for the length of treatment. Some side effects are similar to symptoms of depression (for instance, fatigue and constipation). For this reason, the patient or family should discuss all symptoms with the doctor, who may change the medication or dosage.

Tricyclics also may interact with thyroid hormone, antihypertensive medications, oral contraceptives, some blood coagulants, some sleeping medications, antipsychotic medications, diuretics, antihistamines, aspirin, bicarbonate of soda, vitamin C, alcohol, and tobacco.

An overdose of antidepressants is serious and potentially lethal. It requires immediate medical attention. Symptoms of an overdose of tricyclic antidepressant medication develop within an hour and may start with rapid heartbeat, dilated pupils, flushed face, and agitation, and progress to confusion, loss of consciousness, seizures, irregular heartbeats, cardiorespiratory collapse, and death.

Monoamine Oxidase Inhibitors (MAOIs). MAOIs may cause some side effects similar to those of the other antidepressants. Dizziness when changing position and rapid heartbeat are common. MAOIs also react with certain foods and alcoholic beverages (such as aged cheeses, foods containing monosodium glutamate (MSG), Chianti and other red wines), and other medications (such as over-the-counter cold and allergy preparations, local anesthetics, amphetamines, antihistamines, insulin, narcotics, and antiparkinsonian medications). These reactions often do not appear for several hours. Signs may include severe high blood pressure, headache, nausea, vomiting, rapid heartbeat, possible confusion, psychotic symptoms, seizures, stroke, and coma. For this reason, people taking MAOIs *must* stay away from restricted foods, drinks, and medications. They should be sure that they are furnished, by their doctor or pharmacist, a list of *all* foods, beverages, and other medications that should be avoided.

Precautions to be Observed When Taking Antidepressants

When taking antidepressants, it is important to tell all doctors (and dentists) being seen—not just the one who is treating the depression—about all medications being used, including over-the-counter preparations and alcohol. Antidepressants should be taken only in the amount prescribed and should be kept in a secure place away from children. When used with proper care, following doctors' instructions, antidepressants are extremely useful medications that can reverse the misery of a depression and help a person feel like himself again.

Antianxiety Medications

Everyone experiences anxiety at one time or another—"butterflies in the stomach" before giving a speech or sweaty palms during a job interview are common symptoms. Other symptoms of anxiety include irritability, uneasiness, jumpiness, feelings of apprehension, rapid or irregular heartbeat, stomachache, nausea, faintness, and breathing problems.

Anxiety is often manageable and mild. But sometimes it can present serious problems. A high level or prolonged state of anxiety can be very incapacitating, making the activities of daily life difficult or impossible.

Phobias, which are persistent, irrational fears and are characterized by avoidance of certain objects, places, and things, sometimes accompany anxiety. A panic attack is a severe form of anxiety that may occur suddenly and is marked with symptoms of nervousness, breathlessness, pounding heart, and sweating. Sometimes the fear that one may die is present.

Antianxiety medications help to calm and relax the anxious person and remove the troubling symptoms. There are a number of antianxiety medications currently available. The preferred medications for most anxiety disorders are the benzodiazepines. In addition to the benzodiazepines, a non-benzodiazepine, buspirone (BuSpar), has recently been approved for generalized anxiety disorders. Antidepressants are also very effective for panic attacks and some phobias and are often prescribed for these conditions. Antidepressants are also sometimes used for more generalized forms of anxiety, especially when accompanied by depression.

The most commonly used benzodiazepines are alprazolam (*Xanax*) and diazepam (*Valium*), followed by chlordiazepoxide (*Librium, Librax, Libritabs*). Benzodiazepines are relatively fast-acting medications. Most will begin to take effect within hours, some in even less time. Benzodiazepines differ in duration of action in different individuals; they may be taken two or three times a day, or sometimes only once a day. Dosage is generally started at a low level and gradually raised until symptoms are diminished or removed. The dosage will vary a great deal depending on the symptoms and the individual's body chemistry.

Benzodiazepines have few side effects. Drowsiness and loss of coordination are most common; fatigue and mental slowing or confusion can also occur. These effects make it dangerous to drive or operate some machinery when taking benzodiazepines—especially when the patient is just beginning treatment. Other side effects are rare.

Benzodiazepines combined with other medications can present a problem, notably when taken together with commonly used substances such as alcohol. It is wise to abstain from alcohol when taking benzodiazepines, as the interaction between benzodiazepines and alcohol can lead to serious and possibly life-threatening complications. Following the doctor's instructions is important. The doctor should be informed of all other medications the patient is taking, including over-the-counter preparations. Benzodiazepines increase central nervous system depression when combined with alcohol, anesthetics, antihistamines, sedatives, muscle relaxants, and some prescription pain medications. Particular benzodiazepines may influence the action of some anticonvulsant and cardiac medications. Benzodiazepines have also been associated with abnormalities in babies born to mothers who were taking these medications during pregnancy.

With benzodiazepines, there is a potential for the development of tolerance and dependence as well as the possibility of abuse and withdrawal reactions. For these reasons, the medications are generally prescribed for brief periods of time—days or weeks—and sometimes intermittently, for stressful situations or anxiety attacks. For the same reason, ongoing or continuous treatment with benzodiazepines is not recommended for most people. Some patients may, however, need long-term treatment.

Consult with the doctor before discontinuing a benzodiazepine. A withdrawal reaction may occur if the treatment is abruptly stopped.

Symptoms may include anxiety, shakiness, headache, dizziness, sleeplessness, loss of appetite, and, in more severe cases, fever, seizures, and psychosis. A withdrawal reaction may be mistaken for a return of the anxiety, since many of the symptoms are similar. Thus, after benzodiazepines are taken for an extended period, the dosage is gradually tapered off before being completely stopped.

Although benzodiazepines, buspirone, or tricyclic antidepressants are the preferred medications for most anxiety disorders, occasionally, for specific reasons, one of the following medications may be prescribed: antipsychotic medications; antihistamines (such as *Atarax*, *Vistaril*, and others); barbiturates such as phenobarbital; propanediols such as meprobamate (Equanil), and propranolol (Inderal, Inderide).

Children, the Elderly, and Pregnant, Nursing, or Child-Bearing Age Women: Special Considerations

Children, the elderly, and pregnant and nursing women have special concerns and needs when taking psychotherapeutic medications. Some effects of medications on the growing body, the aging body, and the childbearing body are known, but much remains to be learned. Research in these areas is ongoing.

While, in general, what has been said in this text applies to these groups, below are a few special points to bear in mind:

Children

- Mental disorders in children may present symptoms that are different or less clear-cut than the same disorders in adults. Younger children, especially, may not talk about what's bothering them, but this may be a problem with older children as well. For this reason, having a doctor, other mental health professional, or psychiatric team examine the child is especially important.

- When a child is taking medication, active monitoring by all caretakers (parents, teachers, others who have charge of the child) is essential. Children should be watched and questioned for side effects (many children, especially younger ones, do not volunteer information). They should also be monitored to see that they are actually taking the medication.

430

- All types of medications described in this text may be used with children, although some specific medications are not used, and the use of others is more limited than with adults.

- One type of medication not covered in this text is stimulants. Two stimulants methylphenidate (*Ritalin*) and dextroamphetamine (*Dexedrine*) are more commonly prescribed for children than adults. They are successfully used in the treatment of attention deficit hyperactivity disorder (ADHD). ADHD is a disorder usually diagnosed in early childhood in which the child exhibits such symptoms as short attention span, excessive activity, and impulsivity. A child with ADHD should take a stimulant medication only on the advice and under the careful supervision of a physician.

The Elderly

- The elderly tend to be more sensitive to medications. They also generally have more medical problems, which may complicate the prescribing of some medications. Even healthy older people eliminate some medications from the body more slowly than younger persons and therefore require a lower or less frequent dosage to maintain an effective level of medication.

- The elderly may sometimes accidentally take too much of a medication because they forget that they have taken a dose and take another dose.

- The elderly and those close to them—friends, relatives, caretakers—need to pay special attention and watch for adverse (negative) physical and psychological responses to medication.

- The elderly tend to take more medications (including over-the-counter preparations and home or folk remedies), so that the possibility of negative drug interactions is higher.

Pregnant, Nursing, or Childbearing-Age Women

- In general, during pregnancy, all medications (including

psychotherapeutic medications) should be avoided where possible, and other methods of treatment should be tried.

• A woman who is taking a psychotherapeutic medication and plans to become pregnant should discuss her plans with her doctor; if she discovers that she is pregnant, she should contact her doctor immediately. During early pregnancy, there is a possible risk of birth defects with some of these medications, and for this reason:

—Lithium is not recommended during the first 3 months of pregnancy.
—Benzodiazepines are not recommended during the first 3 months of pregnancy.

The decision to use a psychotherapeutic medication should be made only after a careful discussion with the doctor concerning the risks and benefits to the woman and her baby.

• Small amounts of medication pass into the breast milk; this is a consideration for mothers who are planning to breast-feed.

• A woman who is taking birth-control pills should be sure that her doctor is aware of this. The estrogen in these pills may increase side effects of some antianxiety medications and/or reduce their efficacy to relieve symptoms of anxiety.

For more detailed information, talk to your doctor or mental health professional, consult your local public library, or write to the pharmaceutical company that produces the medication or the U.S. Food and Drug Administration, 5600 Fishers Lane, Rockville, MD 20857.

Index of Medications

To find the section of the text that describes the medication you or a friend or family member is taking, find either the generic (chemical) name and look it up on the first list, or the trade name and look it up on the second list. If you do not find the name of the medication on the label, ask your doctor or pharmacist for it. (Note: some drugs, such as amitriptyline and chlordiazepoxide, are marketed under numerous trade names, not all of which can be mentioned in a brief publication such as this. If your medication's trade name does not appear in this list, look it up by its generic name or ask your doctor or pharmacist for more information.)

Alphabetical Listing of Medications by Generic Name

The following list gives the generic name followed by the trade name(s) for each medication.

Antipsychotic Medications

- chlorpromazine; Thorazine
- chlorprothixene; Taractan
- clozapine; Clozaril
- fluphenazine; Permitil, Prolixin
- haloperidol; Haldol
- loxapine; Daxolin, Loxitane
- mesoridazine; Serentil
- molindone; Lidone, Moban
- perphenazine; Trilafon
- pimozide (for Tourette's Syndrome); Orap
- thioridazine; Mellaril
- thiothixene; Navane
- trifluoperazine; Stelazine
- trifluopromazine; Vesprin

Antimanic Medications

- carbamazepine; Tegretol
- lithium carbonate; Eskalith, Lithane
- lithium citrate; Cibalith-S

Antidepressant Medications

- amitriptyline; Elavil
- amoxapine; Asendin
- bupropion; Wellbutrin
- desipramine; Norpramin, Pertofrane

433

- doxepin; Adapin, Sinequan
- clomipramine; Anafranil
- fluoxetine; Prozac
- imipramine; Tofranil
- isocarboxazid (MAOI); Marplan
- maprotiline; Ludiomil
- nortriptyline; Aventyl, Pamelor
- phenelzine (MAOI); Nardil
- protriptyline; Vivactil
- tranylcypromine (MAOI); Parnate
- trazadone; Desyrel
- trimipramine; Surmontil

Antianxiety Medications

(All of these antianxiety medications except buspirone are benzo-diazepines)

- alprazolam; Xanax
- buspirone; BuSpar
- chlordiazepoxide; Librax, Libritabs, Librium
- clorazepate; Azene, Tranxene
- diazepam; Valium
- halazepam; Paxipam
- lorazepam; Ativan
- oxazepam; Serax
- prazepam; Centrax, Vestran

Alphabetical Listing of Medications by Trade Name

The following list gives the trade name followed by the generic name for each medication.

Antipsychotic Medications

- Clozaril; clozapine
- Daxolin; loxapine
- Haldol; haloperidol
- Lidone; molindone
- Loxitane; loxapine

- Mellaril; thioridazine
- Moban; molindone
- Navane; thiothixene
- Orap (for Tourette's Syndrome); pimozide
- Permitil; fluphenazine
- Prolixin; fluphenazine
- Serentil; mesoridazine
- Stelazine; trifluoperazine
- Taractan; chlorprothixene
- Thorazine; chlorpromazine
- Trilafon; perphenazine
- Vesprin; trifluopromazine

Antimanic Medications

- Cibalith-S; lithium citrate
- Eskalith; lithium carbonate
- Lithane; lithium carbonate
- Lithobid; lithium carbonate
- Tegretol; carbamazepine

Antidepressant Medications

- Adapin; doxepin
- Anafranil; clomipramine
- Asendin; amoxapine
- Aventyl; nortriptyline
- Desyrel; trazodone
- Elavil; amitriptyline
- Ludiomil; maprotiline
- Marplan (MAOI); isocarboxazid
- Nardil (MAOI); phenelzine
- Norpramin; desipramine
- Pamelor; nortriptyline
- Parnate (MAOI); tranylcypromine
- Pertofrane; desipramine
- Prozac; fluoxetine
- Sinequan; doxepin
- Surmontil; trimipramine
- Tofranil; imipramine

- Vivactil; protriptyline
- Wellbutrin; bupropion

Antianxiety Medications

(All of these antianxiety medications except buspirone are benzo-diazepines)

- Ativan; lorazepam
- Azene; clorazepate
- BuSpar; buspirone
- Centrax; prazepam
- Librax; chlordiazepoxide
- Libritabs; chlordiazepoxide
- Librium; chlordiazepoxide
- Paxipam; halazepam
- Serax; oxazepam
- Tranxene; clorazepate
- Valium; diazepam
- Vestran; prazepam
- Xanax; alprazolam

At one time, two combination medications not included in the above list were often prescribed, but are prescribed only occasionally today. They are: a combination of amitriptyline (antidepressant) and perphenazine (antipsychotic) marketed as *Triavil* or *Etrafon*; and a combination of amitriptyline (antidepressant) and chlordiazepoxide (antianxiety) marketed as *Limbitrol*.

References

AHFS Drug Information, 91, Gerald K. McEvoy, Editor. Bethesda, Maryland, American Society of Hospital Pharmacists, Inc., 1991.

Bohn J., and Jefferson, J.W., *Lithium and Manic Depression:A Guide*. Madison, Wisconsin, Lithium Information Center, rev. ed. 1990.

Goodwin, Frederick K. and Jamison, Kay Redfield. *Manic-Depressive Illness*. Oxford University Press, New York. 1990.

Johnston, H.F. *Stimulants and Hyperactive Children: A Guide.* Madison, Wisconsin, Lithium Information Center, 1990.

Medenwald, J.R., Greist, J.H., and Jefferson, J.W. *Carbamazepine and Manic Depression: A Guide.* Madison, Wisconsin, Lithium Information Center, rev. ed., 1990.

Physicians' Desk Reference, 45th edition, Edward R. Barnhart, Publisher. Oradell, NJ, Medical Economics Data, 1991. (available in public libraries).

Schizophrenia Bulletin (Issue Theme: New Developments in the Pharmacologic Treatment of Schizophrenia), Volume 17:4, 1991, David Shore and Samuel J. Keith, Editors. (available in most medical libraries).

Chapter 36

Lithium

If a doctor has prescribed lithium for you or someone close to you, you may wish to know more about the medication: Is it safe? Will it cause discomfort? Most importantly, will it work? Chances are you've been told that lithium may prevent future bouts of your illness. You can benefit from this remarkable effect only if you continue to take the drug exactly as the doctor prescribes. You may have to take it for long periods of time, perhaps indefinitely. That means lithium is as important to you as insulin is to a diabetic or other kinds of daily medications are to people with high blood pressure. Like a diabetic or hypertensive person, you may question whether you need to continue taking the medication day after day, especially if you feel well. But lithium can save your life as surely as those other drugs save theirs. This text will help you learn more about lithium.

Lithium: Mineral and Drug

Pure lithium, like sodium, calcium, or potassium, is a naturally occurring mineral. Lithium is found abundantly in certain rocks and the sea and in minute amounts in plant and animal tissues. Lithium also shows up in water, notably in the springs and spas where in earlier times people "took the waters," bathing in and drinking the lithium-rich water for its soothing effects. Whether lithium actually calmed 19th-century ladies and gentlemen has never been docu-

NIH Pub. No. 93-3476.

mented. What we do know is that, from time to time since antiquity, doctors have noticed that lithium can control overexcitement in some of their patients.

Today, lithium is administered to patients as a lithium salt, usually as lithium carbonate or lithium citrate, which is taken by mouth in capsule, tablet, or syrup form. Pharmaceutical companies often assign a "trade name" to their products. Examples of trade names for lithium are Cibalith, Eskalith, Lithane, and Lithobid.

Some companies use only the chemical name, that is, lithium carbonate or lithium citrate.

Modern physicians rely on these various forms of lithium to treat serious mental illness. Properly administered, it is one of the most powerful medications available for mood disorders. [For more information about mood disorders, see Part III of this volume.]

The Development of Lithium Treatment

John Cade, an Australian physician, introduced lithium into psychiatry in 1949 when he reported that lithium carbonate was an effective treatment for manic excitement. Unfortunately, Dr. Cade's discovery coincided with reports of several deaths from the unrestricted use of lithium chloride as a salt substitute for cardiac patients. Four patients died, and several developed toxic reactions. It was not known at that time that lithium can accumulate to dangerous levels in the body or that lithium has to be used with special caution in patients with cardiac disorders.

As a result of these experiences, lithium was virtually neglected in this country until the early 1960s. Research by European psychiatrists, especially Dr. Mogens Schou in Denmark, hastened acceptance of lithium in the United States. Renewed interest in the compound led to numerous clinical trials, including pivotal studies conducted by NIMH. These studies showed how lithium could be used safely and effectively to treat psychiatric disorders.

In addition, research—both in animals and humans—showed that lithium influences several functions in the body, including the distribution of sodium and potassium, which regulate impulses along the nerve cells. Lithium can affect the activity of neurotransmitters and biological systems because it alters the way in which a variety of messages are transmitted after they reach their target. Although scientists have many promising leads, they have yet to explain the biochemical actions of depression.

In 1970, the U.S. Food and Drug Administration (FDA) approved lithium as a treatment for mania. Four years later, the FDA also approved the use of lithium as a preventive, or prophylactic, treatment for manic-depressive illness.

Lithium's Uses

Psychiatrists use lithium in two ways: to treat episodes of mania and depression and to prevent their recurrence. Lithium can often subdue symptoms when a patient is in the midst of a manic episode, and it may also ameliorate the symptoms of a depressive episode. The single most important use for lithium, though, is in preventing new episodes of mania and depression. Lithium is also being used experimentally to treat other disorders.

Manic and Depressive Episodes

Lithium is highly effective in treating acute episodes of mania, especially when symptoms are mild. Patients going through severe manic episodes need to be calmed as quickly as possible, however, and lithium may take 1 to 3 weeks to achieve its full effect. Therefore, physicians most often treat very disturbed patients by first combining lithium with a different type of drug, a tranquilizer, such as haloperidol or chlorpromazine. When lithium has had a chance to act, the tranquilizer may be gradually withdrawn. Lithium can normalize the manic disorder without causing the drugged feeling that often occurs with tranquilizers. Also, tranquilizers may produce troublesome side effects that limit their usefulness as a long-term treatment.

Lithium is also effective in treating depressive episodes in some patients with manic-depressive illness. For these patients, some doctors prefer to treat mild to moderate depressive episodes with lithium alone because of the possibility that conventional antidepressant drugs such as imipramine may trigger a hypomanic or manic attack. If the depression is severe, treatment is usually begun with a conventional antidepressant in combination with lithium. That same combination is sometimes used in unipolar depressions that do not respond to antidepressant medications alone.

Lithium's Role in Preventing Manic and Depressive Episodes

As noted, lithium's greatest value is in preventing or reducing the occurrence of future episodes of bipolar disorder. The effectiveness of this lithium prophylaxis or lithium prophylactic treatment has been demonstrated in more than two decades of careful research. In related research, several major studies indicate that lithium can decrease the frequency or severity of new depressive episodes in recurrent unipolar disorder. This suggests that lithium may also have prophylactic value in treating this mood disorder. Conventional antidepressants also have been shown to be effective prophylactic treatments for recurrent unipolar depression.

In prophylactic treatment, lithium is administered after a manic or depressive episode to prevent or dampen future attacks. Some patients respond quickly and have no further episodes. Others respond more slowly and continue to have moderate mood swings even months after therapy is started. These highs or lows usually become progressively less severe with continued lithium treatment; often they disappear. With other patients, lithium may not prevent all future manic and depressive episodes, but may reduce or lessen their severity so that the individual can continue to lead a productive life.

There are patients who are not helped at all by lithium. About one in ten patients with bipolar disorder who takes lithium does not respond to the medication, but continues to have manic-depressive episodes at the same frequency and severity as before. Doctors cannot predict with certainty how lithium will work in any individual case. This can be determined only by actual use of the medication.

When deciding whether a patient should start lithium prophylactic therapy, a psychiatrist or other physician considers the likelihood of a new episode in the near future; the impact that the episode might have on the patient, family, and job; the patient's willingness to commit himself or herself to a long-term treatment program; and the presence of medical conditions that may rule out lithium treatment. Usually, a doctor prescribes lithium prophylactic therapy only after a patient has had two or three well-defined episodes requiring treatment. Patients who have had only a single attack, mild attacks, or a long interval between episodes—for example, over 5 years—usually do not receive prophylactic treatment unless the second episode would be life threatening or highly disruptive to the patient's career or family relations.

Such rules, though, serve as only broad guidelines. Patients must act as the doctor's partner in weighing the circumstances and making the decision. Each patient should understand the reasons for lithium prophylaxis as well as the benefits and risks and be an informed participant in the treatment program.

When lithium fails or when a patient has another medical condition that precludes its use, the doctor may consider an alternative prophylactic drug treatment. First, however, he or she will reevaluate why lithium failed: Was dosage adequate? Did the patient take the medication as prescribed? Does the patient have a problem with thyroid function? Many patients with mood disorders have malfunctioning thyroid glands, a problem that can be successfully treated with a thyroid hormone or related preparations without withdrawing lithium.

For manic-depressive patients, the anticonvulsant drugs carbamazepine (trade name Tegretol) and valproate (trade name Depakote) seem to be the best alternatives to lithium. Sometimes the anticonvulsant drugs are given alone, sometimes in combination with lithium, to prevent or dampen future episodes.

Patients with unipolar disorder who fail on lithium often are given an antidepressant drug alone or in combination with lithium. A severe episode may be treated with electroconvulsive therapy. Information on alternatives to lithium treatment can be found in the literature listed at the end of [this chapter].

Other Disorders

Lithium may also be useful for treating other mental illnesses. Research psychiatrists have evaluated lithium as a treatment for a variety of psychiatric disorders, including schizophrenia, schizoaffective disorder, alcoholism, premenstrual depression, and periodic aggressive and explosive behavior. Lithium appears to produce the best responses in patients who have mood swings, a tendency to have intermittent bouts of illness, or a family history of mood disorder.

A Checklist for Patients Taking Lithium

1. Take the medication on a regular basis as prescribed by the doctor. Ask the doctor for instructions on what to do if one or more doses are missed. Unless the doctor advises otherwise,

do not catch up on a missed dose by doubling the next dose. This may produce a dangerously high blood level of lithium.

2. Obtain regular blood tests for lithium levels.

3. Have the doctor take blood tests for lithium levels 12 hours after the last dose. Inform the doctor if it has been less than 11 hours or more than 13 hours since the last dose.

4. Inform the doctor if other medications are being taken, since they can change lithium levels.

5. Notify the doctor whenever there is a significant change in weight or diet. It is especially important to tell the doctor if you plan to begin a rapid weight-loss diet, since lithium levels in the body may be drastically affected.

6. Advise the doctor about any changes in frequency of urination, loss of fluids through diarrhea, vomiting, excessive sweating, or physical illness, particularly if there is a fever, because adjustment of dosage or further testing may be required.

7. If planning to become pregnant, advise the doctor.

8. If another doctor is being seen or an operation is planned, be sure to inform that doctor that you are taking lithium.

9. Because it may take time for mood swings to be completely controlled by lithium, try not to get discouraged. Continue taking the medicine as prescribed until advised otherwise by the doctor. However, be sure to notify the doctor of recurrences in mania or depression because it may be necessary to increase the dose or to receive additional medication for a time. Psychotherapy can help you to recognize manic or depressive episodes early in their course, as well as help you to express and understand your feelings about having manic-depressive illness.

10. Ask the doctor any questions about the treatment program or any procedures that you do not understand. A well-

informed patient and family are important factors contributing to a successful treatment outcome. Also, if your psychotherapist is someone other than the doctor prescribing the medication, it is important for the two professionals to exchange information about your progress and problems as needed.

Lithium's Side Effects

Most patients do not experience serious side effects when they begin lithium therapy. Initially, the patient may have slight nausea, stomach cramps, diarrhea, thirstiness, muscle weakness, and feelings of being somewhat tired, dazed, or sleepy. A mild hand tremor may emerge as the dose is increased. These effects are normally minimal and usually subside after several days of treatment. But some of the initial side effects may carry over into long-term therapy and others may emerge. Some patients continue to have a slight hand tremor. Many drink more fluids than usual—without always being aware of it—and urinate more frequently, while still others may gain weight. Weight gain often can be controlled with proper diet. Crash diets should be avoided, however, since they may adversely affect lithium levels. Also, to avoid excessive weight gain, excessive amounts of drinks with high sugar content should be avoided.

In patients who have low amounts of thyroid hormone, enlargement of the thyroid gland may develop, but this condition is generally not serious if monitored closely by a physician. It can be successfully treated with supplementary thyroid medication without withdrawing lithium.

Because of physiological changes in kidneys observed in some lithium-treated patients, any past or current kidney disorder or changes in frequency of urination should be reported to the physician. Long-term lithium therapy can also worsen certain skin conditions, especially acne and psoriasis, and may produce edema, or swelling, which is due to accumulation of water in tissues.

Lithium must be taken with care, with attention to taking the proper dose, having regular blood tests, and reporting changes in diet, exercise, and the occurrence of illness. Toxic levels of lithium in the blood can cause vomiting, severe diarrhea, extreme thirst, weight loss, muscle twitching, abnormal muscle movement, slurred speech, blurred vision, dizziness, confusion, stupor, or pulse irregularities. Sudden physical or mental changes should be reported to the doctor immediately. These problems can almost always be avoided when the doctor's instructions are followed carefully.

Periodic Blood Tests

The amount of lithium needed to treat or prevent manic and depressive symptoms effectively differs greatly from one patient to another. The doctor determines how much lithium a patient needs by taking a sample of blood from time to time. The blood is analyzed to determine how much lithium is present. Testing for the lithium blood level is a vital part of treatment with lithium. It aids the doctor in selecting and maintaining the most effective dose. Just as important, lithium blood levels assure the doctor that a patient is not taking a toxic dose—that is, a poisonous dose.

Lithium is an unusual drug because the amount needed to be effective is only slightly less than the amount that is toxic. For that reason, patients must be very careful not to take more lithium than prescribed.

Lithium levels in the blood can change even when the patient takes the same dose every day: The concentration of lithium can increase when a person becomes ill with another medical condition, especially influenza or other illnesses that result in fever or changes in diet and loss of body fluids. Surgery, strenuous exercise, and crash diets are other circumstances that can lead to dangerously increased lithium levels in the blood. The doctor should be informed of illness or changes in eating habits, and a regular blood testing schedule should be set up and followed rigorously.

If a patient stops taking lithium for only one day, the blood level of the drug falls to half that needed for effective therapy. A forgotten dose should not, however, be taken with the regular dose the next day, because it could raise the lithium level too much. Furthermore, the lower lithium level that results from missing one dose is unlikely to jeopardize therapeutic response.

Because the blood level of lithium rises rapidly for a few hours after swallowing a lithium pill and then slowly levels off, having a blood test right after taking the drug can mislead the doctor into thinking that the dose is too high. To gauge the average blood level accurately, it is important to have blood drawn about 12 hours after the last dose of lithium. Otherwise, the results will be misleading and possibly dangerous. Most patients take their nighttime dose of lithium and then come to the doctor's office the next morning to have a blood test before taking their first dose for the day. Some patients are able to take their full daily dose at bedtime and don't have to worry about the morning dose when getting a blood level.

Precautions in Taking Lithium

Lithium is excreted from the body almost entirely by the kidneys. If, for some reason, the kidneys are unable to get rid of the proper amount of lithium, the drug may accumulate to dangerous levels in the body. The excretion of lithium in the kidneys is closely linked to that of sodium. The less sodium, or salt, in the body, the less lithium is excreted, and the greater chance of lithium buildup to toxic levels. Diuretics cause the kidneys to excrete sodium; as a result, lithium levels rise. The reason that many illnesses can increase lithium levels is that increased sweating, fever, a low salt diet, vomiting, and diarrhea all result in less sodium present in the body, thus producing higher levels.

Lithium should not be taken by patients with severely impaired kidney function. Patients with heart disease and others who have a significant change in sodium in their diet or periodic episodes of heavy sweating should be especially careful to have their lithium blood levels monitored regularly.

For women in the fertile age range, the possibility of harmful effects on the unborn child may pose problems for continued use of lithium. Children of mothers who received lithium during the first 3 months of pregnancy have been reported in some, but not all, studies to have a slightly increased frequency of malformations of the heart and blood vessels. Even though this risk is low and uncertain, it is strongly recommended that women discontinue lithium during the first 3 months of pregnancy. The decision to stop the medication, however, must be weighed against the possible consequences of an untreated manic or depressive attack, which may result in injury, physiological stress, dehydration and malnutrition, sleep deprivation, or possibly even suicide. Because of the risk of postpartum depression or mania, lithium is sometimes restarted during the final weeks before birth is expected. Women should not breast feed when they are taking lithium, except in rare circumstances when the potential benefits to the mother outweigh possible hazards to the child.

Taking Lithium: How Long?

When fully effective, lithium can control manic-depressive illness for the rest of a person's life. But it is not a cure. Like antihypertensive medications for controlling high blood pressure, lithium should not be discontinued without consulting the physician.

Unfortunately, some patients stop taking their lithium when they find that it diminishes the wonderful sense of well-being they felt when hypomanic; most resume taking their medication when disabling manic episodes return.

Other patients discontinue lithium because they feel they no longer need it. Such reasoning is perfectly understandable. When a person remains well week after week, there is a tendency to forget to take lithium or to deliberately stop taking the medication, believing that the illness has been cured. Lithium's effects, however, last only when patients regularly take the medication. If patients stop taking lithium—no matter if they've been taking it for 5 weeks or 5 years—the chances of having another manic or depressive attack increase. In fact, patients who stop taking the medication are just as likely as patients who have never been treated to fall back into a manic or depressive episode.

This does not mean, though, that all patients must take lithium for a lifetime. After a long period of treatment without a recurrence of mania or depression, the doctor and patient may consider withdrawal of medication under close supervision. That decision will depend upon several factors, including the impact that a subsequent episode may have on the patient's marriage or other significant relationships, career, and general functioning; the likelihood that an emerging recurrence will be detected early enough to prevent a full-blown attack; and the patient's tolerance of lithium.

Information Resources

Suggested Reading

Bohn, J., and Jefferson, J. *Lithium and Manic Depression: A Guide*. Rev. ed. Madison, WI: Lithium Information Center, University of Wisconsin, 1990.

Fieve, R. *Moodswing: The Third Revolution in Psychiatry*. Rev. ed. New York: William Morrow and Company, 1989.

Gold, M. *The Good News About Depression*. New York: Villard Books, 1987.

Goodwin, F.K., and Jamison, K.R. *Manic-Depressive Illness*. New York and Oxford: Oxford University Press, 1990.

Jefferson, J., and Greist, J. *Valproate and Manic Depression: A Guide*. Madison, WI: Lithium Information Center, University of Wisconsin, 1991.

Jefferson, J.; Greist, J.; Ackerman, D.; and Carroll, J. *Lithium Encyclopedia for Clinical Practice*. Rev. ed. Washington, DC: American Psychiatric Press, Inc., 1987.

Johnson, F.N., ed. *Handbook of Lithium Therapy*. Lancaster, England: MTP Press Ltd., and Baltimore, MD: University Park Press, 1980.

Johnson, F.N. *Depression and Mania: Modern Lithium Therapy*. Oxford: IRL Press, 1987.

Medenwald, J., Greist, J.; and Jefferson, J. *Carbamazepine and Manic Depression: A Guide*. Rev. ed. Madison, WI: Lithium Information Center, University of Wisconsin, 1990.

Post, R., and Uhde, T. Refractory manias and alternatives to lithium treatment. In: Georgotis, A., and Cancro, R., eds. *Depression and Mania*. New York: Elsevier, 1988.

Prien, R.F., and Potter, W.Z. National Institute of Mental Health workshop report on treatment of bipolar disorder. *Psychopharmacology Bulletin* 26(4):409-427, 1990.

Schou, M. Lithium treatment of manic-depressive illness: Past, present, and perspectives. *Journal of the American Medical Association* 259:1834-1836, 1988.

Schou, M. *Lithium Treatment of Manic-Depressive Illness: A Practical Guide*. Rev. ed. New York and Basel: Karger, 1989.

For More Information on Mood Disorders and Lithium

There are a number of consumer advocacy and support organizations for people with mood disorders. The underlying philosophy of these organizations is that the best helpers are often those who have experienced similar problems. These groups typically provide a variety of forms of practical help for dealing with problems that their members share in common. Organizations that have chapters in many communities are:

The National Alliance for the Mentally III
2101 Wilson Boulevard, Suite 302
Arlington, VA 22201
(703) 524-7600; 1-800-950-NAMI

National Depressive and Manic Depressive Association
730 N. Franklin, Suite 501
Chicago, IL 60610
(312) 642-0049; 1-800-826-2632

National Mental Health Association
1021 Prince Street
Alexandria, VA 22314-2971
(703) 684-7722; 1-800-969-NMHA

For further information on lithium contact:

Lithium Information Center
Dean Foundation
8000 Excelsior Drive, Suite 203
Madison, WI 53717-1914
(608) 836-8070

—by Robert F. Prien, Ph.D., and
William Z. Potter, M.D., Ph.D.

Chapter 37

Mutual-Help Groups

For many human problems there are no easy answers or easy cures. Even after the best professional help has been obtained, a person may be left with difficulties too great to handle alone. In this situation, millions of people have found much-needed personal support in mutual-help groups. It is within these groups, whose members share common concerns, that they are offered an important aid to recovery, the understanding and help of others who have gone through similar experiences. This [chapter] lists some of the groups that offer solace and assistance to those who must deal with mental illnesses, addictive behaviors, and other emotional problems.

What Is Mutual Help?

Mutual help has been a mainstay of life for as long as families have existed. As social beings, all of us need to be accepted, cared for, and emotionally supported. We also find it satisfying to care for and support those around us. Within the most natural "mutual-help networks"—made up of our families and friends—we establish the one-to-one contact so important to our happiness and well-being. We often take this informal support for granted, but it clearly influences our ability to handle distressing events in our lives. Many of our daily conversations are actually mutual counseling sessions in which we exchange the reassurance and advice that help us deal with routine

DHHS Pub. No. (ADM) 89-1138.

stresses. In fact, scientists have found that this sort of emotional support can help prevent ill health and that it promotes recovery when an illness or accident does occur.

The supportive relationships we establish with family and friends, however, constitute only some of the interpersonal networks that help sustain us through life. As we develop socially and intellectually, we tend to associate with others who have similar interests and beliefs. These associations include religious congregations, civic and fraternal organizations, and social clubs: in them, members benefit from a shared identity and a sense of common purpose. Some groups are aimed primarily at social enjoyment. Others come together to bring about social change. Through combined efforts, the group can often promote or accomplish what the individual cannot. Yet each member's presence and participation adds to the strength of the group.

Why the Need for Mutual-Help Groups?

The twentieth century has produced social changes which affect our traditional patterns of support. Living in a highly mobile society, we may not enjoy the benefits of a permanent community and longstanding stable relationships. People today are apt to live in more than one home before adulthood. As adults, they may hold a series of jobs requiring them to form new friendships in new locations. Their families, once close, are now separated by distance. The emotional and practical support they gave is no longer available and may not be forthcoming from new neighbors and friends. And, perhaps most significantly, divorce is separating millions of families each year. Despite these changing social patterns, our needs for stability and support remain constant. We are likely to feel a sense of isolation, questioning "What role do I play in such a vast, impersonal world? Where can I find other people like me?" To overcome this sense of isolation, to exercise more control over the quality of their lives, and to get help with serious mental disorders, millions are turning to mutual-help groups.

What Is the Purpose of Mutual-Help Groups?

The estimated half-million mutual-help groups in existence deal with almost every human problem. There are three types of formal groups: (1) the self-care groups for those suffering physical and mental illness (there is at least one group for nearly every major disease); (2) the reform groups for addiction behaviors (particularly the "anonymous" groups such as Alcoholics Anonymous, Gamblers Anonymous, and Overeaters Anonymous); and (3) advocacy groups for certain minorities (handicapped, elderly, mentally ill, etc.). Names and addresses of support groups in any of these categories can be obtained from self-help clearinghouses such as those listed in this [chapter].

In spite of the enormous diversity of the problems they address, all mutual-help groups have the same underlying purpose: to provide emotional support and practical help in dealing with a problem common to all members. There is a special bond among people who share the same troubling experience; it begins when one person says to another, "I know just how you feel." Knowing that someone else truly understands one's feelings by virtue of having "been there" brings a sense of relief; one's pain is no longer a burden borne alone. Stepping into the security of such a group can be like coming home for those who have been too long isolated by their private and painful concerns. Each mutual help group provides an atmosphere of acceptance that encourages members to share their sorrows, fears, and frustrations. They can then begin to communicate more openly, view their problems more objectively, and find more effective coping strategies.

How Do Mutual-Help Groups Operate?

The structure of mutual-help groups and the way they serve their members depend primarily on their goals. Each local group determines its own programs and meeting schedules. Typically, groups hold regular meetings in church halls, public buildings, or other no-rent or low-rent facilities. Many small groups meet in a member's home. Programs for those meetings can include group discussions, study groups, visiting speakers, and other activities that inform the members and help to build their confidence. Along with the personal support gained from meeting together, the groups may offer additional services. Newsletters published by both parent organizations and local groups report individual success stories, treatment updates, and other information about the group's concerns. Some groups maintain a "hotline" so that those in need will have constant access to information and an understanding listener. Others, particularly those focusing on addictive behavior or emotional disorder, use a "buddy system" so that members can count on one-to-one encouragement between meetings. Some groups, such as those that deal with a rare disease and have only a few members in each part of the country, have a correspondence referral system to put members in touch with one another. Although some mutual-help groups receive funding from Government health agencies and public contributions, many are entirely self-supporting through members' voluntary contributions or minimal dues (average: $10-$15 yearly). Since the groups are run by members for members, there are seldom any professional salaries or overhead costs (although an office administrator or secretary is sometimes necessary). Some groups will even refuse outside contributions on the grounds that it would compromise their independent status.

What Happens at a Mutual-Help Group Meeting?

For the millions currently utilizing and contributing to mutual-help groups, the process began with a tentative exploration, a first meeting. Of course, the prospect of exposing a previously concealed pain may be frightening; thus many approach their first group meeting with their defenses up. All new members wonder what the group can do for them and what it will ask in return. Experienced members, aware of these mixed emotions, encourage new members to feel relaxed and welcome. A veteran member may begin a conversation and offer literature that outlines the group's purposes. In an atmosphere that is friendly, compassionate, and accepting, new members soon realize that their participation is purely voluntary, with no strings attached. There is an unwritten code of confidentiality within the group, and each member's privacy and dignity is respected. Everyone is given the freedom to draw on the strength of the group as needed and to extend support to others when possible. Even in the groups which have a series of steps to recovery (such as the "Anonymous" organizations), members proceed at their own pace, within their own limits. Group disapproval of those who stumble in the march toward recovery is rare because everyone knows how difficult it can be. In fact, mutual-help groups use the knowledge gained from a conflict or crisis as a valuable tool for building better ways to manage such problems in the future.

To those new to a mutual-help group, being with others like themselves, who are successfully getting on with life despite their problems, can be the best encouragement of all. Who are the "others" who provide the positive example that keep the group together? If they have passed a crisis or gained confidence in coping with their hardship, what further need do they have for shared support? While there are no levels of distinction among the members in a group, there are always those who are stronger, more experienced, more committed to the group's goals and more able to give of themselves. These people often assume leadership roles, continuing to receive comfort and encouragement while helping others. There is a natural tendency among those who have derived benefit from the group to want to perpetuate the cycle of being helped and helping. For those helpers who lead, organize, reach out to others, and bolster the group's morale by their own example, reward comes in seeing the progress of others. Says one group member, "I've been there and know what it's like. I could have been saved 20 years of misery if there had been a group to help me."

What About Professional Help?

Mutual-help groups do not intend to replace physicians, therapists, and other skilled professionals. Rather, the groups function in the belief that many of our physical and mental health needs go beyond the bounds of formal care measures. Some who have received treatment for an illness have taken only the first step toward recovery; adjusting to a long convalescence becomes the greater challenge. Others must deal with a lifelong handicap or chronic illness. For both, the practical problems of everyday life can be overwhelming. In particular, those who have a mental or emotional illness require the continuing support of others to help them along the road to recovery. These ongoing problems do not signify a failure on the part of professional caretakers but indicate that there are limits to their ability to serve our needs.

Some mutual-help groups avoid formal professional guidance or consultation, although many have benefitted from the informal help of professionals. Despite the distance maintained between the groups and their professional counterparts, each acknowledges the role of the other: groups typically encourage their members to seek or continue with the professional help they need, and many physicians and other service providers strongly endorse group programs as an appropriate extension of care.

Finding the Mutual-Help Group That You Need

You may already have heard about a mutual-help group that deals with your concerns. There are a number of ways to get more information about groups that may interest you. Some of the larger groups are listed by subject in the phone directory, and the names and phone numbers of many more are available from hospitals and local health and social-service agencies. If you're interested in an organization that does not have a group in your area, the central office will provide information on organizing one. Directories of mutual-help groups can usually be found in public libraries, and more comprehensive information and assistance, including how to organize a group, can be found through the organizations and reference books listed.

The important thing to realize is that mutual-help groups are there for you. They're economical and effective. And they can reassure you that you are not alone: there are others who understand your problem and are eager to share their experience and support with you.

The following organizations offer support to people with mental or behavioral problems.

AIDS Referral
1620 Eye St., NW
Washington, DC 20006
(202) 293-7330

The U.S. Conference of Mayors publishes a brochure, *Local AIDS-Related Services National Directory*, a listing of over 2,000 AIDS groups.

AL-ANON Family Group Headquarters
1372 Broadway
New York, NY 10018
(212) 302-7240

For relatives and friends of persons with alcohol problems. Includes ALATEEN.

Alcoholics Anonymous
P.O. Box 459
Grand Central Station
New York, NY 10163
(212) 686-1100

For men and women who share the common problems of alcoholism.

Alzheimer's Disease and Related Disorders Association
P.O. Box 5675
Department PX1
Chicago, IL 60680
1-800-572-6037 (in Illinios)
1-800-621-0379 (Nationwide)

Offers assistance and information to Alzheimer's families through its 188 chapters nationwide.

American Association of Suicidology
2459 South Ash
Denver, CO 80222

For those who have experienced the suicide of someone close.

Association for Children and Adults with Learning Disabilities
4156 Library Rd.
Pittsburgh, PA 15234

For individuals—children and adults—who suffer from a learning disability.

American Narcolepsy Association
P.O. Box 1187
San Carlos, CA
(415) 591-7979

Provides information and referrals to people with sleep disorders.

Autism Society of America
1234 Massachusetts Ave., NW
Washington, DC 20005
(202) 783-0125

For both adults and children who have autism.

The Compassionate Friends
P.O. Box 3696
Oak Brook, IL 60522-3696
(708) 990-0010

For bereaved parents: peer support.

Depression after Delivery
P.O. Box 1282
Morrisville, PA 19067
(215) 295-3994

For women experiencing Postpartum Depression.

Emotions Anonymous
P.O. Box 4245
St. Paul, MN 55104
(612) 647-9712

For persons with emotional problems: a Twelve-Step Program adapted from the Alcoholics Anonymous Program.

Families Anonymous
P.O. Box 528
Van Nuys, CA 91408
(818) 989-7841

For concerned relatives and friends of youth with drug abuse or related behavior problems.

Narcotics Anonymous
P.O. Box 9999
Van Nuys, CA 91409
(818) 780-3951

For narcotic addicts: peer support for recovered addicts.

The National Alliance for the Mentally Ill
2101 Wilson Blvd., Suite 302
Arlington, VA 22201
(703) 524-7600

For families and friends of seriously mentally ill individuals; provides information, emotional support, and advocacy through local and State affiliates.

National Association of Anorexia Nervosa and Associated Disorders
Box 7
Highland Park, IL 60035
(312) 831-3438

Offers assistance to anorexics/bulimics and their families.

National Coalition Against Domestic Violence
P.O. Box 15127
Washington, DC 20003-0127
1-800-333-SAFE

National organization of shelters and support services for battered women and their children.

National Depressive and Manic Depression Association
Merchandise Mart
P.O. Box 3395
Chicago, IL 60654
(312) 939-2442

For depressed persons and their families.

National Foundation for Depressive Illness, Inc.
P.O. Box 2257
New York, NY 10116
(212) 620-0098; 1-800-248-4344

Provides referrals to support groups.

National Mental Health Association
1021 Prince St.
Alexandria, VA 22314-2971
(703) 643-7722

Citizens advocacy group concerned with all aspects of mental health and mental illnesses.

OCD Foundation, Inc.
P.O. Box 9573
New Haven, CT 06535
(203) 772-0565, 772-0575

For sufferers of obsessive-compulsive disorders and their families and friends.

Orton Dyxlexia Society
724 York Rd.
Baltimore, MD 21204
(301) 296-0232; 1-800-ABC-D123

For persons interested in the study, treatment, and prevention of the problems of specific language disability.

Parents Anonymous
6733 South Sepulveda Blvd., Suite 270
Los Angeles, CA 90045
(213) 410-9732

For parents who have abused their children.

Parents United
P.O. Box 952
San Jose, CA 95108
(408) 280-5055

For abused children and for adults who were abused as children.

Phobia Society of America
133 Rollins Ave., Suite 4B
Rockville, MD 20852
(301) 231-9350

For people who suffer from phobia and panic attacks.

Recovery, Inc.
802 North Dearborn St.
Chicago, IL 60610
(312) 337-5661

For former mental patients: peer support.

Tardive Dyskinseia/Tardive Dystonia National Association
600 East Pine St.
Seattle, WA 98122
(206) 522-3166

For tardive dyskinesia or tardive dystonia sufferers.

Self-Help Centers and Clearinghouses

Information about self-help groups can be obtained from self-help centers and clearinghouses. Some of these are listed below.

California Self-Help Center
2349 Franz Hall, UCLA
405 Hilgard Ave.
Los Angeles, CA 90024-1563
(213) 825-1799
California residents: 1-800-222-5465

California Self-Help Center, continued

Publishes *Self-Help Group Resources Catalog: A Guide to Print, Audio, and Visual Materials and Services for Starting and Maintaining Self-Help Groups.*

The National Mental Health Consumers' Self-Help Clearing-house
311 South Juniper St., Room 902
Philadelphia, PA 19107
(215) 735-6367

Provides technical assistance and information and referral services to further the development of consumer-run mental health self-help groups.

National Self-Help Clearinghouse Graduate School and University Center
City University of New York
33 West 42nd St.
New York, NY 10036
(212) 840-1259

Newsletter; free brochure.

Self-Help Clearinghouse
St. Clares—Riverside Medical Center
Denville, NJ 07834
(201) 625-7101

Publishes *The Self-Help Source Book*, listing 500 national organizations.

Self-Help Clearinghouse of the Greater Washington Area
7630 Little River Turnpike, #206
Annadale, VA 22003
(703) 941-5465

Provides information, referral, and support services to self-help groups in the Greater Washington Area.

Self-Help Center
1600 Dodge Ave, Suite S-122
Evanston, IL 60201
(312) 328-0470

Publishes in conjunction with the American Hospital Association *Directory of National Self-Help/Mutual Aid Resources*.

Chapter 38

Electroconvulsive Therapy (ECT)

Introduction

Electroconvulsive therapy (ECT) is a treatment for severe mental illness in which a brief application of electric stimulus is used to produce a generalized seizure. In the United States in the 1940s and 1950s, the treatment was often administered to the most severely disturbed patients residing in large mental institutions. As often occurs with new therapies, ECT was used for a variety of disorders, frequently in high doses and for long periods. Many of these efforts proved ineffective, and some even harmful. Moreover, its use as a means of managing unruly patients, for whom other treatments were not then available, contributed to the perception of ECT as an abusive instrument of behavioral control for patients in mental institutions for the chronically ill. With the introduction of effective psychopharmacologic medications and the development of judicial and regulatory restrictions, the use of ECT has waned.

The treatment is now used primarily in general hospital psychiatric units and in psychiatric hospitals. A National Institute of Mental Health hospital survey estimated that 33,384 patients admitted to hospital psychiatric services during 1980 were treated with ECT, representing approximately 2.4 percent of all psychiatric admissions.

Consensus Development Conference Statement, Volume 5, Number 11; U.S.G.P.O. 1985: 491-242-21264.

Although ECT has been in use for more than 45 years, there is continuing controversy concerning the mental disorders for which ECT is indicated, its efficacy in their treatment, the optimal methods of administration, possible complications, and the extent of its usage in various settings. These issues have contributed to concerns about the potential for misuse and abuse of ECT and to desires to ensure the protection of patient's rights. At the same time, there is concern that the curtailment of ECT use in response to public opinion and regulation may deprive certain patients of a potentially effective treatment.

In recent decades, researchers intensified efforts to establish the effectiveness of ECT and its indications, understand its mechanism of action, clarify the extent of adverse effects, and determine optimum treatment technique. Despite recent research efforts yielding substantial information, permitting professional and public evaluation of the safety and efficacy of ECT, the investigation of ECT has not generally been in the mainstream of mental health research.

To help resolve questions surrounding these issues, the National Institutes of Health in conjunction with the National Institute of Mental Health convened a Consensus Development Conference on Electroconvulsive Therapy on June 10-12, 1985. For 1-1/2 days, experts in the field presented their findings, and an audience, including health professionals, former patients, and other interested persons, discussed the issues. A consensus panel representing psychiatry, psychology, neurology, psychopharmacology, epidemiology, law, and the general public considered the scientific evidence and agreed on answers to the following questions:

1. What is the evidence that ECT is effective for patients with specific mental disorders?

2. What are the risks and adverse effects of ECT?

3. What factors should be considered by the physician and patient in determining if and when ECT would be an appropriate treatment?

4. How should ECT be administered to maximize benefits and minimize risks?

5. What are the directions for future research?

1. What is the evidence that ECT is effective for patients with specific mental disorders?

Published controlled studies of ECT permit evaluation of its short-term efficacy in severe major depressions (delusional and endogenous), in acute mania, and in certain schizophrenic syndromes. The available controlled clinical trials do not extend beyond the treatment of the acute episode (i.e., about 4 weeks). These studies are difficult to compare because they have used differing diagnostic systems and research designs. Further, they have measured outcome only in terms of symptom reduction, not the quality of life and social functioning.

Depression

Studies of ECT in depression have used various control conditions for comparison, including "sham" ECT (e.g., all of the elements of the ECT procedure except the electric stimulus), tricyclic antidepressants (TCA), monoamine oxidase inhibitors (MAOI), combinations of antidepressants and neuroleptics, and placebos. The efficacy of ECT has been established most convincingly in the treatment of delusional and severe endogenous depressions, which make up a clinically important minority of depressive disorders. Some studies find ECT to be of at least equal efficacy to medication treatments, and others find ECT to be superior to medication. Not a single controlled study has shown another form of treatment to be superior to ECT in the short-term management of severe depressions. It must be noted, however, that those studies that found ECT to be superior to medication were not designed to study the persistence of this advantage of ECT beyond the short term. Moreover, the available evidence suggests that relapse rates in the year following ECT are likely to be high unless maintenance antidepressant medications are subsequently prescribed. Several studies suggest that ECT reduces symptoms in severely depressed patients who previously have not responded to adequate trials of antidepressant medication. The literature also indicates that ECT, when compared with antidepressants, has a more rapid onset of action.

Delusional Depression

ECT is highly effective in the treatment of delusional depression. It is superior to either antidepressants or neuroleptics used alone and is at least as effective as the combination of antidepressants and neuroleptics. ECT is often effective in patients who have previously failed to respond to medication. The duration of therapeutic effect beyond the initial acute episode is not clear.

Endogenous/Melancholic Depression

The severe endogenous/melancholic depressions are characterized by early morning awakening, marked weight loss, psychomotor retardation and/or agitation, diurnal variation, and lack of reactivity. ECT is at least as effective as TCA and more effective than sham ECT in the short-term treatment of these severe endogenous/melancholic depressions. ECT appears to be more effective than MAOI in the treatment of severe depressions, but available studies have generally used relatively low MAOI doses. There is evidence for the efficacy of ECT in those endogenous depressives who have not responded to an adequate trial of antidepressants. The long-term efficacy of ECT with endogenously depressed patients is not known.

Other Depression

The majority of depressed persons encountered in medical and psychiatric settings do not have the severe endogenous/melancholic or delusional depressions described above. ECT is not effective for patients with milder depressions, i.e., dysthymic disorder (neurotic depression) and adjustment disorder with depressed mood. Patients with major depression that is nonendogenous/nonmelancholic have not yet been extensively studied. Because of this, it is unclear whether their response to ECT would be more like those with dysthymic disorders or those with endogenous/melancholic features.

Acute Manic Episode

ECT and lithium appear to be equally effective for acute mania, and either is superior to hospitalization without somatic therapy. A treatment regimen in which ECT is used for the acute episode, followed by lithium maintenance, does not appear to be associated with an increased risk of early relapse compared with lithium treatment alone.

Schizophrenia

Neuroleptics are the first line of treatment for schizophrenia. The evidence for the efficacy of ECT in schizophrenia is not compelling but is strongest for those schizophrenic patients with a shorter duration of illness, a more acute onset, and more intense affective symptoms. ECT has not been useful in chronically ill schizophrenic patients. Although ECT is frequently advocated for treatment of patients with schizophreniform psychoses, schizoaffective disorders, and catatonia, there are no adequate controlled studies to document its usefulness for these disorders.

Other Disorders

There are no controlled studies supporting the efficacy of ECT for any conditions other than those designated above (i.e., delusional and severe endogenous depression, acute mania, and certain schizophrenic syndromes).

2. What are the risks and adverse effects of ECT?

To maximize the benefits of ECT and minimize the risks, it is essential that the patient's illness be correctly diagnosed, that ECT be administered only for appropriate indications, and that the risks and adverse effects be weighed against the risks of alternative treatments. Risks and adverse effects of ECT can be divided into two categories: (1) Those medical complications that can be substantially reduced by the use of appropriately trained staff, best equipment, and best methods of administration and (2) those side effects, such as spotty but persistent memory loss and transient posttreatment confusion, that can be expected even when an optimal treatment approach is used. In this report, we will focus on the risks still present with adequate treatment techniques.

In the early days of ECT, mortality was a significant problem. The commonly quoted overall mortality rate in the first few decades was 0.1 percent or 1 per 1,000. Over the years, safer methods of administration have been developed, including the use of short-acting anesthetics, muscle relaxants, and adequate oxygenation. Present mortality is very low. In the least favorable recent series reported, there were 2.9 deaths per 10,000 patients. In another series, 4.5

deaths per 100,000 treatments were reported. Overall, the risk is not different from that associated with the use of short-acting barbiturate anesthetics. The risk of death from anesthesia, although very small, is present and should be considered when evaluating the setting for performing ECT.

In the past, up to 40 percent of patients suffered from various complications, the most common being vertebral compression fractures. With present techniques, these risks have been virtually eliminated. In one recent study of almost 25,000 treatments, a complication rate of 1 per 1,300 to 1,400 treatments was found. These included laryngospasm, circulatory insufficiency, tooth damage, vertebral compression fractures, status epilepticus, peripheral nerve palsy, skin burns, and prolonged apnea.

During the few minutes following the stimulus, profound and potentially dangerous systemic charges occur. First, there may be transient hypotension from bradycardia caused by central vagal stimulation. This may be followed by sinus tachycardia and also sympathetic hyperactivity that leads to a rise in blood pressure, a response that may be more severe in patients with essential hypertension. Intracranial pressure increases during the seizure. Additionally, cardiac arrhythmias during this time are not uncommon (but usually subside without sequelae). Thus, certain patient groups that would be adversely affected by these manifestations are at increased risk.

There are two categories of central nervous system effects: The immediate consequences of the ECT seizure and the more enduring effects, both of which are affected by the treatment course. Immediately after awakening from the treatment, the patient experiences confusion, transient memory loss, and headache. The time it takes to recover clear consciousness, which may be from minutes to several hours, varies depending on individual differences in response, the type of ECT administered, the spacing and number of treatments given, and the age of the patient.

The severity of this acute confusional state is greatest after bilateral sine wave treatment and least when nondominant unilateral pulsed ECT is administered. Severity also appears to be increased by longer seizure duration, close spacing of the treatments, increasing dosage of electrical stimulation, and each additional treatment.

Depressive disorders are characterized by cognitive deficits that may be difficult to differentiate from those due to ECT. It is, however,

470

well established that ECT produces memory deficits. Deficits in memory function, which have been demonstrated objectively and repeatedly, persist after the termination of a normal course of ECT. Severity of the deficit is related to the number of treatments, type of electrode placement, and nature of the electric stimulus. Greater deficit occurs from bilateral than from unilateral placement. Sine wave current has been found to impair memory more than pulsed current.

The ability to learn and retain new information is adversely affected for a time following the administration of ECT; several weeks after its termination, however, this ability typically returns to normal. There is also objective evidence, based on neuropsychological testing, of loss of memory for a few weeks surrounding the treatment; such objective tests have not firmly established persistent or permanent deficits for a more extensive period, particularly for unilateral ECT. However, research conducted as long as 3 years after treatment has found that many patients report that their memory was not as good as it was prior to the treatment. They report particular difficulties for events that occurred on average 6 months before ECT (retrograde amnesia) and on average 2 months after the treatment (anterograde amnesia). Because there is also a wide difference in individual perception of the memory deficit, the subjective loss can be extremely distressing to some and of little concern to others.

There are other possible adverse effects from ECT. Some patients perceive ECT as a terrifying experience; some regard it as an abusive invasion of personal autonomy; some experience a sense of shame because of the social stigma they associate with ECT; and some report extreme distress from persistent memory deficits. The panel heard eloquent testimony of these attitudes from former patients who had been treated with ECT. It is clear, however, that these attitudes are not shared by all ECT patients. The panel also heard moving testimony from former patients who regarded ECT as a wholly beneficial and lifesaving experience. There are insufficient systematic studies to permit any definitive assessment of the prevalence of these various perceptions among ECT patients.

Numerous ECT studies have been conducted with animal models. Many of these suffer from methodological shortcomings. In studies that have been controlled for fixation artifacts, hypoxia, and other methodological problems, neuronal cell death has not been detected. Cerebral vasospasm and alterations in capillary permeability are of short duration and of insufficient magnitude to lead to neuronal cell death. The precise mechanism of the anterograde and retrograde memory deficit has not been established; it may represent alterations in neuronal function that are not detectuble with present methods. Computerized axial tomography (CAT) studies of patients who have had ECT are very preliminary and open to alternative interpretations. Definitive studies of *in vivo* brain metabolism with positron emission tomography (PET) and studies of tissue changes detectable by magnetic resonance imaging (MRI) remain to be done.

3. What factors should be considered by the physician and patient in determining if and when ECT would be an appropriate treatment?

The consideration of ECT is most appropriate in those conditions for which efficacy has been established: Delusional and severe endogenous depressions, acute mania, and certain schizophrenic syndromes. ECT should rarely be considered for other psychiatric conditions. The decision whether to offer ECT to an individual patient should be based on a complex consideration of advantages and disadvantages for ECT and for each treatment alternative. Whether to use ECT should be based or a thorough review of severity of the patient's illness, medical indications and contraindications, and nonresponsiveness to other treatments. It should be emphasized that for certain patients with very specific and narrow indications, ECT may be the only effective treatment available. In certain circumstances of acute risk to life or of medical status incompatible with the use of other effective treatments, ECT may be the first treatment.

The panel is concerned that ECT only be administered for the benefit of individual patients. Institutional factors (such as financial pressures created by prospective systems or staff convenience) should play no role in the decision to administer ECT.

Severity

Given a diagnosis for which the efficacy of ECT has been established, the immediate risk of suicide (when not manageable by other means) is a clear indication for the consideration of ECT. Acute manic episode—especially when characterized by clouded sensorium, dehydration, extreme psychomotor agitation, high risk for serious medical complications or death through exhaustion, and nonresponse to pharmacological interventions—are also clear indications for ECT. The severe and unremitting nature of the patient's emotional suffering, or extreme incapacitation, are also important considerations.

Medical Indications and Contraindications

The patient's medical status is often the determining consideration in the use of ECT. ECT may be necessary when the patient has medical conditions that preclude the use of TCA, MAOI, lithium, and neuroleptics. ECT should be considered in patients with severe depression or psychosis during the first trimester of pregnancy. Conversely, ECT is contraindicated for increased intracranial pressure, while space-occupying lesions in the brain, a recent history of myocardial infarction, and large aneurysms are relative contraindications for ECT. A personal history of nonresponsiveness to, or debilitating side effects (medical or psychological) from, ECT are also possible contraindications.

Nonresponsiveness to Other Treatments

ECT should be considered when alternative pharmacological and/or psychotherapeutic treatments have been given an adequate trial without efficacious response. When a patient is nonresponsive to other treatments, factors such as severity of the illness, its natural course, and the risk of other treatments worsening the course (as, for example, antidepressant medications precipitating a manic episode) need to be taken into account.

Informed Consent

When the physician has determined that clinical indications justify the administration of ECT, the law requires, and medical ethics demand, that the patient's freedom to accept or refuse the treatment be fully honored. An ongoing consultative process should take place. In this process, the physician must make clear to the patient the nature of the options available and the fact that the patient is entitled to choose among those options.

No uniform "shopping list" can be drawn up regarding the matters that should be discussed by patient and physician to assure a fully informed consent. They should discuss the character of the procedure, its possible risks and benefits (includinq full acknowledgement of posttreatment confusion, memory dysfunction, and other attendant uncertainties), and the alternative treatment options (including the option of no treatment at all). Special individual needs may also be relevant to some patients, for example a personal situation that requires rapid remission to facilitate return to work and to reduce family disruption. In all matters, the patient should not be inundated with technical detail; the technical issues should be translated into terms meaningful and accessible to the patient.

It is not easy to achieve this ideal of "informed consent" in any aspect of medical practice; and there are special difficulties that arise regarding the administration of ECT. In particular, the patients for whom this procedure is medically appropriate may be suffering from a severe psychiatric illness that, although not impairing their legal competency to consent, may nonetheless cloud judgment in fully weighing all of the available options. Such judgmental distortion does not justify disregarding the patient's choices; rather it makes it all the more important that the physician strive to identify and clarify the options that the patient alone is entitled to exercise.

The consent given by the patient at the outset of treatment should not be the final exchange on this issue but should be reexamined with the patient repeatedly throughout the course of the treatment. These periodic reviews should be initiated by the physician and not depend on patient initiative to "rescind" consent.

There are several reasons for this repeated consenting procedure: because of the relatively rapid therapeutic effect of the procedure itself, the patient after initial treatments is likely to have enhanced judgmental capacities; the risks of adverse effects increase with repeated treatments, so that the question of continued treatment presents a possibly changed risk/ benefit assessment for the patient; and because of the short-term memory deficits that accompany each administration of ECT, the patient's recollection of the prior consenting transaction might itself be impaired, so that repeated consultations reiterating the patient's treatment options are important to protect the patient's sense of autonomy throughout the treatment process. Moreover, if the patient agrees, the family should be involved in each step of this consultative process.

In a small minority of cases, a patient will lack adequate legal capacity to consent to the proposed procedure. In such cases, timely court proceedings are necessary if treatment is to be provided. Legislation in a few states dictates that ECT may in no circumstance be provided to an involuntarily committed patient. The panel believes that such absolute bans are unduly restrictive and make treatment impossible for patients who might obtain more benefit, at acceptable levels of risk, from ECT than from alternative treatments.

It may be desirable for physicians with patients for whom the prospect of ECT is a foreseeable but not immediate possibility to discuss this in advance with the patient when his or her judgment appears least compromised by the underlying disease process. Such advance discussion would serve as a nonbinding guide both to the patient and physician and would be another means to enhance the patient's autonomous choice in weighing the risks and benefits of this procedure and its alternatives.

4. How should ECT be administered to maximize benefits and minimize risks?

Once the patient and the physician have decided that ECT may be indicated, the patient should undergo a pretreatment medical examination that includes a history, physical, neurologic examination, EKG, and laboratory tests. Medications that affect the seizure threshold should be noted and decreased or discontinued when clinically feasible. MAOI should be discontinued 2 weeks before treatment, and patients should be essentially lithium-free. Severe hypertension should be controlled before beginning treatment. Because some patients with compromised cardiovascular status will be receiving ECT, cardiac conditions should be evaluated and monitored closely. Educating the patient and the family through discussion and written and/or audiovisual material describing the procedure is necessary prior to obtaining written informed consent.

An area should be designated for the administration of ECT and for supervised medical recovery from the treatment. This area should have appropriate health care professionals available and should include equipment and medications that could be used in the event of cardiopulmonary or other complications from the procedure.

A health professional specifically trained and certified in the use of brief anesthetic procedures should administer the anesthesia. The treatment team should include nursing personnel trained in ECT procedures and recovery.

Typically, ECT is administered as follows: the treatment is given in the early morning after an 8- to 12-hour period of fasting. Atropine or another anticholinergic agent is given prior to the treatment. An intravenous line is placed in a peripheral vein, and access to this vein is maintained until the patient is fully recovered. The anesthetic methohexital is given first followed by succinylcholine for muscle relaxation. Ventilatory assistance is provided with a positive pressure bag using 100 percent oxygen. The EKG, blood pressure, and pulse rate should be monitored throughout the procedure. Stimulus electrodes are placed either bifrontotemporally (bilateral) or with one electrode placed frontotemporally and the second electrode placed on the ipsilateral side (unilateral). Bilateral ECT may be more effective in certain patients or conditions. It has been established, however, that unilateral ECT, particularly on the nondominant side, is associated with a shorter confusional period and fewer memory deficits. Also, a brief pulse stimulus is associated with fewer cognitive defects than the traditional sine wave stimulus. Seizure threshold varies greatly among patients and may be difficult to determine; nevertheless the lowest amount of electrical energy to induce an adequate seizure should be used. Seizure monitoring is necessary and may be accomplished by an EEG or by the "cuff" technique. In this technique, a blood pressure cuff is placed on an arm or leg and is inflated above systolic pressure prior to the injection of a muscle relaxing agent. In unilateral ECT, the cuff should be on the same side as the electrodes to ensure that a bilateral seizure occurred.

The number of treatments in a course of therapy varies. Six to twelve treatments are usually effective. In the United States, the usual frequency is three times weekly; in the United Kingdom, the standard practice is two treatments weekly. Regressive ECT (a large number of treatments given within a short period for the purpose of achieving a persistent organic brain syndrome) is no longer an acceptable treatment form. Multiple-monitored ECT (several seizures during a single treatment session) has not been demonstrated to be sufficiently effective to be recommended. There are no controlled studies on the periodic use of ECT after remission of the acute episode or as a maintenance regimen to prevent recurrence of new episodes. Following ECT, most depressed patients should be continued on antidepressant medication or lithium to reduce relapse.

The panel is concerned that there are only limited data on the manner and extent of ECT administration in the United States and on the training of personnel involved in it. A national survey should be undertaken to assemble basic facts about the status of ECT treatment.

Medical school curricula should include education in the use of ECT. Psychiatric residency programs should include complete ECT training indications, contraindications, risks, clinical management, informed consent, and evaluation of outcome. The American Board of Psychiatry and Neurology should include questions about ECT in its oral and written examinations.

The panel believes it is imperative that appropriate mechanisms be established to ensure proper standards and monitoring of ECT. Hospitals and centers using ECT should establish review committees modeled on other medical-surgical review committees and should formulate rules and regulations to govern the privileging of physicians giving the treatments. Stringent peer review consistent with Joint Commission for the Accreditation of Hospitals' standards should monitor ongoing utilization of ECT. Periodic inspection of the equipment is also essential. As experience accumulates, consideration should be given to the adequacy of existing monitoring and review mechanisms.

5. What are the directions for future research?

ECT has been underinvestigated in the past. Among the most important immediate research tasks are:

- Initiation of a national survey to assemble the basic facts about the manner and extent of ECT use, as well as studies of patient attitudes and responses to ECT. Better understanding of negative, positive, and indifferent responses should result in improved treatment practices.

- Identification of the biological mechanisms underlying the therapeutic effects of ECT and the memory deficits resulting from the treatment.

- Better delineation of the long-term effects of ECT on the course of affective illnesses and cognitive functions, including clarification of the duration of ECT's therapeutic effectiveness.

477

- Precise determination of the mode of electrode placement (unilateral versus bilateral) and the stimulus parameters (form and intensity) that maximize efficacy and minimize cognitive impairment.

- Identification of patient subgroups or types for whom ECT is particularly beneficial or toxic.

Conclusion

Electroconvulsive therapy is the most controversial treatment in psychiatry. The nature of the treatment itself, its history of abuse, unfavorable media presentations, compelling testimony of former patients, special attention by the legal system, uneven distribution of ECT use among practitioners and facilities, and uneven access by patients all contribute to the controversial context in which the consensus panel has approached its task.

The panel has found that ECT is demonstrably effective for a narrow range of severe psychiatric disorders in a limited number of diagnostic categories: delusional and severe endogenous depression and manic and certain schizophrenic syndromes. There are, however, significant side effects, especially acute confusional states and persistent memory deficits for events during the months surrounding the ECT treatment. Proper administration of ECT can reduce potential side effects while still providing for adequate therapeutic effects.

The physician's decision to offer ECT to a patient and the patient's decision to accept it should be based on a complex consideration of advantages and disadvantages of ECT compared with alternative treatments. An ongoing consultative process, requiring time and energy on the part of both patient and physician, should occur.

Much additional research is needed into the basic mechanisms by which ECT exerts its therapeutic effects.

Studies are also needed to better identify subgroups for whom the treatment is particularly beneficial or toxic and to refine techniques to maximize efficacy and minimize side effects. A national survey should be conducted on the manner and extent of ECT use in the United States.

These recommendations reflect the consensus of the panel. We have been careful to narrowly delineate when and how, in our judg-

Chapter 39

New Directions for
ECT Research

Introduction

[In addition to this introduction, this chapter includes three] papers presented originally at the *New Directions for ECT Research*, a workshop sponsored by the National Institute of Mental Health (NIMH). [They are: Indications for the Use of ECT; The Mode of Action of ECT; and, Treatment Optimizaion with ECT.] The workshop, and this report, continue a tradition wherein the NIMH has employed its "convening power" repeatedly over the past two decades to stimulate and guide research on electroconvulsive therapy.

In 1972, the NIMH convened a conference on the psychobiology of convulsive therapy, an initial effort to examine scientific evidence accumulated over the previous two decades on the basic mechanisms of action, broad psychological and biological effects, and the specific clinical efficacy of ECT. That session and its proceedings, edited by Max Fink, Seymour Kety, James McGaugh, and Thomas Williams, stand as a milepost in the study of ECT (Fink et al. 1974). By the early 1970s, the "psychopharmacology revolution" had led to comparisons of the efficacy and safety of medications and other somatic treatments that were used to treat mental disorders during the 1940s, 1950s, and 1960s. As Fink has recounted (1979), these early comparisons led rather quickly to the virtual abandonment of several once widely-used

Excerpts from *Psychopharmacology Bulletin*, Vol. 30, No. 3; NIH Pub. No. 94-3707.

approaches, including lobotomy and insulin coma. ECT, however, was shown to be as effective and, in some populations, more effective than existing medications. Consequently, it retained its stature even as conventional psychopharmacologic strategies were refined, experimental drugs were introduced, and other non-pharmacologic somatic and psychosocial treatments were developed. Thus, the first NIMH conference was significant insofar as it (1) legitimized ECT as a component of "modern" psychiatric treatment, and (2) underscored the need for research on ECT to be every bit as sophisticated and rigorous as that conducted in any other sphere of mental health science.

In 1978, Gerald Klerman, then head of the Alcohol, Drug Abuse, and Mental Health Administration (ADAMHA), designated treatment assessment an agency priority. In response, NIMH convened a second ECT research conference, this one focused on the short- and long-term physiological and psychological impact of ECT, and on assessing the procedure's efficacy in a wide range of psychiatric disorders. In that same year, the American Psychiatric Association (APA) Task Force on ECT would issue its first report (1978), finding convulsive therapy to be a safe and effective treatment. Next, working under an NIMH grant, Richard Abrams assembled a group to conduct, in 1981, a state-of-the-science review of ECT research and to recommend research needs and opportunities (Abrams & Essman 1982).

In early 1985, the Institute sponsored the International Conference on Electroconvulsive Therapy, which was convened and organized by the New York Academy of Sciences and the New York State Psychiatric Institute. Six months later, NIMH, in collaboration with the NIH's Office of Medical Applications of Research, convened a Consensus Development Conference on Electroconvulsive Therapy. Under the chairmanship of Robert Rose, the Consensus Conference strongly affirmed the role, appropriateness, and efficacy of electroconvulsive therapy in the treatment of specific mental disorders and, again, prioritized specific research needs (NIH 1985). [See Chapter 38.]

The workshop articles presented in this issue provide further evidence of NIMH's long-held commitment to ensuring that research on ECT is as sophisticated and rigorous as that conducted in any other sphere of basic and clinical mental health science. Beyond that, this continuation of the NIMH's involvement in this area is particularly timely and important. I might note that electroconvulsive therapy has been a personal interest of mine for many years, not only as a scientific and clinical issue, but also because ECT so vividly marks the progress we have made, and challenges we yet face, in reducing the stigma attached to mental illness and its treatment, and replacing ignorance with understanding. Clinical efficacy notwithstanding, ECT always has been particularly vulnerable to fragile public attitudes. Over the years, a small cadre of people who cling to the notion that mental illness does not exist have used—and fostered—misperceptions about this treatment very effectively in furtherance of an antipsychiatry "myth of mental illness" agenda.

Over the past couple of years, however, we have had cause to be encouraged by a dramatic shift in public attitudes about mental illness, and the extent of this shift is nowhere more profoundly evident than in attitudes toward electroconvulsive therapy. These advances in public knowledge and acceptance of mental illness can be attributed to several factors.

One is NIMH's return to the National Institutes of Health. The placement of research on mental illness and behavior in the mainstream of biomedical science sent a strong message that mental illnesses are as scientifically and clinically valid as other medical conditions under the NIH aegis. For the Institute to be back at the NIH—where, of course, it was initially established some 45 years ago—is powerfully destigmatizing. Separate is not equal, and having mental health and illness programs sequestered in a separate agency implied that these programs were not the equal of other biomedical science. This is not the case, either in the quality of biomedical or behavioral research supported by NIMH or in the quality of treatments available for mental disorders.

More recently, a key indication of the dramatic shift in public attitudes has been the approach to mental illness taken by the Clinton Administration in its health care reform activities. This is the third administration, following Kennedy's and Carter's, to have an explicit interest in mental health and mental illness. This time, moreover, the interest is very up-to-date and sophisticated. Consider, for example, the following statement made repeatedly by candidate Clinton:

> With the increasing evidence that many mental illnesses have a biological or chemical basis and are treatable, there is no legitimate rationale for distinguishing between "mental illness" and "physical illnesses" in terms of research dollars, individual entitlements, and insurance reimbursement. (communication, February 1992)

The statement is very different from the "we are in favor of mental health" sort of statements that were characteristic—perhaps, unavoidably—as recently as two decades ago when there was much less of a knowledge base than today. This one statement does not capture everything the Clinton Administration has said on the topic of mental illness/mental health, but it was first and has been most repeated.

These leadership developments have parallelled a significant change in public attitudes. Last year, all three major news magazines—*Time, Newsweek,* and *U.S. News & World Report*—had cover stories on mental illness and the brain. But more important than the mere fact of these stories was their internal consistency: all three reflected the mainstream consensus that guides our fields today—a consensus that emphasizes the interaction of biological vulnerability and psychosocial stress. Furthermore, two autobiographical books about mental illness made the "best sellers" list—William Styron's *Darkness Visible* and Patty Duke's *A Brilliant Madness.*

An even more dramatic indicator of the beginning of a sea change in public attitudes is personified in Bob Boorstin, a Special Assistant to the President, who has been very forthcoming about his own experience with manic depressive illness and its successful treatment. This would simply not have happened just a few years ago. Contrast Senator Tom Eagleton's experience in the early 1970s, with that of Lawton Chiles, who, two years ago, was elected Governor of Florida after acknowledging that he was being treated for depression. It is true that Senator Eagleton had been treated with ECT and was disadvantaged by that stigma, but even that is beginning to change; Dick Cavett has spoken publicly about the success of this treatment in fighting his depression, and he is still on the air.

Now the question is, are we going to be able to take advantage of this change in public attitudes? Are we going to be able to use the change productively in our activities concerned with the current major event in the field—that is, health care reform? The changes being discussed have tremendous implications for mental illness treatments, for ECT specifically, and, in turn, for further addressing the stigma issue.

In developing the Health Care Reform Task Force, the Administration created a mental health/mental illness team under the leadership of Mrs. Tipper Gore, itself an important signal to the field. To staff this activity, the Administration has drawn on NIMH expertise, particularly in the area of services research. A major area of focus has been to develop the data needed to rebut three destructive myths about mental illness: That it is not definable, that it is not treatable, and that it is so pervasive that coverage would break the bank. Actually, there exist very convincing data—better, in fact, than exist in many other areas of health—that these are simply myths. Not only have we been able to show that the diagnosis of mental illness is as reliable as diagnoses in any other areas of medicine, but also we have generated solid estimates of the costs of mental illnesses, particularly severe mental illnesses; the costs of covering their treatment under a national program; and what the costs are to the health care system and the economy, including the cost of failing to treat them. The data have essentially transformed the nature of the debate about including mental illness in health care reform. That is, whether there will be coverage for mental illness is not a question, albeit the breadth of coverage is still open to debate.

As health care reform discussions continue, there will be more focus, across medicine, not only on the efficacy of treatments, but also on treatment effectiveness in actual clinical settings, and on efficiency (i.e., the cost-benefit ratio). To this point—that is, the proportion of practice supported by controlled clinical trials—psychiatry actually compares quite favorably with other areas of medicine. In that regard, ECT is a treatment which has benefitted recently from an increasingly solid foundation of rigorous clinical research. This should ensure that the therapy will be included as a legitimate, reimbursable treatment. Toward that end, ECT is mentioned in the recent report of the NIMH's National Advisory Mental Health Council to the Congress on mental illness in health care reform (NAMHC 1993; Frank et al. 1993; Depression Guideline Panel 1993).

This progress notwithstanding, continuing research on ECT is vitally important. One reason that ECT has been vulnerable over the years to mischaracterization and stigmatization stems from the fact that it has been a black box, scientifically speaking; that is, it was difficult to get a handle on it theoretically. Although ECT worked, it lacked the theoretical underpinnings often necessary to attract the intellectual interest that brings a discovery fully into the mainstream. Today, however, a number of advances have opened up opportunities for fundamental research on mechanisms. For example, work focusing on brain kindling and sensitization models is being explored imaginatively and instructively in studies of recurrence in mental disorders, especially in the area of affective disorders. The known anti-kindling effects of ECT clearly are germane in this line of research. Questions about the role of ECT as a "synchronizer" in a dysregulated biological system complement questions about circadian dysrhythmias in recurrent affective disorders. These theoretical issues have brought ECT to the attention of scientists who might not otherwise be involved in its study, and they underscore other important practical clinical concerns; for example, the timing of maintenance ECT, which is widely practiced in some parts of Europe, albeit with a sparse research base. The question of how to maintain remission achieved with ECT is important and urgent, and, indeed, is the focus of an ongoing NIMH multicenter study. The so-called continuation phase in the treatment of depression is as important as the acute treatment phase; if a medication has not been used, or has not been effective, knowing what to do to maintain recovery is critical.

At the clinical level, scientific psychiatry now has tools capable of refining our understanding of the mechanisms of action of ECT. With new brain imaging technologies, for example, we can observe, over time, brain changes that may be associated with ECT. In addition to elucidating mechanisms, this information is proving invaluable in rebutting the mythology about brain damage which has been so widely touted by the anti-psychiatry forces.

The issue of transient cognitive impairments has been controversial, and is the object of vigorous research. The questions addressed recently by Dr. Sackeim in the New England Journal of Medicine (Sackeim et al. 1993) concerned with such fundamentally important matters as bilateral or unilateral electrode placement, or stimulus intensity with respect to efficacy and cognitive impacts afford a sense of the vitality in the clinical research sphere. As a result, not only is an impressive knowledge base accumulating, but, as importantly, the field is developing standardized questions and research methodologies that promise to be very influential in putting to rest the many misconceptions about the impact of ECT on brain and memory. An unassailable research methodology is crucial. In the wake of any transient memory loss, an individual tends to pay more attention to memory from that point forward. This has been shown, for example, in head injury cases. Once a person has had that experience, there is a tendency to focus on memory function, and attribute the transient memory loss to whatever circumstances precipitated the problem. Novel research designs such as those developed by Squire (1986) can minimize the problem, but additional research is needed.

Despite that problem, we need also to remember the dramatic data, cited by Potter and Rudorfer (1993), indicating a very high level of patient satisfaction with ECT; that is, the expressed willingness by some 80 percent of severely depressed patients to have the treatment again if needed. Comparative data on other repeat procedures in other areas of medicine would be interesting. Perhaps the Agency for Health Care Policy and Research might support a project to obtain patient satisfaction data across the spectrum of medical and surgical procedures. That 80 percent figure may be viewed as a bottom line assessment of a risk/benefit ratio. And it is interesting, in this regard, that the highest utilization of ECT is in private hospitals with high income, upper middle class clients. The lowest use of ECT is in public systems where the political forces are much more potent. A high "user satisfaction" rating from very successful people who want to get treated quickly and effectively is quite noteworthy. That fact has not been lost at the NIMH, where the premier public and professional education campaign about depression—the Depression/Awareness, Recognition and Treatment (D/ART) program—is increasing its emphasis on ECT as a frequent first-line treatment in the management of this illness. It is noteworthy, too, that the patient-run National Depressive and Manic Depressive Association has issued a strong position statement endorsing the use of ECT (NDMDA 1992).

Publication of the article by Sackeim and colleagues (1993) in the prestigious *New England Journal of Medicine*, with an accompanying editorial (Potter & Rudorfer 1993), testifies to the acknowledgement of the legitimacy of ECT, but also underscores educational needs that persist within the scientific community. (That is, I recently was reminded that *Convulsive Therapy*, a first-rate specialty journal which holds an important place in our research and clinical enterprise, is not, at present, included in the principal citation and reference services provided by the National Library of Medicine, Index Medicus and MEDLINE. I and others have initiated efforts to correct this omission.)

Workshops such as the one presented here are important and helpful to NIMH in its task of research priority setting—and this is much more true when the budget is tight, as it is now for all of NIH, than it might have been in recent years when the NIMH's budget grew at an annual rate of 10 to 15 percent. While it is unlikely that double-digit annual growth will re-occur in the near future, neither is it likely that the zero growth the Institute now is experiencing will persist.

Thus, the report of the workshop and recommendations for new directions in ECT research presented in this issue of the *Psychopharmacology Bulletin* is a timely contribution to future advances in this important scientific arena.

References

Abrams, R, and Essman, W, eds. *Electroconvulsive Therapy: Biological Foundations and Clinical Applications*. New York: Spectrum Publications, 1982.

American Psychiatric Association. *Electroconvulsive Therapy: Task Force Report 14*. Washington, DC: The Association, 1978.

Depression Guideline Panel (DGP), *Depression in Primary Care: Volume 2. Treatment of Major Depression. Clinical Practice Guideline, Number 5*. Rockville, MD: U.S. Department of Health and Human Services, Public Health Service, Agency for Health Care Policy and Research, AHCPR Pub. No. 93-0551. April 1993.

Fink, M. *Convulsive Therapy: Theory and Practice*. New York: Raven Press, 1979.

Fink, M; Kety, S; McGaugh, J; and Williams, T, eds. *Psychobiology of Convulsive Therapy*. New York: Winston-Wiley, 1974.

Frank, E; Karp, JF; and Rush, AJ. Efficacy of treatments for major depression. *Psychopharmacol. Bull.* 29(4):457-475, 1993.

National Advisory Mental Health Council. Health care reform for Americans with severe mental illnesses: Report of the National Advisory Mental Health Council. *Am. J. Psychiatry* 150:1447-1465, 1993.

National Depressive and Manic Depressive Association. Statement regarding electroconvulsive therapy (ECT). Robert M.A. Hirschfeld, M.D., Chair, Scientific Advisory Council. Chicago: NDMDA. February 1, 1992.

National Institutes of Health. Electroconvulsive Therapy. Consensus Development Conference Statement. *JAMA* 254:2103-2108, 1985.

Potter, WZ, and Rudorfer, MV. Electroconvulsive therapy: A modern medical procedure. *New Engl. J. Med.* 328:882-883, 1993.

Sackeim, HA; Prudic, J; Devanand, DP; Kiersky, JE; Fitzsimons, L; Moody, BJ; McElhiney, MC; Coleman, EA; and Settembrino, JM. Effects of stimulus intensity and electrode placement on the efficacy and cognitive effects of electroconvulsive therapy. *New Engl. J Med.* 328:839-846, 1993.

Squire, LR. Memory functions as affected by electroconvulsive therapy. In: Malitz, S, and Sackeim, HA, eds. *Electroconvulsive Therapy: Clinical and Basic Research Issues*. New York: New York Academy of Sciences, 1986. pp. 307-314.

—by Frederick K. Goodwin, M.D.

The above section was written while Dr. Goodwin was Director of the National Institute of Mental Health (NIMH), Rockville, MD. He currently is Professor of Psychiatry and Director, Center on Neuroscience, Behavior, and Society at the George Washington University Medical Center, in Washington, DC, and Senior Scientific Advisor to the Director, NIHM; Frederick K. Goodwin, M.D., 2300 I Street, NW, Room 514, Washington, DC 20037.

Indications for the Use of ECT

Introduction

The practice of convulsive therapy recently celebrated its 60th birthday. The first treatment was given by Meduna, on January 24, 1934, in Budapest, Hungary. He used a chemical induction of the seizure. The modification to electroconvulsive therapy, made by the Italians in 1938, made the treatment more facile, but did not materially change the treatment as one that is dependent on the induction of repeated seizures.

This fact was emphasized in the naming of the journal *Convulsive Therapy* rather than *Electroconvulsive Therapy* because while the electricity makes some contribution, it does so mainly to the secondary effects, such as on cognition, and not to efficacy. Electricity is not an essential part of treatment.

Indications for the Use of Electroconvulsive Therapy (ECT)

We have greatly extended the clinical indications for ECT in the past decade. Our criteria are generally accepted in the clinical community, even though only some uses are supported by well-designed studies. For many indications, our data are limited to case reports and our professional consensus. In this review, I will identify what are generally accepted indications for ECT, some unusual applications that clinicians believe may be useful, and my suggestions for studies that warrant our attention in the next decade.

Caveats

There is an immediate problem with the language of clinical diagnosis. Presently, we depend on the "operational" and descriptive nosology of mental disorders described by Feighner and colleagues (1972) and in *DSM-III* (*Diagnostic and Statistical Manual of Mental Disorders, Third Edition*—APA 1980) and *DSM-III-R* (*Diagnostic and Statistical Manual of Mental Disorders, Third Edition, Revised*—APA 1987). These criteria were developed in the context of the "medical model" in clinical psychiatry. They were driven by the successes of clinical psychopharmacology and are useful mainly for decisions about pharmacotherapy. But these diagnostic criteria are difficult to apply in decisions about ECT. Severity of illness, an essential criterion for the decision to use ECT, is not a consideration in *DSM-III*. We usually reserve ECT for patients who are so ill as to require hospital care. Patients may be labeled as having major depression if their mood is altered, regardless of the presence or absence of vegetative features and whether or not they are able to function in society. The same diagnosis is given to one who is sad and unhappy, with obsessional thoughts, yet able to work as well as the severely delusional, negativistic, cachectic, mute, melancholic, or demented patient requiring full nursing care.

Patients with catatonia exemplify another problem. Such cases are only classified in *DSM-III* and *DSM-III-R* as schizophrenia, catatonic type (295.2x). But patients with catatonia often have a history of mania, or depression, or suffer from a systemic disorder like lupus erythematosus. When *DSM* criteria are applied, these patients must be lumped into the class of schizophrenia, catatonic type. Patients with schizophrenia are usually treated with neuroleptic drugs, even though such drugs may be ineffective in patients with catatonia. ECT and benzodiazepines, which seem to be specifically helpful in relieving catatonia, are precluded under the common belief that neither ECT nor benzodiazepines are effective for schizophrenia. In *DSM-IV* (APA 1994), catatonia is recognized as a separate entity "catatonic disorder due to a general medical condition" (293.89), in addition to its subtype of schizophrenia. Catatonia is also a specifier of both major depressive and bipolar disorders.

Established Indications for ECT

Since *DSM-IV* criteria are the standard, we first look at the diagnoses for which ECT is ordinarily accepted as effective (Table 39.1). Somehow, ECT has proven useful across all affective diagnoses. The present pigeon-holing of affectively ill patients is irrelevant to the decision to use ECT. The diagnoses of atypical psychosis and schizophrenia are included, in part, because efficacy for acute disorders are reasonably well documented.

TABLE 39.1. Diagnoses For Which ECT Is Effective (*DSM-IV*)

Major depression:
> Single episode (296.2x)
> Recurrent (296.3x)

Bipolar major depression:
> Depressed (296.5x)
> Mixed (296.6x)
> Not otherwise specified (296.70)

Mania (Bipolar disorder):
> Mania (296.4x)
> Mixed type (296.6x)
> Not otherwise specified (296.70)

Atypical psychosis (298.90)

Schizophrenia:
> Catatonia (295.2x)
> Schizophreniform (295.40)
> Schizoaffective (295.70)

Catatonia:
> Schizophrenia, catatonic type (295.2x)
> Malignant catatonia (293.89)
> Neuroleptic malignant syndrome (333.92)

Other conditions may have a strong affective component and may be unusually responsive to ECT (Table 39.2). These conditions may be difficult to distinguish from the generally accepted indications, and we may be erring in listing another class from *DSM-IV* because the cutting criteria are so weak.

TABLE 39.2. Diagnoses For Which ECT May Be Effective or Have Application

Other Conditions:
> Organic delusional disorder (293.81)
> Organic mood disorder (293.83)
> Psychotic disorder, Not Otherwise Specified (298.90)
> Obsessive compulsive disorder (300.30)
> Dysthymia (300.40)
> Agitation in severe mental retardation (318.10)
> Neuroleptic-induced parkinsonism (332.1)
> Neuroleptic-induced tardive dyskinesia (333.82)

This widespread applicability of ECT to widely diverse conditions has led some authors to view ECT as non-specific, much in the way that they view the analgesic effects of aspirin or morphine. For others, however, (and I include myself in this latter group), the fact that the efficacy of ECT and the criteria we use to select patients cuts across our classification scheme is a flag that the separated illnesses have a common psychopathology: the phenotypic diversity reflects a genotypic homogeneity. But that is another problem. It is sufficient to say that the evidence, although variable for the different classes, compels consideration for ECT in each of the affective disorders. The 1990 APA Task Force report on ECT uses another typology, not based on DSM criteria. The authors describe primary indications and secondary indications (Table 39.3) for ECT. The primary indications are conditions in which a "life-saving" component is identified, or the interesting instance of "patient preference." ECT is considered a primary treatment—one to be given without a prior course of other therapy—in patients so suicidal as to compel continuous observation; or in patients in manic delirium, catatonic stupor, or catatonic excitement, especially when these conditions are so dangerous to the patient or others that they require continuous observation, restraints, isolation, or parenteral feeding. Inanition that is so severe as to be life-threatening is an-other example. Some psychiatrists prefer ECT as a primary treatment in patients with delusional depression, in first-episode acute schizo-phrenia in young adults, and in rapid-cycling manic patients because psychoactive drugs are often less effective than ECT.

TABLE 39.3. 2.2.1 Primary and 2.2.2 Secondary Use of ECT

Primary

"Situations where ECT maybe used prior to a trial of psychotropic agents include, but are not necessarily limited to, the following:

a) where a need for rapid, definitive response exists on either medical or psychiatric grounds; or
b) when the risks of other treatments outweigh the risks of ECT; or
c) when a history of poor drug response and/or good ECT re-sponse exists for previous episodes of the illness; or
d) patient preference."

Secondary

"In other situations, a trial of an alternative therapy should be consid-ered prior to referral for ECT. Subsequent referral for ECT should be based on at least one of the following:

a) treatment failure (taking into account issues such as choice of agent, dosage, and duration of trial);
b) adverse effects which are unavoidable and which are deemed less likely and/or less severe with ECT;
c) deterioration of the patient's condition such that criterion 2.2.1(a) is met."

What is Clinical Practice?

Clinicians usually consider ECT in affectively ill patients who have failed adequate trials of other treatments. Medication trials are both easier to administer and less expensive, and are clearly the first choice of treatment. There is some argument, however, as to how many trials, with how many drugs, in how many combinations, for whatever length of time, is an adequate trial of medication. Perhaps, as ECT becomes more freely available, we will come to use a standard for therapy resistance to drugs as suggested in the clozapine trials—two drug periods, in adequate dosage, for 4 to 6 weeks each.

If we focus on the presence of psychosis as a criterion for ECT, however, we find, much as we did for affective states, that the range of psychotic conditions for which ECT is demonstrably useful is quite broad (Table 39.4).

TABLE 39.4. Psychoses For Which ECT May Be Effective

Major depression with psychotic features:
>   Single episode (296.24)
>   Recurrent (296.34)

Bipolar major depression with psychotic features:
>   Depressed (296.54)
>   Mixed (296.64)
>   Not otherwise specified (296.74)

Mania (Bipolar disorder):
>   Mania (296.44)
>   Mixed type (296.64)
>   Not otherwise specified (296.74)

Atypical psychosis (298.94)

Schizophrenia:
>   Catatonia (295.2x)
>   Schizophreniform (295.40)
>   Schizoaffective (295.70)

Psychoses, especially those of acute onset, and those unresponsive to sedation or the use of antipsychotic drugs may be relieved by ECT. Some psychoses are considered schizophrenic, some schizophreniform, or some schizoaffective. Others are an aspect of a severe affective disorder and are described as manic delirium, manic psychosis, major depression with psychosis, or toxic delirium. ECT seems to be effective in each of these acute psychotic conditions, regardless of the associated symptomatology and the functional cause. The controversy about the efficacy of ECT in schizophrenia is based on our difficulty in defining schizophrenia in patients with acute disorders, coupled with our belief that antipsychotic drugs are effective (and ECT is not) in this condition. In part, the belief that ECT is ineffective in schizophrenia derives from studies in chronic mentally ill patients. (The question of efficacy of ECT in schizophrenia will be discussed later.)

Catatonia, a disorder characterized by motor and thought disorders, is particularly responsive to ECT (Fink 1990). This is true regardless of etiology. Catatonia may be a feature of systemic disorders (such as lupus erythematosus, typhoid fever), toxicity of neuroleptics (malignant neuroleptic syndrome), or a phase of schizophrenia, bipolar disorder, or major depressive disorder. In "malignant catatonia" ECT has been lifesaving (Geretsegger & Rochowanski 1987; Hermle & Oepen 1986; Mann et al. 1986; Nolen & Zwaan 1990; Philbrick & Rummaus 1994). Some authors, notably Rosebush and colleagues (1990) and Pataki and coworkers (1992) find the incidence of catatonia higher than ordinarily described; indeed, these authors replicate the studies of Abrams and Taylor (1976) who found catatonia a common feature in patients with severe affective disorders. Further, Rosebush finds lorazepam very effective in relieving catatonia. But for those who are unresponsive, ECT is still required. Is there a clue to mechanism of action of ECT in the similarity of the effects of benzodiazepines, barbiturates, and ECT in catatonia?

There are some idiosyncratic applications for ECT. The motor manifestations of parkinsonism, like those of catatonia, may respond to ECT (Douyon et al. 1989; Fink 1988). Such use is experimental, but trials for the severely incapacitated are warranted. Some clinicians have used ECT to relieve the overt signs of tardive dyskinesia. Study of such an application, like that of parkinsonism, will be helpful in delineating the central effects of ECT. There is a special application of ECT in the management of an active and severe psychosis in the first two trimesters of pregnancy where fears of drug induced teratogenicity may compel an alternate treatment. Some authors find ECT useful in the agitated elderly or severe mentally defective, especially those with self-injurious behavior, and in the elderly demented where there is a strong history of affective disorder, and there is a possibility that the dementia syndrome may be an example of the reversible dementia defined as pseudo-dementia.

Conditions for Which ECT May or May Not Be a Consideration

The indications cited so far are justified by some clinical studies but mainly by case material and consensus. There are other conditions, however, for which we know relatively little about the efficacy or safety of ECT; they are surrounded by a negative air, and it is customary to argue that ECT is not warranted (Table 39.5).

TABLE 39.5. Behaviors For Which ECT Is Believed To Be Ineffective

- Severe character pathology
- Substance abuse and dependence (including alcoholism)
- Sexual identification disorders
- Psychoneuroses (hysterical disorder, Briquet's syndrome, hypochondriasis, panic or anxiety disorders, pain syndromes, obsessive-compulsive disorders)
- Chronicity of illness without flagrant psychopathology

Like other innovations in medicine, when convulsive therapy was introduced and found safe and easy to administer in dementia praecox, clinicians tried it in other conditions which lacked effective therapy. Some trials were unusually successful, as in the relief of involutional melancholia, agitated depression, and mania; others failed, and even had adverse consequences, as in severe neuroses and hypochondriasis, drug dependence, and sexual identification disorders. A particularly distressing example is in the use of ECT as a last resort in patients with severe somatization disorder, hypochondriasis, obsessive compulsive, and panic disorders. In such cases, patients have been referred for ECT when all treatments have failed, including experimental treatments and polypharmacy. We lack evidence for the efficacy of ECT in such conditions (and for some there is even evidence of a worsening of the condition). Use of ECT in such conditions should be limited to proper experimental studies. But, in truth, we do not know whether ECT may or may not be useful in these conditions, and we may usefully inquire whether there may be a basis for their reassessment in the light of our present experience of the general efficacy of ECT in affective and psychotic states.

Conditions that Warrant Prospective Study

In the absence of systematic study and an effective therapy, we are faced with mental disorders for which ECT may have a clinical role, but neither adequate clinical studies, nor case material are of help (Table 39.6). The recent awareness that ECT may be effective in psychoses as well as depressive mood states has been helpful in redirecting my thinking about mechanisms of action of ECT. I suggest that the study of these conditions is warranted for reason of practical applicability and for our speculations about mechanisms.

TABLE 39.6. Conditions That Warrant Prospective Study

Acute schizophrenia
Child and adolescent hospitalized behavior disorders
Rapid cycling bipolar disorder
Alcohol dependence
Maintenance ECT in various disorders

Schizophrenia. In returning to the question of the efficacy of ECT in schizophrenia, many believe that ECT is ineffective. Such a view arises from its presumed lack of efficacy in longterm hospitalized patients with moderate to minimal "positive" pathology, who have been labeled as having schizophrenia under earlier classification schemes. Meduna's 1937 report of convulsive therapy describes its relative inefficacy in patients who had been ill longer than 2 years, with few active signs of psychosis. Recent experience supports the inefficacy of ECT in patients with chronic forms of psychosis, but even such a caveat may occasionally be disregarded if the patient exhibits an active psychosis with a range of positive symptoms.

Friedel (1986) described the successful treatment of cases of severe schizophrenia with thiothixene and ECT. That report led Gujavarty and colleagues (1987) to review their experience with psychotic patients. When ECT was added to antipsychotic drug treatment in patients labeled as having schizophrenia (with positive symptoms of delusions, hallucinations, or paranoid ideation), the long-term results were successful. The latest convert to this point of view is Herbert Meltzer. Sajatovic and Meltzer (1993) report favorable results in the relief of schizophrenic symptoms in an open trial of combined loxapine and ECT in patients who had failed clinical trials of both antipsychotic drugs alone, and of clozapine. Meltzer's complaint, however, is that the changes are not persistent. He describes a feeble attempt at maintenance ECT, with eventual relapse in almost all his patients when he was unable to deliver maintenance ECT on a schedule that the patients required.

The study of ECT in schizophrenia, alone or combined with antipsychotic drugs, will be useful for at least two theoretical questions. Is schizophrenia a distinct structural brain disorder with a genetic fault and a fatalistic outcome? If the illness can be aborted by ECT, we can focus on the ECT process more broadly than as a process in affective illnesses only. If we can only abort the illness by the combination of ECT and antipsychotic drugs, such data would argue that availability of drugs to the brain may be impeded in some subjects and that its availability is enhanced by the changes in the blood brain barrier. Surely, there are other theoretical justifications for the study of ECT in patients with schizophrenia.

Children and Adolescents. It is not known whether ECT has a place in the treatment of psychoses of childhood or adolescence. Many recall the experience of Lauretta Bender, the pioneer who established the child psychiatry unit at Bellevue Hospital before the second World War. Faced with the most psychotic and unmanageable children of the city, without the benefit of our drug therapies, Bender used what she could to manage behavior—insulin coma, barbiturates, amphetamines, leucotomy, Metrazole seizures, and ECT. In her followup study of 100 schizophrenic children treated with induced seizures, she reported positive behavioral changes as a lessening of disturbance, excitability, withdrawal, and anxiety. Remission occurred in a few children who exhibited syndromes similar to those of adults in whom ECT was considered useful. She noted that the basic schizophrenic process, including motility disturbance, vegetative lability, disturbances in thought and language, and perceptual motor patterning were not modified by ECT. Intellectual functioning was not impeded by the treatment, and the electroencephalogram continued to indicate maturation.

No authors have described a similar experience. The antipathy to the use of ECT in children is so marked, that few texts of child and adolescent psychiatry even mention it, and few therapists are willing to consider ECT in this population. A study of the efficacy of ECT in affectively ill and psychotically ill children would contribute to the following two theoretical issues. If prepubertal children respond like adults, then we can argue that the post-pubertal endocrine systems play less of a role in mechanism. If they do not, we can argue that endocrine issues are important in the affective illnesses of adulthood and of the elderly. At the least, assessment of ECT in the severely mentally disabled may yield some untapped therapeutic benefit.

Rapid Cycling Bipolar Disorder. Evidence for the efficacy of ECT in patients with mania relies on a few prospective comparisons of ECT with lithium therapy. But its use in these conditions is based mainly on clinicians' experience with individual cases. "Rapid cycling" bipolar patients are often resistant to drug therapies. But some clinicians report favorable results with ECT, especially when ECT is maintained over long periods of time. If ECT is effective in reducing the rate of cycling, or the recurrent attacks can be aborted by continuation or maintenance ECT, we will be forced to reassess our views of the biochemical alternations of mania and depression, as well as provide a practical solution for a very difficult problem.

Alcoholism and Drug Dependence. Some clinicians view alcohol dependence as secondary to a depressive mood disorder, or believe that dependent persons develop a secondary depressive disorder. With either view, antidepressant drugs are often applied, occasionally with success. Is it not reasonable to examine the efficacy of the most effective antidepressant, ECT? Failure of the trials with lithium or tricyclic drugs may not have been the result of poor theory, but of drug effects which are relatively ineffective as antidepressants. The popular expectation of inefficacy as well as political and psychosocial conditions have discouraged adequate clinical trials.

Maintenance ECT. Throughout the literatures both clinical and lay, a quixotic element in the antipathy to the use of ECT is the complaint that the beneficial results are temporary. In the early years of ECT, it was customary to continue or maintain patients on outpatient ECT. Patients were treated at weekly, biweekly, or monthly intervals, with occasional periods of more intensive treatments. Such treatments continued for months or even years after the acute episode had been relieved. (It is such continuation treatments that aroused much public and professional ire in the belief that such treatment was unnecessary and was done mainly for monetary gain.) With the introduction of psychotropic drugs, this practice disappeared. The reasons given include the disuse of ECT, the belief that drugs could replace ECT, the lack of effective drug trials after ECT, and fear of causing brain damage. ECT is the only treatment in psychiatry that is stopped just as soon, often too soon, as the symptoms show some relief and that ending the course places the patient, even the most responsive patient, at hazard for relapse. Replacement with drugs, often the same which had been ineffective before ECT, is often ineffective. Continuation and maintenance ECT were endorsed by the APA Task Force (1990), based on some recent retrospective data. But here, too, we lack adequate prospective data.

The need for data on maintenance ECT is compelling, again for both practical and theoretical reasons. The practical is our desperate need to reduce relapse after ECT. The theoretic is even more compelling. We will soon embark on studies of the mechanism of ECT. We can focus our assessments on the acute events, either in brain chemistry or body physiology. But there is such a plethora of bodily changes induced by repeated seizures, that the identification of even a single event in the therapeutic chain has not yet been achieved. A more reasonable approach would be the search for changes in brain chemistry or body physiology that persist during the post-treatment period, and that can be assessed in those patients who remain well and those who relapse. If we plan prospective studies of any application of ECT, a component of continuation and maintenance ECT should be included.

In summary, our understanding of the elements of a safe and effective seizure has increased. Our practice has become technically more complex, but the techniques are reasonably well described such that most students can easily learn how to treat a patient adequately and safely. The accepted indications are well-defined, and the APA Task Force designation of primary and secondary indications, and support for continuation and maintenance ECT, has done much to improve the climate for treatment in academic centers.

But little has been done to develop an understanding of the ECT process. The theoreticians of the past 50 years have been focused on the antidepressant qualities of ECT, but the studies of the past decade have demonstrated efficacy in mania, schizophrenia, parkinsonism, catatonia, and neuroleptic malignant syndrome, to name conditions that are not considered "depressive states." Before we can adequately understand the ECT process, more work must be done to establish which psychopathologies are responsive to ECT. In summarizing the accepted indications for ECT, I noted other mental disorders that warrant study: schizophrenia, affective disorders and psychoses in childhood and adolescence, rapid cycling bipolar disorder, and alcoholism. These conditions warrant study in prospective trials, first to elucidate the indications themselves, but also to provide a basis for a better understanding of what may be in the therapeutic chain and what may not. In this vein, studies of maintenance and continuation ECT warrant special consideration insofar as they will provide evidence of what is needed to extend the duration of ECT effects.

Conclusion

Despite an extensive experience of more than half a century, the selection of patients for ECT is a complex calculus, based on the severity of illness and symptom expression of the patient, the training and skill of the psychiatrist, and the availability of treatment facilities. The nosology of *DSM* and the recommendations of the American Psychiatric Association and Royal College of Psychiatrists (1989) are approximate guidelines. The new guidelines also argue that, for some conditions, ECT may be considered a primary treatment; no longer is it necessary to await the failure of other treatment trials. While many accept ECT as a treatment for major depressive disorders, the indications are much broader and we must consider its effects in mania, psychosis, and catatonia in any theoretical consideration. This progression has challenged theoreticians to develop models of the therapeutic chain that are broader than the prevailing hypotheses of the role of biochemical events in depressive disorders. As a result of clinical experience, there is a defined need to undertake controlled prospective studies of ECT in acute schizophrenia, emotional disorders of children and adolescents, rapid cycling bipolar disorders, alcoholism and drug dependence; and most challenging, the techniques for maintenance and continuation ECT.

References

Abrams, R, and Taylor, MA. Catatonia, a prospective clinical study. *Arch. Gen. Psychiatry* 33:579-581, 1976.

American Psychiatric Association. *DSM-III: Diagnostic and Statistical Manual of Mental Disorders*. 3d ed. Washington, DC: American Psychiatric Press, 1980.

American Psychiatric Association. *DSM-III-R: Diagnostic and Statistical Manual of Mental Disorders*. 3d ed., revised. Washington, DC: American Psychiatric Press, 1987.

American Psychiatric Association. *DSM-IV: Diagnostic and Statistical Manual of Mental Disorders*. 4th ed. Washington, DC: American Psychiatric Press, 1994.

American Psychiatric Association. *The Practice of Electroconvulsive Therapy: Recommendations for Treatment, Training and Privileging. A Task Force Report*. Washington, DC: APA Press, 1990.

Consensus Development Conference. Electronconvulsive therapy. *JAMA* 254:103-108, 1985.

Douyon, R; Serby, M; Klutchko, B; and Rotrosen, J. ECT and Parkinson's disease revisited: A 'naturalistic' study. *Am. J. Psychiatry* 146:1451-1455, 1989.

Feighner, JP; Robins, E; Guze, SB; Woodruff, RA; Winokur, G; and Munoz, R. Diagnostic criteria for use in psychiatric research. *Arch. Gen. Psychiatry* 26:57-63, 1972.

Fink, M. ECT for parkinson disease? *Convulsive Ther.* 4:189-191, 1988.

Fink, M. Is catatonia a primary indication for ECT? *Convulsive Ther.* 6:1-4, 1990.

Friedel, RO. The combined use of neuroleptics and ECT in drug resistant schizophrenic patients. *Psychopharmacol. Bull.* 22:928-930, 1986.

Geretsegger, C, and Rochowanski, E. Electroconvulsive therapy in acute life-threatening catatonia with associated cardiac and respiratory decompensation. *Convulsive Ther.* 3:291-295, 1987.

Gujavarty, K; Greenberg, LB; and Fink, M. Electroconvulsive therapy and neuroleptic medication in therapy-resistant positive-symptom psychosis. *Convulsive Ther.* 3:185-195, 1987.

Hermle, L, and Oepen, G. Zur differentialdiagnose der akut lebensbedrohlichen Katatonie und des malignen Neuroleptikasyndroms-Ein kasuistischer Beitrag. *Fortschr. Neurol. Psychiatr.* 54:189-195, 1986.

Mann, SC; Caroff, SN; Bleier, HR; Welz, WK; Kling, MA; and Hayashida, M. Lethal catatonia. *Am. J. Psychiatry* 143:1374-1381, 1986.

Meduna, L. *Die Konvulsionstherapie der Schizophrenie*. Halle: Carl Marhold, 1937.

Nolen, WA, and Zwaan, WA. Treatment of lethal catatonia with electroconvulsive therapy and dantrolene sodium. *Acta Psychiatr. Scand.* 82:90-92, 1990.

Pataki, J; Zervas, IM; and Jandorf, L. Catatonia in a university inpatient service. *Convulsive Ther.* 8(3):163-173, 1992.

Philbrick, KL, and Rummaus, TA. Malignant catatonic. *J. Neuropsych. Clin. Neurosci.* 6:1-13, 1994.

Rosebush, PI; Hildebrand, AM; Furlong, BG; and Mazurek, MF. Catatonic syndrome in a general psychiatric population: Frequency, clinical presentation, and response to lorazepam. *J. Clin. Psychiatry* 51:357-362, 1990.

Royal College of Psychiatrists. *The Practical Administration of Electroconvulsive Therapy (ECT)*. London: Gaskell, 1989. 30 pp.

Sackeim, HA, ed. Mechanisms of action. *Convulsive Ther.* 6:207-310, 1989.

Sajatovic, M, and Meltzer, HY. The effect of short-term electroconvulsive treatment plus neuroleptics in treatment resistant schizophrenia and schizoaffective disorder. *Convulsive Ther.* 9:167-175, 1993.

Weiner, RD, and Coffey, CE. Indications for the use of electroconvulsive therapy. In: Francis, AJ, and Hales, RE, eds. *Review of Psychiatry, VII*. Washington, DC: APA Press, 1988. pp. 458-481.

—by Max Fink, M.D.

The above section was written by Dr. Max Fink, Department of Psychiatry and Behavioral Sciences, School of Medicine, State University of New York at Stony Brook, Health Science Center-T 10, Box 457, Stony Brook, NY 11794.

The Mode of Action of ECT

In the two decades since the first conference of this type was held in Dorado Beach, Puerto Rico, in 1972 (Fink et al. 1974), we have expanded our knowledge of the technical aspects of ECT. We determined that seizures are essential to the ECT process and that real ECT differs from sham-ECT, reduced the cognitive effects of ECT by changing electrode placement, induction currents, number and frequency of treatments, and dosing strategies; improved the safety of seizures induced in patients with severe systemic disorders; and extended the indications for its use.

We are now assured that ECT induces unique and specific changes in the brain with defined behavioral effects. We are assured that repeated seizures affect mood, thought, and memory, as well as the vegetative aspects of behavior.

We have learned a lot about the details of the ECT process, but we lack a coherent hypothesis of the way repeated seizures affect behavior. We have not been shy in putting forth hypotheses of the mode of action. In 1972, at Dorado Beach, the considered theories were focused on three effects of the process: the changes in memory, in brain electrophysiology, and in cerebral neurohumors. By 1979, with the publication of my textbook, the interest in neurohumors and their receptors dominated our thinking, as these became the dominant models of the mode of action of antidepressant drugs (Fink 1979). To these we should add the hypotheses based on neuroendocrine changes, kindling, and the special interest in hemispheric localization of mood and thought. These themes were played out again in 1985 at the New York Academy of Sciences (Malitz & Sackeim 1986) and in the special issue of *Convulsive Therapy* edited by Harold Sackeim in 1989. The importance of the rise in seizure threshold and the role of GABAergic systems was a new theme.

Each hypothesis is based on a single aspect or a single technique of examination of the ECT process. Unfortunately, such focal thoughts have not been fruitful. Kety in 1972, I in 1979, Ottosson in 1985, and Sackeim in 1989 each identified aspects of the ECT process that were considered "essential" that is, probably in the therapeutic chain (Fink 1979; Kety 1974; Ottosson 1986; Sackeim 1989). But these views have not been very productive, in part, because they did not clearly define the psychopathology for which the effects were sought. In 1979, I focused on antidepressant activity and so noted that ECT requires the induction of grand mal seizures (at the time, Crow and other British authors were challenging the merit of seizures); that it is effective after 6-9 seizures (the effective changes were additive); that the presence of vegetative signs and neuroendocrine imbalance were the best predictors of favorable outcome and their reversal were the best signs of recovery; and argued that antidepressant activity resulted from the increased release of endogenous hypothalamic peptides, to which I gave the name "antidepressin."

In 1985, Ottosson saw the effect on melancholia as the target effect, and that the effect which was considered favorable in schizophrenia and psychosis was the clouding of consciousness, a view that was challenged by Mukherjee (1989).

Sackeim (1989) highlighted the separation of our patients from the great numbers treated with psychoactive drugs by their severity of illness and their drug therapy resistance. Three aspects assured differences from pharmacotherapy—the physiological effects are not contaminated by drugs, the treatment is punctate in delivery, and it can be delivered so as to have effects on anatomically distinct brain areas.

What aspects of the ECT process should be considered today in developing a more coherent theory?

Specificity of ECT. While we are impressed with the antidepressant effects of ECT, we find that mania, psychosis, catatonia, and even motor disorders are directly affected by ECT. We can no longer seek to explain an antidepressant effect alone. Nor can we argue from the phenotypic classifications of *DSM-III* (American Psychiatric Association 1980). If we view ECT as a non-specific effect, like the analgesic effects of aspirin or morphine, then we may have to give up the classification of many severe mental illnesses and talk of a unitary psychosis. But it is more likely that ECT does have specific brain effects and that these affect individuals differently because each substrate differs—both in individual biology, history, and psychology. I am reminded of the ubiquitous nature of the effects of *Treponema pallidum* on behavior—a single cause with diverse manifestations that cut across many aspects of psychopathology. We need to look for a common abnormality that can be altered by ECT among those with depression, mania, and psychosis. From our present knowledge, we will have to give longer courses of adequate treatments to ensure persistent effects.

A seizure is essential to the process. It is also essential that these have to be repeated over some weeks to have a temporary effect, and over months for a long lasting effect. As Sackeim has so elegantly shown, we can define the parameters of a therapeutic seizure—one that has a persistent behavioral effect—and as Calev and his coworkers have shown, the seizure and the behavioral consequences can be enhanced by caffeine (Calev et al. 1993). From a history of the successful induction of seizures by pentylenetetrazol and flurothyl, nothing about electricity is essential for the treatment, but that some aspects may augment or minimize the therapeutic effects (e.g., dosing and electrode placement being the most studied). The observations of less effective and more effective seizures, and our ability to augment seizures with caffeine, provide two avenues to properly controlled studies.

Behavioral effects vary with the psychopathology investigated. The effects on mood, psychosis, and vegetative symptoms vary with the severity of the disorder. It is no longer acceptable to depend on simple memory tests and rating scales of depression to assess therapeutic outcome. We need detailed assessments of the time course for changes in mood, affect, vegetative measures, thought, and motor activity. When we correlate the changes in chemistry and physiology with specific changes in behavior, we will be able to define the specific effects of seizures.

Behavioral effects of ECT are poorly sustained by drugs, continued ECT is an important, indeed probably an essential, part of treatment. A prejudice against the use of ECT and our fear of cognitive effects leads many to give the shortest course of ECT possible. When studying the effects of such courses, we have had great difficulty in assessing the changes in body chemistry and physiology, in part, I believe, because the changes have not been stabilized. A few years ago, I collected cerebrospinal fluid (CSF) from severely depressed patients undergoing ECT and asked Drs. Nemeroff and Bissette at Duke University to measure three brain peptides. CSF levels of corticotropin releasing factor (CRF) and beta-endorphin decreased, while somatostatin increased. The changes were small, however. The samples were taken before ECT and after ECT #5-6 (Nemeroff et al. 1991). I believe that the effects were not stabilized at that time, and our results were unclear. Perhaps the unclear results of studies of other peptides, such as the neurophysins, ACTH, prolactin, luteinizing hormone (LH), growth hormone (GH), and thyroid stimulating hormone (TSH) result from the failure to study patients after the behavioral changes have been stabilized.

The central effects of ECT and drugs are different, and should not be expected to be the same. It is no longer useful to add the effects of ECT (and ECS) to a table of effects of drugs and argue for their similarities. No psychoactive drug developed so far has the generalizability or specificity or efficacy of ECT. The best that we can get from our chemical studies are techniques for study.

I cannot be more specific as to where to look for an explanation for the dramatic effects of ECT on behavior. After seeking an explanation for 35 years, I remain optimistic that we will be able to define the central changes that make ECT so useful and so effective, and thereby replace this intrusive and expensive treatment with a simpler chemical treatment.

We should continue the studies of the neuroendocrine effects of seizures, and the behavioral effects of peptides. There is so much more to be learned about the role of the hypothalamus, pituitary, thyroid, and adrenal glands in behavior. These are most likely in the therapeutic chain, at least for the effects of ECT on mood and vegetative functions. Thyroid functions and the importance of TRH, the endorphins, and the neurophysins each have their advocates at this time as substances in the therapeutic chain. They deserve more study (Fink 1993).

We should look at the cholinergic system again. This system plays important roles in motor activity, and some authors argue that disturbances in this system are central to changes in cognition. Acetylcholine is involved in the development of electroencephalogram (EEG) slow wave activity, a sign that seizures have occurred and a sign of the persistence of seizure effects (Fink 1966). Like GABA, for which a connection to the cessation of seizures is suggested, acetylcholine should be studied for its electrophysiologic connections in relation to persistent mood change. Observations on the persistent changes in cholinesterases (and monoamine oxidases) have not been examined with the detail our present methods can provide. Perhaps the rise in seizure threshold and persistent EEG slow wave activity, which seem related to GABA and acetylcholine levels, are more than epiphenomena of the treatment course.

There is a putative clue in the effects of both ECT and benzodiazepines on the motor and thought behavior of patients with catatonia. We have known for decades that the mutism, negativism, and rigidity of catatonia can be temporarily resolved with barbiturates, and more recently with benzodiazepines. ECT remains an effective agent for reversing catatonia. Looking for a clue to the similar effects of benzodiazepines and ECT, some authors have focused on the rise in seizure threshold and anticonvulsant effects of both.

Many authors will argue that studies of ECT should properly begin with studies of the biochemical effects of ECS in rats; in molecular neuroscience; and in the similarities between the effects of drugs and ECT in animal systems, focusing on receptors and neurohumors. At best, these studies cannot add much information about human physiology and behavior for the many reasons specified by numerous authors in numerous treatises—the differences in physiology between rats and men, between one rat strain and others, between rats and mice, and between the normal animal and the sick human. There is also the difficulty in replicating a systematic series of treatments in humans in animals.

Others will argue that we need more study: of the brain effects of ECT, with a greater emphasis on newer analytic methods, including SPECT, MRI, and PET, or the detailed study of cognition, and greater efforts to reduce the effects; or the need to reduce the risks of seizures by studies of antihypertensives or other anesthetics or other muscle relaxants. These efforts are salutary and should clearly continue. But the essential need today is for the further study of the mode of action of ECT in studies in our patients—studies which apply the knowledge of the laboratory to the measures in man (Fink 1993). We now have a greater knowledge of the adequacy of certain seizures, of the need for prolonged treatments, and the need to parcel out different behavioral effects rather than global changes. The next decades should be as fruitful for the increase in our knowledge about the mechanism of ECT as the past decade has been about our knowledge of an effective seizure and the reduction in cognitive effects of seizures.

References

American Psychiatric Association. *DSM-III: Diagnostic and Statistical Manual of Mental Disorders*. 3d ed. Washington, DC: American Psychiatric Press, 1980.

Calev, A; Fink, M; Petrides, G; Francis, A; and Fochtmann, L. Caffeine pretreatment enhances clinical efficacy and reduces cognitive effects of electroconvulsive therapy. *Convulsive Ther.* 9:95-100, 1993.

Fink, M. Cholinergic aspects of convulsive therapy. *J. Nerv. Ment. Dis.* 142:475-484, 1966.

Fink, M. *Convulsive therapy: Theory and Practice.* New York: Raven Press, 1979. 306 pp.

Fink, M. Convulsive therapy: The mode of action of ECT. *Convulsive Ther.* 9:192-197, 1993.

Fink, M; Kety, S; and McGaugh, J. *The Psychobiology of Convulsive Therapy.* Washington, DC: V.H. Winston & Sons, 1974.

Kety, S. Biochemical and neurochemical effects of electroconvulsive shock. In: Fink, M; Kety, S; and McGaugh, J, eds. *Psychobiology of Convulsive Therapy.* Washington, DC: V.H. Winston and Sons, 1974. pp. 285-292.

Malitz, S, and Sackeim, HA, eds. Electroconvulsive therapy: Clinical and basic research issues. *Ann. N.Y. Acad. Sci.* 462:1-424, 1986.

Mukherjee, S. Mechanism of the antimanic effect of electroconvulsive therapy. *Convulsive Ther.* 5:227-243, 1989.

Nemeroff, CB; Bissette, G; Akil, H; and Fink, M. Neuropeptide concentrations in the cerebrospinal fluid of depressed patients treated with electroconvulsive therapy. Corticotrophin-releasing factor, beta-endorphin and somatostatin. *Br. J. Psychiatry* 158:59-63, 1991.

Ottosson, J-O. Clinical perspectives on mechanism of action. In: Malitz, S, and Sackeim, HA, eds. Electroconvulsive therapy: Clinical and basic research issues. *Ann. NY Acad. Sci.* 462:357-366, 1986.

Sackeim, HA, ed. Mechanisms of action. *Convulsive Ther.* 6:207-310, 1989.

—by Max Fink, M.D.

The above section was written by Dr. Max Fink, Department of Psychiatry and Behavioral Sciences, School of Medicine, State University of New York at Stony Brook, Health Science Center-T 10, Box 457, Stony Brook, NY 11794.

Treatment Optimization With ECT

Abstract

Although electroconvulsive therapy (ECT) is considered to be an effective and safe treatment, as with any treastment, both therapeutic outcome and adverse effects can be expected to vary considerably across patients. It is incumbent upon the practitioner to be aware of factors that serve to influence the benefits and risks associated with this treatment modality. This article provides a brief, clinically oriented overview of many of these factors, including those that may be useful in response prediction, as well as technical modifications of the ECT procedure itself. In addition, a number of suggestions are made concerning promising future avenues of research in this area.

Introduction

The concept of treatment optimization with electroconvulsive therapy (ECT) can be broadly viewed along the dimensions of maximizing therapeutic response and minimizing adverse effects. Although much work of this sort has already been accomplished over the nearly six decades that have passed since the inception of convulsive therapy, a great deal more remains to be done. The continued viability of this treatment modality may depend on the extent to which it can be shown that an acceptable risk-benefit analysis truly favors ECT over treatment alternatives. Not only are the forces of health care reform demanding that increased attention be paid to such considerations for all treatments, but regulatory efforts at both the State (e g., California and Texas) and Federal level (e.g., Food and Drug Administration) have made it amply clear that the evidence in support of ECT must be compelling to justify its survival.

This article will attempt to briefly review the area of treatment optimization with ECT; what has been done, what work is presently being carried out, and, most importantly, what areas should be the focus of future research. While the ECT of today is far safer and more effective than that used a half century ago, one can hope that the same can be said 50 years from now as well.

The Maximization of Therapeutic Response

Major Depression. There is widespread agreement that major depression is by far the primary diagnostic indication for referral to ECT (Weiner & Coffey 1988). However, recent practice guidelines have recognized that the decision to refer a patient to ECT should not be based solely on diagnostic issues, but also on factors such as symptomologic severity, urgency of the presentation, the extent to which treatment alternatives have either been ineffective or poorly tolerated, and patient preference (American Psychiatric Association 1990). The choices of whether and when each type of treatment is indicated must be made on the basis of an individualized analysis of the applicable risks and benefits for all treatment alternatives. However, the available information on which such an analysis depends is often insufficient to make a truly optimum choice.

Traditionally, it has been believed that the two strongest predictors of ECT response are the presence of melancholia (*DSM-IV*; American Psychiatric Association 1994) and mood-congruent delusions. However, most recent data indicate that the presence of melancholia is not of predictive importance (Prudic et al. 1989). In addition, while the existence of delusions remains a good predictor of ECT response, it is not clear whether this increased efficacy reflects a distinct depressive subtype or whether it merely indicates a particularly high level of overall severity. Further, there continues to be an absence of well-controlled data demonstrating whether ECT is more effective in the presence of psychosis than a combination of antidepressant and antipsychotic medication.

The absence of pre-existing illness also appears to be of importance in the prediction of response to somatic treatment (Weiner & Coffey 1988). Evidence now suggests that individuals with a severe primary major depressive episode (i.e., uncomplicated by significant coexisting mental or physical illness) are very likely to respond well to somatic treatment and particularly likely to respond to ECT (with an estimated remission rate of 80 to 90 percent, versus 60 to 70 percent for an antidepressant drug trial).

A commonly held belief is that refractoriness to pharmacologic interventions during the present episode does not diminish the likelihood of later response to ECT. In fact, recent data suggest that drug refractory patients are less likely to respond to ECT (Devanand et al.

1991). However, the likelihood of response to yet another drug trial may be diminished as well, and no one has yet shown which treatment modality is affected to the greatest extent.

During the 1950s and 1960s, there was a major effort to develop composite scales for prediction of response to ECT. The most widely used of these was the Newcastle Scale (Carney et al. 1965). Unfortunately, none of these scales proved superior to clinical judgment. Another historically active area in terms of establishing predictors of ECT response has been the use of biological markers. Here, as well, success has been found to be wanting. However, much work of this type continues, primarily involving neuroendocrine challenge tests and neurobiologic probes sensitive to specific neurotransmitter systems, as well as investigation of the neurochemical and neurophysiological response to the ECT treatments themselves (Krystal et al. 1993; Nobler et al. 1993; Scott 1989).

Mania. Only a small fraction of patients with mania are referred for ECT in the United States. Primarily for this reason, it has not been until recently that controlled studies of ECT versus antimanic pharmacologic agents have been carried out (Small et al. 1988). Such studies, though few in number, have corroborated the clinical belief that ECT is effective in this condition, not only on a first-line basis, but also in treatment refractory cases (most likely to a lesser degree). As one might expect, there is little at present in the literature concerning differential prediction of response between ECT and alternative treatments.

Schizophrenia and Related Conditions. The use of ECT in schizophrenia has moved from overutilization to underutilization (Small 1985). Until recently, most ECT studies in this type of population have concentrated on primary use (i.e., in patients who are not treatment refractory by history). The results of these studies suggest that individuals with acute, affective, and/or catatonic symptomatology do about as well as those who receive antipsychotic pharmacologic agents. More contemporary work, focusing on refractory patients, has also explored the role of antipsychotic drugs in the potentiation of ECT response (see below), although issues such as ability to maintain a remission, likelihood of improvement, and predictive factors remain to be investigated. While there appear to be sufficient data that chronically impaired patients do relatively poorly with ECT, such individuals also tend to do poorly with medication as well; therefore, if there is even a small (10-20%) chance of remission, a trial may be worthwhile, at least when positive or psychotic symptoms are prominent.

How Can an ECT-Induced Therapeutic Remission Be Maintained? Another topic of relevance to optimizing therapeutic response with ECT involves the maintenance of therapeutic gains after the course of ECT has been completed. A course of ECT does not, and cannot be expected to, prevent relapse. Furthermore, the risk of relapse is high, particularly during the first year (Sackeim et al. 1990). The efficacy of psychopharmacologic continuation therapy, a mainstay of prophylactic treatment, has recently been questioned, particularly for its use in patients who were refractory to pharmacologic agents during the index episode. The primary alternative, continuation/maintenance ECT (Kramer 1990), has yet to be subjected to controlled studies, including those designed to clarify the optimum timing of such treatments.

Can the Therapeutic Response to ECT Be Potentiated?

Efforts to increase the therapeutic potency of ECT have persisted since the early days of this treatment modality. The following examples, will be discussed: number and rate of treatments, stimulus electrode placement, stimulus dosing, and pharmacologic potentiation.

Number and Rate of Treatments. There is no evidence that a fixed number of treatments should be used with ECT. The number of treatments necessary to induce a therapeutic remission varies considerably across individuals. Patients rarely respond fully before the 4th or after the 18th treatment, although the typical range is 6 to 12 treatments (American Psychiatric Association 1990). The decision to stop or alter the ECT course is made either when a therapeutic plateau has been reached or when no response exists after a set number of treatments (most commonly at least 6). Giving additional treatments after a therapeutic plateau has been reached does not appear to be of general benefit, although it is still unclear whether such a practice might be helpful when there has been a history of early relapse.

ECT is, by tradition, generally given 3 times per week in the United States and 2 times per week in Europe and some other countries, with variations in the rate based on both the need for a rapid response and the severity of ECT-associated adverse cognitive effects (American Psychiatric Association 1990). Recent data suggest that more frequent ECT will bring about a more rapid remission, but at the cost of increased cognitive effects (Shapira et al. 1991).

Multiple Monitored ECT (MMECT). MMECT is a treatment variation in which multiple seizures (usually 2-5) are induced within each session of anesthesia (Roemer et al. 1990). Although it is clear that the total number of seizures required to induce a therapeutic response is greater with MMECT than with standard ECT, the number of treatment sessions, and therefore the duration of treatment course, appears to be less. However, MMECT has also been associated with an increased risk of both cognitive and cardiovascular sequelae, as well as a heightened incidence of prolonged seizures. Unfortunately, well-controlled studies designed to delineate the true efficacy and safety of MMECT have not yet been carried out.

Stimulus Electrode Placement. Recognizing that ECT-related memory impairment represented a major impediment to the acceptance of ECT, Lancaster and colleagues (1958) showed that stimulating the cerebral hemisphere opposite to that involved with language functioning produced significantly less adverse memory effects than the more traditional bifrontotemporal (BL) placement. Thus began the era of unilateral nondominant (ULND) ECT. However, beginning with Lancaster's work, and continuing to the present, there has also been evidence that ULND ECT is, at least in some patients, less effective, in terms of likelihood, speed, degree, and/or persistence of response, than BL ECT (Abrams 1986). Although this difference has been reported to be greatest in mania, there is not complete agreement on this issue (Mukherjee et al. 1988).

To an extent, suboptimal techniques account for part of the reported diminished efficacy advantage for ULND ECT. For example, it is now clear that a frontotemporal to high centroparietal location affords a relatively low level of scalp current shunting and thereby a low seizure threshold (Sackeim 1991). This situation makes it easier to attain a moderately suprathreshold stimulus dosing level, and therefore also easier to maximize treatment adequacy (see below). Still, it cannot be assumed that optimum stimulus electrode placement has yet been achieved. Resolution of this problem is confounded by our lack of understanding as to which neural pathways activated by the seizure are responsible for mediating the therapeutic action of ECT (Sackeim 1991).

Stimulus Waveform. The type of electrical stimulus waveform used with ECT is now known to affect treatment response. As one might expect, the most efficient type of waveform for initiating a seizures the brief pulse stimulus (Weiner 1982), closely resembles the signal by which neurons themselves communicate: the action potential. This brief pulse stimulus consists of an interrupted series of rapidly rising and falling bursts of current. For a variety of reasons it has not been until the last one or two decades that devices incorporating the brief pulse stimulus have been widely available. In terms of benefits, not only is seizure threshold (the amount of electrical charge necessary to induce a seizure) lower with a brief pulse stimulus than with the more traditional sine wave stimulus (the same shaped signal as line current), but adverse cognitive effects and EEG abnormalities are diminished as well (Weiner et al. 1986a, 1986b). For all of these reasons, the brief pulse stimulus has largely replaced alternative waveforms in many countries, including the United States.

The pulse stimulus is characterized by several electrical parameters, including modality (constant current, voltage, and/or energy), directionality (pulse polarity), pulse width, frequency (proportional to number of pulses per unit time), duration (length of the entire train of pulses), and peak pulse intensity. Given the number of parameters involved, it has thus far proved difficult to fully study their relative effects and arrive at optimum choices for clinical practice. Constant current stimulus delivery is more physiologic than either constant voltage or constant energy (Sackeim et al. 1994). In terms of directionality, all existing U.S. ECT devices make use of a bidirectional stimulus, most likely to avoid polarization effects that would otherwise exist. Human efficacy and safety studies of polarization effects have never been carried out, although unidirectional stimuli have been widely used for many years, and at least a rough equivalence in seizure threshold exists between uni- and bidirectional pulses (Weaver & Williams 1986). Other studies have demonstrated that pulse widths of

0.5 msec or less may be associated with diminished efficacy, but this finding has been called into question (Sackeim et al. 1994). Finally, comparisons of the relative effects of other parameters (i.e., pulse frequency, duration of the pulse train, and peak pulse intensity) have also not provided definitive guidance as to optimum parameter choice.

Stimulus Dosing. The dosing of the electrical stimulus (in terms of electrical charge, a composite measure of stimulus intensity) is in some ways analogous to the dosing of pharmacologic agents. Therefore, it is surprising that this topic has not drawn much attention from researchers until recently. In this regard, Sackeim and coworkers (1987, 1993) found that relative stimulus intensity (i.e., the intensity with respect to a given patient's seizure threshold) is related to both therapeutic outcome and adverse cognitive effects, particularly for ULND ECT. Specifically, these investigators established that barely suprathreshold stimuli were less effective and were also associated with less severe amnestic changes than more moderately suprathreshold stimuli. These findings have recently been corroborated by work in our own department (unpublished observations). The reason for these dose-dependent effects is unclear, but may be related to differences in site of initiation of the induced seizures and/or the seizure generalization process (Sackeim 1991).

On the basis of Sackeim's findings, optimum stimulus dosing should involve an estimation of seizure threshold at the time of the first treatment, followed by use of a sufficiently suprathreshold stimulus at successive treatments. In fact, knowledge about relationships between seizure threshold and factors such as gender, stimulus electrode placement, and age have made it easier to develop clinically implementable paradigms for seizure threshold estimation (Sackeim et al. 1991). Unfortunately, the optimum choice of "moderately suprathreshold" stimulus dose is unknown; if it is too low, efficacy may be diminished, whereas if it is too high, adverse cognitive effects are increased. In the absence of definitive data, a recommended level is 150 to 250 percent over the estimated seizure threshold for ULND ECT and 50 to 100 percent for BL ECT.

The choice of dosing at successive treatments is confounded by the existence of a variable rise in seizure threshold over the series of treatments, a phenomenon that makes ongoing determination of relative stimulus dose impossible to gauge without re-estimation of seizure threshold. However, such re-estimation exposes the patient to additional marginally suprathreshold ECT treatments. To avoid this problem, dose-related ictal EEG changes can be used to assess the extent to which the seizure is suprathreshold. At present, most practitioners use a seizure duration criterion (usually greater than 25 seconds by motor and/or electroencephalographic response) as a measure of seizure "adequacy," in spite of the fact that such a criterion has only marginally supportive data (Ottosson 1960; Weiner et al. 1991). More recent work, however, has suggested that other, more complex, electrophysiologic measures may be more pertinent to the determination of seizure adequacy, although the optimum choice of electrophysiologic parameters remains to be established (Krystal et al.1993; Nobler et al. 1993; Weiner et al. 1991).

Additional possibilities for future consideration include the following: a pulse delivery system that is time-locked to the transient EEG response to each pulse, the introduction of sensory stimulation (e.g., stroboscopic flashes) time-locked to the occurrence of stimulus pulses, the application of focal noninvasive electrical or electromagnetic stimulation, and pharmacologic or physiologic potentiation. While the former three possibilities may presently be outside the realm of technical feasibility, the latter will be discussed below.

Pharmacologic Potentiation of Therapeutic Response

A variety of means to lower seizure threshold and/or increase seizure duration already exist. The most widely used of these are hyperventilation and caffeine, both of which prolong seizure duration but probably do not lower seizure threshold (Calev et al. 1993; McCall et al. 1993). However, for reasons already mentioned, agents that lower seizure threshold, rather than just prolong seizure duration, are theoretically more desirable. In the past, the pro-convulsant drug pentylenetetrazol (Metrazol) has been effectively used for this purpose (Thigpen & Cleckley 1984). The fact that barbiturate anesthetics used with ECT (e g., methohexital (Brevital) and pentothal) elevate seizure threshold has led to the consideration of alternative anesthetic agents, such as ketamine (Ketalar), that do not exhibit such properties (Lunn et al. 1981). Unfortunately, ketamine may be associated with a transient emergent hallucinosis and raises cardiovascular risks in some individuals.

The matter of whether concurrent use of psychotropic agents increases the effectiveness of ECT has been of great interest. The use of antidepressant agents for this purpose was tested in the 1960s with negative results (Weiner & Coffey 1988). Still, the possibility that such a combination might be of benefit in patients who had previously failed to respond to ECT has not been ruled out. Lithium appears to be associated with increased neurotoxic effects and no enhancement of efficacy when combined with ECT (Small & Milstein 1990), although its value in individuals with a history of an ECT-associated switch from depression to mania has not been examined. Benzodiazepines and other drugs with anticonvulsant properties make seizures more difficult to induce and may also have a further negative effect on treatment outcome (Pettinati et al. 1990). The primary exception to the general rule of avoiding ECT/psychotropic combinations is the use of antipsychotic agents in conjunction with ECT in patients with schizophrenia and related conditions. Recent evidence indicates that this combination is more effective than either treatment alone (Hertzman 1992). Even more recent is the suggestion that the "ultimate" treatment for refractory schizophrenics with prominent positive symptoms may be the combination of ECT and clozapine (Landy 1991).

Other drugs for which preliminary data have suggested a potentiating effect on treatment efficacy include caffeine, yohimbine, and thyroid hormone. However, in each case, corroboration will be necessary before clinical application is indicated (Calev et al. 1993; Sachs et al. 1986; Stern et al. 1991). The underlying bases for such effects are unknown, but may involve activation of certain neurotransmitter systems (e.g., monoamine) or even facilitation of seizure generalization.

The Minimization of Adverse Effects

Serious risks of ECT are rare, but they include: mortality, major anesthetic complications, cardiovascular decompensation, injuries related to motor convulsion, spontaneous seizures, and severe persistent cognitive deficits. Less serious, and more common, risks include headaches and muscle pain, and transient cognitive deficits (except for an occasional persistent difficulty in recalling some recent memories during and just before the index episode of illness). Serious risks associated with pharmacologic alternatives are also rare but may include mortality, cardiovascular decompensation, spontaneous seizures, injuries relating to orthostatic hypotension, hematopoietic suppression, liver or kidney toxicity, idiosyncratic drug reactions, delirium, and tardive dyskinesia (with neuroleptic agents) (uncommon unless used for a prolonged time interval). More common but less severe risks of pharmacologic agents include a wide variety of somatic effects that depend on the specific agent. Some examples are dry mouth, sedation (or insomnia), constipation, urinary retention, weight gain (or anorexia), nausea, dizziness, confusion, anxiety, orthostatic hypotension, tachycardia and other electrocardiographic changes, and mild allergic reactions. More common but less severe risks of pharmacologic agents also include interactions with other drugs the patient may be taking concurrently.

The risks of both ECT and drugs increase in likelihood as well as severity with concurrent medical illness. An advantage for ECT, however, is that some of the most serious risks are temporally limited to a period when a high level of medical monitoring is in place, and are therefore easier to detect and manage before dangerous complications ensue. With pharmacologic agents, the period of risk is more prolonged and complications are less likely to be detected as quickly. A number of technical tools to diminish the risk with ECT now also exist (see below). On the other hand, such opportunities are more limited in the pharmacologic domain. With the increased use of ECT in the elderly, the extent of age-related risk factors also needs further study, in particular for cardiovascularly compromised individuals and those with pre-existing cerebral dysfunction. There is evidence, for example, that patients with basal ganglia lesions on magnetic resonance imaging scans have an increased risk of delirium with ECT (Figiel et al. 1991).

Because the occurrence of amnesia following ECT is of such concern, it would be useful to have some means of predicting those who are most likely, not only to sustain such an effect, but also to be troubled by it. In addition to pre-existing cerebral disease, a number of nonorganic factors have been suggested, although none of these have yet been adequately substantiated. These include obsessive personality features (particularly with respect to cognitive dysfunction), a history of either more than expected physiologic or non-physiologic side effects to multiple pharmacologic agents, the existence of a substrate for the development of secondary gains following a transient ECT-associated amnesia, and a strong expectation by the patient or their family that problems of this sort will occur. Further research into

519

the nature of such factors, along with the investigation of means to ameliorate their influence, should also be carried out.

The Role of Treatment Modifications in the Minimization of Risk With ECT

Cardiovascular Risks. The risks of ECT in patients with pre-existing cardiovascular conditions such as hypertension, coronary artery disease, and arrhythmias can be substantially diminished by appropriate pharmacologic agents. The choice of agent should be based on knowledge of both the patient's condition and the anticipated physiologic changes that accompany ECT. The most notable of these changes result from the sympathetic surge that accompanies the seizure, and include hypertension, tachycardia, and increase in myocardial oxygen demand. Other changes include parasympathetic effects that transiently appear immediately following the electrical stimulus and again as the seizure ends, and the secondary sympathetic activity that often takes place as the patient awakens. Unfortunately, there is no general agreement as to optimal agents for the control of these changes.

Risks Involving Cerebral Function. Existing tools used to minimize the adverse cognitive effects associated with ECT involve the following: keeping the number and frequency of ECT treatments to the minimum necessary to induce a remission over a clinically reasonable timeframe; using ULND electrode placement and moderately suprathreshold brief pulse stimuli; making sure that the patient is well-oxygenated throughout the procedure; and ameliorating any cardiovascular risks that might serve to compromise cerebrovascular integrity.

Future research should be focused on pharmacologic means of minimizing cognitive losses with ECT. Thus far, the results of most clinical trials of putative antiamnestic agents have been disappointing (Krueger et al. 1992). In this regard, recent positive findings with both caffeine and thyroid hormone require corroboration (Calev et al. 1993; Stern et al. 1991). In addition, further investigation of the cognitive effects of variations in the stimulus waveform and its various component parameters, as well as with different stimulus electrode placements, should also be carried out.

Conclusions

The practice of ECT today involves an appreciation of how therapeutic outcome can be maximized and adverse effects can be minimized. However, many aspects of treatment optimization have not yet been well delineated, and others have likely not even been considered. Further research in a number of these areas will be crucial to the achievement of an optimally safe and effective treatment.

References

Abrams, R. Is unilateral electroconvulsive therapy really the treatment of choice in endogenous depression. *Ann. N.Y. Acad. Sci.* 462:50-55, 1986.

American Psychiatric Association. *DSM-IV: Diagnostic and Statistical Manual of Mental Disorders.* 4th ed. Washington, DC: American Psychiatric Association, 1994.

American Psychiatric Association. *The Practice of ECT Recommendations for Treatment, Training, and Privileging.* Washington, DC: American Psychiatric Association, Inc., 1990.

Calev, A; Fink, M; Petrides, G; Francis, A; and Fochtmann, L. Caffeine pretreatment inhances clinical efficacy and reduces cognitive effects of electroconvulsive therapy. *Convulsive Ther.* 9:95-100, 1993.

Carney, MWP; Roth, M; and Garside, RF. The diagnosis of depressive syndromes and the prediction of ECT response. *Br. J. Psychiatry* 111:659-674, 1965.

Devanand, DP; Sackeim, HA; and Prudic, J. Electroconvulsive therapy in the treatment-resistant patient. *Psychiatr. Clin. North Am.* 14:905-923, 1991.

Figiel, GS; Coffey, CE; Djang, WT; Hoffman, G Jr; and Doraiswamy, PM. Brain magnetic resonance imaging findings in ECT-induced delirium. *J. Neuropsychiatry Clin. Neurosci.* 2:53-58, 1991.

Hertzman, M. ECT and neuroleptics as primary treatment for schizophrenia (Editorial). *Biol. Psychiatry* 31:217-220, 1992.

Kramer, BA. Maintenance electroconvulsive therapy in clinical practice. *Convulsive Ther.* 6:279-286, 1990.

Krueger, RB; Sackeim, HA; and Gamzu, ER. Pharmacological treatment of the cognitive side effects of ECT' A review. *Psychopharmacol. Bull.* 28:409-424, 1992.

Krystal, AD; Weiner, RD; McCall, WV; Shelp, FE; Arias, R; and Smith, P. The effects of ECT stimulus dose and electrode placement on the ictal electroencephalogram: An intraindividual crossover study. *Biol. Psychiatry* 34:759-767, 1993.

Lancaster, NP; Steinert, RR; and Frost, I. Unilateral electroconvulsive therapy. *J. Ment. Sci.* 104:221-227, 1958.

Landy, DA. Combined use of Clozapine and electroconvulsive therapy (Case report). *Convulsive Ther.* 7:218-221, 1991.

Lunn, RJ; Savageau, MM; Beatty, WW; Gerst, JW; Staton, RD; and Brumback, RA. Anesthetics and electroconvulsive therapy seizure duration: Implications for therapy from a rat model. *Biol. Psychiatry* 16:1163-1175, 1981.

McCall, WV; Reid, S; Rosenquist, P; Foreman, A; and Kiesow-Webb, N. A reappraisal of the role of caffeine in ECT. *Am. J. Psychiatry* 150:1543-1545, 1993.

Mukherjee, S; Sackeim, HA; and Lee, C. Unilateral ECT in the treatment of manic episodes. *Convulsive Ther.* 4:74-80, 1988.

Nobler, MS; Sackeim, HA; Solomou, M; Luber, B; Devanand, DP; and Prudic, J. EEG manifestations during ECT Effects of electrode placement and stimulus intensity. *Biol. Psychiatry* 34:321-330, 1993.

Ottosson, JO. Experimental studies of the mode of action of electroconvulsive therapy. *Acta Psychiatr. Scand.* 35:1-141, 1960.

Pettinati, HM; Stephens, SM; Willis, KM; and Robin, SE. Evidence for less improvement in depression in patients taking benzodiazepines during unilateral ECT. *Am. J. Psychiatry* 147:1029-1035, 1990.

Prudic, J; Devanand, DP; Sackeim, HA; Decina, P; and Kerr, B. Relative response of endogenous and non-endogenous symptoms to electroconvulsive therapy. *J. Affective Disord.* 16:59-64, 1989.

Roemer, RA; Dubin, WR; Jaffe, R; Lipschutz, L; and Sharon, D. An efficacy study of single- versus double-seizure induction with ECT in major depression. *J. Clin. Psychiatry* 51:473-478, 1990.

Sachs, GS; Pollack, MH; Brotman, AW; Farhadi, AM; and Gelenberg, AJ. Enhancement of ECT benefit by yohimbine. *J. Clin. Psychiatry* 47:508-510, 1986.

Sackeim, HA. Optimizing unilateral electroconvulsive therapy (invited commentary). *Convulsive Ther.* 7:201-212, 1991.

Sackeim, HA; Decina, P; Kanzler, M; Kerr, B; and Malitz, S. Effects of electrode placement on the efficacy of titrated, low-dose ECT. *Am. J. Psychiatry* 144:1449-1455, 1987.

Sackeim, HA; Devanand, DP; and Prudic, J. Stimulus intensity, seizure threshold, and seizure duration: Impact on the efficacy and safety of electroconvulsive therapy. *Psychiatr. Clin. North Am.* 14:803-843, 1991.

Sackeim, HA; Long, J; Luber, BA; Moeller, JR; Prohovnik, I; Devanand, DP; and Nobler, MS. Physical properties and quantification of the ECT stimulus: I. Basic Principles. *Convulsive Ther.* 10:93-123, 1994.

Sackeim, HA; Prudic, J; Devanand, DP; Decina, P; Kerr, B; and Malitz, S. The impact of medication resistance and continuation pharmacotherapy on relapse following response to electroconvulsive therapy in major depression. *J. Clin. Psychopharmacol.* 10:96-104, 1990.

Sackeim, HA; Prudic, J; Devanand, DP; Kiersky, JE; Fitzsimons, L; Moody, BJ; McElhiney, MC; Coleman, EA; and Settembrino, JM. Effects of stimulus intensity and electrode placement on the efficacy and cognitive effects of electroconvulsive therapy. *N. Engl. J. Med.* 328:839-846, 1993.

Scott, AI. Which depressed patients will respond to electroconvulsive therapy? The search for biological predictors of recovery. *Br. J. Psychiatry* 154:8-17, 1989.

Shapira, B; Calev, A; and Lerer, B. Optimal use of electroconvulsive therapy: Choosing a treatment schedule. *Psychiatr. Clin. North Am.* 14:935-946, 1991.

Small, JG. Efficacy of electroconvulsive therapy in schizophrenia, mania, and other disorders. I. Schizophrenia. *Convulsive Ther.* 1:263-270, 1985.

Small, JG; Klapper, MH; Kellams, JJ; Miller, MJ; Milstein, V; Sharpley, PH; and Small, IF. Electroconvulsive treatment compared with lithium in the management of manic states. *Arch. Gen. Psychiatry* 45:727-732, 1988.

Small, JG, and Milstein, V. Lithium interactions: Lithium and electroconvulsive therapy. *J. Clin. Psychopharmacol.* 10:346-350, 1990.

Stern, RA; Nevels, CT, Shelhorse, ME; Prohaska, ML; Mason, GA; and Prange, AJ Jr. Antidepressant and memory effects of combined thyroid hormone treatment and electroconvulsive therapy: Preliminary findings. *Biol. Psychiatry* 30:623-627, 1991.

Thigpen, CH, and Cleckley, HM. Electroconvulsive therapy with enhancement by pentylenetetrazol. *Am. J. Soc. Psychiatry* 4:25-27, 1984.

Weaver, LA Jr, and Williams, RW. Stimulus parameters and electroconvulsive therapy. *Ann. N.Y. Acad. Sci.* 462:174-185, 1986.

Weiner, RD. The role of stimulus waveform in therapeutic and adverse effects of ECT. *Psychopharmacol. Bull.* 18:71-72, 1982.

Weiner, RD, and Coffey, CE. Indications for use of electroconvulsive therapy. In: Frances, AJ, and Hales, RE, eds. *Review of Psychiatry, Volume 7*. Washington, DC: American Psychiatric Press, Inc, 1988. pp. 458-481.

Weiner, RD; Coffey, CE; and Krystal, AD. The monitoring and management of electrically induced seizures. *Psychiatr. Clin. North Am.* 14:845-869, 1991.

Weiner, RD; Rogers, HJ; Davidson, JR; and Kahn, EM. Effects of electroconvulsive therapy upon brain electrical activity. *Ann. N.Y. Acad. Sci.* 462:270-281, 1986*a*.

Weiner, RD; Rogers, HJ; Davidson, JR; and Squire, LR. Effects of stimulus parameters on cognitive side effects. *Ann. N.Y. Acad. Sci.* 462:315-325, 1986*b*.

—by Richard D. Weiner, M.D., Ph.D.

The above section was written by Richard D. Weiner, M.D., Ph.D., Box 3309, Durham University Medical Center, Durham, NC 27710.

Index

Index

R

racing thoughts 197, 207, 221
ranitidine 168
rape 9, 317, 382, 387, 394
rapid cycling 225, 237, 497, 499, 501
rapid eye movement 156, 157, 226
rapid heartbeat 261, 302, 419, 425, 427
rashes 419, 424
reactive mood 157
real-life exposure 255
reality-oriented therapy 77
rearranging objects 274
rebellion 175
receptors 88, 90, 94, 126, 127, 134, 135, 262, 263, 504, 508
recovering mental patients 52
Recovery, Inc. 271, 411, 461
recreation 61, 238, 277
recreational therapy 10
recurrent brief depressive disorder 160, 161
recurrent depressions 151
reduction in emotional expressiveness 68
refugees 393
refusal of services 39
regressive behaviors 375
regressive ECT 476
rehabilitation 31, 37, 53, 77, 83, 87, 122, 123, 178, 398, 404-406, 408
relapses 65, 75, 82, 90, 95, 97, 118, 119, 121, 123, 135, 140, 151, 233, 234, 256-258, 277, 309, 348, 420, 467, 468, 476, 498, 500, 513, 523
relaxation 62, 186, 255, 285, 286, 292, 309, 313, 403, 476
remission 151, 152, 154, 224, 474, 476, 486, 498, 511-514, 520
remoxipride 97, 117
renal damage 243
renal function 81, 224, 239, 291, 346, 423, 445, 447, 519
renal tubular defects 243
repeating 220, 274
repetitive thoughts 9, 260, 273, 343
repressed anger 377
reserpine 166
residential care 79, 80

residential facilities 34, 57
respiratory disorders 252, 255, 358, 502
rest 55, 61, 62, 91, 126, 161, 354, 356, 448, 486
restaurants 57, 312
"restless legs" syndrome *see* nocturnal myoclonus
restlessness 76, 88, 91, 117, 149, 174, 232, 283, 355, 360, 364, 419, 426
restraints 75, 116, 492
retirement 4, 186, 354
retrograde amnesia 471
retrograde ejaculation 94
rheumatoid arthritis 165
risperidone 97, 117
Ritalin® 431
rituals 9, 260, 274, 275, 277, 279, 298, 340, 341
rocking 7
role models 285
Roxiam® 97
running away 176, 178, 375
rural communities 19-23, 38, 391

S

sadness 4, 5, 26, 148, 150, 155, 164, 165, 174, 176, 177, 184, 214, 231, 260, 355, 360, 373, 422
safety risks 197
schizoaffective disorders 68, 115, 140, 155, 443, 469, 491, 494, 503
schizophrenia 6-8, 10, 16, 17, 65-85, 87-90, 94-144, 274, 325, 328-330, 332, 335, 355, 392-394, 401, 402, 416, 418, 421, 437, 443, 469, 490, 491, 493-495, 497, 498, 500, 501, 503, 505, 512, 518, 521, 523
    causes of 99, 129, 143
    nonparanoid forms 106, 330
    paranoid form 106
    risk of schizophrenia 70-71, 101, 113, 114
    symptoms 7, 66-70, 74, 81, 89, 94, 98, 99, 101, 106, 129, 142
    treatment 75, 77, 80, 81, 83, 87, 95, 116, 117, 121, 123, 437
Schizophrenia Bulletin 84, 85, 99, 332, 437